RE-THINKING
THE ADMINISTRATION
OF JUSTICE

edited by Dawn H. Currie and Brian D. MacLean

Editing: Robert Clarke
Cover photo courtesy of Heritage House Publishing, Vancouver
Design and production: Brian MacLean
Printed and bound in Canada

A publication of:
Fernwood Publishing
Box 9409 Station A
Halifax, Nova Scotia
B3K 5S3

When books are co-authored by authors of different genders, it is the policy of Fernwood Publishing to list women first rather than follow the usual alphabetical sequencing. The fact that the male author/ editor appears after the female does not imply subordinate status. This procedure is intended to counteract the common assumption that the female author/editor is subordinate.

Canadian Cataloguing in Publication Data

Main entry under title:

Re-thinking the administration of justice

Includes bibliographical references.
ISBN 1895686-01-6

1. Sociological jurisprudence. 2. Law -- Canada.
I. Currie, Dawn, 1948- II. MacLean, Brian, 1950-

KE429.R47 1992   340' .115'0971   C92-098576-9

for Herb, Marg, Sal, and the loving memory of Doug

Foreword

At the Centre and on the Periphery: Criminal Justice Research in Canada

Canadian Scholarship in the field of criminal justice has been both innovative and challenging. To name just a few selected texts: the pioneering work of Clarke and Lewis (1977) on rape, the important intervention of Varda Burstyn and her associates (1985) in the pornography debate, or, more recently, DeKeseredy's and Hinch's exhaustive analysis of violence against women (1991), the continuing work of John Lowman (1992) in the area of prostitution, and the excellent joint Canadian/U.S. collection of recent developments in critical criminology edited by Brian MacLean and Dragan Milovanovic (1991). Together with this book, they illustrate the flourishing development of critical work in a country with a comparatively small population adjacent to the United States — the major producer of criminal justice research and theory in the world — yet open to ideas from Europe, particularly Britain and France.

Social theory does not emerge out of the blue; it develops in distinct social and economic situations and is influenced by specific material problems in the context of a particular array of ideas and socially defined problems. Academic debate has both an interior and exterior history. The interior history is the interchange between scholars buttressed by the material strength of departmental hierarchies and the underpinning of journal and publication outlets, together with access to external funding. But however much this academic debate is seen by its participants as autonomous, the interior dialogue is propelled by the exterior world. The dominant ideas of a period , whether establishment or radical, the social problems of a particular society, the Government in power and the political possibilities existing in a society, all shape the interior discourse of the academic. Nowhere is this more evident than in criminology and the sociology of law. Exterior problems of crime, of lawmaking, of political options and current ideas all profoundly shape the theories emanating from the interior world of academic criminology and legal scholarship. Both the establishment academic, propelled by the direction of local and national government funding, and the critical scholar contesting the ever-changing orthodoxies of theory and practice, clash on a terrain determined by the specificity of their society. It is no accident therefore — to take three radical currents — that abolitionist theory takes root in the liberal welfare democracies of Scandinavia and the Netherlands (Hulsman, 1986; Scheerer, 1986); that realist theory emerges in a Britain concerned with a radical reappraisal of social democracy (Young and Matthews, 1992); and that legal guaranteeism (Ferrajoli, 1989) enthuses Latin American criminologists in countries where the rule of law is precarious and fragile. None of this is to suggest a relativism of theory. Rather it is to point to its reflexivity. That is, theory emerges out of a certain social and political conjuncture; this generates points of sensitivity and areas of blindness which inhibit the development of a general theory applicable to all industrial societies — let alone the Third World. Yet theory, on the other hand, must be sharpened by its sense of locality if it is to take purchase on the particular social and political terrain of which it is a part. To take realism as an example, Ray Michalowski (1991) quite correctly separates out discussion of realism as a general theory and its practical applicability in the United States, as do David Brown and Russell Hogg (1992) in their discussion of the applicability of realism to the Australian context, while DeKeseredy and Schwartz (1992) accurately point to the way in which the merging realist currents in Britain and the United States are shaped by glaring social contrasts between the two countries.

Underlying this debate is the problem of specificity (Young, 1992). Namely that generalizations about crime and justice (e.g. the relationship between unemployment and crime) can only be formulated in specific political and social contexts and cannot be made without specifying the particular social characteristics of the offender and victim in terms of their position on the major social axes of age, class, ethnicity, and gender. It is not possible to simply transpose findings from one country to another or to generalize from men to women, white to black, working class to middle class, and so forth. Such a localism does not preclude generalization, as many postmodernists would argue (e.g Nicholson, 1990); it merely stresses that sociological generalizations must be grounded in the lived realities of the human actors concerned.

In criminology a paradox is that the United States, the major source of criminological ideas, is exceptional in its social and political characteristics when compared to the majority of industrial nations. The extraordinarily high crime rate, the paucity of its welfare State, the minor role of social democracy, the existence of a popular ethos of individualism as expressed in the American Dream, the extent of ghettoization, the range of organized crime, and so forth all distinguish the U.S. from other societies (see. E. Currie, 1985,1990). Furthermore, all of these factors are likely to have a profound effect on theory. The theory of differential association, Mertonian anomie theory, labelling theory, social control theory, are all illuminated if we situate them within this context. None of this represents a call for theoretical isolationism. Rather, it stresses the need for the careful transposition of American theory to other industrial societies. Canadian criminal justice scholars, with a high exposure to the creative ferment of U.S. criminology yet, with an interior intellectual history of politics and social sensibilities, are in a unique position to contrast the problem of specificity and the possibility of synthesis. To be, in short, at the periphery of the United States yet at the epicentre of the debate. This book represents a significant contribution to the task of creating a generalizable theory aware of the particularities of practice in widely differing social and political contexts.

Jock Young,
Head of The Centre for Criminology
University of Middlesex,
London

Preface

Canadian history has been forged against a background of colonization. Therefore, one major difference between our specific history and that of our past colonial overlords is that while our history has been one of resistance, theirs has been one of domination. At first, resistance to colonial imperialism was a physical struggle. Resistance by Indigenous peoples was criminalized and the participants killed or executed — all in the name of 'justice.' Resistance to colonial domination by settler populations in Canada's various regions was similarly criminalized, with execution often used as the solution. As we approach the 21st century, a new form of domination has appeared — this time ideological. Although often couched in terms of 'academic debate,' execution by pen is but a discursive variation of the imperial mindset.[1] The resultant ongoing conflict has remarkable implications for the contemporary administration of justice in Canada, as well as the intellectual traditions by which this administration of justice is understood.

The domination of Canada has been facilitated by the divisive character of our geography, a fact often overlooked by commentators on the Canadian experience. Canada is a geographically immense country with a comparatively small population, fostering local politics and regionalism. In forging our own traditions, therefore, we have had to overcome both geographical divisiveness and the divisiveness fostered by those who facilitate further fragmentation through misobservations about the absence of a Canadian politics of resistance. For many of us this divisive influence is best countered through coalition building. The support for specialist academic journals is limited and many academics have opted for the anthology as a way of producing 'counter-hegemonic' discourse while maintaining links between regions. This book is no exception. Like many others of its kind, this book is an attempt to bring together pockets of critical discourse from across the country in a search for commonalties of experience and ideas. Such attempts are a necessary aspect of a political practice aimed at resisting the forces of fragmentation and revitalizing the struggle for social justice.

---

[1] Ian Taylor's recent indictment of the Canadian academy generally, and Canadian criminology specifically, is an excellent example. (see *British Journal of Criminology*, 30, 1990:103-106)

We have enjoyed the support and assistance from many in producing this modest contribution to such a struggle. Faculty and students at Simon Fraser University, University of British Columbia, Carleton University, and Northeastern Illinois University patiently listened to oral versions of parts of this manuscript and made helpful suggestions on how it might be improved. We should like to thank them for their constructive criticisms. We would also like to thank Walter DeKeseredy, John Lowman, and Dragan Milovanovic as well as three anonymous reviewers for their helpful suggestions on various aspects of the manuscript. Our secretaries, June Freeborn, Christa Rathje, and Carol Wong made the production of the manuscript less difficult than it could have been and our copy editor, Robert Clarke, made the refining of the manuscript a pleasurable experience. We should also like to thank Errol Sharpe from Fernwood Publications for his persistence in seeing this manuscript through to its completion. Finally we would like to thank all of our contributors who, despite our delays, remained supportive and collegial. It is their work which brings this manuscript to fruition.

Dawn H. Currie

Brian D. MacLean

Vancouver

Contents

Foreword   v

Preface   ix

Introduction

1.   Three Traditions of Critical Justice Inquiry:
Class, Gender, and Discourse
Dawn H. Currie, Brian D. MacLean, and Dragan Milovanovic   3

Part One   The Legislative Branch: Lawmaking

2.   Meech Lake: Constitution-Making as Patriarchal Practice
Donna Greschner   45

3.   Abortion Law Reform: A Pendulum That Swings One Way
Dawn H. Currie   60

4.   Crisis Justice for Youth: Making the
Young Offenders Act and the Discourse of Penality
Paul Havemann   86

Part Two   The Judiciary: Law Finding

5.   Wildlife, Domestic Animals, and the
Dene Aboriginal Rights Claim
Michael Asch   115

6.   Due Process in Saskatchewan's Uranium Inquiries
Jim Harding   130

7.   "Sociologically Speaking":
Law, Sexuality, and Social Change
Didi Herman   150

8. Subjectivity and Reality-Construction in Law
    Dragan Milovanovic   169

Part Three The Executive Branch: Policing

9. The RCMP and Its Ancestors:
    Over 100 Years of Willing Service
    Lorne Brown   185

10. In Defiance of the Law of the Land:
    Social Control and the Unemployed Movement in
    the Dirty Thirties in British Columbia
    Louise Gorman Arkle and John McMullan   214

11. Casino Gambling and Organized Crime:
    Towards an Analysis of Police Discourses
    Colin S. Campbell   234

12. Women, Men, and Police:
    Losing the Fight against Wife Battery in Canada
    Dawn H. Currie and Brian D. MacLean   251

13. Reconstituting Social Order and Social Control:
    Police Accountability in Canada
    Dawn H. Currie, Walter S. DeKeseredy, and Brian D. MacLean   276

Bibliography   298

Introduction

Three Traditions of Critical Justice Inquiry

Chapter One

Three Traditions of Critical Justice Inquiry: Class, Gender, and Discourse

Dawn H. Currie/Brian D. MacLean/Dragan Milovanovic

INTRODUCTION

In liberal-democratic social formations, the concept of *justice* occupies a central position in the set of ideological categories through which social reality is both constructed and understood. Virtually no day passes without exposure to the concept of justice in one way or another, often in great variety. In Canada the electronic and visual news media devote considerable time and space to crime and its treatment. Contemporary issues that involve human rights — such as the abortion debate, the pro-democracy movements of Eastern Europe, the events at Tienanmen Square, and the victims' rights movement — are newsworthy stories reported upon with regularity. Movies involving crime, the denial of justice to victims, racism, neofascist organizations, and the related threats to our everyday experience and understanding of justice and *law and order* are among the most popular films at the box office, while murder mysteries and crime novels rank highly on the best-seller lists. Still other issues receive increasing public attention: Child abuse, wife battery, aboriginal land claims, the Canadian/United States Free Trade Agreement, Canadian unity, and the *Charter of Rights and Freedoms* all contribute to public consciousness about a just and fair quality of life in Canadian Society.

While popular conceptions of justice are important to our understanding of life in Canadian society, a careful interrogation of what the term 'justice' implies — and the many meanings with which it is associated — does not necessarily lead to a scientific understanding of the processes by

Dawn Currie is Assistant Professor in Sociology at the University of British Columbia, Brian MacLean is a Criminologist in Vancouver, Dragan Milovanovic is Associate Professor in Criminal Justice at Northeastern Illinois University

which justice is understood or acted upon. We are consistently exposed to ideas such as the principles of natural justice, justice prevails, justice for all, in the interests of justice, and so forth, as if they were self-evident truths and ideals towards which our society strives. But if we attempt to extract from these notions a general concept of justice, we end up with an ideal that stands above and beyond society itself — an image of justice in which some universal, transhistorical state of social well-being exists independently of society — and our task as social scientists and members of society becomes to ensure that this ideal is achieved in everyday life. The problem with such an image is that it separates the concept of justice from the social relations that construct its meaning. The image sustains the conviction that justice is a natural thing existing independently of society.

One central assertion of this book is that all concepts are human constructions. As such, they are subject to modification within a social context, which is itself continually changing. Furthermore, concepts differ from time to time, place to place, and culture to culture. Perhaps even more importantly, the terms we use to denote concepts might well remain constant while the social meanings attached to them vary. For example, a specific concept such as *crime* has changed in its meaning over time, from designating an act that violates a criminal law to designating an act for which a legal category has been assigned "by authorized agents in a politically organized society" (Quinney, 1974: 23). Thus using the term 'crime' without specifying its historical and social context can lead to ambiguity in meaning. Concepts that are less specific and more abstract, such as *freedom,* are applied differently by different groups, and the meanings differ greatly. For example, while President Reagan often referred to the Contra rebels as 'freedom fighters,' the Nicaraguan state defined these very same forces as counterrevolutionary.

Both of these examples share certain similarities. Firstly, as concepts 'crime' and 'freedom' have meanings that are specific to a historical moment, to a cultural, social, and political context, and to the sets of social relations that both construct and use the concepts as relevant to the comprehension of social experience. Similarly, the concept of justice is equally ambivalent if it is not used and understood within its relevant sociohistorical, cultural, and political context. To understand the nature of justice in a given society we must understand the nature of the social relations of that society and the processes by which a conceptual category like justice is both constructed and understood socially. In this manner we can determine how the concept of justice changes over time in accordance with the progressive forces of a society; and how the conception and meaning of justice remain similar over time in accordance with the conservative forces of society.

The task of this book is to examine the administration of justice. Such a task implies that justice is more than a concept or idea. The starting point of our investigation is the recognition that justice is a set of social relations that we can grasp as *legal relations* and that the social actors in this set of relations can be grasped as *juridic subjects.* Our purpose is to carefully examine the social structures whose task it is to administer justice in our society and that have developed out of these relations. Our analysis will suggest that the basis of the administration of justice is contradictory because what is seen by some to be just is seen by others to be unjust. To recognize this contradictory nature of justice is to implicitly assume that legal relations are in some way reflective of power relations. It is precisely this recognition that has motivated a variety of legal scholars, criminologists, and social scientists to oppose the view that legal relations are relations of equality and justice; they advocate instead a full-scale inquiry into the nature of legal relations as relations of power. During the 1970s and 1980s, when critical legal scholarship began to flourish, a dominant theme of investigation was the way in which these power relations are reconstituted within the state. Because such an approach was relatively novel there were a number of false starts, a number of ideas that when pursued led to more questions than answers. To some extent, simplistic analyses of these relations were undertaken and advocated with more seriousness than they perhaps deserved.

One such approach suggested that the state was reflective of the interests of the most powerful segments of society and as such acted as an *instrument* of ruling-class domination of other classes in society. As the critique of *instrumentalism* developed, scholars began to take the view that the state, law, and authority are not the simple instruments of class domination but remain relatively autonomous from the class structure of society. Such a conception of law and the state implies that, once constructed, the state is more or less a separate entity that proceeds to pursue its own interests more or less free from the influence of competing class interests. The problem that arises from this conception is that in its role of facilitating the reproduction of social relations the state somehow seems to operate in the interests of the powerful despite its purported autonomy from the class structure. Consistent with this approach, the concept of *hegemony* gains some significance. For our purposes, 'hegemony' means domination of one class in society by another. By domination we mean political, economic, and ideological control; however, the concept of hegemony also includes the notion that the dominated classes willingly participate in this domination largely because of their adoption of ruling-class ideology, which portrays law as an instrument ensuring fairness, equality, and justice. Thus the notion of hegemony logically leads to an investigation of the way in which the ideology of law and the state is both constructed by the ruling class and subsequently adopted by the working class. The questions to be answered by this approach primarily concern the processes by which the working class is controlled by the ruling class and the role that the state plays in fostering this control. More specifically, how are law and the administration of justice used by the state to secure control of the working class? This line of questioning gained such significance as a tradition of academic inquiry that it came to be known as a separate discipline of *social controlology*.

While controlology played a useful historical role in raising questions about the fairness of the administration of justice, its importance has been called into question. The critique advanced against the social-control paradigm deserves our attention if we are to fully comprehend the significance of contemporary critical lines of inquiry into the nature of justice in our society.

THE TROUBLE WITH CONTROLOLOGY[1]

In a recent examination of the social control literature, Matthews (1989) has found a number of central concepts that, when taken to their logical conclusion, lead us into a 'nothing works' dilemma. Firstly, he argues that the social-control literature describes the development of the formal social-control network as a *widening of the net*. Here the image is of a net being extended over ever-increasing spheres of social life so that more and more people are caught up in this net of formal social control. While the controlologists may be correct in this observation, according to Matthews any attempts to overcome the widening of this net by reforms that turn to community and informal approaches are seen by the controlologists as being simply more of the same. Thus the image that the working classes are continually crushed under the state machinery or *Liberal Boot* (Ratner, 1984) is not only misleading and overly simplistic but also logically leads to the conception that if interventions are attempted the state will use these to its advantage, and, if interventions are not attempted, the state is free to go about its business of bringing the boot down upon the masses. In short, the conclusion that *nothing works* cannot be avoided if one embarks upon this line of discourse. Aside from the *impossiblism* of the controlologists' position, there is an inherent *negativism* in that once in place such a dominant state structure is beyond control from below. The conception that there is a transhistorical or inevitable quality to state domination is unwittingly implicit in this line of argument.

Matthews (1989) outlines an extensive critique of this approach, with these main points:

1. *Conceptual Vagueness.* The term 'social control' itself has been widely recognised as being something of a 'Mickey Mouse' concept. The literature also suffers from globalism and from the uncritical employment of various empirical generalisations.

2. *The employment of polarised and exclusive dichotomies.* Notably formal-informal, public-private, state-market, which are not disaggregated and which are rarely examined in relation to their interconnections and interdependencies.

3. *An underlying commitment to pessimism and impossiblism.* This arises from a number of sources. It is linked primarily to functionalism but can also be the product of setting unrealistic and unrealisable goals. It is also a product of seeing the history of social control as the rise of Unfreedom.

4. *The problem of reform.* This problem arises on the one hand from the commitment to impossiblism ('nothing works') and to the reliance on polarised alternatives. The failure to take reform seriously results in

a limited discussion of possible strategies on the one hand, and often a significant gap between theory and any reforms which might be proposed.

5. *A limited conception of power.* Despite the preoccupation with the work of Foucault the notion of power which is employed in much of the social control literature is crude and often 'pre-Foucauldian.' Power, for example, as a positive and constructive force is largely absent from this analysis.

6. *That the explanation of the changes in control practices is often weak.* Much of the work is descriptive or a 'mapping out' in which the dynamics behind policy movements are left unexamined. Instead, we tend to be offered 'top down' explanations which ignore the complexity of social and political frameworks within which policy materialises. Thus although much of this work is ostensibly radical it remains in a sense peculiarly depoliticised.

7. *That the analysis of social control suffers from an arbitrary separation of crime and control.* This exaggerates the autonomy of central decision-making processes and plays down the demand side of the equation. Importantly, it loses sight of how policies relate to public priorities and changing levels of tolerance. It is therefore unable to evaluate the democratic component in policy-making effectively.

Matthews is not alone in his critique of the directions in which the social-control literature has developed. Stan Cohen, globally recognized as the world's leading contrologist, has found it necessary to criticize the way in which the literature generally has totally misused the concept of social control. He plainly attempts to divorce himself and his work from more vulgarized versions advanced by others taking up the tradition. He writes:

Children (invariably boys) are sometimes given a toy hammer for a present. At first they learn the many good uses of the instrument, like hitting nails into wood; then they discover some other uses and delights like banging on the floor, attacking a baby sibling, enjoying the sound of breaking glass. This is when parents regret buying the present.

In sociology — as elsewhere — concepts are used like hammers. A formless and recalcitrant reality is banged into shape, rendering it manageable and comprehensible. This is both necessary and inevitable; otherwise there would be no need for 'science.' Sometimes, though (like small children with their hammers) the project gets a little out of hand. The concept/hammer is wielded with much imagination and inventiveness, but without much attention to consequences.

In this paper, I consider some such features of the concept of social control as they appear in various radical, critical or revisionist writings about crime, deviance, and the law over the past two decades. (1989:347)

While Cohen (1989) analyses a number of points at which he sees contrology going astray, perhaps of most importance to our argument is the "privileged role given to the working of the modern state" (351). Within this conception of social control there is an overarching apparatus or "master pattern" that gives a logical meaning to the otherwise inexplicable activities of the state as envisioned by these writers. Similarly, the failure to recognize the different operations of the various components of the state apparatus as being both distinct and interconnected leads controlologists to a confused conception of the state. By looking for a monolithic institution in which some overarching ideology prevails, many of them have decontextualized the state, simplifying its structure and mystifying its internal operations. For example, the Canadian state has been conceptualized by Ratner and McMullan as a repressive apparatus in which the relative autonomy of the criminal justice system is used to reinforce ruling class interests:

> The difficulties in sustaining a social formation prone to class struggle and hegemonic discord become more palpable at the operational level of the organizational components of the criminal justice system. In responding to the social frictions generated by class inequalities, the police, courts, and corrections typically act to protect the interests of capital with constitutional restraints. Relative autonomy is especially visible when legal norms are periodically violated by these authorities in order to safeguard bourgeois interests jeopardized by changing trajectories in the class distribution of power. (1987: 109)

For these writers, power is apparently not a social relation but some *thing* distributed within the class structure of society. While they provide us with the notion that the state has certain components, the imagery of their conception suggests that these components act in specific ways and for the same purposes, namely to safeguard bourgeois interests. Thus, despite their analysis of the different components of the criminal justice system, they seem to be arguing that these components always act in harmony towards the same identifiable end and for the same reasons. Perhaps the limitation of this approach is best understood by the fact that while these authors make general claims about the workings of the state, they focus their analysis upon those components of the state which they feel constitute the criminal justice system: police, courts, and corrections.

While the *state control* debate rages on within controlologist discourse, its relevance to our understanding of legal relations becomes decreasingly apparent. Also, while the criminal justice system might consist of the three components of police, courts, and corrections, missing from this formulation is the arena in which 'legal norms' are constructed. Since these norms are the starting point for the analysis by these authors, an analysis of the way in which such norms are constructed seems mandatory for an understanding of the relation between state, capital, and labour.

THREE COMPONENTS OF THE ADMINISTRATION OF JUSTICE

A careful reading of the pitfalls inherent in the social-control literature leads to another central assertion of this book: that the administration of justice, while inclusive of the activities of criminal justice agencies, is much broader than criminal justice. Far from being monolithic in its structure, operation, and ideology, the state consists of a number of components, all of which presuppose a particular configuration of legal relations. Sometimes these components are complementary in their activities; at other times they are contradictory. Sometimes they operate in harmony, sometimes in discord. Sometimes they have a united purpose, often they disagree as to their purposes. For this reason, it is useful for us to distinguish between three broad categories of organized state activity that can be loosely described as components in the state structure and that function differently in the process of the administration of justice.

The *legislative branch* of the state is that aspect of state activity in which legal norms are codified. Sometimes referred to as *lawmaking*, this aspect of state activity legislates codes of legal practices. Here the state is responsible for constructing a criminal code, civil law, legal statutes, a constitution, and a variety of other legal mechanisms that can be broadly defined as legal norms. Analyses of this process can range from the conception of a rational process through which the regulation of society is maintained, to a process in which class struggle and legal relations are crystallized into various legal codes.

The *judiciary* is that aspect of organized state activity in which the legal codes produced by the legislative apparatus are interpreted. Sometimes referred to as *law finding*, this aspect of state activity serves to interpret, apply, and rule upon the meaning of the legal formulations previously produced. Generally seen in Canada as the two-tiered court system, in which the appellate division of the Supreme Court of Canada has the highest authority, this aspect of state activity can also be broadly conceived of as agencies that must make rulings based upon laws passed by the legislative branch. For example, boards of inquiry have authority to interpret specific legislation, but must ultimately succumb to decisions given by different levels of the court system.

The exe*cutive branch* refers to the aspect of state activity that enforces the laws as constructed by the legislature and interpreted by the judiciary. Clearly, agencies such as municipal, provincial, and federal police forces as well as provincial and federal correctional agencies fall within the confines of the executive branch. Other state enforcement agencies can be broadly construed as part of the executive branch as well. An example might be The Combines Investigation Branch, which investigates allegations against corporate infractions of Anti-Combines Legislation (Goff and Reasons, 1978).

While it might be argued that each of these components of the state must operate in harmony to produce the administration of justice in Canada, it can be argued with equal validity that sometimes the specific interests of these three branches collide. For example, the abortion debate in Canada represents a conflict between the legislative branch and the judiciary in terms of which aspect of the state is responsible for attempting to resolve the issue. On the one hand, the judiciary has argued that it is up to parliament to pass legislation; on the other, the legislative branch is reluctant to do so and has attempted to leave such a responsibility to the courts.

The executive branch and the courts often come into conflict with one another. The spate of films in which Dirty Harry, the police officer, is constantly having his hands cuffed by the courts in his quest to protect society from dangerous criminals reflects one aspect of the tensions between the judiciary and the executive branch. The subtext of these films suggests that the courts are continually intervening in police activity in the interests of due process and that in doing so they fail to meet their goal of dispensing justice, because the criminals walk away from the courtroom unscathed. It is not uncommon for the police to argue that the courts are too lenient, while the courts argue that the police abuse their power. One concrete example of such a conflict is the *Royal Commission Inquiry into Metropolitan Toronto Police Practices* (Morand, 1976), when the legislative branch appointed the judiciary to investigate the executive branch. At points in his judgments, Justice Morand clearly states that he finds it difficult to believe that the police might act in ways of which they have been accused (see Part Three of this volume). Yet at another point in his judgments he observes:

> During the course of the inquiry, it became obvious to me that some police officers believe that they are the only remaining barrier between the public who hired them and the anti-social persons who break society's laws. They apparently believe as well that it is necessary for them not only to investigate crimes, but to act as judge and jury. No police officer who testified before the Commission stated this position and I am convinced that the vast majority of police officers do not take this position. Where, however, this view is held by officers, it cannot be tolerated. It is the sole duty of the police officer to arrest and prepare a case for presentation to the court regarding those persons who break society's rules. It is for the courts to determine guilt or innocence and it is for the courts to determine punishment. If society tolerates the police usurping the position of judge and jury and administering punishment for them, then society is no better than the persons who have broken its rules. (Morand, 1976:15)

This case illustrates that when one part of the state sees its role being 'usurped' by another part of the state there is a considerable potential for conflict regardless of the extent to which the social actors in these different locations have or have not adopted 'bourgeois ideology.'

Finally, the executive branch often comes into conflict with the legislative branch. Perhaps the best contemporary example of this conflict in Canada is the capital punishment debate. In 1976 capital punishment was abolished in this country, much to the chagrin of the police who represented one of the strongest retentionist lobbies (Taylor, 1983). In 1987 the issue of capital punishment was again raised as a private member's bill in the House of Commons. Despite the fact that the legislature had abolished capital punishment ten years previously, the police were still in favour of reinstating the death penalty (Comack, 1990). Thus, rather than being harmonious, the relation between the function of the executive branch and the legislative branch of the state was characterized by conflict and strife.

Despite the fact that there is conflict among the three principal components of the state, the administration of justice still emerges as a more or less dominant set of discursive categories and practices so that hegemony is reconstituted. Far from being a simplistic process in which all three components of the state apparatus simply agree on the dominant ideas and practices to be followed, the hegemony produced is more a process of active negotiation between these components in their daily relations than a set of ideas imposed upon them by some monolithic structure. Carriere and Ericson (1989) come to similar conclusions in their analysis of community policing when they argue: "Hegemony is not a static, cage-like structure imposed on 'the soft fibres of the brain' (Foucault, 1977:103) of oppressed people by the powerful." Carriere and Ericson (1987:9) quote Raymond Williams:

> A lived hegemony is always a process. It is not, except analytically, a system or a structure .... It does not just passively exist as a form of dominance. It has continually to be renewed, recreated, defended, and modified. It is also continually resisted, limited, altered, challenged by pressures not all its own.... One way of expressing the necessary distinction between practical and abstract senses within the concept is to speak of the 'hegemonic' rather than 'hegemony,' and of the 'dominant' rather than simple 'domination.' The reality of any hegemony, in the extended political or cultural sense, is that, while by definition it is always dominant, it is never total or exclusive. (Williams, 1977: 112-3)

Following Williams, any understanding of the administration of justice must take into account not just the hegemonic and the dominant, in the way that social controlology has done. Rather, we must attempt to understand the processes by which hegemony is continually resisted, limited, altered, and challenged. Our first step has been to identify the processes by which the three components of the state interact to produce a hegemony rather than enforce one. Our next step is to examine what kinds of inquiry have emerged within the study of justice that are cognizant of the processes by which hegemony is both reconstituted and resisted. Also, such inquiry must recognize the different constituencies that participate in the construction of the hegemonic and the dominant. Three distinct traditions of critical inquiry can be identified for this purpose.

THREE TRADITIONS OF CRITICAL INQUIRY
Critical studies of the justice apparatus and the legal relations upon which it is founded can be broadly grouped within three distinct traditions. While each of these traditions has made a significant impact upon social-scientific inquiry generally and are therefore distinguishable from each other, each also draws to some extent upon the concepts and ideas offered by the other traditions. Thus, while distinct and separate, these traditions often intersect.

Historical materialism or *Marxist political economy*[2] has a lengthy history and has provided social science with a set of conceptual tools from which social inquiry has benefited greatly. From the mid-1960s, this tradition has been gaining significant attention and has emerged as a dominant form of critical social inquiry. Central to its conceptual panoply are the concepts of the *relations of production* and the *forces of production*. The 'forces of production' refer to the material factors by which material reality is constructed and reproduced. In capitalist society, these forces include the labour power, raw materials, technology, and other resources that constitute the production of commodities for profit. The 'relations of production' refer to the way in which the forces of production are organized. In a capitalist society some people own the productive property, and derive their subsistence from that property, while others own only their labour power which they must sell in the market in order to subsist. *Class* refers to the position a person occupies within this system of ownership. Thus the two great classes are *capital*, the owners of productive property, and *labour*, the non-owners who sell their labour power to capital. While there are a number of variations in how these basic concepts are developed within this tradition, common assertions are that class domination provides the basis for a state apparatus that ultimately serves in the reproduction of the relations of production. Thus the administration of justice within this framework is analysed as the social reproduction and legitimation of property relations.

Feminism[3] also has a long history of scholarship, although it is only since about the mid-1960s that the current body of feminist literature began to develop into the significant intellectual force it represents today. Again, while there are a considerable number of variations within contemporary feminist debate, one concept central to all approaches is the notion of *patriarchy*, as a form of social organization in which domination is secured by a small number of men or an individual male. Central to feminist debate is the notion of sexual inequality in which female members of a particular social formation are dominated in a variety of ways by the male members. Sometimes this domination is material, sometimes social, sometimes economic, sometimes physical; but it is always some combination of these forms. Despite disagreement concerning how male domination of women originates and is perpetuated, most feminists agree that the subordinate position of women in society is a social fact and not a biological one, and that the institutions of society have arisen both as a result of and as agents in the reproduction of unequal social relations on the basis of sex. Thus, for many feminists the administration of justice does not just involve the issue of property ownership, which for the most part is male dominated, but is also a process in which male superiority in society is both legitimated and reproduced.

Discourse analysis or *poststructuralism*[4] is primarily an investigation into language as the expression of dominant forms of thought. For these writers power relations are not only reflected in language; but power relations are also themselves reconstituted primarily through systems of discursive categories and practices. It is the power of language that represents the form by which the dominant is reproduced and primarily the vehicle by which the individual subject is constructed socially. Thus the focus of study for discourse analysis is the discursive context of people's lives. In this way, the process by which the hegemonic and the dominant are legitimated and reproduced is analysed as the 'text' as a form of power. In terms of the administration of justice, discourse analysis is concerned with the logic, language, and ideology of the various forms of domination and control.

All three of these traditions can be seen as critical because they share certain features regarding the nature of social reality. Firstly, each of them goes beyond the level of appearances and attempts to carefully excavate the underlying social relations of those appearances. Secondly, rather than accepting the status quo as given, each of the traditions challenges both appearances and their justifications. The traditions differ in the sense that they each have as the object of their inquiry different aspects of the nature of social relations; however, each tends to draw heavily upon one another as well. For example, Marxist political economy is of little practical or intellectual value if it does not consider the unequal nature of gender relations and the role of female labour in the reproduction of social reality. Thus, while it may view social class as central to the reproduction of social reality, social class has little meaning if it is not informed by the consciousness that gender helps to construct. Furthermore, Marx himself was particularly interested in the ways by which human consciousness was socially constructed. Central to his critique of the political economy of his time was the argument that the ideological constructs of bourgeois society were used by political economists to interpret history and thus arrive at the conclusion that what now exists is an inevitable given. In this way the nature of capitalist domination was secured.

Feminism often draws upon the concepts given by historical materialism and discourse analysis. Thus a good deal of feminist discourse uses concepts such as class, forces and relations of production, and so forth. As well, feminist inquiry often draws upon *semiotics* or the philosophy of language as a way to understand how male rationality is reproduced and enforced in the process of social reproduction.

Finally, a discourse theory that is not grounded in the material conditions of class and gender relations makes little sense. Such a discourse theory would see language as living and in this personification of language people would be used as weapons by words in the struggle of opposing discourses. A more relevant form of discourse analysis is to attempt to analyse the nature of power relations and inequality as material facts in which language and discursive categories figure prominently.

Class / Power: The Political Economy of Justice

While the literature on the political economy of justice is voluminous, the studies can be grouped into three broad areas: law, the courts, and law enforcement and corrections. Central to such studies are the concepts of class, property, exploitation and accumulation, although how these concepts are linked and analyzed by different traditions of Marxist political economy tends to vary. Marx himself never produced a theory of social class, although the concept is central to his writings. Furthermore, although Marx planned to develop an intensive analysis of the capitalist state, he died before undertaking such a task. The result has been that more recent scholars have debated the way in which a Marxist theory of law and the state might be developed, and a number of different schools of thinking on this important point can be identified within the broader tradition of Marxist scholarship. It is clear that if we are to understand the nature of the administration of justice within a Marxist framework, a clearly articulated theory of law and the state in capitalist society is the starting point. Unfortunately, no such clear articulation exists.

The Legislative Branch: The Political Economy of Lawmaking

For many Marxists, the relations that embody private ownership of productive property form the basis for an analysis of the state and law. The central question is: What role does law play in both the legitimation of private property and the social inequality that private property represents? For some, the answer to this question is that the state and law are simply instruments through which the owning class subordinates the working class. Thus the state and law are instruments of class domination and will always express what is in the best interests of the owning class. This school of thinking, *instrumentalism*, has been criticized by numerous Marxists who argue that such a conception of law and the state is not only vulgar and simplistic but can also be proved to be empirically incorrect. These writers cite historical examples, such as the *Ten Hours Bill*, in which the state has either intervened or passed legislation to protect the interests of the working class. Thus, far from being a simple agent of social reproduction in the interests of capital, law and the state are much more complex and *relatively autonomous* from the pressures of either of the major classes and their interests.

The conception of the state as a structure with its own dynamics and interests as a social entity relatively autonomous from the class structure can also be refuted empirically. The fact that most capitalist states are dependent on private capital for state functioning, for example, is best illustrated by the fact that most capitalist states have developed a method of deficit financing in which their very existence is dependent upon the success of the political economy; however, focusing upon the economic aspects of the relation between state and capital does not often fully explain the political aspects of state functioning.

With such an empirical observation comes the idea that the state is really a product of the struggle between classes. In this conception, the state responds most readily to those groups that have fared best in the struggle. For the most part the successful group is capital; but labour has also been effective at different moments in history in getting its interests encoded in legislation. The difficulty with this *class conflict model* of law and the state, however, is that not enough attention has been paid to the economic aspects of the relation between the state, law, capital, and labour.

This brief overview of the logic of arguments debated in Marxist political economy is enough to demonstrate that different approaches have strengths and weaknesses, but that none is sufficient on its own to capture the precise nature of the complexity of law and the state. All of these approaches agree that somehow law and the state facilitate the reproduction of power relations in society, but the nature of those relations and the precise manner in which social inequality are reproduced is debated. Also, there seems to be little agreement among these Marxists as to what role law plays in transforming society. The dilemma here appears to be that if law and the state combine to legitimate and reproduce unequal property relations while providing a political climate in which the private accumulation of wealth can take place, then law and the state cannot in any sense be seen as providing an avenue for social emancipation. In this view, law is seen as oppressive. The other side of the coin is that law and the state have been used historically to improve the position of the working class and other disenfranchised groups. In emphasizing this view, law is seen as an "unqualified human good" or as a vehicle of social change. The state and the rule of law are seen as progressive.

Some writers have expressed dissatisfaction with these currents of Marxist political economy and have accused them all of being one-sided. These writers suggest that there is a logic to capitalist development that comes to be expressed in different legal forms. Far from being *economistic*, these writers fully recognize that such forms are not universal. Rather, while there are certain *laws of motion of capital* that can be "identified with the precision of a science," how such processes develop is *historically specific* and dependent upon the nature and strength of the class struggle at any specific historical moment and within a particular state. Thus it is next to impossible to predict precisely how the state and law will operate in different concrete situations.

For example, all capitalist societies face the problem of unemployment. It is a law of motion of capital that unemployment will rise and fall in accordance with cycles of capitalist development. Having said this, however, it is not clear how any particular society copes with unemployment. In Western European societies, workers have struggled to produce a commitment by the state to maintaining a welfare apparatus that caters to some extent to the needs of the unemployed. In the United States, welfare systems are less well developed. The result is that unemployed workers in the U.S.A. are more likely to be imprisoned, while in Europe some level of subsistence is maintained via the welfare apparatus. It is perhaps for this reason that the United States has one of the highest rates of incarceration in the world while the rates in Western European societies are among the lowest. Thus in this version of Marxist political economy, *the capital logic* school, law and the state are analysed as being historically specific. In this formulation economic processes and political processes combine in a unique way to produce specific variations of the way in which law and the state develop. In this view law and the state are seen as being both oppressive and progressive. Law is potentially both a vehicle of domination and a vehicle of emancipation. This contradictory nature of law is due to the contradictory nature of the state and the social relations that the state presupposes.

In all of these variations of Marxist political economy, the theoretical assertions about the nature of law and the state and the nature of the social relations upon which these institutions are based can only be empirically tested in the way that law is interpreted by the judiciary and enforced by the executive branch. Thus much of the empirical investigations of Marxist studies of justice have attempted to determine what role class plays in the administration of justice.

The Judiciary: The Political Economy of Law Finding

Studies in the political economy of law finding look for class biases in how the courts administer the law. There are a variety of ways in which such a study might be pursued, but to a large extent the differential treatment of individuals and powerful corporations by the courts has received considerable attention from the Marxists. Henry (1986) reports that in their quest for profits, corporations continually violate laws that restrict their activities in the interests of public safety; these corporations are rarely dealt the same severe punishments that individuals might receive for similar acts.

As an example Henry demonstrates that the Richardson-Merrel company produced a drug, MER/29, which was approved by the FDA in 1960. During the first year of production alone Richardson-Merrel grossed over $7 million from the sale of this drug; however, shortly thereafter over five hundred individuals developed cataracts after using the drug. As a consequence of ingesting the unsafe product, one of these consumers, Sidney Roginsky, also developed scaling and rashes and his hair began to fall out. In a civil suit the jury determined that the company had submitted falsified results of the testing of this product to the FDA and that various corporate officials were aware of this, including the vice-president. Roginsky was awarded $17,500 in damages and $100,000 in compensation because it was evident that Richardson-Merrel had purposely and knowingly marketed a product that was approved on the basis of false evidence. Nevertheless, the decision was reversed by a judge at an appeal. The judge ruled that although he recognized that Richardson-Merrel was culpable, it would not be fair to allow the compensation. He produced three reasons for this decision. Firstly, he stated that the marketing of MER/29 was a single error. Secondly, he noted that because many people had filed claims against the company, the company would go bankrupt if all the complainants received punitive damages. Finally, he reasoned that if such awards were given the resultant reduction in profit would fall upon the innocent stockholders of the company.

Henry observes that each of the reasons given in this case are erroneous. Firstly, there were many steps involved in the fake testing and its concealments, so it is difficult to understand how the actions of so many executives can be considered as a single fault. Secondly, the courts would not hesitate to jail individuals who were guilty of offences resulting in similar public harm. Once jailed, these persons would have no income, and it is well known that the stigma fostered by incarceration would minimize their opportunities of employment once released. Henry reasons that such consequences are similar to individual bankruptcy. While this outcome has not deterred judges from incarcerating individuals in the past, it seems to have prevented the Richardson-Merrel company from being punished in this case. Finally, the stockholders of the company benefited financially from the sale of the unsafe product, and with such a benefit comes responsibility. Henry further reasons that when people invest in corporations, they should make it their business to learn the nature of the corporate activity with which they are associating themselves. For these reasons, Henry concludes that a pro-business bias can be identified in the court's decision in this case. Here the power and influence of the corporation has resulted in a reduction of penalty compared to what an individual from the working class would receive for inflicting similar harms upon society.

The Richardson-Merrel case is not an isolated one. In their study of corporate crime in Canada, Goff and Reasons (1978) found that although many Canadian corporations were guilty of infractions against anticombines legislation, the nature and severity of punishment imposed by the courts on those corporations were in no way sufficient to deter further infractions. Furthermore, these authors found that the larger the corporation, the less likely it was for a punishment to be imposed. Therefore, this study also provides evidence to suggest that the law finding aspect of the administration of justice tends to favour one class at the expense of the other, indicating that the power relations in which social inequality is embodied have considerable influence on the activities of the courts. In another article Goff and Reasons (1986) suggest that there are nine categories of activity in which members of the working class are regularly victimized with impunity by powerful organizations. It appears that when the judiciary does investigate such activities, it is often more likely to rule in favour of the powerful.

Sometimes the courts do rule in favour of the less powerful. These decisions are often overturned, as in the case of MER/29, and sometimes laws are reformed to make the restrictive activity legitimate. In 1983 in Canada, a tripartite system in which prison officials, the Royal Canadian Mounted Police (RCMP), and the parole services colluded to continue incarceration for prisoners due for release received considerable public attention. Prisoners on mandatory supervision (MS) can be returned to prison at the discretion of their parole supervisor if the supervisor deems that the prisoner has either violated or *will* violate a condition of release. Thus prisoners under MS need not violate either an existing law or a condition of their release to be reincarcerated. *'Gating'* was the practice in which prisoners due for release on MS would have their parole suspended without ever having been released. The parole supervisor would initiate a suspension warrant to be served by the RCMP. On the day of release the prisoner would be showered, dressed in civilian clothing, and taken to the front gate of the prison, where the RCMP would be waiting to serve the suspension warrants. The prisoner would be transferred to the custody of the RCMP, who would serve the warrant and recommit the prisoner to the custody of the prison administration, who would then take the prisoner back into the prison as a parole violator — all without the prisoner ever having been actually released (MacLean and Ratner, 1987).

The practice of gating was eventually ruled illegal by the Supreme Court of Canada because it operated against the principles of natural justice; but in accepting the decision the solicitor general, Robert Kaplan, made the commitment to have parliament make the practice a legal one (MacLean and Ratner, 1987). In 1986 Parliament passed *Bill C-67* and *Bill C-68* into law, essentially legalizing the practice of gating and giving the National Parole Board the authority to deny the mandatory release of prisoners. The example of gating illustrates that even when the more powerful organizations in our society are ruled against in the courts, they often have the influence to change legislation so that it no longer operates against their specific interests.

In 1982 the *Charter of Rights and Freedoms* was proclaimed in Canada, and according to one of its architects, Roy Romanow, the purpose of the *Charter* was to provide a vehicle by which the poor and less powerful classes in society could be protected from the powerful. Essentially the *Charter* guarantees equal treatment to everyone, rich or poor, and provides a mechanism for action when such equality has been violated. Critical legal scholarship has been developing in Canada as a result of the *Charter*. After several years of *Charter* decisions, these writers argue that the courts are more likely to rule in favour of the powerful organizations than they are to rule in favour of the working class. Indeed, Romanow himself admits that what was intended to be a 'shield for the poor' ended up being a 'sword for the rich.' So it is with the contradictory nature of law and the state. Despite the fact that the law guarantees equality in theory, in practice law functions within a political economy in which the more powerful segments of society benefit.

The Political Economy of the Executive Branch

The study of the political economy of the executive branch has been to a large extent the study of how the unemployed labour force is disciplined and controlled by the owning class. Much of this work has been instru-mentalist in its orientation, although not necessarily. Whatever the theoretical framework, however, social class also figures prominently in Marxist studies of the executive branch. Although the executive branch consists of both law enforcement and corrections, in North America more attention has been directed at the correctional arm than at the police. In the attempt to fill this gap, in its investigation of the executive branch this book will later focus specifically on the police.

Perhaps the most critical studies of social class and policing have taken place in the United Kingdom, where the movement for the local accounta-bility of the police has sparked considerable debate and research. In 1978 Stuart Hall et al. undertook a case study of how class relations were reinforced by the police. Essentially the writers argued that police engage in a practice called *focused policing*. This policing style involves the disproportionate policing of poorer neighbourhoods and communities, which means that those most likely to be caught and arrested for street crime will be from the poor, working-class, and multiracial communities. In this way, far from being a simple process of focused policing, policing practices involve the enforcement of dominant class interests and the social construction of an ideology conforming to those dominant class interests. In their study of the mugging crisis in England, these writers found that as a result of policing practice, a false conception of a serious increase in mugging was produced and reinforced in the police statistics. They argued that the image of an assailant who is young, black, and male is embedded within the term mugging. By focusing their efforts on the poor, black community, the police not only made more arrests, which were subsequently reflected in their statistics, but these statistics themselves also became the basis for a moral panic and demands by the public to heavily police the black community.

Hall et al. conclude that such control campaigns are both the result of policing practices and a method of manufacturing public support for disproportionate policing of the black community. Because the dominant order sees young, black males as representing the greatest political threat, largely due to the high levels of unemployment and economic discrimination characterizing these communities, the establishment would benefit from a more heavy-handed policing of those communities. But unless valid reasons for such practices were developed, the action would be seen as unfair. Thus, the relation between policing and control campaigns was identified as a central element in the manufacture of public consent for what amounts to unfair policing. In this way unequal class interests are reinforced by a police force that appears to be acting in the public interests, but that is actually partisan in its practices. Policing or law enforcement as practised represents the enforcement of class domination and hegemony, not the equality guaranteed by law.

In North America, the most prevalent work of Marxist studies of the executive branch involves theories and studies of punishment and corrections. This tradition can be traced back to the writings of Georg Rusche and Otto Kirchheimer (Platt and Takagi, 1980) who pioneered the study of punishment and labour market variations. In their *Punishment and Social Structure* (1939), these writers advanced the notion that the nature of production in a given society was related to the kind of punishments used by that society. In a feudal society execution was used most often because workers were abundant. As commodity production emerged and capitalist relations became dominant, production became subject to periodic fluctuations in the labour market. At times there was a shortage of labour and at other times there was an oversupply. During the period of labour oversupply, in the interests of maintaining a cheaper supply of labour for exploitation during periods of labour shortage, prisons arose and gradually replaced execution as the predominant form of punishment. According to Rusche and Kirchheimer the *principle of less eligibility* guided the construction and maintenance of prisons. This principle states that the conditions in the prison must be worse than the worst conditions of existence in 'free' society; otherwise people living in squalor would flock into the prisons.

Some researchers have attempted to test the principle of less eligibility empirically. In one study, Jankovic (1980) deduces from the work of Rusche and Kirchheimer that, firstly, there should be a relationship between economic conditions and the severity of punishment: "When the economy is bad, punishments should be more severe." He also deduces that, if these authors are correct, we should expect to find a direct relationship between unemployment trends and prison populations. In other words, as unemployment rises and an oversupply of labour is produced, we should find greater use of imprisonment as a form of punishment. Jankovic's study produced statistically significant findings in support of the idea that prison populations increase during periods of high unemployment despite the level of criminal activity. What these findings suggest is that whether or not unemployment leads to crime, crime is dealt with more severely by the courts when there is an oversupply of labour. Thus the significance of this finding is not that unemployment necessarily leads to crime, which would then explain higher prison populations. Rather, when the rate of crime is held constant, prison populations still increase during periods of high unemployment, indicating that the courts increasingly make use of carceral forms of punishment when the unemployed labour force is larger.

While there are numerous difficulties with both the theoretical work of Rusche and Kirchheimer and the empirical studies it has generated, there can be little doubt that their work has inspired a good deal of study of the political economy of punishment. Indeed, Box (1987) cites 11 studies in which the relation between unemployment and punishment was investigated, and there are numerous others that have been since completed or are currently in progress. Central to all of these studies is the notion that the political economy of capitalist development continually reproduces *problem populations* (Spitzer, 1975), which represent the greatest threat to established power relations and must be disciplined and controlled if those power relations are to be maintained. In this conception, the executive branch fulfils the function of enforcing class interests that have through other aspects of the administration of justice come to be represented in legal codes. Thus the study of the executive branch within this tradition is the study of how one class is controlled by another class through its ability to influence the enforcement apparatus of the state.

Absent from most Marxist studies of the different components of the administration of justice is an analysis of gender. Although the concept of class as central to such work cannot be denied, recent feminist scholarship has successfully pointed out that while class might be an important aspect of social inequality, class domination is not the only form of domination in capitalist society. Social inequality is manifest in a number of ways, and power relations are more extensive than those involving class power as studied by Marxist political economy. One such set of ignored power relations is patriarchal, in which one group of people — men — dominates another group of people — women. Once we recognize that such a set of power relations is a significant aspect of inequality in our society, we must examine how these power relations are also reproduced by the administration of justice.

Gender / Power:
Feminist Challenges to the Study of Justice

From her observation that every avenue of power in society, including the coercive power of the state, is in male hands, Millett (1970) defined *patriarchy* as "the rule of the father." Feminists since have disagreed about exactly how this power of men over women operates and is maintained.[5] Although these writers themselves are increasingly dissatisfied with academic categorization of feminist theory, there are predominantly three approaches that systematically explore the nature of patriarchal relations to develop general theories of women's oppression (see Donovan, 1986; Tong, 1989). The first is liberal feminism, which views patriarchy primarily as operating through the unfair rules and practices of gender stereotyping, which perpetuate sex-role dualisms throughout society and disadvantage women. Liberals believe that these rules governing society are based on mistaken or outmoded ways of thinking. Because they view rules themselves as inherently neutral, liberals do not challenge the rules themselves but, rather, emphasize the need for their reform. Radical feminists, on the other hand, associate patriarchal rules directly with the interests of men. This is because they equate patriarchy with the benefits that men derive from the appropriation of women's sexuality and procreative labours. This appropriation occurs through heterosexual relations, especially those within the family. From this perspective patriarchy benefits men both individually and collectively, making it unlikely that they will relinquish privileges embodied by current institutions and the rules of operation of those institutions. Finally, reflecting the influence of Marxist theory and method of inquiry, socialist feminists reject both the liberal emphasis on the cultural sphere of ideas and the radical view of men as sharing a universal interest, arguing instead that we must identify the material basis for the oppression of women within social institutions. Beginning from Engels's recognition that history consists of both the production of daily life and the reproduction of generational life, within socialist feminist debates patriarchy is inextricably linked to class and embraces relations of production and reproduction (as well as the relationship between the two).

Feminism and the Legislative Branch

Reflecting the emergence of the contemporary women's movement, the past two decades have witnessed feminist legal reform in Canada.[6] Central to this struggle was changing the symbolic representation of women as juridic subjects. The *British North America Act* of 1867 — as the foundation upon which Canadian society was built — stipulated that only 'persons' could vote, be appointed Senators, or become lawyers and judges. Given that women were legally not 'persons,' they could not exercise these rights. While the status of women as 'persons' was won in the courts by 1929, this blatant example of legal sexism continues to remind feminists today of the important role of law and the necessity for its reform. Beginning in 1970 a growing body of feminist jurisprudence has identified ways in which law and its administration are biased against women, particularly in the areas of employment, the family, the *Criminal Code* and constitutional rights (see Atcheson, Eberts, and Symes, 1984).

The longest tradition of feminist legal scholarship is grounded in classical liberal theory. While 'enlightenment' philosophers such as Rousseau and Locke excluded women from rights of citizenship on the grounds that women lacked rational and moral thought, during the eighteenth century Mary Wollstonecraft argued that men and women have the same intellectual and moral core: When women do reason differently or incorrectly — as many feminist writers at that time believed they did — it is simply due to their lack of proper training. Following the enlightenment tradition, feminists linked the notion of natural rights with women's emancipation (see Rossi, 1973). Accepting the liberal view that law is inherently neutral, reformers campaigned for the elimination of stereotypical differentiation of women and men and for legislation making it illegal to discriminate against individuals on the basis of their sex. While U.S. struggles crystallized around the latter in the form of the *Equal Rights Amendment*, Canadian feminist struggles focused primarily on the former. Family law in particular has been criticized for perpetuating the legal view of women as subordinate to husbands and primarily responsible for the raising of children (see Boyd and Sheehy, 1989). While the struggle for women to retain earnings and property upon marriage began in the nineteenth century, the increasing divorce rate during the 1960s made apparent the hidden costs of marriage to women. By assuming the unpaid role of mother and wife, women relinquish serious commitment to the labour force, becoming both economically and psychologically dependent upon husbands. With marriage being redefined — both in law and popular culture — as a union *not* binding for life, this dependency translated into a lifetime handicap for divorced women. This is because ownership of matrimonial property was legally interpreted as established through direct financial contribution. As a consequence, women found upon divorce that they were not necessarily entitled to assets acquired during marriage. On this basis women's groups across Canada became involved in a nationwide lobby for reform of family law. This struggle has been effective in eliminating references to traditional views of the 'proper' roles for men and women within marriage and the notion of the unity of the family under the legal identity of the husband. Reflected in the use of gender-neutral language, the terms 'husband' and 'wife' have been replaced with 'spouse,' and the word 'parents' has been substituted for 'mother' or 'father' (see Currie, 1989). Implicit in the outdated language is men's primary responsibility to provide a home and women's destiny as the rearing of children. The general effect of reform has been to redefine marriage as a contractual partnership of equals rather than a sacramental obligation. A similar approach resulted in these types of reforms in employment law and criminal law (see Burt, 1988; Baines, 1988).

As well as removing ideological language and assumptions that perpetuate social differences between the genders, patriation of the Constitution in 1980 provided the opportunity to enshrine the principle of equality in a new *Canadian Charter of Rights and Freedoms* (see Kome, 1983). Although successful, the struggle was not an easy one: Even in the 1980s sexual equality had to be negotiated, fought for, and defended at every stage. While Hosek (1983: 295) provides an impressive list of demands that women's groups fought for but did not secure, sections 15(1) and 28 of the *Charter* express commitment to the goal of sexual equality:

15 (1) Every individual is equal before and under the law and has the right to the equal protection and equal benefit of the law without discrimination and, in particular, without discrimination based on race, national or ethnic origin, colour, religion, sex, age or mental or physical disability ...

28 Notwithstanding anything in this Charter, the rights and freedoms referred to in it are guaranteed equally to male and female persons.

With the security of this *Charter*, the efforts of liberal reform appear to have been successful: Most of Canada's laws had been scrutinized for sexist bias and women are guaranteed equal treatment both within and before the law. By the close of the 1980s, legal rights for Canadian women were basically secure. Through a century of struggle women can own property on the same basis as men; they have gained access to professions; they can vote in elections and sit in the Senate; three women now sit in the Supreme Court of Canada; and Canadian women have access to formal redress in the case of alleged discrimination.

Feminism and the Judiciary

Despite feminist victories, by the 1990s Canadian women were becoming painfully aware of the difference between the symbolic value of law and the material effect of its application. Because the judiciary continues to be dominated by men and patriarchal attitudes about women, the interpretation and application of even gender-neutral laws have been a disappointing experience for Canadian women. A good example of the way in which patriarchal attitudes influence the application of law is provided by the refusal of women into the legal profession in Canada. Annie Macdonald Langstaff, one of the first Canadian women to apply for admission to the bar, was refused in 1915 on the grounds that "to admit a woman, and more particularly a married women, as a *barrister*, that is to say, as a *person who pleads cases at the bar before judges or juries in open court and in the presence of the public*, would be nothing short of a direct infringement upon public order and a manifest violation of the law of good morals and public decency" (in Baines, 1988: 163).

While present-day readers may consider this a 'quaint' reminder of Victorian attitudes towards women, our courts continue to interpret law from a white, middle-class male perspective, thereby discriminating against women. Boyle (1984), shows how sexual assault provisions in the *Criminal Code* have been interpreted and applied in a way that protects 'the falsely accused male.' She documents technical aspects of law that allow judicial discretion as a source of unfair judicial decision-making: the 'chaste/unchaste distinction' as a testament of the credibility of the victim who is reduced to the role of Crown 'witness'; the 'marital immunity' clause which was not removed until 1983; the requirements for corroborating evidence; and the tolerance of questioning the victim on her past sexual conduct and reputation. While these examples point to the clear need to improve the evidentiary and procedural rules in a rape trial, they belie the patriarchal definition of issues that accompanies sexual assault. In contrast to the reality that the majority of rapes are committed by acquaintances or relatives, the dominant view within the courts is that a 'rapist' is a stranger who physically coerces the victim to have intercourse. Cases that do not fit this model are not considered by the court to be rape, or else are subject to less severe penalties, as reasoned by Judge Cross (1975):

> One reason why the maximum punishment for rape is life imprisonment is that the common man considers rapists to be very wicked people. Someone who believes, albeit without reasonable cause, that the woman is consenting may well be stupid and insensitive, but he is not wicked in the sense which the rapist is wicked.... Let us consider carefully what the maximum punishment should be, and above all let us not call the crime 'rape.' (in Manitoba Association of Women and the Law, 1988)

While this type of law finding has become the impetus for further reform of procedures of criminal law, the contradictory effects of liberal reform in family and constitutional law are only now becoming apparent. Adjudication of family law based upon the *assumption* of equality has in fact operated to disadvantage women. Removing references to women as economic dependents and notions that children are best cared for by mothers has resulted in diminished financial obligation by husbands for previous wives and children while improving the chances that custody decisions will favour fathers. The problem is that the image of the contemporary family as conveyed by reformed family law stands in direct contradistinction to the *reality* that many women with children are not employed, that the overall earning potential of women is a fraction of that of men's, and that women still carry the primary burden of responsibility for childcare irrespective of their employment status. As a result of the mere declaration of marriage as an equal partnership, women with or without children became expected to be self-sufficient, so that the administration of reformed family law has had the paradoxical effect of acting against the interests of individual women (see Manitoba Association of Women and the Law, 1988).

Unfortunately, some of the best examples of this contradiction can be found in decisions under the new *Charter* that blatantly contradict the spirit of equality. In 1986 a District Court judge invoked equality provisions of the *Charter* to strike down the *Criminal Code* prohibition against incest on the grounds that it results in a crime for men and not for women. Thus a man who had intercourse with his 11-year-old stepdaughter was acquitted because the *Criminal Code* did not apply to stepmothers who had intercourse with stepsons. In another similar decision, in 1985, a District Court judge found that statutory rape in the criminal code — sexual intercourse with a female partner under the age of fourteen — was of no force and effect because the prohibition applied only to men (both cases discussed in Mandel, 1989: 258-9). Finally, a B.C. Provincial Court judge blocked a paternity suit by a single mother, declaring that all such suits are contrary to the *Charter*. In this latter case the Court of Appeal did find sex discrimination, but saved the statute in question on the grounds that it "provides a basis for shifting the financial responsibility for the child from the public to the private domain."

While it is possible to talk about victories for women secured by the *Charter* (see Baines, 1988), there are both empirical and theoretical reasons to predict that *Charter* decisions on equality will not be any less contradictory than the outcomes of law reform. Given these developments, it is not surprising that Canadian feminist legal scholars are becoming increasingly disenchanted with liberal-democratic notions of the 'rule of law.' Some feminist legal scholars have argued that women should abandon abstractions of law to focus more carefully on the actual results of law finding. Boyd and Sheehy (1989) thus call this school 'result equality feminism.' As an example, Smith (1986) maintains that all proposed legislation should be tested for its effects before its implementation. To ensure equitable results, the benefits and burdens should be measured against the group with the greatest needs as the norm. Radical feminists maintain that it is no mere coincidence that justice currently favours men's interests, rejecting the view that law is inherently neutral or that it can be used as suggested by Smith. Influenced by the works of U.S. psychologist Carol Gilligan and radical feminist lawyer Catherine McKinnon, radicals maintain that law itself is a masculine paradigm and male mode of action that *necessarily* supports male supremacy (see Greschner, 1986; Lahey, 1984). From this position, writers posit the need for an alternative morality — based upon the feminine principles of care, connection, and community — upon which law *should* be based. In this way, a bifurcation has appeared between an applied 'feminist legal realism' and a speculative 'feminist legal utopianism.'

In similarly assessing the disappointments of liberal reform, socialist feminists reject a narrow focus on law and law finding themselves. They argue that these processes can only be understood within the broader context of society and social inequality. They point out that the achievement of a formal legal equality does nothing to change the concrete relations between men and women. For example, Fudge argues that: "The success of this litigation demonstrates the courts' willingness to accept arguments advocating formal legal equality when issues of obvious symbolic, though of little material, import are raised.... However, the attainment of such formal equality does nothing in itself to further substantive equality for women either within or outside of marriage" (Fudge, 1987: 514). From this perspective, socialist feminists argue that the limitations of legal reformism reflect the fundamental contradictions of a 'democratic' society stratified along the lines of class, race, and gender. As Marx noted, individuals can be equalized in law only by abstracting away the differences that distinguish them in real life. In this way, equality in law stands in contradistinction to the reality of the substantive inequalities that groups face in society. While some legal reforms undoubtedly enhance the immediate position of many women, we must not mistake legal reform as the solution to women's secondary position. No matter how extended and democratized, legal rights cannot address fundamental inequalities in society — inequities that can be addressed only through real material transformation.

Feminism and the Executive Branch

In contrast to the expanding literature on 'women and the law,' relatively little work has been done on the executive branch of the justice system.[7] This is particularly true for women and prisons, especially within the Canadian context. For the largest part, this neglect reflects the fact that women are a minority of designated 'criminals' in patriarchal cultures. The Royal Commission on the Status of Women (RCSW), for example, reported that in 1967 women made up approximately 12.5 per cent of those convicted of indictable offences in Canada (RCSW, 1970: 366). Reflecting the relatively 'minor' nature of their offences, 37.6 per cent of these women received suspended sentences, 46.7 per cent received fines, while only 15.7 per cent were imprisoned. As a consequence, women continue to form only a small fraction of prison populations. Statistics Canada reports that women accounted for just over 17 per cent of adults charged with criminal offences in 1988, up slightly from 15 per cent in 1979 (Statistics Canada, 1990). Not surprisingly, one of the few books on women in the Canadian penal system is aptly titled *Too Few to Count* (Adelberg and Currie, 1987). Hidden by this focus on numbers, however, is the racist nature of Canadian corrections. The RCSW, for example, found that Indian or Metis women made up anywhere from 46 per cent (Oakalla Prison Farm, BC) to 100 per cent (The Pas Correctional Institution for Women, Manitoba) of women in prisons during 1966.

The relatively small number of women in prisons does not mean that policing is not an issue for Canadian women. A number of writers have documented the way in which women's sexual behaviour within both the private and the public spheres has been more closely scrutinized than that of men (Chesney-Lind, 1985/86, 1974; Geller, 1987). Reflecting this mandate, policing has focused upon, firstly, the sexual behaviour of young girls through the 'status offences' of the old *Juvenile Delinquency Act* and, secondly, the public sexuality of adult women through the regulation of prostitution. Ironically, while the 'common prostitute' may be prosecuted for soliciting men for sexual purposes or even for loitering in order to do so, soliciting or accosting women for sexual purposes by men has only been an offence in Canada since 1985 and then only selectively enforced (Lowman, 1990). As a consequence, sexual harassment is a common experience for women, although it is not legally identified as a limitation upon their equality and freedom (McNeill, 1987; Kelly, 1987; Jones, MacLean, and Young, 1986).

Even in cases of criminally defined assault women do not receive the full protection of the law through policing. While the actual number of sexual assaults on women has always been a matter of dispute, Statistics Canada reports rates of 10.2 and 28.5 incidences per 100,000 population for rape and indecent assault on women respectively for the year 1982. At the same time, this report acknowledges that only 39 per cent of sexual assaults on women ever get reported to the police. Even then, rape is showing the greatest increase in all violent crimes. During the decade between 1971 and 1982, the incidence of reported rape increased by 29 per cent. Against common patriarchal wisdom, women are far more likely to be sexually assaulted by someone they know — boyfriends, husbands, fathers, and other family relations — than by the proverbial stranger (see Green, Hebron and Woodward, 1987; Hall, 1985). Added to sexual assault is the recent recognition of the extent of wife battery in Canada. In the first national study of domestic violence, the Canadian Advisory Council on the Status of Women estimated that at least 24,000 Canadian women were battered by husbands or lovers during 1978 (MacLeod, 1980). It is now commonly accepted that one in ten women living with men is battered every year (ibid.: 16). Criminologists have subsequently expended a great deal of energy exacting the measurement of violence against women, especially by intimates (see Chapter 12).

At the same time as they documented the widespread frequency of violence against women, feminists and researchers alike have noted that the police response has been one of non-arrest, in the cases of wife battery, and down-criming, in the case of sexual assault. Requests for protection by battered wives have been dealt with as 'domestic disputes' — temporary and non-serious disagreements between partners, best resolved without police intervention. In the case of rape, researchers (see Clark and Lewis, 1977; Gunn and Minch, 1988) have found that once reported, complaints are likely to be discounted by police or categorized as less serious offences. As a consequence of this practice, 30 per cent of reported rapes during 1982, for example, were classified by the police as 'unfounded,' compared to 6 per cent of all other violent offences (Manitoba Association of Women and the Law, 1988). Examining the handling of rape cases by police, writers note that victims deemed 'deserving' of patriarchal protection are young, chaste, and white (see Clark and Lewis, 1977). Reflecting developments in other advanced industrialized nations, therefore, women began to complain that policing operates to protect male offenders rather than their female victims.

As a feminist concern, policing highlights the contradictions inherent in the notion that there can be justice for women in a patriarchal culture. At the same time, because it shifts the struggle for justice from the ideological/symbolic realm to the real world of women, the issue of policing highlights the fundamental — and possibly unresolvable — differences between feminists as to the practical agenda. To liberals, police inaction is a clear violation of women's right to equal protection under the law, as guaranteed in the *Charter*. Accepting the view of law as symbolic of dominant values, liberal feminists have campaigned for the criminalization of domestic violence, arguing that mandatory arrest — as one example of a more positive policing practice — would act as deterrence. They further note that because individual policemen are members of the dominant culture, it is not surprising that they subscribe to sexist, as well as racist, ideologies concerning rape and wife battery. On this basis, liberals have campaigned successfully for programs of police education, the recruitment of female officers to work in particular with female victims of crime, and more sensitive handling of cases during their investigation.

In contrast to the liberal campaigns for reform of policing, radical feminists see violence as the 'normal' component of heterosexual relations. Characterizing violence against women by fathers, husbands, and other patriarchs as fundamental to a patriarchal order, radicals argue that it is therefore inherently contradictory to conceptualize justice in terms of men policing male violence against women. For this reason and as a result of sexist treatment by police, radical feminists working with victims of male violence in Vancouver, for example, refuse to liaise with police. While a radical feminist literature on policing in Canada is virtually non-existent, a number of important books on this theme have appeared in Britain. The writers point out that women are often the targets of policing mandates (Dunhill, 1989) and that because the police themselves benefit from the regulation of women it is unlikely that they will shed their sexist attitudes and behaviours. At the same time, the researchers do not find female policing to be an answer. Female recruits have been described as being as aggressive as their male colleagues if not worse (Mcauley, 1989; Heaven and Mars, 1989), while Radford (1989) argues that because the policing of prostitution and rape benefits the status quo, it is impossible for feminists to work with male authorities on terms that will not compromise women's interests. While it is less clear from a radical perspective how violence against women can be eradicated, most of these writers maintain that the current reality demands tighter surveillance and punishment of masculine aggression. Radical feminists in both Britain and Canada — as well as the United States — have therefore supported liberal campaigns for feminist 'law and order.' As a feminist struggle for justice, the law and order agenda is defended on a number of grounds: Women only want the same kind of justice that has been given to other victims of crime; feminism is not responsible for problems with the current form of *male* justice, it only asks for the law to be applied consistently, against men; the use of criminal legislation against violence against women establishes the principle of women's dignity as a people by recognition of violence against them as a major crime; and, finally, although law will not diminish crimes and harsher sentencing will not alter the general picture, the use of the justice system can become an occasion for public debates that increase cultural and political awareness of violence against women (see Pitch, 1985: 43).

Against this backdrop, socialist feminists have more recently called for a more holistic approach to feminist analyses of police (see Chapters 12 and 13). While not denying that the policing needs of women are real needs, these writers are alarmed at how the current focus upon violence against women can feed into a reactionary law and order lobby. Snider (1991), for example, is critical of how liberal and radical campaigns against violence against women have led to lobbying for new criminal offences, making arrests, charges, and convictions easier, and increasing punishment (1991: 239). Elsewhere Currie (1990) explores how expansion of policing as the state's response to wife battery reflects the more general trend in Canada towards the 'institutionalization' of women's issues. Central to feminist critiques of male violence against women is the issue of unequal distribution of societal resources and power. Within a discourse that concerns legal rights, police protection, and criminal justice, this issue is transformed into a technical matter that can be safely met within the current system without any significant changes in relations of power. For this reason, the effect of intervention could well be the strengthening of the very same processes and institutions that give rise to the demand for justice in the first place. A further problem is that this intervention gives an impression that women's needs and their demands for 'justice' have been dealt with, so that in the public's mind feminist demands have been satisfactorily addressed, which makes it more difficult and less acceptable to criticize or lobby for more changes. In this way, while the need for protection from male violence is a real need, satisfying this need through policing or the courts has been conflated with solving the problem.

Feminism has provided us with a powerful set of conceptual tools we can use to gain a critical understanding of the nature of domination and inequality in society and of how these are legitimated within the administration of justice. However, if, as some feminists argue, the administration of justice is an expression of male rationality, then an analysis of the processes by which ideas are both constructed and reproduced becomes necessary, because ideas are themselves the material through which rationality is expressed. When we recognize that ideas are conceptual categories that are discursive, and that these discursive structures are the filters through which reality is comprehended, it becomes necessary to investigate how these discursive structures pertain to structures of domination and their legitimation within the administration of justice.

Knowledge / Power: Discourse Analysis and Justice

Discourse analysis is rapidly becoming a prominent form of critical inquiry. It offers new tools for a critical examination of the criminal justice system, conceptions of justice, and lawmaking and law finding practices.

The beginnings of a discourse analysis — sometimes more simply referred to as a semiotic analysis — can be traced to the Swiss linguist Ferdinand de Saussure. After he died in 1913 Saussure's lecture notes were published in *Course in General Linguistics* (1916). At the outset he states his claim: "Language is a system of signs that express ideas.... A science that studies the life of signs within society is conceivable; it would be part of social psychology; I shall call it semiology.... Semiology would show what constitutes signs, what laws govern them" (1966: 16).

Saussure conceptualizes signs as made up of two entities: the *signifier*, which stands for the sound, the acoustic-image, or the psychic imprint; and the *signified*, the actual concept referred to. If we say the word tree, for example, it conjures up the image of this object. The word 'tree' really stands for an absence — the actual tree. Thus signifiers can be conceptualized as the presence of an absence. Saussure argues that the relationship between the signifier and signified is in most cases not motivated, that is, there is no inherent relationship between the word 'tree' and the image it evokes. These relationships are constructed through sociopolitical practices.[8] Language can be further distinguished according to speech (the spoken word), or *'parole,'* and the dictionary meanings of words, *'langue'* of a particular society or group. *Langue* stands for the abstract forms that may be used (particular words and their meanings) which pre-exist individual users. *Parole* stands for the actual or concrete speeches or utterances constructed. Finally, Saussure provides us with two key axes, the intersection of which contributes to meaning constructions.

The 'paradigmatic axis' stands for a vertical dimension in which each word (signifier) stands in some relationship with each other. For example, we have synonyms, antonyms, homonyms, or words with the same prefixes, suffixes, and so forth. The essence of meaning at this level is the relationship between these signifiers, namely their play of differences. Each word stands in some relationship to each other word along this axis. For example, the word 'voluntary' may be understood in relationship to its contrary, 'involuntary,' or its similarities: 'choice,' 'free will,' 'volitional,' etc. In law, there are different degrees of voluntary behaviour. With the category of homicide, for example, come differences according to negligence or premeditation. The second axis is the 'syntagmatic axis,' the horizontal dimension. Here words are placed in a specific order, structured grammatically by a particular code of a language. For example, in our culture we normally say "The little red brick house," but not "The red brick little house."

For meaning to be constructed — that is, for a particular signified, or image, to be generated — we must look at how the two axes intersect. For example, as we construct a particular sentence or utterance, we not only move sequentially in a linear order, the syntagmatic dimension, but also at each point along this line we have a vertical dimension that appears where the play of differences of signifiers offers choices. Consider the prosecuting attorney who makes the following remark in a trial proceeding: "The defendant maliciously, and in a premeditated manner, inflicted gross bodily harm on the victim." As we move along this linear sequence of signifiers, each word provides us with an instance in which a vertical dimension exists along which we may have chosen other words to use in the utterance, in the speech produced. Instead of 'maliciously' the prosecutor could have used the words 'negligently' or 'with wanton disregard.' Instead of 'gross' the prosecutor could have used 'substantial,' 'significant,' 'massive'. The prosecutor has also had to arrange each word in a particular sequence. She or he could not have said, "The defendant maliciously, and in manner harm, inflicted premeditated bodily gross the on victim," because this would be nonsensical. Meaning comes about only because the words are placed in a particular way in a narrative form, guided by a code, often learned semiconsciously through socialization. The paradigmatic and the syntagmatic intersect, then, to produce particular signifieds and hence meaning.

The U.S. philosopher Charles Sanders Peirce has offered a competing model of discourse in his eight-volume set, *Collected Papers* (1931). Rather than seeing the sign as composed of the signifier and signified, Peirce saw a triadic relationship: the 'sign,' the 'interpretant,' and the 'object.' Thus he added the referent, the actual object implicated in the use of a particular sign. The sign is similar to the signifier of Saussure, the interpretant is similar to the signified. Notice that for Saussure the signified, which is the concept, still does not mean the actual object. In language-use the object never appears in its originality. Although this is also true for Peirce, he would want to warn us of its existence and absence in language use. Finally, for Peirce, the interpretant has an additional aspect beyond that envisioned by Saussure. It is infinitely commutable. That is, the interpretant, the mental effect or the concept generated, acts as a sign that in turn conjures up yet another interpretant, producing yet another sign that produces a particular mental effect, and so forth. This is an endless process.

Roland Barthes (1974) is best noted for his separation of the signifier into its connotative and denotative aspects. The actually intended signified is its denotative aspect. But each signifier generates a *second-order* signifying system; this is its connotative dimension. The word 'cop,' for example, can be defined denotatively as a law enforcement official. For some segments of the population, however, its connotative understanding — the second-order signifying system — may also conjure up the image of a bully, lackey, head-buster, and represser. The denotative dimension could therefore be termed the 'first-order' signifying system. Thus whenever we make use of particular signifiers, we intend to generate a particular meaning or a sequence of concepts placed in a thematic whole; however, we often unwittingly generate other meanings. Barthes suggests that particularly with this 'second-order' signifying system, one must look for an explanation to political-economic factors in situating the signifieds that are actually aroused in the mental apparatus of the hearer/listener of a particular utterance. For Barthes, class interests and values invariably dictate the content of this second-order signifying system. Here we enter the domain of ideology, the system of ideas that are generated, circulated, and reinforced within a political economy and in support of it.

Benjamin Whorf has provided us with the notion of the *linguistic relativity* principle. In his influential book, *Language, Thought, and Reality* (1956), Whorf indicates that the world we perceive follows the organizing categories of language itself:

> Each language is not merely a reproducing instrument for voicing ideas but rather is itself the shaper of ideas, the program and guide for the individual's mental activity, for his analysis of impressions, for his synthesis of his mental stock in trade.... We dissect nature along lines laid down by our native languages. The categories and types that we isolate from the world of phenomena we do not find there because they stare every observer in the face; on the contrary, the world is presented in a kaleidoscopic flux of impressions which has to be organized by our minds.... We cut nature up, organize it into concepts, and ascribe significances as we do, largely because we are parties to an agreement to organize it in this way — an agreement that holds throughout our speech community and is codified in the patterns of our language. (213)

In his insightful analysis of the differences between the standard forms of Indo-European and Hopi Indian language, Whorf indicates profound differences in the conception of the world that is reflected. Consider our use of language and how the basic unit is constructed in terms of a subject, verb, and object/predicate. We say "He is running," or "He is riding a bicycle," or "It is lightning." Implied in the language we use is that the subject is determining or causing the action by his/her freedom of will. For the Hopi of the Southwestern United States, one word would be used to describe the same event. They would say "running," "bicycling," or "lightning." Implied in their language is that the world is so interconnected that we cannot arbitrarily divide it up in terms of a causing entity (the subject) and objects, which exist awaiting to be moved or acted upon. This thought is alien to their thinking, and their language is reflective of this state of affairs. Consider the applicability to law finding practices, particularly to a trial proceeding, which attempts to construct the 'what happened.' In Western societies courts are preoccupied with the connection between an actor and some deviant act that actor may have done. The two, the act and action, are separated in a court of law, and the only question, beyond whether the defendant did it or not, is the degree of choice exercised. Thus trying to determine *mens rea* (state of mind), the courts attribute to the subject various degrees of the capacity to formulate choice. But choice is assumed to exist in the first instance: This is captured in the notion of *the reasonable man in law*, which, for the Hopi, is alien. Hopi cannot separate the actor from the action because these conditions are seen as one — a totality. Action is a composite of forces; a person is subjected to a number of forces that produce an event. Elevating the subject to a self-determining, controlling entity that determines destiny has no place in the Hopi language.

Friedrich Nietzsche had much to say about the *semiotic fictions* provided by language, and much of his thought is being integrated into the current postmodernist perspective. Nietzsche has influenced such thinkers as Freud, Weber, Lacan, and Derrida. Particularly in *Twilight of the Idols and the After-Christ* Nietzsche indicates the *four great errors* brought about by language itself (1968: 47-54). Language, he tells us, provides the fiction that:

1. the existence of an actor is separable from action,

2. that once an actor is separated from the action, a determining self-centred consciousness appears, and thus cause can presumably be attributable to him/her,

3. that a unique cause, or causes, can be found as a sufficient explanation of the action, and

4. that freedom of the will activates action.

Nietzsche argues:

> We separate ourselves, the doers, from the deed, and we make use of this pattern everywhere — we seek a doer for every event.... *Our understanding of an event* has consisted in our inventing a subject which was made responsible for something that happens and for how it happens. (Nietzsche, 1967: 295-6)

And elsewhere:

> We have not got away from the habit into which our senses and language seduce us. Subject, object, a doer added to the doing, the doing separated from that which it does: let us not forget that this is mere semiotics and nothing real. (Nietzsche, 1967: 338)

In sum, for Nietzsche language itself provides us with a ready supply of answers to the complex question of being human.

In recent years the French linguist Emile Benveniste has become a central figure in discourse analysis, particularly by way of his *Problems in General Linguistics* (1971). Benveniste theorizes that discourse and subjectivity are inseparable, that "language provides the very definition of man" (1971: 224). In particular, his examination of the use of personal pronouns has had enormous influence. He argues, for instance, that "I" and "you" are distinguishable from other pronouns such as "he," "she," and "it" in that they are only "filled-in" by their actual use in discourse; otherwise they point to nothing in particular; they are empty, or floating signifiers. The "I" of a particular utterance, then, stands for the subject. It represents the subject in his or her absence:

> Consciousness of self is only possible if it is experienced by contrast. I use *I* only when I am speaking to someone who will be a *you* in my address. It is this condition of dialogue that is constitutive of *person*, for it implies that reciprocally *I* becomes *you* in the address of the one who in his turn designates himself as *I*.... Each speaker sets himself up as a *subject* by referring to himself as *I* in his discourse. (Benveniste, 1971: 224-5)

Thus, for Benveniste the "I" and "you" are reciprocally connected; they are inseparable, and language provides the materials out of which identities are constructed. The actual use of "I" in a particular utterance, in speech, designates the speaker, but in his/her absence. That is, when I use "I" in discourse my whole being does not suddenly appear, but only a representative, the "I" of discourse. The "I" acts therefore as a signifier; it stands for the producer of the discourse itself. This leads Benveniste to postulate the existence of two actual "I"s: The "I" used in a particular utterance, in a particular statement, and the "I" that remains hidden but is the producer of the statement itself (1971: 218). These are two distinct planes. It is now current practice to refer to the discursive "I," the "I" of a particular statement as the *sujet d'énoncé*, and the "I" of its production as *le sujet d'énonciation*. Benveniste elaborates on this thesis in his chapter on "Language in Freudian Theory" (1971) and indicates that two axes unfold in discourse, the unconscious and the conscious. Whereas in conscious discourse, "The subject makes use of the act of speech and discourse in order to 'represent himself' to himself as he wishes to see himself and as he calls upon the 'other' to observe him" (1971: 67), another discourse that lies within the unconscious unfolds simultaneously at a latent level. Much as in Freudian psychoanalysis, the latent level, the deep structure is only approachable by way of the manifest level, the spoken language itself. Thus, building on Freud's monumental insights, particularly in *The Interpretation of Dreams*, Benveniste indicates that there exists a split subject, and that the subject of speech, the actual speaking subject who uses the personal pronoun "I," does not coincide with the producer of the statement, the unconscious subject.

Building on the insights of Freud, Benveniste, Jakobson, the Hegelian Kojève, and the structuralist anthropologist Claude Levi-Strauss, Jacques Lacan was to revolutionize our understanding of discourse in its relationship to subjectivity (Lacan, 1977, 1981) — despite his exceptionally difficult prose, bordering on the unintelligible. In Paris, France, from the 1950s to the 1970s, Lacan delivered a series of seminars, attended by some of the foremost scholars of our time — Foucault, Althusser, Barthes, Derrida, Ricoeur, Kristeva, Guattari, to name a few. In fact, in many ways he provided much of the groundwork for the contemporary perspective, heavily entrenched in discourse analysis, referred to as postmodernism. Here, too, in postmodernism there has been a decentring of Hegel and a rediscovery of Nietzsche. As Milovanovic argues in Chapter 8, Lacan's contributions have been profound. Lacan questions the notion of subjectivity developed after the Renaissance, a subject that is said to be *centred*, in control, determining, self-conscious, and self-directing. These are all myths for Lacan. Rather, the subject is *decentred*, more determined than determining, and a product of discourse itself. The child's entrance into the world is marked by an increasing reliance on language. The child learns to use signifiers that refer to absences. The child too is a signifier, standing for an absence — the actual producer of a statement. According to Lacan, the child is inaugurated into the Symbolic order, language, and culture, by way of an initial 'fort-da' game. Drawing from Freud's observations, Lacan indicates that the young child experiences anxiety when the mother leaves, and happiness when she returns. Soon, the child invents a game, duplicating the process, throwing out a cotton reel, uttering the word 'fort' (gone), and pulling the reel back, uttering the word 'da' (there) with its reappearance. This duplicates the anxiety and happiness witnessed by the child with the mother coming and going. But now the child has gained mastery for, because of the substituted game, she or he is separated forever from the direct experience itself. Language provides mastery, control, and, at the same time, a separation, an alienation from the Real. For Lacan, the unconscious is structured like a language. It consists of 'letters,' signifiers that 'float' within the unconscious awaiting use. But they are charged with effect. Building on Freud — in fact fundamentally changing many of his original concepts — Lacan tells us that the subject is structured by language itself. He tells us again and again that the signifier can only be defined as the subject of another signifier. That is, even the subject is a signifier who finds him/herself captured in signifying chains, strings of signifiers, that are constructed by unconscious forces, particularly those originating from felt 'lacks' that arouse 'desire.'

For Lacan the two main organizing principles of the unconscious, and hence language, are *metaphor* and *metonymy*. Metaphor, the vertical dimension, stands for the coming together of two or more concepts to form an image that implies both. Metonymy, the horizontal dimension, can be defined as something, a part, standing for a whole, or something else. When we say "thirty sails" to refer to thirty ships, we have used a shorthand method to indicate a more complex picture. For Lacan, the intersection of these two axes produces meaning. Desire, the force that activates the psychic apparatus to action — being born of repression and felt 'lack' particularly experienced with the child entering the Symbolic sphere, the world of language (see Chapter 8) — finds its way into metonymic constructions. In fact, Lacan tells us desire is metonymy. Language conveys unconscious wishes, and desire finds an outlet, even if it is in disguised form, through language. We are never in total control of our speech. Desire creeps through always. This often appears in more obvious form in the Freudian slip. Just as the dream was a rebus, a picture puzzle for Freud in his psychoanalytic approach, speech, for Lacan was a harbinger of desire.

Contemporary discourse analysis is being infused with yet another dimension, the political-economic. The 'new turks' are such figures as Deleuze and Guattari (1987), Kristeva (1984), and Lecercle (1985). They criticize Lacan and his predecessors for their lack of a critical materialistic analysis of discourse and their conservative notions of desire. Discourse for the new turks is inherently ideological. Entrance into the Symbolic order produces an irreversible loss; the pre-symbolic is celebrated as the site for spontaneity, creativity, plenitude, transcendence. The Symbolic order conveys the thought system that contributes to the perpetuation of given hierarchical, exploitive modes of production. Deleuze and Guattari, for example, indicate that discourse is a form of a disciplining mechanism that moulds subjects into appropriate gender roles, outlooks, and motivations. They repeatedly inform us that "We are desiring machines." That is, discourse, a conveyer of a particular thought system, channels creative psychic energy, the libido of Freud, along lines that contribute to the perpetuation of the political-economic system. Thus the Oedipus complex is but an example of the repressive tendencies of an exploitive system that seeks to imprison men and women in particular roles supportive of capital logic. The internal logic of capitalism produces the subjects it needs. What is repressed is other yearnings; these do not have a language within which they can be expressed. Kristeva (1984) and Lecercle (1985) have indicated how two languages exist: On one hand is the language of the body, the 'scream,' an individual expression of passions, drives, yearnings originating from the body, a form of 'desire'; on the other is the formal language we must use to express ourselves, the materialistic dictionary language that provides us with signifiers already laden with a particular ideology and values (Lecercle, 1985: 41-45).

The Russian theorist Volosinov has provided a pragmatic approach to language, particularly in his *Marxism and the Philosophy of Language* (1986; see also Bakhtin, 1981). In his classic study, Volosinov tells us, "A sign does not simply exist as a part of a reality — it reflects and refracts another reality" (1986: 10). For Volosinov every sign conveys an ideological evaluation; that is, every sign reflects a particular belief system of a particular segment of a population. The content of the sign, the signified, according to Volosinov, comes about because of the unique set of political-economic forces to which a society is subject. The nature of the sign is its 'multi-accentuality'; that is, a sign is really a composite of competing signifieds — each group in a society attempts to give a sign an accentuation, a meaning reflecting its particular viewpoint and interest. However, it is the dominant class that wishes to 'uni-accentuate' the sign, giving it a meaning that is supportive of its dominant position (1986: 23). The clash of opposing interests produces a dynamic flux — a rich mixture of meanings (signifieds) — but the dominant segments of society attempt to render this rich flux static to further their dominant position. By way of the media, the school system, and the structure of the family in capitalist society, a particular ideology, a particular system of uniquely accented signs (signifieds) is perpetuated. Subjects in a social formation are restricted, then, in the very materials used for expression; hence, discourse can only take place within a particular narrowly circumscribed sphere, a locus of circumscribed signifieds. The repressed classes are separated — alienated from the very discourse they must use, particularly in the legal sphere. Also, the implications of the Volosinov/Bakhtin pragmatic thesis is that the empirical subject (the construct of positivistic sciences) and the juridical subject (the 'reasonable man in law') are fictions; they are one-sided depictions of human possibility; they are static categories well suited as substitutable parts in the machinery of capitalism (Milovanovic, 1990a).

Discourse Analysis and the Legislative Branch: Lawmaking

The legislative branch, lawmaking, is especially susceptible to discourse analysis. Legislators, who are predominantly legally trained, must make decisions; they must conceptualize and promulgate laws. But laws convey ideology; in fact, for many, law *is* ideology. Legislators make use of discourse, but predominantly in one form, the dominant *linguistic co-ordinate system* (Milovanovic, 1986, 1987). Elsewhere, Milovanovic has argued that discourse analysis must be sensitive to the idea that many discursive regions exist. In particular, we may identify the dominant, juridic, pluralistic, and oppositional linguistic co-ordinate systems (Milovanovic, 1986, 1988a). Each discursive region can be considered a bounded sphere in which signifiers float, awaiting use. To communicate to others necessitates that the subject places him/herself within a particular linguistic co-ordinate system and then borrows (appropriates) from the particular narrowly accented signs that are available. Thus legislators find themselves in the dominant framework, one supportive of the status quo. They insert themselves within this framework that produces few accented signs arising from real human beings in the lower classes struggling to exist. The world, the reality that they create, always pre-exists and is simply reconfirmed in legislative decisions concerning new laws.

Such conceptions as the calculating and determining subject, and the assumed attributes of responsibility, accountability, and blameworthiness always pre-exist in the dominant discourse. Take, for example, the *juridic subject*, the so-called *reasonable man/woman in law.* Pashukanis has shown (1980; see also Milovanovic, 1989) that commodity exchangers in the competitive marketplace of capitalism, during the multitude of exchanges, produce what is known as phenomenal forms, appearances, due to the form of interactions that take place there. That is, through the constant exchange of commodities certain appearances develop; the appearance of free will, equality, and proprietorship interests. These, in turn, are given idealized expression in law in the form of the juridic subject, the abstract bearer of rights. Legislators work with this as a given, not understanding the underlying dynamics in the production of the legal subjects. For example, the *Fourteenth Amendment* to the *U.S. Constitution* includes the so called 'equal protection clause,' which states that equally situated individuals should be equally treated. The law endows the subject with *formal* rights, but neglects gross economic inequalities. By focusing on the appearances (all are free to become unequal through their own activity and all are equal in the eyes of the law) rather than on the substance (gross economic inequalities) the law cloaks exploitive practices. Discourse analysis undoes what has been done. It reveals that the discourse that legislators make use of is supportive of dominant practices, even though the legislators are not fully conscious of the dynamics of inserting themselves in particular linguistic co-ordinate systems and its effects. They make use of a cleansed, sterilized, decontextualized discourse that centres on the abstraction, the juridic subject, not real human beings in struggle.

Examples of the exploitive practices of law are plentiful (see Kairys, 1982). Legal discourse, for example, has been shown to contribute to circumscribed thought processes in such areas as labour relations law (Klare, 1982), race discrimination law (Freeman, 1982), women's subordination in law (Taub and Schneider, 1982), constitutionally protected speech (Kairys, 1982), contract law (Gabel and Feinman, 1982), torts (Abel, 1982) and copyright law (Coombe, 1989a). In each case, the judiciary creates particular accented signs (the sphere of linguistic production) that subsequently become the locus (the sphere of linguistic circulation), in which subjects, to do law, must insert themselves and appropriate given value-laden signs in creating reality in narratively constructed form, in story-telling. The dominant and legal linguistic co-ordinate systems reflect a particular reality, and lawmaking is situated within this framework.

Discourse Analysis and the Judiciary: Law Finding

The judiciary lends itself to further investigation by the tools provided in discourse analysis. In the advanced form of the capitalist mode of production, the state-regulated form, in which the state is much more interventionist than its predecessor of the nineteenth century (the laissez-faire form) mainly because of the need to overcome inherent crises tendencies (Habermas, 1984), the judiciary makes increasing use of a *balancing of interests* formula. The higher courts will balance the government's interest in some regulation or contemplated right and the interests of the citizen affected by governmental action, specifying the appropriate balance to be struck and hence specifying the rights available to different subjects (Milovanovic, 1987). In the nineteenth-century laissez-faire form of capitalism, the courts were minimally involved in the economic sphere, and the abstraction created — the juridic subject — was respected. The twentieth-century form, however, necessitated the promulgation of new rights; in fact, rights are constantly changing because of the inherent instability of interest balancing. Thus, we envision the higher courts as not only specifying rights, but also providing specific content to signifiers. Signifieds, in other words, are accented in precise ways. In the act of specifying just what an acceptable constitutionally protected interest consists of, the higher courts are constructing the appropriate signifieds, the legal definitions of terms (See Milovanovic, 1986, 1987, 1988a, 1988b). This is not an arbitrary, unmotivated process. Rather, some inputs are entertained by the courts, some are not. Disenfranchised, minority groups, women, and marginal groups will have few of their *accentuations* accepted for 'balancing,' unless they become organized. This is one level.

At the second level, once codification by the higher courts has taken place, the sphere of linguistic production, these terms with the appropriate legal meanings (signifieds) enter the domain of linguistic circulation, or more precisely the juridic linguistic co-ordinate system. To do law henceforth is to situate oneself within this domain and to make use of the signifiers available. A certain conception of reality will be constructed through the use of the elements available; another reality will be non-justiciable, not even constructed in law. Subjectivity, too, is constructed in the process. Balbus's classic study (1973) of the rebellions in the 1960s in the U.S. indicated that the rebels were 'cooled out' and denied their political agenda by being forced to use legal discourse or the legal linguistic co-ordinate system. To do otherwise placed the rebels at risk in court processing. Rebels and their legal supporters all played the game, all accepted the legal discourse as the appropriate boundary of discourse, and hence the rebellions were seen as acts of common criminality rather than revolutionary activity. An oppositional linguistic co-ordinate system did not materialize. Rebels were denied a discourse within which they could insert themselves to provide verbalizations and articulations of system injustices (also see Bannister and Milovanovic, 1990).

In his study of 'jailhouse lawyers,' Milovanovic (1988b) found that inmates who taught themselves law and practised it inadvertently accepted the legal framework and its discourse in constructing the 'what happened?' Hence they unintentionally contributed to the perpetuation of a legal system that they claim represses them and their fellows. Along the same theme, Bennet and Feldman indicate in *Reconstructing Reality in the Courtroom* (1981) that certain segments of the population are at risk during trial proceedings because they are incapable of mustering up the symbols that are reflective of the dominant reality and hence are more likely to be seen as telling suspect stories; consequently they will be found guilty.

Two recent theorists — Peter Goodrich in *Legal Discourse* (1987) and Bernard Jackson in *Semiotics and Legal Theory* (1985) and *Law, Fact and Narrative Coherence* (1988) — have extended a semiotic analysis of law. Goodrich has persuasively argued that the judicial sphere is characterized by the perpetuation of ideology supportive of dominant groups. Through law school training neophyte law students learn the appropriate grammar of law, the appropriate legal definitions of signs, and, more subtly, how to (and why to) subordinate themselves to the legal apparatus (see Kennedy, 1982). Law students incorporate a distinct method of reasoning, a specific language, and when they enter their future practice they are always already receptive to using the higher court's accentuations of the sign. To do law is to insert oneself in this legal discourse and to construct the 'what happened?' out of the elements offered by this discourse, by this linguistic co-ordinate system.

Jackson's more recent work (1988) takes a different approach in explaining narrative construction in law. His claim is that legal discourse is non-referential, meaning that signifiers used in law only make reference to other signifiers, which in turn make reference to others, etc. At rare points is the direct world dealt with. Rather, opposing lawyers in trial proceedings, or higher courts in adjudicating appeal cases, situate themselves in a circumscribed legal sphere and construct a logical picture, in narrative constructions that only make reference to the formal elements of story-telling, not to what actually happened in the streets.

In his Chapter 8 here, Milovanovic argues that subjectivity itself is being constructed in law-finding practices. Gaps in stories presented are filled in or *sutured* by available elements in the legal discursive sphere in order to construct not only believable stories but logical, coherent, centred subjects that are said to be the authors of particular deviant acts. The centred subject is created anew in these trial proceedings.

Discourse and the Executive: The Semiotics of Control
In the realm of the executive branch, the domain of the enforcement of law or the administration of justice itself, much work awaits to be done in using discourse analysis. The most penetrating examination has been done by Peter Manning in *Symbolic Communication* (1988). His study was concerned with how emergency 911 phone calls are codified and how the codification mobilizes police in the streets. What he spells out is a complex process by which raw data (the telephone call to the police) are worked over, conceptualized into categories reflecting a hierarchy of priorities, which then become the basis of action or inaction. His analysis implies that in modern societies we more and more abdicate, or are denied, the ability to construct reality; we increasingly rely on organizational structures to rationally construct reality for us. Modern society is in a crisis of meaning construction. Authoritative powers are increasingly monopolizing the process of constructing meaning. Organizations such as the police, making use of 911 emergency calls, essentially take floating signifiers — the calls by the citizen — and anchor, or give precise content (the signified), to them. Essentially, as in Bernard Jackson's analysis of story-telling in law, the police handling of 911 phone calls results in the creation of coherent narrative texts. 'Administrative rationality' guides the construction process. Stable meanings are constructed by taking a multitude of presumedly unorganized data — the call to the police — and fitting it into a coherent story of what *must have* happened.

We can extend this analysis to justice rendering generally. Since more than 90 per cent of court cases are resolved through the guilty plea, and since about 70 per cent of this is due to plea-bargaining and its constraints, we may say that ours is a system of bureaucratic justice having little to do with justice rendering in a more general sense (Thomas, 1988). Plea-bargaining is a secretive process; dialogue that takes place, even though more informal, still does not produce a conception of reality that 'counts.' That is, the formal trial is a symbolic recreation of the boundaries of a society, established primarily by the dominant group.

Manning shows that what guides the process of reality construction is a 'tacit knowledge' of how events take place (1988: 215). According to Manning, story construction relies on a metaphysics that is not verbalized. He tells us, "It is likely that scenes of a basic sort orient coding and interpretation across the subsystems" (1988: 217). These anchor the otherwise perpetual sliding of meaning, the sliding of signifieds under signifiers, giving them stability and a coherent explanation. The answer to the 'what happened?' in essence is a text, a coherent narrative construction, that, in Jackson's thesis, is non-referential. The text 'floats' in the organizational world and is often devoid of any reference to the real world dynamic of what actually happened. What increasingly takes place, however, is that organizations, such as those administering the 911 emergency calls, assume the role of creating reality, irrespective of what really happened in the streets. It is as if two texts unfold: the real and the text produced by administrative rationality. More and more this rationalistic construction dominates our lives (also see Habermas, 1984). We are but signifiers in the panoptic machine.

An important analysis of how prison and court officials read jailhouse lawyers' litigation has been presented by Jim Thomas (1988: 145-51, 158-175). Various prison and court workers screen cases and more often look for specific cues that may indicate improprieties — 'failure to state an adjudicable claim,' 'failure to exhaust all state remedies prior to federal filings,' etc. But these readings more often rely on extra-legal factors such as the pragmatics of the organizational structure (for example, the particular relationship between the court and the prison, availability of prison space, availability on the court calender), or personal biases (for example, whether the particular screener is favourably predisposed or not towards prisoner litigation; Thomas, 1988: 169). The prisoner litigant, on the other hand, tells stories and attempts to persuade the reader to "infer the preferred interpretation as one of staff impropriety and 'deprivation of liberty or property'" (ibid.: 134). As Thomas writes: "The prisoner story resembles a narrative dictionary by which prisoners key their lexicon to the audience by taking a set of facts, as they perceive them, and retranslating these to correspond to the frame by which they believe the audience might be persuaded to act" (133).

In sum, discourse analysis indicates that the executive branch is one in which texts are constructed and acted upon. The particular ideologies or pragmatics of the organizational setting guide the construction process. Reality construction takes place within a narrowly constructed system of relevancies.

CONCLUSION

In this chapter we have argued that to properly understand the administration of justice we must conceptualize the three branches of the state as they actually operate. Unlike the perception of the state as an overarching superstructural monolith that impinges a particular hegemony on the minds of the public — as inferred by the controlologists — the state should be viewed as a collection of different organized practices that operate in such a way as to construct and reconstruct a particular view that is often resisted and modified. For the administration of justice, this means that the legislative branch, the judiciary, and the executive branch interact in complicated ways. Sometimes these interactions are harmonious and sometimes they are contradictory, but they always produce a definitive set of organized practices, which embody the administration of justice.

Underlying such practices is a set of material social relations that are unequal but legitimated through the administration of justice. To critically deconstruct and analyse these relations and the administration of justice they engender, three critical traditions of inquiry have emerged: Marxist political economy, feminist inquiry, and discourse analysis. While each of these traditions is distinct, each also heavily relies upon the concepts provided by the other traditions, and a thoroughly critical approach should be sensitive to the arguments all of them present.

NOTES

1. For a good discussion of the limitations of controlology, see Lowman and Palys, 1991.

2. For a more detailed overview of how the method of historical materialism and the concepts of political economy have been used by criminologists, see MacLean (1986b).

3. For good general introductions to the analytical approaches of feminists see Donovan (1986) and Tong (1989).

4. For a more general introduction to postmodernism and poststructuralism see Sarup (1989).

5. For an overview of the various ways in which the notion of patriarchy has been used by feminists and the various analytical problems associated with the concept, see Fox (1988).

6. For a more detailed overview, which also includes a discussion and critique of postmodern influences, see Currie and Kline (1991).

7. Canadian feminists have not focused on the lawbreaking of individual women. As discussed in this overview, the tendency has been to concentrate on women as victims of criminal activity. This reorientation transforms criminology to such an extent that some British writers (Gelsthorpe and Morris, 1988; Smart, 1990) maintain that we should abandon attempts to delineate a specifically 'feminist' criminology. LaBerge (1991) maintains that the invisibility of women within Canadian criminology, which is only now being addressed, is due to the fact that criminologists, historically, did not define crime in a way that made it appear to be relevant to women, on the one hand, and that feminists, until recently, did not prioritize issues of criminal justice, on the other hand. For overviews of the female offender see RCSW (1970) and Hatch and Faith (1989/90).

8. For a discussion of how this approach helps us to understand how meaning is constructed in pornography and the implications of this understanding in campaigns for censorship, see Currie (1992).

Part One

THE LEGISLATIVE BRANCH: LAWMAKING

Chapter Two

Meech Lake: Constitution-Making as Patriarchal Practice

Donna Greschner

The Meech Lake Accord offers a particularly relevant study of lawmaking in progress. As Donna Greschner notes, almost all women's and Aboriginal organizations denounced the amendments proposed by the Accord. Greschner examines the basis for this opposition and explores the process through which Meech Lake was negotiated — a process that could have the contradictory result of undermining the rights for women secured only in 1982 and with much struggle. The problem with Meech Lake is that it undermines the importance placed upon sex equality as an organizing ideal of Canadian polity by Sections 15 and 28 of the Charter of Human Rights and Freedoms. This jeopardy arises through the juxtaposition of two clauses in the proposed amendments to the constitutional text: Section 2, which states that the Constitution of Canada shall be interpreted in a manner that recognizes the linguistic duality of Canada and the existence of Quebec as a distinct society within Canada; and Section 16, which states that Section 2 does not affect the provisions concerning Aboriginal peoples and multiculturalism. In other words, the Accord implies that linguistic duality and Quebec's distinctiveness are not as important a feature of Canadian life as Aboriginal rights and multiculturalism, but are more important than sex equality. The fear of women's groups is that women stand to lose the symbolic, rhetorical, discursive power of the priority of equality. Greschner analyses how this loss could negatively affect women.

To understand how such a threat to sex equality could arise, Greschner outlines two specific problems that underlie the Canadian constitution. The first concerns the way in which Canadian federalism is grounded in the concept of territory or "real property." The second concerns the exclusion of women from Canadian constitution-making. While this is not to say that the involvement of women would necessarily render constitutional amendment an equitable proc-

Donna Greschner is Professor of Law at the University of Saskatchewan

cess, it is important to recognize that the leading parliamentary opponent to Meech Lake was Sharon Carstairs, leader of the official opposition in Manitoba. Greschner notes that unlike the passage of ordinary law, which requires first, second, and third readings to allow debate, an amendment to the Constitution is approved through simple resolution. Perhaps ironically, it is more difficult for the Saskatchewan legislature to amend the Abandoned Refrigerators Act, for example, than to agree to Constitutional changes. In conclusion, what feminism demands of justice, therefore, is nothing less than changes in the notions of representation, political leadership, and responsible government.

A PREFATORY EPILOQUE

This essay was completed in March 1989, and the *Meech Lake Accord* died on June 23, 1990, in Winnipeg. For two weeks in June, Elijah Harper, an Aboriginal member of the Manitoba Legislature acting on behalf of the provincial First Nations, refused his consent to accelerated legislative consideration of the Accord. The recently elected Newfoundland premier, Clyde Wells, a staunch opponent of the Accord who had rescinded Newfoundland's legislative approval, then cancelled a second vote in the Newfoundland Assembly because of the Accord's failure in Manitoba.

The events after March 1989 do not disprove the thesis that men rule the constitutional world, but they illustrate sharply the inappropriateness of exclusively gendered language to describe the persons comprising the state. Speaking abstractly of 'men' submerges the racism embedded deeply and painfully within contemporary patriarchy. Elijah Harper's actions, and the rarity of an Aboriginal voice within the state, are an acute reminder that the state is the creature of white men and that non–Aboriginal men also exercise power most often, if at all, as outsiders. Since March 1989, a few more non-Aboriginal women have taken positions within the state: Audrey McLaughlin as the leader of the federal New Democratic Party; Beverley McLachlin as the third woman appointed to the Supreme Court of Canada; Kim Campbell as the first female Minister of Justice for Canada; and a record number of women as cabinet ministers in the Ontario New Democratic government. The most powerful woman in the history of constitution-making remains Sharon Carstairs. Her early opposition to the Accord galvanized despondent critics, and her persistence gave Elijah Harper the opportunity to say no. The demise of Meech Lake in Manitoba occurred because of a lucky coincidence of circumstances involving an Aboriginal man and a non-Aboriginal woman, both outsiders on the inside's periphery, both exercising not the insider's power of setting agendas but the outsider's limited power of saying no.

Afterwards, once again the country began searching its constitutional soul, with six jurisdictions having at least one committee inquiring into constitutional reform (Greschner, 1991a). In the face of threatened Quebec separatism, the debates focus on the division of power among Quebec, the federal government, and other provinces. However, the failure of the Accord has directed more attention to the process of constitution-making and the constitutional position of Aboriginal peoples. The promotion of

Aboriginal self-government will benefit not only Aboriginal women but all women, if we listen to Aboriginal wisdom in the renovation of constitutional process and substance. The Manitoba chiefs and Harper made their political decisions in June by consensus, a method in stark contrast to the secret manipulations of the first ministers (Greschner, 1991b) and one more consistent with feminist principles. The traditional Aboriginal relationship to 'Mother Earth' that still informs aboriginal political structures and decision-making is neither feudal nor patriarchal. It is not based on absolute ownership and hierarchy in caretaking, responsibility, and respect. Imagine what a constitution and its attendant political and economic systems would look like if grounded in the Aboriginal concept of Mother Earth. Listening attentively to the voices of Aboriginal women and men may not only improve the Constitution, but also save the land.

INTRODUCTION

The *Meech Lake Accord* is a set of proposed amendments to the Constitution negotiated by the prime minister and the ten provincial premiers — eleven men — in April and June of 1987.[1] The stated purpose of the Accord is to change the Constitution in a manner satisfactory to the government of Quebec and thus achieve, finally, Quebec's agreement to amendments enacted in 1982. Almost all women's groups have been critical of the Accord. They argue that women's equality rights, articulated and protected in the Constitution in 1982 only after a long and arduous campaign, are jeopardized by the textual priority the Accord gives to the recognition of Canada's linguistic duality and Quebec's distinct society (Smith, 1988; Mahoney, 1988). They point out that other provisions in the Accord have the potential to harm women. For instance, the proposed changes to the federal spending power could hamper the development or continuation of social programs, such as daycare and medicare, of benefit to all women and poor women in particular (National Action Committee, 1987). Although other groups representing both disadvantaged women and men, such as Aboriginal organizations, have also voiced their disapproval of the Accord, Parliament and eight of the ten provincial legislatures had adopted the Accord as of July 7, 1988.[2] Only rejection of the Accord by one of the two remaining provinces, Manitoba or New Brunswick, would stop its deleterious effects on women. Both provinces, having held elections since June 1987, now have different premiers than the men who agreed to the Accord.

How could amendments be proposed to the Constitution that threaten the interests and the newly minted constitutional equality rights of over half of the population? In other words, how could Meech Lake happen? For women familiar with the history of constitutional change, the Accord is not a complete surprise. Constitution-making has been a male prerogative since well before 1867, the year of Confederation. Mary Eberts's comment about constitutional change in the 1980s aptly describes the past century: "Constitutional decisions of great significance to women are made by men without notice to women, without consultation, and in the absence of any essential awareness of women's interests" (Ad Hoc Committee, 1988: 145). The great battle in 1980-81 for a sex equality clause in the Constitution, a victory now known as the "taking of 28" (Kome, 1983), was the first time, ever, that women were able to achieve an addition to the constitutional text. Meech Lake shows the difficulty, if not the too-frequent impossibility, of even stopping adverse constitutional amendments. To our dismay, we see clearly now that the triumph of section 28 was an anomaly rather than a harbinger of a more inclusive approach to constitutional politics (Whyte, 1988: 263-266).

The short answer to how Meech Lake could have happened is that men still rule the constitutional world. But a fuller exposition of how Meech Lake happened serves two purposes. First, by illuminating the obstacles preventing women from participating in constitutional politics, the case proves the need for a foundational rebuilding of political structures and processes. Second, Meech Lake is a story about the Canadian state. Feminism has not yet developed a theory of the modern state (MacKinnon, 1983). One prelude to a feminist theory of the state is an understanding of the current operation of the different components of the state. Another is attention to the state's personnel. As Burstyn (1985) points out, personnel cannot be ignored in theorizing about the methods, ideology, and functions of the modern state. To chronicle how Meech Lake happened, to describe some parts of the state and the real men who wield and benefit from state power, is to concretize and personalize the abstract concept of the state.

THE SUBSTANCE OF THE *MEECH LAKE ACCORD*

Perhaps the first question to ask is why so many women's groups see the *Meech Lake Accord* as an important site of women's struggles. Even if the concept of a constitution is not necessarily antifeminist (Greschner, 1986), why expend energy now fighting for a better Constitution when we urgently need more shelters for battered women? Conceptually, the Constitution is the linchpin of the legal system and the formal political system. It establishes or recognizes basic institutions of the state, such as the executive and the legislature, delineates their powers, and enunciates some fundamental principles of the polity. As explicitly stated in section 52(1) of the *Constitution Act*, 1982, the Constitution is the supreme law of the land and any law not in conformity with it is of no force and effect. Practically, although the arid phrases of the Constitution may seem far removed from the daily concerns of the rural farm woman in Saskatchewan or the garment worker in Toronto, what the Constitution says — and does not say — can make a difference in women's lives. For instance, the federal government used its spending power to introduce a universal mothers' allowance program in 1944, replacing the widely divergent provincial programs (Burt, 1988). Furthermore, we must pay attention to the Constitution because it can be used against us. In the late 1970s, for example, a feminist lobby helped stop a proposed transfer of divorce jurisdiction from the federal to the provincial governments, a change that would have had adverse consequences for women, particularly poor women with children (Bowman, 1981).[3]

Moreover, the Constitution has an important symbolic function. Its ideals and ideas become part of our national discourse, part of our cultural lexicon, shaping our future and reinventing our past. Consider the aspirations and grievances of Aboriginal women and men. In 1982 for the first time their existence as *peoples* became a formal part of the national consciousness.[4] The Constitution finally saw them as agents, as subjects, as peoples, not merely as objects of federal control casually listed after bankruptcy, patents, and copyrights in the constitutional catalogue of governmental powers. Their dreams of sovereignty are unfulfilled and their constitutional power remains cramped, but constitutional visibility has been achieved at last.

Only in 1982 was sex equality haltingly articulated in the Constitution; indeed, only in 1982 was gender even recognized by the Constitution. The *Charter of Rights and Freedoms*, being Part I of the *Constitution Act, 1982*, guarantees in section 15 the right not to be discriminated against on the basis of sex, while the opening words of section 28 state the priority given to sex equality: "Notwithstanding anything in this Charter, the rights and freedoms referred to in it are guaranteed equally to male and female persons." These are critical symbolic statements for political discourse. When rights are taken away from women, when we are treated as inferior, when opportunities are denied to us, we can point to sections 15 and 28 and make the political argument that we are guaranteed sex equality and that we are guaranteed equality notwithstanding anything else.[5] We can point to the discontinuity between the promise of section 28 and the reality of our lives. Sometimes we will be able to take the further step and make a legal argument that the sex equality provisions stop any government from taking away our rights and freedoms, but the political argument may prove the most powerful. Several years ago, my university publicized a new sexual harassment policy as necessitated by the spirit, if not the legal niceties, of sections 15 and 28. Another illustration of the symbolic power of the two sections is the sign in a private men's club in 1982, announcing that in the spirit of the new Constitution the club would admit women as full members.[6] In the *spirit* of the Constitution: The club had no legal obligation to abide by the Charter,[7] to follow the stated public commitment to sex equality, or to bring its reality in line with principle, but it did.

The first concern of women with the *Meech Lake Accord* is that two provisions disturb the importance given to sex equality as an organizing ideal of the Canadian polity. Section 2 of the Accord states that the Constitution of Canada shall be interpreted in a manner recognizing the linguistic duality of Canada and the existence of Quebec as a distinct society within Canada. Section 16 then states that section 2 does not affect the provisions of the Constitution concerning Aboriginal peoples and multiculturalism. The inference is that section 2 can negatively affect anything not mentioned in section 16. Conspicuously absent from section

16 is equality generally and sex equality in particular. In other words, section 16 says linguistic duality and Quebec's distinctness are not features of our collective life as important as Aboriginal rights and multiculturalism, but are more important than sex equality. Sex equality is now of lesser importance than the items mentioned in sections 2 and 16. The fear of women's groups is obvious. What we have lost, a critical political loss, is the symbolic, rhetorical, and discursive power of the priority of equality.

We may also lose a lot legally. Women argued that section 16 increases the chances that governments will take away what little equality women have now. In litigation involving a competition between sex equality and the promotion of a distinct society (for Quebec) or linguistic duality (for anglophone Canada), sex equality now stands a greater chance of losing because of section 16 (Ad Hoc Committee, 1988:146).

The branch of the state charged with deciding the legal competition between sex equality and territorial or linguistic distinctiveness is the judiciary. Its power to adjudicate constitutional disputes includes giving authoritative interpretations of the constitutional text. Moreover, since judicial interpretation of the words changes over time, it can be as important a method of constitutional change as formal political agreements to make additions or deletions to the text.[8] The meaning judges will give to sections 2 and 16 will determine the extent of the Accord's negative effect on women's equality rights and thus the very meaning of equality for women, both in the immediate and long-term future.

The judiciary remains a male preserve. The Supreme Court of Canada has had two women members in its lengthy history. Pierre Trudeau appointed Madame Justice Bertha Wilson in 1982 and Brian Mulroney appointed Madame Justice Claire L'Heureux-Dubé in 1987. Moreover, the current 22 per cent (two out of nine) female membership is an aberration. Women constitute only 6 per cent of judges appointed by the federal government and only 4.6 per cent of judges appointed by provincial governments, even though we have been a significant part of the legal profession for the past 15 years (Baines, 1988). Several provincial appellate courts, in practice the final courts for the overwhelming majority of cases, still have no women judges. The absence of women on the bench means that our claims about the meaning and priority of sex equality will be heard primarily by men.

The continuing masculine dominance of the judicial branch of the state has long been a concern for women. Suspicions about the legitimacy of the judicial system will continue at least until women constitute 50 per cent of all judges. So the question is: Who appoints judges? For the lowest level of courts in each province, the provincial cabinet makes appointments, which means in practice that the attorney-general (sometimes called the minister of justice) makes the selection. All provincial attorneys-generals have been men until Brian Peckford appointed Lynne Verge as Newfoundland's attorney-general in 1985. For the higher courts in each province and the federal courts, the federal cabinet receives recommendations on appointments from the minister of justice. As of March 1989, no woman has held the post of federal minister of justice. The executive power of appointment seems untrammeled. No public consultation occurs,[9] no legislature approves the appointments, and no legal restrictions limit the executive decision except the requirement that judges be lawyers. To add to the obstacles placed before women, judgeships are often, if not usually, meted out as a political reward (Canadian Bar Association Report, 1985). Hence, the exclusion of women from the inner circles of power within political parties also operates as a bar to participation in this branch of the state. Perhaps the primary reason why the Supreme Court of Canada has the highest percentage of women judges ever is the recent absence of political patronage as a criteria for selection of judges to that court.

The Accord's only provision about judicial appointments requires the federal minister of justice to select judges for the Supreme Court of Canada from lists prepared by provincial governments. Provincial premiers did not demand this power because they wanted to make the Court more representative of the gender composition of the country, but because they perceived a bias within the Court during the 1970s. They thought the Court was favouring the federal government in battles with the provinces. They want to ensure that the Court's members will incline towards maintaining or augmenting provincial powers. Notice that the provincial *government* has been given the power to nominate candidates. The executive, most likely the premier and the attorney-general, will exercise this power without any obligation to have public consultation or even to submit the names to the provincial legislatures. For women, what little has changed may be for the worse (Whyte, 1988: 265).

The remaining substantive provisions of the Accord also relate to the division of powers between the federal and provincial levels. They graphically illustrate that an understanding of the state in Canada must begin with the reality of 11 different states. As Sandra Burt (1988:153) reminds us, "In Canada, the most significant structural characteristic of the political system is the division of powers between the federal and provincial levels." Accordingly, we must be cautious about the applicability of state theories from Britain, a unitary state, or the United States, federalist in name but highly centralized in practice.

Federalism grounds constitutional politics in the concept of territory, in land, in what lawyers call real property. It divides state powers not only by physical boundaries, by longitude and latitude, but also on two different planes: ten provincial units, with no physical overlap, and one national unit superimposed over all the other ten units. Just as homesteaders had control over their 160 acres and suburbanites have control over their lots, so too the ten provincial governments have control over physical terrain and the people on it. Federalism assumes that a person's interests are, to a large extent, coterminus with the other persons who live within the provincial borders and share the same provincial address. Interests of persons not peculiar to a particular place are recognized within the national government, which Canadians call the federal level. Federalism is the political version of condominium property ownership. Each province owns one condo; while the federal government owns the common terrain, such as the corridors between condos (in legal terms, 'interprovincial trade') and the roof overhead ('national interest'), and provides most of the utilities necessary for warmth and light (such as pensions, or medicare). Given the absolute primacy of control over, and divisions of, real property in politics — historically, conceptually, and practically — it is no accident that the only mention of equality the first ministers inserted into the *Meech Lake Accord* speaks of the equality of provinces, not of people.

Both the federal and provincial levels of the state contain the various components of state power. While legislative division of power between the federal and provincial levels cannot be ignored, of greater importance for women has been cooperation and conflict between the 11 executive branches, particularly since the advent of the welfare state. Federal-provincial relations at the executive level determine the shape and speed of initiatives from medicare to daycare to welfare to equality rights. Agreements on every matter under the sun are written by bureaucrats, signed by ministers and rubber-stamped by legislatures only if necessary. The daily executive interactions among the 11 governments are the very real context within which women must operate. Lest we forget, the taking of 28 was a battle fought against the *executive* arms of government. And women had the advantage of the federal executive's commitment in principle to a sex equality clause, thus making easier the job of convincing the recalcitrant provincial executives (Burt, 1988: 149).

The remaining clauses in Meech Lake, as with the clause on judicial appointments, in essence give power to the provincial governments at the expense of the federal government. In the past 20 years, although several provinces have made significant innovations in social programs, the federal government has shown more responsiveness to women's concerns than has the average provincial government (Doerr, 1981). Yet Meech Lake would have weakened the primary instrument of federal initiatives, the spending power. In practical terms, Meech Lake means that women in some provinces will not have the benefits enjoyed by women in other provinces, and that the women's movement will need increasingly to lobby 11 governments for policy improvements. Meech Lake makes a woman's provincial address more important than ever. Practically and symbolically, the augmented power of the provinces retrenches the politics of real property at the expense of the politics of rights and group consciousness (Cairns, 1988). The lens through which Meech Lake refracts questions of power is geography, not gender.

That owning property produces a sense of smug exclusivity, the desire to prevent others from having the same power, is shown in the provisions on new provinces. The land mass of Canada also has two territories, the Northwest and Yukon, but their governments were not invited to the Meech meetings nor were they partners in the agreement: absent, but not forgotten. The 11 ministers included a provision in Meech Lake requiring the consent of all provinces before either territory becomes a province, thus giving each first minister absolute control over the admission of any new members to the club.[10] The ministers are not about to let someone buy into the condo unit even if the person already has the price of admission; namely, control over a land mass. What hope, then, is there for women, historically excluded from any control over property of any kind?

THE PROCESS OF MEECH LAKE

The process of reaching agreement at Meech Lake began in 1982 when the Quebec government refused to sign the package of constitutional amendments that became the *Constitution Act, 1982*. The 1980-81 round of constitutional talks were undertaken because during Quebec's referendum debate of 1980 federal politicians promised that if the people of Quebec voted 'no' to sovereignty-association they would revise federalism to take better account of Quebec's concerns. Hence, the refusal of the Quebec government to sign the deal was a major political problem. Quebec was legally bound by the 1982 changes but without its formal assent the Quebec government saw the revised Constitution as devoid of legitimacy in the province.

When Brian Mulroney became prime minister in 1984, striking a constitutional deal acceptable to the government of Quebec was a major item on his political agenda. He needed the consent of other provincial governments because the 1982 amendments required the agreement of seven provinces representing over 50 per cent of the population for most future constitutional amendments.[11] In May 1986, the Bourassa government, also willing to bargain, enunciated five conditions for its agreement. The other nine premiers accepted the conditions as the agenda for constitutional talks at a conference in Edmonton in August 1986. Before and after these public announcements, over the course of 14 months, federal bureaucrats visited various provincial governments for discussions about constitutional matters, while the Quebec government also sent emissaries to other provinces. The meetings were secret. I remember talking to one provincial civil servant who would not even tell me who the participants were (other than himself) or what were the topics. Meetings of bureaucrats continued until the Meech Lake meeting of first ministers on April 30, 1987, and between April 30 and June 3, 1987, when the first ministers at their second meeting approved the final text. Bureaucrats prepared the groundwork, floated ideas, produced drafts and gave advice.

By virtue of the importance of the subject-matter, the bureaucrats would be high-ranking civil servants, deputy or associate deputy ministers, and exclusively or predominantly men. In 1987, women were a mere 8.7 per cent of the executive category and 13.2 per cent of the senior management category of federal public servants (Morgan, 1988). The interviews Morgan conducted reveal the fear, hostility, and active resistance of men (how many men she does not say) towards the advancement of women in the civil service. Her work also shows that in our understandable concern with the systems, structures, and organizations that oppress women, we cannot ignore blatant prejudice and misogyny. The systems may still be the manifestation of, and the mask for, deep-seated beliefs about the proper place and inferiority of women.

For the two meetings of first ministers that produced the Accord, no transcript or record of governmental delegations provides information about the number, identity, and gender of the civil servants. Only members of Parliament or legislatures are listed as participants in the transcript from the June 3, 1987, conference announcing the deal. All are men, from the nine-man federal team to the one-man Newfoundland delegation composed of Premier Peckford (First Ministers Conference on the Constitution: Verbatim Transcript, 1987).[12] We will need to retrieve the unofficial history of Meech Lake to find the women erased by the official record, to discover the number of women involved and the extent of their influence. In the meantime, we cannot assume that the proportion of women in every delegation was equal to the ten per cent proportion of women in the executive category in the federal government, because women in this category are clustered in less powerful posts (Morgan, 1988: 56), and constitution-making involves lots of power. Even if ten per cent or more of the bureaucrats were women, and they were sensitive to the effects of the proposals on women, they may have been incapable of making a difference. The experience of one woman civil servant in the 1980-81 negotiations attests to the hostility and apathy of men towards women's concerns, even when the process was visible and the women's movement had the opportunity to lobby politicians.[13]

The importance of bureaucrats in designing the *Meech Lake Accord*, however, cannot be overly stressed because the first ministers took an exceptionally active role. They met in private at Meech Lake, excluding all of their advisors. They agreed to items that had apparently not been part of Quebec's original demands or the subject of bureaucratic talks (Schwartz, 1987:2-3). The first ministers are all white men who lead the ruling political parties. As leaders of the ruling party, they automatically become heads of the executive branches of government in their respective jurisdictions. When ultimate executive power is exercised, they are the ones who do the exercising.

Feminist political theorists consider political parties the biggest barrier against women's effective political participation (Domgalski, 1986; Burstyn, 1985). A host of factors within political parties exclude women from positions of power in the organizations. When women have assumed leadership positions, it has been in provinces with parties so moribund that no man wanted the job. The Manitoba Liberal Party and the Nova Scotia New Democratic Party were politically irrelevant when Sharon Carstairs and Alexa McDonough became their respective leaders. It is at least plausible to hypothesize that the presence of women leaders at Meech Lake would have made a difference. Sharon Carstairs, the primary parliamentary opponent to Meech Lake, leads the Official Opposition in the Manitoba legislature after resuscitating the Manitoba Liberals and is opposed to any amendments that threaten women's equality rights.

The executive branches have no constitutional obligation to receive input into the terms of a constitutional change. The process of constitution-making knows nothing of referenda and very little of the public constitutional convention. The only conference mentioned in the Constitution is the First Ministers Conference, the cabal that gave us Meech Lake.[14] These conferences need not even be open to the public. When they are, as with the June 3, 1987, conference, they can be snappy endorsements of secret deals worked out over late-night coffee, nothing more than opportunities for first ministers to make speeches and pat themselves on the back. The Accord will institutionalize this closed, elitist process even more deeply by requiring a constitutional conference of first ministers every year.

When the first ministers agreed to the Accord, it was only an agreement among 11 men. For the deal to have legal force, to become a binding part of the Constitution, it needs approval by Parliament and the legislatures of each province.[15] In theory this stage of the process gives voice to the people through their elected representatives and checks unfettered power by democratic control. It is tempting, however, to stop the Meech Lake story at this point and say nothing about Parliament or the legislatures because they have become almost politically irrelevant in the process of constitution-making. Their approval may be a legal requirement but they collaborate in being treated as a political nuisance by the executive. When the first ministers returned from Meech Lake, they used their considerable power to ensure that the Accord would receive speedy legislative approval. Each is first minister, after all, because his party controls the majority of the seats in the elected assembly. Once the executive branch — the premier or prime minister — agrees to a constitutional change, party discipline virtually guarantees legislative approval. In Canada parties are extraordinarily disciplined because of one principle of responsible government, specifically that a majority vote against a government motion is a non-confidence motion that defeats the government and causes an election.

To add procedural insult to democratic injury, the formal process can be indecently fast. The assembly's legal consent is indicated by the passage of a resolution. Unlike the passage of an ordinary law, which requires first, second, and third reading to allow time for debate, reflection, and amendment, an amendment to the Constitution is approved by one simple vote. It is more difficult and time-consuming for the legislature of Saskatchewan to pass an amendment to the *Abandoned Refrigerators Act* than to agree to fundamental constitutional change. Indeed, in British Columbia, the government introduced the Meech Lake resolution and received legislative approval within one day.

Although under no constitutional obligation to do so, a Special Joint Committee of the House of Commons and the Senate held public hearings during the summer of 1987 (with three regular women members and fourteen regular male members). To call the hearings a sham and a waste of time and money, almost a slap in the face to democratic principle, would still not capture the outrage, bitterness, and intense sense of futility felt by the Accord's critics who travelled to Ottawa that summer (Cairns, 1988). The Prime Minister had announced often and loudly that not one word of the Accord would be changed unless the Committee found an egregious error. The Committee, not surprisingly, did not find one. It did not even bother to listen to women's groups; as Baines (1987) shows in her perspicacious analysis of the Committee's report, the Committee's members did not hear or understand the words of the women who spoke before them. The treatment of women's groups before the Committee was a classic example of patriarchy at work.

Several provincial legislatures, such as Ontario, also conducted hearings, but again on the explicit premise that changes would not be contemplated. None were.

Thus, the only small burp in the legislative digestion of the first ministers' Meech Lake meal was the appointed Senate at the federal level, which delayed approval until a few months after the House of Commons had passed the resolution. The will of nine of the eleven men could have taken legal effect almost instantaneously. Only the intervention of elections in Manitoba and New Brunswick prevented the Accord from becoming law quickly. New Brunswick held public hearings to determine the new government's position on the Accord, and public hearings will also be conducted in Manitoba, the only legislature with a self-imposed statutory obligation to hear the public's views before voting on a constitutional amendment. Whether or not these two provinces will reject the Accord remains an open question. The rhetoric from the nine signers remains bellicose, with Mulroney continuing to state categorically that any change to Meech Lake would mean the death of Canada. The two premiers of the hold-out provinces have already withstood tremendous pressure to agree to the Accord before the expiry date of June 23, 1990. The fate of the Accord will depend in large measure on the tenacity of Sharon Carstairs, for as leader of the Official Opposition in the province with the only minority government, she wields power that would not exist if the Manitoba government controlled a majority of seats in the legislature. If she succeeds in producing changes to the amendments, or stopping them altogether, she will have exercised more direct power in formal constitution-making than any other woman, ever.

If elected assemblies were not politically irrelevant, would they make any difference? Parliament and the provincial legislatures are also overwhelmingly dominated by men, an expected statistic given the well-known difficulties faced by women within the established political parties (Domagalski, 1986). Rather than reiterate these problems, I want to highlight a more fundamental problem with the electoral system that prevents women from having an effective voice. Constituencies are determined solely by geography. How our vote is counted — that is, the people our votes are counted with — is determined by where we live. Again we see the land on which a person lives equated with her interests, the continuing legacy of the historical importance of real property in the political system. A geographic system does not encourage the representation of women; rather, it divides women by telling us that our interests are closest to the interests of the men who live in the same area. But it is not at all obvious that every woman's primary interests are the same as the men who live in the neighbourhood rather than the other women in the city or the province or the country. And if women do form a feminist consciousness and try to exercise organized political power in a constituency, the first-past-the-post rule requires us to possess significant support before we are able to elect a representative that really does represent our views (Boyle, 1984). As long as we have geographic constituencies represented by the one person receiving the largest number of votes, we will wait a long time for women's emancipation.

CONCLUSION

Studying Meech Lake shows MacKinnon's proposal that "the state is male" to be not only normatively but literally true: Men are the state. Constitutional politics is rooted in the historically masculine concept of property of which women were the first instantiations. This politics is played out primarily by the executive branch of the state, by leaders of geographical units who fight over powers to control property. The modern state, analysed usually by feminists as an instrument, manifestation, or correlate of capitalism, remains grounded in the precapitalist notions of feudalism. As a political and social system, feudalism was the first recorded form of condominium property ownership. Feudalism was a land-based system in which the king and his lords shared powers, and in which the vassals' life was determined by the particular land on which they lived and hence the landowning lord who had power over them. First Ministers constitute the new feudal king and lords, expecting blind obedience from their serfs, noticing women only if and when it suits them. In the constitutional context, First Ministers would not be boasting to appropriate the claim of the last French feudal monarch: "*L'état, c'est nous.*"

By noting the absence of women in the constitutional process, I am not saying that more women would have made a profound difference, although like Burstyn (1985), I find it hard to believe that if 50 per cent of the participants had been women, the process and substance would not have been very different. Feminism is not satisfied by a *coup d'état* — a mere change in leaders at the pinnacle of the political pyramid. Plotting how the state is male has shown how it is male according to its basic method and division: a method of reposing almost absolute power in a leader; and a division by territory or property, which women were legally prevented from holding until recently and are still excluded from by economic circumstance. In 1867, a property-oriented system of politics would still have seemed natural to the men of property who were the fathers of Confederation. What feminism demands is nothing less than changes in the notions of representation, political leadership, and responsible government.

The *Meech Lake Accord* was reached because of the stated desire of politicians to bring Quebec into the constitutional family. Supporters of Meech Lake will say of this paper, as they say of every criticism, that it fails to take account of the paramount need to have a legitimate constitution for Quebec. Legitimacy of the Constitution for Quebec is important but not the only issue. Women never agreed to the original documents of Confederation — the fathers of Confederation did not allow us to speak — or to any of the amendments. When will it be time to consider the legitimacy of the Constitution for women? Such a strange notion of family this is — excluding the mothers. Or is it the reality of the patriarchal family writ large?

March, 1989. I would like to thank Debra Greschner, Renaldo Murphy, and Martha Shaffer for comments on an earlier draft of this chapter.

NOTES

1. The initial agreement, reached on April 30, 1987, at Meech Lake, was altered somewhat at a second meeting of the 11 first ministers in Ottawa on June 3, 1987. The amended text is called the *Meech Lake Accord.*

2. The first provincial legislature to register its approval was the National Assembly of Quebec on June 23, 1987; the eighth was Newfoundland on July 7, 1988. At the federal level, the House of Commons approved the resolution on October 26, 1987, and the Senate on April 21, 1988.

3. The two most critical problems for women were maintenance orders and custody disputes (Bowman, 1981). If divorce jurisdiction had been transferred to the provinces, enforcement of maintenance orders in one province of orders made in another province would have been even more difficult and expensive, at a time when 70 per cent of maintenance orders were not paid by husbands and many husbands moved from the province granting the divorce to avoid payment. Extra-provincial enforcement of custody orders would also have become far more costly and time-consuming, again at a time when taking a child out of the province was a quick way for the non-custodial parent (usually the father) to obtain custody or use de facto custody as a bargaining chip for maintenance and property division. Since Bowman wrote her analysis, legislation has sought to help women and children with the enforcement of maintenance and custody orders by establishing more national regimes, precisely the opposite direction of the proposals in the late 1970s.

4. Sections 25, 35 and 35.1 of the *Constitution Act, 1982.*

5. I am not saying that the language of equality and inequality captures fully the phenomenon of women's subordination; the language of oppression, occupation, and colonization is far more apt, particularly in describing the sexual exploitation of women. The point is, as Majury (1987) notes, that the discourse of equality offers strategic possibilities for women's liberation because of its entrenchment in the *Charter of Rights and Freedoms.*

6. I owe this example to Catharine MacKinnon.

7. The courts have interpreted section 33 of the *Charter*, which states that governments and legislatures are bound by the *Charter*, as excluding all 'private,' that is, non-governmental, institutions and organizations from the Charter's ambit.

8. Besides judicial interpretation and formal amendment, constitutions can change through the development of conventions. Conventions are political practices that deviate from the formal written text of the Constitution because of the perceived need by politicians to adhere to more important principles. A full analysis of conventions is beyond the scope of this chapter; suffice it to say that since women have been politicians in very small numbers, they have helped formulate conventions only in a small way, if at all.

9. Advisory committees, aptly named as they have no legal power, have been established by several provinces to give opinions on candidates for judicial appointments, but they do not hold public hearings or publicize their assessments.

10. This provision has been called despicable (Schwartz, 1987:126) for good reason. The injustice done to the predominantly Aboriginal women and men of the North — preventing them from becoming truly self-governing because of the self-interest of provincial leaders — is highly offensive to democratic principles, a perpetuation of a racist colonialism.

11. The *Meech Lake Accord* requires the agreement of all ten provinces and Parliament because it changes several provisions in the *Constitution Act, 1982,* that require unanimity.

12. Brian Peckford, with the only female attorney-general in the country, was one of only three first ministers who came to the meeting without his attorney-general.

13. Edythe MacDonald (1988: 7-8), a federal public servant at the time of the constitutional negotiations, recounts how a committee of public servants decided in November of 1981 to have s.28 made subject to the override clause, only weeks after the provinces and the federal government had agreed, finally, to ratification of the International Convention on the Elimination of all Forms of Discrimination against Women, and in apparent hostility to the agreement of politicians with women's groups for a strong s.28. The public servants, knowledgeable about the Convention and only charged with working out the 'detail' of the *Charter*, still proposed to weaken s.28. At one meeting, MacDonald's deputy minister (a man) refused to allow her to speak on s.28, and she left the committee room 'in anger and frustration,' only to encounter a provincial civil servant who had been strongest in his views that legislatures should be allowed to override s.28. Her statement to him that "the women of Canada would not put up with this treachery" was proved correct, for a massive lobbying effort by women across the country saved s.28 from the override.

14. For conferences on Aboriginal rights and sovereignty, such as the ones already held from 1983–87, section 35.1 requires the prime minister to invite Aboriginal leaders to sit at the conference table with the first ministers.

15. The *Constitution Act,* 1982, requires that all 11 resolutions be passed within three years of the date of the first resolution. As the first resolution was passed by Quebec on June 23, 1987, the last province must agree by June 23, 1990. If this has not happened, the entire process of legislative approval starts over.

Chapter Three

Abortion Law Reform:
A Pendulum That Swings One Way
Dawn H. Currie

While early feminists almost unequivocally accepted the legislative forum as a means of achieving sexual equality, after a century of legal struggle acrimonious debate surrounds the nature of law and the impact of legal reformism. In this chapter, Dawn Currie provides an overview of the ways in which legal reform concerning abortion has resulted in contradictory outcomes for Canadian women. As one particularly important example, she explores the Supreme Court decision of January 1988. While declaring the current Abortion Act a violation of women's right to "life, liberty, and security of the person" as guaranteed by the Charter of Rights and Freedoms, this decision paradoxically resulted in greater restrictions on women's access to abortion services. To explain this outcome, Currie reviews Canadian abortion law and reforms in 1969, which acted largely as a legitimation of existing medical practices. Within this context, although abortion was discussed as a private matter and in terms of women's rights, legislative reforms brought abortion under medical control, laying the ground for further politicization.

While public opposition to abortion before the 1969 Act was limited to the Catholic Church, the period since has been characterized by increasing public interest in abortion as a public issue and the polarization of debates into "pro-choice" versus "pro-life" positions. Because each position is grounded in the advocacy of individual rights — those of women versus those of the fetus or of men — these positions appear to be irreconcilable. What remains obscured, however, is the fact that both support the status quo: similar to "pro-life," the current "pro-choice" position also reinforces parenting and family values. This is because abortion practice represents a personalized and case-by-case solution to "unwanted" pregnancy, which is a structural feature of Canadian society and is unlikely to be eliminated through individual behaviour, as anti-abortionists

---

Dawn Currie is Assistant Professor in Sociology/Anthropology at the University of British Columbia

imply. From this structural perspective, the current demand for abortion is unlikely to recede, so law will not determine whether or not abortions will occur. Rather, the law will determine the form that abortions will take. Given the nature of the demand, it is unlikely that abortion will become illegal. Rather, the struggle is whether abortion practice will be a universally available service funded by socialized medicine or an individualized practice, determined by the "ability to pay." Currie examines recent struggles over health care, which suggest that Canada is moving towards an individualized practice. This point is obscured, however, by current debates on abortion. As long as abortion is discussed as a constitutional and moral issue, the underlying contradictions will remain obscured, displacing the struggle for justice from the material to the ideological level. In conclusion, Currie discusses the limitations of current struggles for reproductive freedom as the legal right to state-provided technologies of con(tra)ception and abortion.

INTRODUCTION

In Canada, as elsewhere, the 1980s witnessed increasing agitation to restrict women's access to employment, daycare, sex education, abortion, shelters, and other similar services. Given the electoral successes of conservative parties during this period, the events of January 28, 1988, may appear all the more monumental. In a 5 to 2 ruling, the Supreme Court of Canada declared that the 1969 Abortion Law violates a woman's right to 'life, liberty, and the security of the person.' Invoking the *Charter of Rights and Freedoms*, Chief Justice Dickson transformed unwanted pregnancy from a regrettable misfortune to an injustice: "Forcing a woman by threat of criminal sanction to carry a fetus to term unless she meets certain criteria unrelated to her own priorities and aspirations is a profound interference with a woman's body" (*Maclean's*, February 8, 1988).

Ending almost 20 years of struggle on the part of pro-choice advocate Dr Henry Morgentaler, this ruling of abortion as a private matter beyond state regulation gave the appearance that Canadian women had secured 'reproductive freedom.' As the jubilation subsided, however, women found that rather than being guaranteed access to abortion, they have been placed under greater restrictions. With funding of health care being a provincial matter,[1] one by one the provinces announced policies on the performance of abortion. While justice officials in Manitoba and Ontario dropped all outstanding charges against Morgentaler, in British Columbia the health minister declared that the medical services plan in his province would pay only for abortions approved by a therapeutic abortion committee within an accredited hospital. Thus, although the provinces of Ontario and Manitoba announced their intentions to uphold the spirit of the Supreme Court decision, other premiers used the opportunity to attempt to thwart women's 'right to choose.' Although it may be argued that Dickson intended to guarantee abortion as a right of citizenship by referring to the Canadian *Charter*, a woman's access to safe abortion reflected her provincial jurisdiction.[2] Reproductive 'freedom' was back to square one.

While this contradictory outcome of legal battles reflects the division and separation of federal versus provincial jurisdictions in the *BNA Act* of 1867, our purpose here is to identify the contradictions involved in addressing the social issue of abortion through legal apparatus. To do so, we must review the history of Canadian abortion law and its reform. Within the context of the debates that have accompanied this legislation, the patterns of abortion practice suggest that, despite widespread claims by anti-abortionists that abortion threatens traditional values and institutions, in Canada the practice (as opposed to the rhetoric) of abortion operates to perpetuate family and parenting values. This is reflected in both *'pro'* and *'anti'* abortion campaigns. The problem is that while public debates portray abortion as a personal failure giving rise to the need for social intervention, at the material level abortion is a socially generated problem that currently requires personal resolution. For this reason, abortion has proved to be a conservative rather than radical practice because it solves the problem of 'unwanted' pregnancy at the individual level without addressing the processes that render pregnancy 'problematic' in the first place. Because these processes remain unaddressed, the law does not determine whether abortion will continue to be a widespread practice. Rather, law determines the form that abortion will take. While the socially created demand for abortion means that abortion is unlikely to become criminalized, current struggles will determine whether the costs of abortion services will be carried by the individual or the state — a struggle that extends beyond the terms of reference of the current abortion debate. In the final analysis, the current discourse that frames the struggle for abortion law reform is regressive rather than progressive: As long as abortion remains linked in the public's mind to a struggle between the legal rights of women versus those of the fetus (or men), underlying contradictions remain obscured, which means that the struggle for justice becomes displaced from the material to the ideological level.

ABORTION ACT(ION): ABORTION LAW IN CANADA

Canadian abortion law is rooted in the British *Offences Against the Person Act* of 1861. Section 58 of this Act made it a felony punishable by life imprisonment for anyone to unlawfully procure an abortion, while Section 59 made it a misdemeanour punishable by imprisonment for three years to supply any instrument, poison, or 'noxious thing' for an abortion (Currie, 1988). Because the term *'unlawfully'* was never clarified, ambiguity existed as to whether there were circumstances when abortion could in fact be legal. The most common situation would be abortion to save the life of the mother. However, this exception was not actually stipulated until 1929, when British parliament passed the *Infant Life (Preservation) Act*, which made abortion lawful if done in good faith for the preservation of the mother.

With the establishment of Confederation in 1867, except where nullified by local colonial law, Canada inherited British criminal and civil legislation. Since before Confederation, three offences regarding abortion have existed in Canadian legislation:

1. Anyone using any means with intent to procure the miscarriage of a female person whether she is pregnant or not *(maximum penalty, life imprisonment plus fine);*
2. A pregnant female person using or permitting to be used any means with intent to procure her own miscarriage *(maximum penalty, two years imprisonment plus fine);*
3. Anyone unlawfully supplying or procuring anything knowing it to be intended to be used with intent to procure the miscarriage of a female person, whether she is pregnant or not *(maximum penalty, two years imprisonment plus fine).* (Ryan, 1981: 362)

After 1955 the word *'unlawfully'* was omitted, even though it had appeared in the previous legislation. Its absence gave rise to interpretations that Canadian law therefore did not permit abortions for *any* reason whatsoever, even to save the mother's life. Valk (1974) suggests that this omission played an important role in changing the attitude of the medical community in favour of abortion law reform. Adding to the three direct references to abortion, Section 150 of the Canadian *Criminal Code* linked birth control and abortion by prohibiting the sale, distribution, and advertisement of "any means, instructions, medicine, drug or article intended or represented as a method of preventing conception or causing abortion or miscarriage" (Valk, 1974: 28). As we shall see, this law can be also credited with adding momentum to public support for reform of the *Criminal Code.*

By the end of the 1950s, calls for the liberalization of abortion law began to appear in the Canadian media.[3] In August 1959, *Chatelaine* — a popular women's magazine — featured an article entitled *"Should Canada Change Its Abortion Law?" Chatelaine* received support for this story from *The United Church Observer* and *The Globe and Mail.* While the United Church approved of therapeutic abortions for reasons of physical or mental health, it did not support abortion as a means of family planning or as relief for the unmarried mother. *The Globe and Mail* subsequently became a formidable proponent of legalized abortion, arguing that patterns of illegal abortions testified to the fact that women were already following a moral standard that was at odds with the legal code. Along these lines the *Globe* repeatedly asserted that abortion was a question of private morality and, therefore, that law should not be concerned with it. When the Pearson government refused to commit itself on the revision of the law, the *Globe* attempted to strengthen this sentiment by documenting the extent to which abortions were already being carried out in a number of hospitals for reasons other than saving the life of the mother. During this campaign, a thalidomide scandal added momentum to the call for abortion law reform among the general public and the medical community. By 1964, 349 babies with gross deformities had been born worldwide to women who had been prescribed the sedative Distaval. The celebrated cases of Sherri Finkbine and Suzanne Vandeput in particular drew public sympathy for abortion,[4] and physicians were placed in the untenable position of being seen as responsible for a tragedy that required an illegal solution.

The first professional body to raise the question of abortion reform in a systematic way was the Canadian Bar Association (CBA). At an annual meeting in September 1963, CBA members proposed a resolution for the amendment of the *Criminal Code* to legalize abortion, outlining three grounds for legal abortions: danger to the mother's life or health; unwanted pregnancy due to rape or a similarly unlawful act; and danger of a mentally or physically defective child (Valk, 1974: 14). Notably, this resolution did not include the socioeconomic grounds that had been recommended in Britain (see Hindell and Simms, 1971). Due to ensuing controversies, voting was deferred until 1965 when it was suggested that the view of the medical community be ascertained. Like the legal profession, the Canadian Medical Association began discussions of therapeutic abortion in 1963, and in the same year the Ontario Medical Association authorized a study of the technical and medical aspects of abortion. The investigators recommended that operations terminating a pregnancy be lawful if performed "to preserve the life or the physical or mental health of the mother" *and* if performed in a properly qualified place and manner, after consultation with an abortion committee. Emphatically, the committee wanted it understood that it did not "encourage *wide* liberalization" of abortion procedures but "rather [intended] to make them legal and to provide ... better precautionary standards for the protection of both the public and the profession" (Valk, 1974: 18). With slight modifications, this proposal was adopted by the Canadian Medical Association in November 1965.

From this point onward, the movement for abortion reform was characterized by a rapid growth in public interest. While Britain moved into its final legislative phase, Canada initiated reform in 1967 by referring the matter to a House of Commons Standing Committee on Health and Welfare, which heard briefs from a broad range of organizations. At that time articulate and organized opposition to revision of the law was virtually non-existent apart from the Roman Catholic Church. Against Catholic opposition, *The Globe and Mail* continued the line of argumentation established earlier: Laws not being observed should be removed; the law should not represent religious morality; opposition to a revision of the law comes solely from Roman Catholics; a Catholic minority is attempting to impose its views upon the nation; and reform of the law would not require anyone to do anything against their conscience (Valk, 1974: 41). In presenting its case the *Globe* reminded readers, "As many as 300,000 illegal abortions are performed in Canada every year" (*The Globe and Mail*, Oct. 11, 1967). The Commons hearings revealed that many people were ready to accept abortion whenever the life or health of the mother was endangered, as well as in cases of criminal assault and possible deformity. However, although a Gallup Poll showed that 71 per cent of Canadians favoured the legalization of abortion in these cases, there was little support for going as far as the British legislation, which included 'social grounds.'[5] Very few people were willing to argue that women should be allowed 'abortion on demand.' Most stressed instead the ways in which abortion could contribute to an increased 'quality of family life.' Groups advocating liberalized abortion drew attention to the commonsense observation that "An unwanted child runs a higher risk of drawing resentment and even maltreatment, physically or emotionally, from his parents than a wanted child" (Pelrine, 1971: 54).

In December 1967 the Standing Committee presented the government with an Interim Report advising revision of the law. The report noted that the existing law was ambiguous and contradictory. It proposed that the Standing Committee continue with further research, including crosscultural studies in other countries. On the "understanding that the government may wish to introduce some legislative changes," it recommended in the meanwhile that the *Criminal Code* be amended to "allow therapeutic abortion under appropriate medical safeguards where a pregnancy will seriously endanger the life or the health of the mother" (Valk, 1974: 55). Two days later, an Omnibus Bill to amend the *Criminal Code* was introduced into the House of Commons. The supporters of the bill, which was drafted under the direction of justice minister Pierre Elliott Trudeau, claimed that it would bring the law into line with modern thinking on matters of private morality. The Omnibus Bill included over one hundred items ranging from drunken driving to lotteries, marijuana, cruelty to animals, homosexuality, the dissemination of birth-control materials, and abortion. Trudeau saw no reason to allow a free vote on any part of the bill.

In terms of abortion the proposed legislation mirrored the proposals in the Interim Report, although it did not qualify the threat to the mother's life and health as having to be 'serious.' While general press coverage of the Omnibus Bill was positive, outspoken criticism of the abortion clause came from the Catholic press, especially the English-language weeklies. When hearings of the Standing Committee resumed in January 1968, there was evidence of growing opposition. The first meeting of the resumed hearings received the Hamilton Right to Life Committee, a group newly formed for the expressed purpose of opposing broader grounds for abortion. The Hamilton Committee was followed by the London Society for Protection of the Unborn, which presented as evidence illustrations of various stages of fetal development — including a picture of a fetus sucking its thumb. The Catholic Hospitals Association argued that the Bill would irrevocably divide physicians and hospitals into 'dissenting' and 'consenting' camps, and recommended a 'conscientious exemption' clause similar to that in the British legislation. The Canadian Catholic Conference opposed open-ended definitions of 'health,' discussing instead 'the common good.' Meetings concluded with the Presbyterian brief: "Abortion is murder."

After 29 meetings, 35 briefs, and 93 witnesses, the Standing Committee on Health and Welfare presented its Final Report to the House of Commons on March 13, 1968. The report recommended amendment to permit abortion when continuation of a pregnancy "will endanger the life or seriously and directly impair the health of the mother." As a point of emphasis, the Committee indicated that a clear and direct serious threat to the mother's health must be present, adding that it "intended *health* to mean physical and mental health and not the wider definition given by the World Health Organization"[6] (Valk, 1974: 80).

With re-election of a Liberal government in 1968, the new justice minister, John Turner, announced that the Omnibus Bill would be reintroduced, with the cabinet deciding whether to allow free votes on some of its provisions.[7] While the bill was passed by the House of Commons on May 14, 1969, by a vote of 149 to 55, it was not passed without struggle. Debates started with the second reading on January 23, 1969, and concluded with the third and final reading in mid-April. The third reading did not finish until a month later, due to a filibuster by the Ralliement des créditistes directed against the clause on abortion. Motivations for supporting the bill were varied and often contradictory. While Mark MacGuigan (Liberal, Windsor-Walkerville), for example, personally opposed abortion because he believed "the fetus is an actual human being from the beginning," he nevertheless supported the abortion clause because it legitimated what was, in reality, the status quo in most parts of Canada. In his opinion, the present law did not permit the "abortions that were now taking place in hospitals ... according to the best canons of medical practice" (Valk, 1974: 105). As Pelrine (1971) points out, with the exception of Grace MacInnis (NDP, Vancouver-Kingsway), the House of Commons debate was an all-male one that often exhibited antiwoman sentiments. Douglas Hogarth (Liberal, New Westminster), for example, argued that unborn life "should not be destroyed *merely at the whim and fancy* of the mother," although he did support the notion that a woman "ought to be able to rid herself of a pregnancy she does not want as a result of a crime against her body"[8] (Valk, 1974: 106). Adding to the blatant sexism of the proceedings was the remark of créditiste leader Réal Caouette: "If such a bill had been passed fifty years ago, the Chinese would perhaps have taken over our country" (in Pelrine, 1971: 37).

Against this backdrop, the final Abortion Bill was passed as Section 251 of the Canadian *Criminal Code*.[9] This section makes abortion illegal except where five conditions are met: The abortion must be performed in an accredited or approved hospital; all applications for abortion must be approved by a Therapeutic Abortion Committee (TAC)[10]; TACs must consist of three qualified medical practitioners; a majority of the TAC must certify in writing that "In its opinion, the continuation of the pregnancy would or would be likely to endanger [the] life or health of the woman"; the abortion must be performed by a qualified medical practitioner who is not a member of the TAC; the decisions of this committee may be reviewed by the provincial attorney-general.

In the final analysis, Canada's abortion 'reform' resulted in conservative legislation that merely afforded medical practitioners legal protection for already existing abortion practices. During the hottest debates *The Globe and Mail* brought attention to the fact that hospitals were already performing then-illegal abortions for 'health' reasons, estimating that 300,000 abortions were being conducted every year (*The Globe and Mail*,

Oct. 11, 1967). From readings of parliamentary debates, it is clear that the intention of the government was to be restrictive. At one point justice minister Turner flatly stated, "The Bill has rejected the eugenic, sociological, or criminal offense reasons ... [with] abortion to be performed only where the health or life of the mother is in danger." The word *danger*, he concluded, "imports or connotes the elements of hazard, peril, or risk ... the meaning of the word *endanger* is every bit as clear and significant as the meaning of [the previously suggested] words *seriously* and *directly impair*" (Campbell, 1977/78: 225). By restricting legal abortions to those performed by a qualified medical practitioner after approval by the TAC of an approved hospital, control over abortion was firmly entrenched in the hands of the medical profession. As later debates revealed, like their parliamentary colleagues many of these professionals simply distrust women's motives. While the rhetoric of reform emphasized abortion properly as a *private* matter, in reality abortion was rendered a *medical* matter — a contradiction that also underlies the later struggles for further transformation of abortion practice.

AFTER THE ACT: ABORTION PRACTICE IN CANADA

Public criticism of the 1969 Abortion Law began as soon as the Act was passed, with denunciations of the shortcomings already identified during the parliamentary debates. In September 1975, justice minister Otto Lang commissioned a committee to study the working of the new Act. Chaired by sociologist Dr Robin Badgley, this investigation (known as the Badgley Commission) collected and compiled a broad range of information on abortion practice in Canada.[11] Given a fact-finding mandate, the purpose of this committee was to ascertain whether the procedures set out in the abortion law were working equitably across Canada. Its terms of reference did not include policy recommendations, even though its final 474-page report confirmed what was already suspected about the failure of the new law.

In summation the report concluded: "The procedure provided in the Criminal Code for obtaining therapeutic abortion is in practice illusory for many Canadian women" (Badgley, Caron and Powell, 1977: 141). In particular, single mothers with low incomes who were poorly educated and less familiar with the workings of the health services reported that they would have preferred to have an abortion, if they had known how to proceed. In terms of geographical inequality, about two-thirds of the people living in the Maritimes (except Nova Scotia) did not have an eligible hospital in the community where they lived. In Nova Scotia, Quebec, and Saskatchewan, about half of the population lived in communities with eligible hospitals, while about two-thirds of the population of Ontario lived in centres with eligible hospitals. Ineligibility resulted from the exclusion of small hospitals due to the requirements for establishing a TAC consisting of not less than three members, all of them qualified medical practitioners.[12] In this way hospitals with medical staffs of three or fewer physicians were automatically excluded. Of the 1,348 civilian hospitals in

TABLE 3-1: Regional Disparities in Abortion Practice, Canada, 1982

Province	Number of Abortions	Number of Hospitals with TACs	Abortion Rate*
Newfoundland	379	5	4.3
Prince Edward Island	6	1	1.3
Nova Scotia	1741	12	14.2
New Brunswick	221	9	2.3
Quebec	9698 **	32	10.3
Ontario	31379	99	25.2
Manitoba	1723	8	10.1
Saskatchewan	1631	10	9.6
Alberta	6556	24	16.0
British Columbia	12712	58	29.6
Yukon	102	1	22.1
Northwest Territories	171	2	19.8
Canada	66319	261	17.8

*Abortions per 100 live births (estimated)
**Hospital Figures only
SOURCE: *Childbirth by Choice Trust*, 1985

TABLE 3-2: Profile of Abortion Patients, Canada, 1975 – 1989

	1975	1977	1979	1981	1983	1985	1987	1989
Total Number	49033	57131	64569	64554	61326	60518	61635	70705
Marital Status				*Percentages*				
married	31.4	29.0	24.7	23.0	22.4	21.8	21.8	22.5
single	58.4	60.2	64.0	65.8	66.1	66.8	67.3	65.2
other	10.2	10.8	11.3	11.3	11.5	11.3	10.9	12.3
Age								
under 20	31.3	30.8	30.4	28.3	24.9	22.9	21.9	21.4
20-24	29.1	30.3	31.5	32.3	33.3	33.5	31.8	21.4
25-29	19.4	19.4	19.3	19.9	20.8	21.5	22.5	23.2
30-34	10.7	11.2	11.3	12.0	12.6	13.0	14.0	14.4
35-39	6.4	5.8	5.4	5.5	6.4	7.0	7.5	8.0
40 plus	3.1	2.6	2.0	2.0	2.0	2.1	2.3	2.2
Previous Abortions								
none	90.9	91.1	91.7	91.8	91.4	90.6	–	–
one	5.1	4.9	4.7	4.6	5.0	5.3	–	–
two plus	1.8	1.6	1.3	1.3	1.3	1.3	–	–
unknown	2.2	2.3	2.3	2.3	2.3	2.7	–	–

SOURCE: *Report of the Committee on the Operation of the Abortion Law* (1977)
and Statistics Canada, 1986, 1991

operation during 1976, at least 331 had less than the required number of physicians. From the point of view of merely the distribution of physicians, therefore, 24.6 per cent of hospitals in Canada did not have a medical staff large enough to establish a therapeutic abortion committee (Badgley, Caron and Powell, 1977: 102). In addition, no hospital was *required* to establish such a committee: Of the 1,348 hospitals in 1976, only 20.1 per cent had established a TAC. This means that while the majority of Canadian hospitals did not perform abortions, large hospitals with liberal policies were forced to turn away patients who qualified. This regional disparity, which followed the 1969 Act, persisted into the 1980s, as shown in Table 3-1.

One of the results of the disparities is an exodus of women to the USA for the purpose of obtaining an abortion. According to the Badgley Report, approximately 3,200 women in Canada were being referred to U.S. abortion clinics each year (Campbell, 1977/78: 229). This migration was to become all the more dramatic during the 1980s: While 56 abortions were performed in the USA on Saskatchewan women in 1981, by 1985 this figure had reached almost 300, reflecting the shutdown of abortion services across the province (*The Leader Post*, Sept. 23, 1986). For this reason, the levelling off (and eventual decline) of the demand for abortion implied by Table 3-2 may not reflect a decline in need, but rather a denial of services.

While the requirement of a TAC was identified by the Badgley Commission as contributing to national inequalities of access, this same requirement was also a major factor in the bureaucratic delays that most women faced in obtaining abortion. An average interval of eight weeks between initial consultation and the performance of the operation increased the risk of health complications associated with second-trimester abortions. This delay means that 61.4 per cent of abortions in Canada are performed during 9 to 12 weeks gestation, compared to only 38.3 per cent in the USA, where 51.6 per cent of terminations are completed before nine weeks (*Childbirth by Choice Trust*, 1985).

Finally, the Badgley Report (updated with data from Statistics Canada) allows us to reconstruct the pattern of therapeutic abortion since the 1969 Act, as summarized in Table 3-2. While it is difficult — if not impossible — to compare the rates presented here to previous abortion practice, most authors suggest that these rates reflect a real increase in the rate of abortion rather than merely a shift from the illegal to legal section. Peaking in 1979-81, the reported rate has since declined. During this period, however, the social profile of the 'typical' patient has changed very little. As shown in Table 3-2, the typical abortion patient is young (under 25 years of age) and unmarried, has no previous induced abortions or deliveries, and is aborted under the umbrella of psychiatric rather than strictly medical grounds.[13] The picture of the usual patient which emerges is the 'normal' woman, rather than the harried and overstrained mother of an already large family or the woman traumatized by sexual assault or the anticipation of an abnormal birth. While feminists continue to cite this as evidence of the widespread need for abortion, these 'facts' fuelled an outcry from elements of the more conservative public.

The operation of the 1969 Abortion Law provided both *pro* and *anti* abortion forces with grounds for declaring the Act a failure. While opponents to the bill complained that the pattern of abortion practice illustrates that TACs are merely a rubber stamp for 'abortion on demand,' proponents focused upon regional disparities, arguing that these disparities testify to deficiencies undermining the intended principle of universal access. From either position, therefore, contradictions in the operation of the 1969 Act fostered further politicization of the abortion issue.

ABORTION (RE)ACTION: PUBLIC DEBATES ON ABORTION

The hearings of the Standing Committee, together with parliamentary debate, anticipated and demarcated the lines of future controversy concerning abortion in Canada. From the onset the demand for universal abortion services was central to almost all factions of the women's movement. By the 1960s it was argued that gains for women such as access to higher education and expanded employment opportunities mean little to women unable to participate in public life on equal terms with men. The major obstacle facing women in the struggle for equality was perceived to be restriction associated with reproductive roles. From this perspective, women's ability to control their bodies was given an urgency not yet so forcibly expressed. With slogans like 'a woman's right to choose,' reproductive freedom was defined in terms of universal access to safe contraception and abortion — a demand requiring improvements in reproductive technology together with the repeal of restrictive legislation and the expansion of state-funded reproductive services. These demands more or less represent what is referred to as women's 'reproductive rights.' The political aim is to separate sexuality and procreation, a process that writers argue will provide the sexual freedom necessary for the economic liberation of women (see Greenwood and Young, 1976: 106). To date this notion of 'reproductive rights' remains probably the most controversial of all feminist demands.

TABLE 3-3: Opinions About Indications for Induced Abortion

Reason for Abortion:	% Approving	
	Women	Men
Danger to Life	71.0	66.8
Rape, Incest	61.7	58.7
Mental Health	58.9	56.6
Deformity of Fetus	53.2	49.4
Economic Circumstances	21.8	21.7
Illegitimacy	17.6	19.3
Anytime On Request	15.8	23.2
Never	11.4	9.8

SOURCE: *Report of the Committee on the Operation of the Abortion Law* (1977)

While Canadians generally supported the liberalization of abortion, this support was qualified: The vast majority approved of abortion in the statistically unusual cases of danger to the woman's life, criminal assault, or problems of mental health, as shown in Table 3-3. At the time of the Badgley Commission, only 16 per cent of Canadian women and 23 per cent of Canadian men supported the notion of abortion on request.[14] Thus support for abortion did not reflect popular support for feminism as such, but rather for the idea of abortion as a benefit for society at large. The most common argument concerned the benefits of 'wanted' children. Along these lines Pelrine, an outspoken feminist who linked abortion to the liberation of women, openly advocated abortion for the improvement of motherhood:

> Abortion can improve the chances for happiness and fulfillment of the women concerned. If a young unmarried woman becomes pregnant unintentionally, an abortion may absolve her of the need to bear a child who will be an emotional, financial and social burden to her; in the years ahead she may marry and know the joy of bearing children who are wanted. For the married woman with a family, an abortion may allow her to devote a greater measure of care and financial resources to the children she already has. Therefore, the beneficiaries of abortion include not only the woman, but her children present or future; her husband; and, indeed, the society at large. (1971: 55)[15]

In this way, after the 1969 Act 'humanitarian and liberal' rather than 'feminist' ideals fostered the growth of the national and regional organizations, which continued to lobby for further reform.

Known as 'pro-choice,' by the 1970s a network of political groups had consolidated across Canada in support of abortion and committed to the expansion of existing services.[16] Drawing attention to research documenting abortion practice in societies since the beginning of recorded history (see in particular Himes, 1936), these groups have focused upon public education about the need for abortion reform, as well as for other reforms that would give meaning to the slogan *mother(parent)hood by choice*. During times of direct political challenge, the groups have formed the basis of a network for petitioning MLAs while maintaining momentum for demands for more equitable access to abortion across Canada and an end to bureaucratic delays.

In this context Dr Henry Morgentaler[17] became a visible symbol of pro-choice struggle. Morgentaler began his campaign without publicity in 1964 as president of the Humanist Fellowship of Montreal, a precursor to the Humanist Association of Canada. As an outspoken advocate of the repeal of Canada's restrictive abortion law, Morgentaler was besieged by requests from desperate women for the termination of unplanned, unwanted pregnancies. At that time operating outside the law was hazardous, with the only legal abortions being available in England and Japan. Once he resolved to follow the dictates of his conscience, beginning in 1969 Morgentaler embarked upon an almost twenty-year career of civil disobedience, providing abortions upon request in defiance of the *Criminal Code* of Canada.[18] After his first arrest in January 1970, Morgentaler's battle with the courts began in September 1973. During the subsequent 18 years of legal struggle four juries found Morgentaler not guilty of performing illegal abortions or 'of conspiracy to procure a miscarriage.' Nevertheless, the Quebec Court of Appeal overturned his first acquittal in 1974 and sentenced Morgentaler to 18 months in prison, anticipating a scenario that was to become all too familiar over the next decade. By 6 to 3, this decision was upheld by the Supreme Court of Canada, which ruled that the trial judge had erred in law (see Pelrine, 1975). A decade later the Ontario Court of Appeal similarly upheld a crown appeal of the acquittal of Morgentaler by a Toronto jury, this time ordering a new trial.[19] When the case went before the Supreme Court in October 1986, defence lawyer Manning identified seven separate constitutional challenges to the 1969 Abortion Law.[20] By all accounts, Morgentaler and his supporters were braced for defeat (*Maclean's*, Feb. 8, 1988). Not resolved until January 1988, Morgentaler's ordeal has been well documented by a number of writers (see Pelrine, 1975, and Collins, 1985), as has the impact of this case on Canadian jurisprudence (see Dickens, 1976, 1981).

While there was little organized and articulate opposition to abortion reform prior to the 1970s, the 1969 Act brought in its wake the proliferation of anti-abortion or 'right to life' groups across Canada.[21] Beginning from the position that abortion is morally wrong because the fetus is a human being, pro-life groups attack abortion on a number of grounds. To begin with, opponents to abortion argue that with easy access to contraceptives there is simply no need for abortion. By implication, accidental pregnancy reflects shortcomings in the individual's use of available technology, rather than in contraceptive practice itself. In particular, they argue that liberalization of abortion encourages women to use abortion as a method of birth control, a method that harms women physiologically and psychologically and fuels a profit-oriented 'abortion industry.' Thus they portray women as victims of a profit-oriented abortion business. The League for Human Life, for example, declares, "At $300.00 each, an abortionist can easily earn $3,000.00 a day, or $15,000.00 a week" (*The Leader Post*, May 6, 1986). Sensationalizing the fact that most abortions are granted for 'psychological' reasons, opponents to abortion claim that by providing 'abortion on demand,' the 1969 reforms went further than even their originators intended. In this spirit, they portray women as having abortions for 'convenience' or for frivolous reasons. One chief of obstetrics and gynecology for a large metropolitan hospital, for example, argued that women are lazy and irresponsible about birth control, so that "If abortion on demand becomes easy for them, they'll be coming to the hospital for abortions the way they go to the beauty parlour to have their hair done" (quoted in Pelrine, 1971: 84). Anti-abortionists also argue that most 'unwanted' children become wanted and, furthermore, that unwanted babies can be placed for adoption. According to anti-abortionists, legal-ized abortion is likely have a 'domino effect' and euthanasia will also come to be advocated for society's unwanted — the old, the infirm, and the handicapped. All in all, anti-abortionists declare that abortion threatens traditional values and social institutions. They therefore form an active movement for a 'return' to family values, targeting for attack a number of social movements that are seen to undermine the family.[22]

Under the banner of protecting 'life,' a number of national and regional groups advocate the abolition of abortion, sometimes even in the case of rape. While critics of pro-life point out that the majority of Canadians favour abortion, the activities of the pro-life minority are extremely visible. Anti-abortion campaigns blatantly equate abortion with the killing of an unborn child, arguing that by the time of eight weeks conception "The baby responds to painful stimuli" (*The Leader Post* ad, May 6, 1986). A sensationalized film, *The Silent Scream*, depicts a 12-week fetus allegedly screaming in pain as a suction cannula pulls it from the womb. During a 'Respect for Life' week, an Ontario branch of the Right to Life Association ran a campaign telling children that "While *they* were born, some babies never are because someone kills them while they are still in mommy's womb" (*The Leader Post*, May 3, 1985). Added to this kind of publicity is a visibility gained through acts of civil disobedience. Pro-life groups regularly picket outside Morgentaler's abortion clinics and, more recently, launched 'Operation Rescue' in protest against the opening of Vancouver's Everywoman's Health Clinic. By February 1989, 188 arrests during three blockades had been made (see *The Vancouver Sun*, Nov. 4, 5, 1988; Feb. 5, 1989).[23]

At the same time, pro-life groups are committed to the lobbying of political candidates. The Coalition for Life — a group opposing abortion under all circumstances — supports candidates of anti-abortion views, regardless of party. Of these candidates they demand two commitments: that they work towards amending the *Criminal Code* to provide children conceived but not yet born with the same legal protection as everyone else; and that they work towards stopping government funding of any agency that directly or indirectly counsels women to have abortions or engages in abortion referrals (unpublished pamphlet). Subsequently, a number of elected members of parliament have used their appointments to challenge current abortion services. In 1983 Tory backbencher Gay Caswell (Saskatoon, Westmont) presented the provincial legislature with a petition carrying over 15,000 signatures to stop financing abortion through medicare (*The Leader Post*, Nov. 25, 1983). In a memorandum to the PC caucus, Caswell argued that medicare funding so spent is a violation of people's conscience regarding abortion and represents a forced pro-choice position for the taxpayer. Further, she claimed that abortion is not therapeutic but rather convenience surgery, similar to a face-lift. Because Caswell believes that the difference between a woman rejecting or accepting a pregnancy is a matter of a few days or a week, she argues that by being forced to consider payment the woman will have time to reconsider and possibly accept the pregnancy. In 1985 Caswell also brought forth Private Member's Bill 53, Freedom of Informed Choice (Abortions) Bill, an act requiring consent for abortion not only from the woman herself but also from her husband or legal guardian. This consent would only be valid if obtained after the woman and her husband or parents had considered a package of information including a detailed description of the probable physiological and anatomical characteristics of the fetus at the time of abortion, as well as a description of the medical risks of abortion.[24] Similarly, a number of other federal pro-life politicians have brought forward private member's bills to restrict or ban abortion. In 1985 Tory MP John Gormley (Saskatchewan, The Battlefords-Meadow Lake) introduced a bill to amend the *Criminal Code* so a woman could obtain an abortion only if her life was endangered by the pregnancy, and in 1986 Tory backbencher Constantine Mitges (Ontario, Owen Sound) called for a constitutional amendment to extend the *Charter of Rights* to include the unborn.[25] As recently as March 1989, however, the Supreme Court has continued to refuse to rule on the rights of the fetus (*The Globe and Mail*, Mar. 10, 1989).[26]

Outside Parliament a number of individual pro-lifers have used the courts to challenge abortion. In Quebec activists brought private complaints against two doctors performing abortions, while former directors of Vancouver's Lions Gate Hospital have attempted to outlaw the procedure through which abortions are authorized on the grounds that, in practice, Lions Gate provides 'abortion on demand.' One-time Manitoba NDP cabinet minister Joe Borowski, perhaps the most celebrated pro-life activist, began highly publicized legal actions in 1978 that unsuccessfully set out to declare that abortion provisions in the *Criminal Code* are unconstitutional because they contravene Section 7 of the *Charter of Rights and Freedoms*. Borowski also wanted the court to rule that any expenditure of public money to support abortion is illegal. His lawyer, Morris Shumiatcher, argued that because life in the womb is equivalent in all ways to the life of the woman who bears the fetus, as a matter of human rights it cannot be sacrificed for the sake of the woman (Collins, 1985). In appeal to the Supreme Court of Canada, Justice Marjorie Gerwing[27] upheld the ruling by Court of Queen's Bench Justice Matheson reasoning that fetuses are not included in the term 'everyone.' It remained for the Supreme Court decision of Chief Justice Dickson to determine interpretation of the *Charter of Rights and Freedoms* in January 1988.

FROM RHETORIC TO REALITY: ABORTION IN THE 1980s

The defeat of anti-abortion efforts and the subsequent Supreme Court ruling, ironically, have not determined Canadian abortion practice. In reality the 1969 Act ensured that access to abortion would be shaped by medical rather than human rights struggles. While the constitutional challenges of both the *pro* and *anti* lobbies created a climate within which debates are increasingly framed along irresolvable lines, struggles between medical practitioners and provincial regulators of health services are the front line. In this struggle, two practical rather than 'moral' issues are important. The first is extra-billing — a practice falling under the jurisdiction of the provincial ministries of health. Given that insurance payments represent only about one-third of the actual cost of an abortion, extra-billing has been integral to abortion practice. In Alberta, for example, medicare reimbursed physicians about $85 for a therapeutic abortion in 1986. With the average cost falling between $200 and $250, doctors recovered their fee through extra-billing. In a move to reduce its projected $3 billion deficit in 1986, the Alberta government banned extra-billing. To maintain the financial viability of abortion practice, some doctors began to charge for the necessary letter of referral required by therapeutic abortion committees. When Alberta hospital minister Marv Moore threatened disciplinary action, many physicians refused their abortion services. In January 1987, gynecologist Ian Ferguson of Calgary's Foothills Hospital was formally warned by Moore after charging for a medical letter. When the Alberta College of Physicians and Surgeons further threatened Ferguson with professional sanction, four of his colleagues withdrew their services, a move that threatened to halt abortion services at Foothills. While the clinic did remain open, the Alberta Medical Association took its case to the Alberta Court of Queen's bench to determine whether such letters are an insured service. In February 1987, the letters were declared illegal. In this way, by ensuring a rate of renumeration below 'market' value, the provincial ministry restricted access to abortion by forcing physicians to withdraw services — a move re-enacted by other provinces.[28]

The second site of struggle concerns the accreditation and approval of hospitals to perform abortions. 'Accredited' hospitals have the endorsement of the Canadian Council on Hospital Accreditation, while 'approved' hospitals are sanctioned by the provincial ministers of health. Saskatchewan, for example, had ten accredited hospitals in 1980. Although the NDP government did not actively approve hospitals during the 1970s to make access to abortion easier, with the election of the Tories in 1982 the province lost a number of abortion services in regional hospitals. The first challenge had come in November 1981, when a pro-life group called the Hospitals Concerns Committee accused Moose Jaw Union Hospital of performing illegal abortions because that hospital was not properly approved under Section 251 of the *Criminal Code of Canada*. The NDP health minister Rolfes had contacted Ottawa to determine whether he had authority to approve an accredited hospital. Five months and an election later, federal justice minister Jean Chrétien publicly stated that he 'felt' that Union Hospital fulfilled all the requirements of the *Criminal Code* because the hospital staff was qualified and equipped to deal with obstetrical emergencies (*The Leader Post*, Aug. 25, 1982). Because hospital lawyers saw this merely as an 'opinion' in a court of law, they applied for provincial approval. In March 1983, the new provincial health minister and an opponent to abortion, Graham Taylor, announced that he had "decided not to accede to the Board's request" (*The Leader Post*, Mar. 15, 1983). Meanwhile, Prince Albert's Victoria Union Hospital was forced to suspend abortions under a similar threat by anti-abortion groups and Weyburn city council bypassed the Hospital Board of the Weyburn Union Hospital by asking Graham Taylor to dissolve its Therapeutic Abortion Committee.[29]

Within the context of visible anti-abortion support, in a February 5, 1984, memo Graham announced the appointment of a six-member committee to review the operation of abortion in the province of Saskatchewan. The terms of reference for this committee included a review of the preconditions set by each hospital and/or therapeutic abortion committee; a review of the guidelines for the review of applicants; and a review of the decisions made by each committee with the associated rationale. From the onset Graham acknowledged the "possibility that this committee could recommend that Saskatchewan Health Services money not be provided for abortions" (*The Leader Post*, Feb. 14, 1984). When the committee's work was completed in March 1986, Graham refused to release its findings to the general public. In the meantime, noting that abortions had declined from 1,632 in 1982 when the PCs took office to 1,207 by 1984, Graham attributed this to actions taken by the provincial government. In a March 22, 1985, memo from his office, Graham alluded to these actions as the provincial funding of pro-life movements and the establishment of an abortion review committee with a mandate, first, "to ensure that the law is being obeyed; and second, to establish patterns of abortion so we may design educational and consultative programs to reduce further abortions in our province." To the public Graham announced, "We want respect for life in this province and that's what we stand for." The health minister continued by declaring that he had never heard from any woman who said she needed an abortion but could not obtain one (*Star Phoenix*, April 30, 1985). With the end of extra-billing in 1985, the introduction of *Bill 53*, and a premier who publicly vowed "to keep Morgentaler out of the province," by the mid-1980s Saskatchewan — like most other Canadian provinces — faced an 'abortion crisis.'

As the Saskatchewan case illustrates, while *pro* and *anti* forces continue to struggle over abortion as a moral and constitutional issue, within the context of fiscal crisis and momentum for a "return to family values" (see Havemann, Chapter 4), provincial jurisdiction over health allows restriction of access to safe abortion. The ministries of health have at least two avenues for anti-abortion action: the banning of extra-billing as part of broader fiscal restraint; and the ability to withhold the provincial approval of regional hospitals required for the establishment of therapeutic abortion committees. While these actions bring the government into direct conflict with the medical profession, practitioners themselves can withhold services on a number of grounds. Physicians can refuse to sit on TACs for moral, financial, or political reasons, circumventing any legal guarantee of abortion services as a 'reproductive right.' In this way, the fiscal restraint of the 1980s together with the electoral successes of conservative parties anticipated the aftermath of January 28, 1988, so that the success of the Supreme Court decision simultaneously highlights the need for and the limitations of legal reform (see also Gavigan, 1986).

ABORTION AS AN ISSUE THAT WILL NOT "GO AWAY"

If the public debates portray abortion as a private or personal problem that necessitates public intervention, ironically this is a view that is maintained by both supporters and opponents of abortion. Anti-abortionists focus upon unwanted pregnancy as an individual failure given the supposed availability of contraceptive technology. They argue for the rights of the fetus as an 'unborn individual,' making abortion a moral and therefore public issue: specifically, about the right to life of the unborn. While pro-choice activists similarly advocate human rights, this lobby focuses upon the right of individual women (or couples). Here social intervention is seen as a practical issue of providing access to abortion services (also childcare), with decision-making about their use being a personal and private matter. In either case abortion is linked to unwanted pregnancy as a personal issue. For this reason, both positions conceptualize abortion as a matter of individual rights: those of women as opposed to those of the fetus (or of men).

In contrast, this chapter abandons ideological debates in order to explore the material reality of unwanted pregnancy. From women's perspectives, abortion is a socially generated problem currently requiring personal resolution: the current demand for abortion by individual women reflects long-term permanent social changes. From the mid-nineteenth century onwards, the size of families in industrialized economies universally has fallen. While the fertility rate for Canadians was 189 births per 1,000 women in 1871, for example, this figure had halved by 1931 (McLaren, 1978: 322), and has since stabilized at about 56 (Statistics Canada, 1985). The processes underlying this decrease are varied, complex, and the matter of academic debate. Recent declines are associated with an in-creased age at first birth, reflecting the influx of women into postsecondary education and the employment of married women. By the 1980s the 'typical' Canadian household consisted of two working spouses. The social and economic processes responsible for the current 'preference' for a small planned family extend, then, beyond the individuals involved. Therefore, given that no birth control is both effective and safe for the user(s), every sexually active woman is 'at risk' for pregnancies that are not intended. 'Unwanted' pregnancies are a structural feature of Canadian society and the demand for abortion is unlikely to 'go away,' as anti-abortionists suggest. For this reason, the current struggle for legal reform will not determine whether abortion will or will not exist; rather, the struggle is whether abortion will be a universally available service funded by socialized medicine or an individual practice determined by the 'ability to pay.' As the data illustrate, given the current political and economic climate, in practice Canada is moving towards the latter. What interests us here is the way in which 'unplanned' pregnancy, while the consequence of historical forces beyond individual control, is experienced by individuals as a personal dilemma to which abortion provides an individually nego-tiated case-by-case solution. Experienced within this context, individual rights appear as a solution when, in fact, they simply reflect the nature of the problem: Reproductive labour is a personal and private responsibility of women rather than of the collective. Individual rights such as those entrenched in the *Charter* are, paradoxically, not only required but also unable to address the real problem. As a consequence, abortion law reform has been a contradictory experience for Canadians. Where does this lead us in terms of 'reproductive rights'?

THE LIMITATIONS OF LEGAL REFORM: "REPRODUCTIVE RIGHTS"

Within this context, the legal right to abortion has the effect of promising equality while reinforcing processes that perpetuate unequal access to services and medical control over reproduction. This does not mean that we should abandon legal reform altogether, however. Political struggles *are* important in that they determine the overall quality — rather than quantity — of abortion. At the same time, the analysis presented here highlights the limitations of current struggles for reproductive freedom as the legal right to state-provided technologies of con(tra)ception and abortion. To begin with, the fiscal crisis of the past decades illustrates the shortcomings of reproductive freedom defined as state funding of reproductive services. While the continued struggle against cutbacks in expenditures in services is important because those services provide some women with an option they might not otherwise be able to afford, state-provided funding is limited by the fundamental contradiction of the welfare state: Fiscally, the state — like the working classes — increasingly has a vested interest in the viability of capitalism so that the economic needs of the 'welfare' state are tied to a system generating the very problems that programs are designed to ameliorate (see Gorman and McMullan, 1987). In the final analysis, the state is unlikely to initiate major structural changes because of its dependence upon private capital, a problem faced by both NDP and Tory governments. Similarly, reproductive freedom as technological control over reproduction is limited. While medical technology is necessary for the control of human reproduction, medical methods of contraception and abortion are technical solutions to a practical problem of limiting or enhancing our biological capacity for procreation. Technology cannot solve the social problem of excess reproduction, because social and not biological factors underscore 'unwanted' pregnancies. Research indicates that such factors as educational agendas, employment security, inadequate housing, or lack of social supports are the criteria for 'planning' pregnancies as 'wanted' or 'unwanted' (see Currie, 1988). From this perspective, technological improvements in reproduction operate to strengthen rather than challenge the status quo, because they are developed so that individuals adjust their reproductive schedules to existing structures rather than vice versa.

Finally, the struggle for reproductive freedom as one for constitutional rights is limited and contradictory. Women's individual control over reproduction challenges the vested interests of other groups — men, medical professionals, the state, and even other women who defend the traditional role of women — highlighting the context within which reproduction occurs as one of antagonistic relations. Antifeminists counterpose the rights of women against either those of the collective — expressed as the social need for repopulation (especially during times of war) — or those of other individuals — the 'unborn child' or procreative father.

Clearly, the tenor of debates reflects the growing perception that because reproduction takes place within women's bodies, individualism as 'bodily integrity' is irreconcilable with reproduction as a social process, forcing pro-choice debates onto the slippery ground of defending women's right to control their bodies. This defence has taken two different—and at times contradictory—positions, both vulnerable to anti-abortion counterclaims.

The first line of argumentation adopts the framework of natural rights. Petchesky (1984) traces the concept of natural individual rights of bodily self-determination to the Puritan revolution of the seventeenth century. At that time, the notion of 'property in one's person' was linked explicitly to nature and paralleled the connection of natural rights to property, or 'possessive individualism.' Underlying the introduction of the *habeas corpus* of 1628, the principle of natural rights maintained:

> To every individual in nature is given an individual property by nature, not to be invaded or usurped by any: for every one as he is himselfe, so he hath a selfe propriety, else he could not be himselfe, and on this no second may presume to deprive any of without manifest violation and affront to the very principles of nature, and of the rules of equality between man and man. (Quoted in Petchesky, 1984: 3)

Although phrased in masculine terms, this notion of individual selfhood improved the position of women by portraying marriage as a contract and by restricting the chastisement of wives. In effect, the notion of natural rights of person coincides with the notion of self-determination through control over one's body as an essential aspect of being an individual with needs and rights. Originally this notion was a radical critique of the status quo, because it rejected the trend of making bodies into commodities through the emerging capitalist labour market.

The second defence of reproductive rights examines the social context of reproduction by invoking the legitimating principle of 'socially determined needs.' Within this framework the notion of bodily self-determination rests upon recognition of the social position of women and the needs that arise from their location in the social order. Specifically, under the current division of labour between the sexes, women are the ones most affected not only by pregnancy, but also by the demands of childcare. As such, it is women who must have the final say about con(tra)ception, abortion, and childbearing. Further, this control can be defended as a precondition for women to exercise their rights of citizenship given current social conditions. Unlike natural rights, therefore, this position is not absolute in that it recognizes the historical specificity of the need for reproductive rights. A position favoured by Marxist and socialist feminists, it implies that societal transformation may render the need for reproductive rights obsolete, although as Petchesky (1984) points out, we have yet to experience the concrete historical conditions under which we could afford to give up those rights.

In summary, the defence of abortion as one of reproductive rights is not a position characterized by consensus. From either position, however, defences are vulnerable to anti-abortion counterclaims. Attempts continue to be made by opponents of abortion to legislate rights for conceived but as yet unborn children, illustrating how easily the concept of inalienable rights can be extended to the fetus. The result of such action is to limit quarrels to definitions of 'humanity,' shifting debates from examination of material conditions and processes to the ideological realm. Philosophical limitations to the notion of reproductive rights notwithstanding, the experiences of women highlight practical limitations so that writers like McDonnell (1984) argue that reproductive freedom as individual rights needs rethinking. With others, McDonnell argues that reproductive freedom should move away from a strict defence of the right to choose in order to examine 'freedom of choice.' Clearly, the right to be able to choose is not the same thing as making meaningful choices, which requires a material and ideological context within which women's choosing is not constrained 'externally.' The lack of daycare, for example, restricts a choice of motherhood for many women, in the same way that a lack of equal opportunities for employment and career advancement may preclude alternative choices to motherhood. These types of considerations move debates towards the issue of meaningful alternatives, so that the ways in which women's choices are constrained becomes the focus of attention. From this perspective, writers like Brophy and Smart (1985) argue that justice for women should begin from women's experiences rather than from abstract legal notions of 'freedom and equality.' They maintain that out of the disappointments with legal reform we can learn to frame legislation that will benefit women.

From this position of legal realism, two types of legal reforms appear capable of broadening women's choices. The first is the *extension* of rights to address the particular disadvantages faced by women. Included in this type of strategy are issues of job security and promotion as current 'costs' of motherhood for women. Translated into programs of 'affirmative action,' disadvantages accruing from the activity of motherhood — as well as the societal expectation that all women are potential mothers — are negated. In this way, campaigns extend the reach of law into areas traditionally defined as beyond the ordinary operation of legal process, so that this extension requires further changes in the *content* of law. Specifically, legal reforms are seen as requiring recognition of the special conditions of pregnancy and childbirth. Jaggar (1983: 186) notes that because classical jurisprudence links the human individual with the capacity to reason, legal philosophy disregards bodily functions. Thus she argues that the problem with traditional political theory is that pregnancy and childbirth are divergences from a biased male-centred norm; as a consequence the law must address physical as well as mental capacities. From this perspective, the content of rights is used to prevent the disqualification of women that results from their biological condition. This argument has recently been extended beyond maternity to include the physiology of the menstrual cycle.

In total, these strategies together move analyses away from law *per se* to the social and material conditions of motherhood. As such, they represent the beginning of a new definition of reproductive freedom. The problem is that in the final analysis reproductive freedom as societal transformation cannot be achieved through legal rights. This is not due to either the content or scope of law, however: Individual rights are limited because of their *form*. It is not simply that they are individualistic. Rather, bourgeois rights are asocial: Individuals are rendered equal in the eyes of law only through means of their abstraction from the differences and distinctions that mark them off in reality from one another. In this way, in legal theory the individual exists prior to and therefore outside society. As Fine (1986) notes, the basic problem for individual rights in class society is that people lead a double existence: on the one hand, as free and equal individuals; and on the other hand, as unequal and dependent members of civil society. This is what Marx meant when he argued that liberty and equality before the law are only *formal*. In terms of reproduction, individuals are differentiated by more than class, however. Due to the sexual division of reproductive labour individuals are unequal on the basis of gender. This is not due to simply biological aspects of reproduction. It refers to social conditions of reproduction: specifically, the primacy of childcare for women who have children. Currently, the sexual division of childcare labour separates women from collective responsibility and places them into personally antagonistic relationships with the social interests in reproduction. This is why reproductive rights, paradoxically, appear as a solution to the personal problem of planned fertility while in reality they are a manifestation of the underlying fundamental problem. For this reason, similar to reform of family law, attempts to address the issue of 'planned fertility' through reform of abortion law — no matter how grounded in egalitarian principles — will be a contradiction for Canadian women (see Currie, 1989). Despite rhetoric that stresses equal 'responsibility' for children, fathers' responsibility remains an economic one while mothers continue to bear the social costs of reproduction as personal problems — social devaluation and isolation, career immobility, poverty, mental illness.[30] These are the real inequalities of reproduction that the notion of individual rights presupposes and therefore cannot remove. However much extended and democratized, legal rights cannot address current social inequalities of reproduction. Only the elimination of the sexual and class divisions of reproduction can give meaning to the slogan of 'reproductive *freedom*.' Ironically, both *pro* and *anti* campaigns that emphasize personal rights or responsibilities obscure this point. As a consequence, the current rhetoric of abortion discourses continues to transform economic and structural issues to moral and legal ones in the public's mind, shifting struggles from the material to the ideological sphere.

I would like to thank Gillian Creese and Patricia Lee (University of British Columbia) for their comments on this chapter.

NOTES

1. From 1947 to 1968 the federal government was responsible for funding and overseeing a rapidly expanding health-care system. Following the Hall Commission, which implemented universal medicare, the federal government entered into a 50-50 cost-sharing with provincial governments, leaving the allocation of the health budget to each province. Thus, at the same time that generalized health care became a universal right, inequities resulted from regional inequities, reflecting the contradiction between a formal statement of universal health care and substantive regional inequalities in health-care delivery — a theme elaborated in the remainder of this chapter.

2. Although Premier Vander Zalm did all he could to limit women's access to abortion, the B.C. Supreme Court struck down his restrictions on health-insurance coverage for abortion. In Saskatchewan Premier Devine refused to pay for abortions not considered medically necessary, a term he did not define. At the time of writing (May 1988), some hospital abortion committees were still in place in Nova Scotia, while in New Brunswick and Alberta the approval of two doctors was necessary for an abortion to be covered by medicare. In Prince Edward Island, nothing was changed: There were no hospitals performing abortions .

3. In his overview of the emergence of the 1969 Act, Valk (1974) emphasizes the influence of the reform movement in the United States, which predates the Canadian movement somewhat.

4. Sherri Finkbine, an American, attempted to obtain an abortion in 1962 after taking thalidomide tablets in early pregnancy. After being refused by U.S. doctors, Finkbine flew to Sweden where she was granted her request by an official medical board. Examination of the fetus revealed that it was seriously deformed. Although the Vatican condemned the operation as a crime, a national poll showed that Americans supported her action by a majority of five to three. Three months later, in Belgium, Suzanne Vandeput euthanized her newborn daughter, who was deformed as a result of thalidomide. The trial received international coverage. Those involved in the case were acquitted of murder, although the physician was temporarily suspended by the regional committee of the Belgian Medical Association for unethical practice (see Francome, 1984; Luker, 1984).

5. The social grounds of the British Steel bill included Clause 2, which instructed a doctor to take into consideration the patient's "actual or reasonable foreseeable" environment (see Greenwood and Young, 1976).

6. The WHO defines health as: "a state of complete physical, mental and social well-being, and not merely the absence of infirmity or disease" (in Pelrine, 1971: 52).

7. A motion to eliminate Clause 18, the abortion clause, in order to allow the House to have a separate recorded vote, was introduced towards the end of the third reading but was defeated by a vote of 107 against, 36 in favour, with 121 absent members (Valk, 1974: 108).

8 MacKinnon (1985) argues that this type of debate illustrates male interest in abortion as a means to facilitate women's heterosexual availability. While I have not pursued this line of argumentation, it is perhaps instructive to note that more Canadian men than women supported the notion of abortion on request when polled in 1974 (see Table 3-3).

9. Other relevant Sections relating to abortion are:
   - Section 159(2)(c), which makes the selling and advertising of drugs, articles, and other methods intended to cause abortion illegal;
   - Section 252, which makes the selling and procuring of drugs, articles, and other methods intended to cause abortion an indictable offence punishable by a two-year jail sentence. (In 1969 the regulations of the sale and advertisement of contraceptives were removed from Section 252 and included in the *Food and Drug Act*.)
   - Section 221(1), which refers to a person causing death in the act of birth, making it an indictable offence punishable by life imprisonment. Although not intended to refer to abortion, in the absence of any provision in the CCC on the subject of abortion, this subsection could be extended to include abortions.

10. There are differing provincial regulations regarding the formation of TACs.

11. As well as information collected from available statistical sources, the committee visited 140 hospital sites; developed questionnaires for a national hospital survey and survey of hospital staff, a national physician survey, and a national population survey; sent questionnaires to out-of-country abortion centres; and obtained counsel and information from several national and provincial voluntary associations.

12. The practitioner performing the operation cannot sit on the TAC so, in effect, four qualified medical practitioners are required.

13. Campbell (1977/78: 226) reports that 95 per cent of abortions fall into the category of psychiatric grounds.

14. By 1988 this proportion had increased, but remained the minority: 36 per cent of Canadians polled three weeks after the Supreme Court decision of January believed that abortions should be permitted "whenever a woman decides she wants one." In contrast, 23 per cent of Canadians claimed to be pro-life, believing that abortions should only be allowed "except when the mother's life is in danger"; and 39 per cent believed that abortions should be allowed "only in some circumstances" (*Star Phoenix*, March 5, 1988).

15. In this way arguments were very similar to those employed at the turn of the century in support of contraception. At that time, debates surrounded the benefits of racially superior children (see Currie, 1988).

16. Together with less celebrated colleagues (see Ontario Coalition for Abortion Clinics, 1988).

17. Better known organizations whose primary mandate is abortion reform include the Canadian Abortion Rights Action League, Childbirth by Choice, Doctors for Repeal of the Abortion Law, Coalition for Reproductive Choice, and various Abortion Action Committees. At the same time, a number of groups support abortion reform as part of their broader mandate — Advisory Councils on the Status of Women, the Canadian Association of Obstetricians and Gynecologists, the Canadian Federation of University Women, the National Association of Women and Law, Planned Parenthood Federation of Canada, and the United Church of Canada have all joined petitions for abortion law reform.

18. At the time that Pelrine published his biography in 1975, Morgentaler said

he had performed over 5,000 abortions (Pelrine, 1975: 81).

19. Morgentaler's case represents the first time in Canadian history when an accused who had been acquitted by a jury of peers suffered reversal of that acquittal without the benefit of retrial. In June 1975 the federal government announced an amendment to the *Criminal Code* to prevent an Appeal Court from reversing a jury verdict.

20. Much of Manning's case focused on unequal access to abortion and the deleterious effects of bureaucratic delays.

21. These include Choose Life Canada, National Pro-Life Associations, Campaign Life, Birthrite, Coalition for the Protection of Human Life, Catholics United for Life, and Right to Life Societies. As well, a number of organizations, such as REAL Women, include the abolition of abortion in their broader mandate to protect the traditional family and restore family values. More recently, anti-abortion activists sought registry as political parties. Two examples are the Family Coalition Party, formed by Burlington businessman Donald Pennell, a former provincial Liberal Party candidate who ran unsuccessfully in 1975 and is national director of "Campaign Life," and The Christian Heritage Party, a federal party opposed to homosexuality and abortion and calling for an overhaul of Canada's welfare and educational systems.

22. Erwin (1987) reports that close to 90 per cent of anti-abortionists see feminism as well as gay rights as serious threats to the family (cited in *The Leader Post*, April 3, 1987; and *The Globe and Mail*, April 2, 1987). It is instructive to note Vander Zalm's comments in the British Columbia legislature that "the senseless termination of human life at the slightest whim or notion is simply removing yet another stone from the wall of an already crumbling society" (*Vancouver Sun*, Mar. 1, 1988, cited in Lee, 1989).

23. While the civil disobedience that has accompanied both campaigns is beyond the scope of this chapter, the use of the 'defence of necessity' is an important development. While three men — Rev. Ted Colleton, Rev. Alponse De Valk, and Pastor Fred Vaughan — were acquitted of mischief charges in 1986 because Provincial Court Judge Lorenzo Di Cecco reasoned that "citizens have a limited right to try and prevent a criminal act," CARAL critics have pointed out that the Ontario Court of Appeal had recently rejected similar defence on the part of Morgentaler (*The Globe and Mail*, Feb. 11, 1986). During the more recent events in 1989, however, 'defence of necessity' was not accepted by the trial judge. For an overview of these events refer to various articles appearing in *The Vancouver Sun* from November 4, 1988, onwards.

24. After second reading, the Saskatchewan Legislature referred the bill to court for a decision on two questions: whether it conflicted with federal jurisdiction and whether it violated the *Charter of Rights and Freedoms*. The Saskatchewan Court of Appeal declared the bill invalid after three judges ruled that it would conflict with the federal *Criminal Code* (*The Globe and Mail*, Dec. 21, 1985).

25. While such a motion becomes the subject of debate and vote, it has no legal effect. The motion merely calls on the government to 'consider' such a *Charter* amendment.

26. While this chapter, which was initially written within months of the

January 1988 Supreme Court decision, has been revised several times, it has been impossible to incorporate more recent rapid developments. Here I would only draw attention to the court injunction by anti-abortionist judge O'Driscoll on behalf of Gregory Murphy, which would prevent his 'girlfriend' from aborting his 'genetically superior child.' This case reflects an escalation of specific attention to the notion of the 'rights of the fetus,' making it safe to predict that the most important development during the next year or so will concern legislation whether/when abortion should be allowed.

27. The appeal's only female judge.

28. For a discussion of similar struggles over extra billing in Ontario, see *The Globe and Mail*, Feb. 24, 1986.

29. "Alderman" Brenda Bakken, city representative to the hospital board, tried to dismantle the TAC on the grounds that a number of women were being granted abortions for reasons other than because "continuation of the pregnancy would or would be likely to endanger her life or health." The hospital board voted 13-7 against her campaign on June 29. Three months later, Weyburn City Council supported her cause, voting 4-2 to ask Taylor for an order withdrawing ministerial approval (*The Leader Post*, Dec. 17, 1983).

30. For a critical analysis of the new rhetoric about fathers' contemporary role in childcare and the rise of movements for 'fathers' rights,' see Sevenhuijsen and Smart, *The Politics of Custody* (London: Routledge and Kegan Paul, 1989).

Chapter Four

Crisis Justice for Youth:
Making the Young Offenders Act
and the Discourse of Penality

Paul Havemann

While the media often encourages the public perception that the Young Offenders Act of 1983-84 is too lenient towards juveniles, Paul Havemann points out that, in reality, the act has increased the number of young people appearing before the courts. He explores this outcome as being inherent to the justice model upon which the act is based. Accommodating neoliberal, neoconservative, and moral authoritarian ideologies, the act is embedded within discourses that dichotomize "welfare" as opposed to "justice" while prioritizing the latter. In the final analysis this acts to reinforce the coercive powers of the state without destabilizing the alliances in new establishment ideology or jeopardizing popular consent. Havemann links this result to the current fiscal crisis, which renders maintenance of the treatment and welfare rights model untenable while fostering support for an explicitly retributive apparatus that shifts consensus about the nature of youth crime from the notion of structural causes and collective responsibility to that of crime as a lack of discipline requiring retribution and individual accountability.

Havemann explores how this shift was accomplished through an examination of the official transcripts and texts of the Justice and Legal Affairs Committee during the implementation of the Young Offenders Act. In particular, he examines how ideas and words are linked together to trigger deliberate associations. For example, proponents of the justice model linked **individual accountability — due process — determinate sentences** *with justice in a positive association, while the law and order lobby associated* **individual deterrence — discipline — the family as social order,** *and so on. Explicating the ways in which these linkages are constructed, Havemann identifies three ideological themes: "moral panic," which classifies youth as a new, dangerous class and legitimates coercion; "individualism," which emphasizes increased individual accountability and the protection of society while mystifying coercion through the*

Paul Havemann is Professor of Law at University of Waikato, New Zealand

notion of "extra" legal rights; and "familialism," which promotes the home as a paramount unit of social organization and disperses coercion by incorporating the family into the crime-control process. Because the resultant justice model reflects a compromise of ideologies forced by the current crisis, Havemann characterizes contemporary justice for youth as "crisis justice." He points out that despite the liberal "control-talk" of neoprogressives about "diversion, individual rights and accountability, the protection of society and decarceration," which was used to oust the welfare model, the justice model that replaces the old Juvenile Delinquents Act in the form of the Young Offenders Act is far more pernicious and punitive. In conclusion, however, Havemann does not dismiss the possibility of collective struggles that resist the centralization of authority and hierarchical ascriptive categorization.

INTRODUCTION

Official statistics reveal the grim truth about 'justice' for youth. As predicted by some (Havemann, 1986a), the reforms of the welfare state that led to the replacement of the *Juvenile Delinquents Act* of 1908 with the *Young Offenders Act* of 1983-84 has licensed provincial justice systems to enmesh and incarcerate unprecedented numbers of young people. As Table 4-1 indicates, after only two years of operation the number of individuals involved in criminal justice had doubled in some provinces.

This chapter analyses the discourse through which the 'reformed' regime of rules to control marginal youth was constructed. Despite the liberal talk of neoprogressives about "diversion, individual rights and accountability, the protection of society and decarceration," which was used to oust the welfare model, the justice model replacing it is far more pernicious and punitive. This is not a case of 'reforms' gone awry due to political obstructionism, professional self-interest, or to choosing convenience over conscience (Cohen, 1983; Rothman, 1980; Cullen and Gilbert, 1982). Rather, this punitive and pernicious outcome is intrinsic to the justice model. The *Young Offenders Act* both reflects and produces ideological outcomes that are within the framework of the New Right's current transformatory project (Havemann, 1986b; Ratner and McMullan, 1987). In Canada this project will no doubt continue to manifest itself in a variety of ambiguous, contradictory, and complex ways accelerated by free trade (Warnock, 1988). Based upon the present trajectory of change, we situate this particular reform within the dismantling of the liberal welfare state, management of the fiscal and ideological crises via corporatism, and the gradual evolution of an 'exceptionalist state' (Hall et al., 1978; Ratner and McMullan, 1983; Taylor, 1983a, 1987; Panitch and Swartz, 1988; Comack, 1987a). The YOA emerges as the "ideal synthesis of coercion and consent" (Fine, 1984) to manage youth in the crisis produced by this conjuncture (Greenberg, 1983).

The 'justice' model crystallized in the YOA is an ideological compromise of liberal rhetoric and law and order practice. Like other regimes of legal rules, the YOA accommodates "sectional ideologies in the language of universals" (Sumner, 1979: 295). Historically, the sectional ideologies of the juvenile justice industry have been reflected in the often polarized discourse that attempts to reconcile criteria as diverse as needs, rights, just deserts, and crime control. For New Right ideologues this tendency has had the merit of polarizing 'justice' versus 'welfare' and privileging 'justice' as appropriated by the justice model. We can illustrate the semantic process of reconciling these discourses by examining the "Declaration of Principle" of the YOA.

TABLE 4-1: Number of Young Persons Appearing before Courts under the JDA and YOA by Province/Territory, 1981-82 to 1985-86[1]

| | Persons | | | | |
| | Juvenile Delinquents Act[2] | | | Young Offenders Act[3] | |
Province/Territory	1981/82	1982/83	1983/84	1984/85	1985/86
Newfoundland	1,893	1,243	1,621	1,017	1,403
Prince Edward Island	105	95	109	83	242
Nova Scotia	994	844	1,007	900	2,003
New Brunswick	835	753	784	564	1,082
Quebec	5,979	5,875	5,908	5,188	5,894
Ontario	11,672	10,327	10,598	15,691	15,662
Manitoba	4,345	4,034	3,908	3,968	3,944
Saskatchewan	928	926	859	775	2,411
Alberta	4,105	4,010	4,376	4,785	8,251
British Columbia	N/A	N/A	5,270	4,568	5,769
Yukon	83	93	92	N/A	147
Northwest Territories	272	234	291	219	584
TOTAL	**31,211**	**28,434**	**34,823**	**37,758**	**47,392**

1. In the JDA data, adults, persons of unknown ages, and persons over the maximum legislated age for each jurisdiction are included. Similarly, in the YOA data, persons of unknown ages, persons under 12, and persons over the maximum legislated age for each jurisdiction are included. Quebec figures exclude charges laid against young persons under 14 years of age (33 persons in 1981-82; 50 persons in 1982-83; 36 persons in 1983-84). Ontario data was received in aggregate form.
2. All figures under the JDA exclude breach of probation (S.666 C.C.) and returns to court (S.20[3] JDA)
3. All figures under the YOA exclude failure to comply (S.33 YOA) and reviews (S.32 YOA).
Source: Canadian Centre for Judicial Statistics. Statistics Canada, 1987:16.

In Canada, the conjuncture of which the YOA was a product was one in which the fiscal crisis of the welfare state rendered the treatment and welfare rights apparatus untenable while ideological support for an explicitly retributive apparatus consisting of exceptional powers of control was generated by conjuring up the spectre of youth as a new, dangerous class. The principles postulated for a 'justice model' represent the compromise required to allow competing values to appear to be reconciled (Morris and Giller, 1980). Thus the model becomes an instrument contributing to the ideological work of shifting consensus about the causes of and responses to youth crime from a welfare rationale (that is, of structural causes and communal responsibility) towards consensus that the causes of youth crime are lack of discipline and wickedness and that the response must be retribution based upon individual accountability. By identifying typical justice-model principles, table 4-3 reveals the links in a chain of discourse promoting this shift.

TABLE 4-2: Young Offenders Act

	Declaration of Principle
Policy for Canada With Respect to Young Offenders	3.(1) It is hereby recognized and declared that:
Responsibility, Accountability	(a) while young people should not in all instances be held accountable in the same manner or suffer the same consequences for their behaviour as adults, young persons who commit offences should nonetheless bear responsibility for their contraventions;
	(b) society must, although it has the responsibility to take reasonable measures to prevent criminal conduct by young persons, be afforded the necessary protection from illegal behaviour;
Special Needs	(c) young persons who commit offences require supervision, discipline and control, **but, because of their state of dependency and level of development and maturity, they also have special needs and require guidance and assistance;**
Alternative Measures	(d) where it is not inconsistent with the protection of society, taking no measures or taking measures other than judicial proceedings under this Act should be considered for dealing with young persons who have committed offences;
Due Process Rights	**(e) young persons have rights and freedoms in their own right, including those stated in the Canadian Charter of Rights and Freedoms or in the Canadian Bill of Rights, and in particular a right to be heard in the course of, and to participate in, the processes that lead to decisions that affect them, and young persons should have special guarantees of their rights and freedoms;**
	(f) in the application of this Act, the rights and freedoms of young persons include a right to the least possible interference with freedom that is consistent with the protection of society, **having regard to the needs of young persons and the interests of their families;**
	(g) young persons have the right, in every instance where they have rights or freedoms that may be affected by this Act, to be informed as to what those rights and freedoms are; and
Parental Responsibility	(h) parents have responsibility for the care and supervision of their children, and, for that reason, **young persons should be removed from parental supervision either partly or entirely only when measures that provide for continuing parental supervision are appropriate.**

NOTE: Bold type represents the treatment/civil libertarian rhetoric, and regular type represents that of the law and order lobby.

SOURCE: Havemann, 1986a: 232-A

TABLE 4-3: Justice Model Principles and their Application in the Y.O.A.

Taxonomy of Principles for a Juvenile Justice Model	Application of Principles in the Young Offenders Act
Principle of the commission of an offence.	Section 5: Exclusive jurisdiction of youth court over federal criminal offences.
Principle of proportionality of sanctions.	Section 20.26: Dispositions that may be made.
Principles of determinate sentences.	Section 20.
Principle of least restrictive alternatives.	Section 3(1) d, f, h: Policy of Canada with respect to young offenders. Section 4: Alternative measures.
Principle of juvenile's right to Counsel.	Section 11: 'Right to retain Counsel.' Section 3(1)e
Principle of limitations on intervention prior to adjudication and disposition.	Sections 7-8: Limits detention prior to disposition.
Principle of visibility and accountability of decision-making.	Section 39(1): 'Publicity and public at hearings.' Sections 28-33: Review of disposition.
Principle of family autonomy and responsibility.	Section 3 (1) f, h (supra). Section 10: Order requiring attendance of parent. Section 9: Notice to parent in case of arrest.

The ideological work required of the justice model is to narrow the solution of the 'youth-crime problem' to the individual as the unit of blame and to universalize the acceptability of this reversion to child-blaming (the principle of the commission of an offence) by guaranteeing 'equality before the law' through due process under the *Charter*. The fact that these individuals are not adults is reconciled by promoting familial accountability, informal forms of coercion surveillance, and controls such as diversion or limits on intervention by officials: "The justice model essentially creates a mirage of justice in procedural and formalistic terms as a substitute for re-distributive social justice in terms of work, education, income, security, and social and political rights" (Havemann, 1986a).

The discourse of those promoting the justice model makes no pretence that reforms ought to be judged in the redistributive terms of the old Keynesian welfare state consensus. An older form of liberalism, now labelled neoliberalism or neoconservatism, has prevailed, emphasizing individual liberty and accountability. From this perspective, production of the text of the YOA deserves attention since: "A legal enactment is a hybrid form combining power and ideology according to the fixed and hallowed procedures for the creation of law by the instituted executors of social power. It originates within legalizing practices which are political in that they are geared to producing specific power relations" (Sumner 1979: 293). This chapter contextualizes the discourses that legitimated the text, which was to license the way in which power would be wielded over youth. To do this we examine debates put forward by the House of Common's Justice and Legal Affairs Committee while the *Young Offenders Act* was being formulated. No doubt some would accuse us of being 'stranded by mystification' because our conclusions appear to:

> rest on a built-in omniscience about all liberal reform. Armed with the right conceptual apparatus it should have been clear from the beginning that nothing good could have come from the original reform visions. It is obvious that these reforms have undeclared purposes and equally obvious that they will fail because there are underlying historical processes which unfold despite and independent of the intentions and proclamations of reformers. (Cohen, 1987: 365)

Have we succumbed to the dangers of 'radical impossibilism,' 'neoliberal pessimism,' and 'dread of reformism'? Against these charges we would assert that this chapter and its precursor (Havemann, 1986a) echo some 'squeaks of hope,' some cautious reaffirmation of values, if only those locked within liberal dialectics but informed by utopian socialism.

HEGEMONIC TRANSFORMATION
From Welfare to Exceptional State?

> What we have to explain is a move toward authoritarian populism — an exceptional form of state which unlike classical fascism, has retained most (though not all) of the formal representative institutions in place, and which at the same time has been able to construct itself an active popular consent. (Hall et al., 1978: 23)

In Canada, the shift to exceptionalism seems to be occurring less by popular (authoritarian) consent than by unpopular incorporation along U.S. lines (Gross, 1980; Warnock, 1988). The anti-democratic free trade deal aside, evidence of the dismantling of the welfare state abounds: Devine's Saskatchewan; Bennett and Vander Zalm's British Columbia; current assaults on labour rights (Panitch and Swartz, 1988); massive increases in criminal-justice spending and jailing (Comack, 1987a: 234). A number of writers, including Taylor (1987), have examined this transformation, although Taylor misconstrues the process by characterizing Canadian political economy as utopian, anglocentric, and ahistorical (Palmer, 1987) while ascribing weakness to the Canadian 'radical' right. However, when noting "the absence of a developed working class contesting for power" (1987: 212) his focus on liberal democracy as the organizing frame for the contemporary bourgeois order is highly apposite: The present transformation of the Canadian State from liberal welfare democracy via corporatism to exceptionalism is greatly facilitated by a new establishment ideology of the New Right masquerading as liberalism but cloaking neoconservative and moral authoritarian elements. Thus Taylor is partially correct when he argues: "We see liberalism as a politics that encouraged the orderly advance of a free market economy in twentieth century Canada, by legitimating possessive individualism as a desirable form of social relations (over and above the conservative stress placed on moral order and community)" (Taylor 1987: 220).

The moral authoritarian and familialist dimensions of the New Right in Canada ought not to be underestimated, however. We have only to examine provincial support for the 'pro-life' movement and federal paralysis after the 1988 Morgantaler Supreme Court judgment. This judgment and its aftermath reveal quite clearly the amicable contesting for power by neoliberal, neoconservative, and moral authoritarian forms of capitalist-patriarchy (see Currie, Chapter 3).

O'Connor's (1984) analysis of hegemonic transformation in the U.S. context has increasing implications for Canada. The 'coming-out' of an aggressive Right under Reagan and Bush has permitted neoliberals, neoconservatives, and law and order authoritarians to join forces. All of these groups explained the economic crisis of the 1970s and 1980s in terms of excessive state intervention (of the Keynesian welfare variety), which fostered a crisis of individual incentives that undermined the discipline to obey, to save, and to work (O'Connor, 1984: 223). Coincidentally, O'Connor's calculus of 'homo economics' readily translates into the calculus of 'homo criminalis' — the free-willing, maximizing young offender explicit in the *Young Offenders Act*. Likewise, in the state's strategies to reduce government's size but enhance its strength, the family has been re-enlisted as a 'cushion against hard times,' becoming a central link in the control of women and youth.

The apparent volatility of the new establishment ideology combining the mutual contradictions of neoliberalism, neoconservatism, and moral authoritarianism has done little to impede its actual political impact. The predictable outcome of the policies of the 'new establishment ideology' —

as pointed out by the anti-free trade movement — will include accelerated and increasing proletarianization, the feminization of poverty, the transformation of adolescents into both a deviant and a consumer class (a process to which the YOA is admirably suited), the institutionalization of the sick, elderly, and preschool children as well as youth and adult offenders in profit-based enterprises, together with more 'law and order' — the latter being an 'unqualified good' from the stance of monetarist libertarians and moral authoritarians alike (Loney, 1986: 32).

Keynesian welfarism made the polarity of justice and welfare models appear to be more real than it was. Today the appeal of 'justice' rhetoric to the New Right's transformatory project is that by conflating 'justice' and 'welfare,' the rhetoric resonates harmoniously with diverse themes encompassed within new establishment ideology:

> Justice and Welfare reflect two co-existing cultural traces, the one speaking to the idea of rational calculating action, the other to an interventionist ideology of a super-ordinate management of malfunctioning, of establishing social engineering to ensure appropriate pre-conditions for the efficient extraction of surplus value with a politically and morally integrated social order. (Harris and Webb, 1987: 30)

The ideological work to which the 'justice' model contributes appears to be the reinforcement of coercive powers — without destabilizing fragile alliances within the new establishment ideology or forgoing the popular consent still accorded to the legitimation spending of the liberal welfare state. Support for the liberal welfare-state consensus still abounds in the education, pensions, and health-care sectors. Most Canadian governments also appear to assume that there are popular expectations for youth access to due process and special programs. Law and order and welfare austerity also command sectoral support of increasing magnitude. Ideological work in the present era involves managing these contradictions: "The crisis consists precisely in the fact the old is dying and the new cannot be born; in this interregnum a great variety of morbid symptoms appear" (Gramsci, 1971: 276).

Back to Justice

The Justice Model: Liberal Victory or Liberal Defeat?

Critiques (Clarke, 1978; Cohen, 1985; Paternoster and Bynam, 1982; Havemann, 1986a; Hudson, 1987) and even autocritiques (Greenberg, 1983; Morris and Giller, 1983) of the justice model now abound. In the U.K., Canada, and the U.S. the results of their insertion as an organizing framework for juvenile justice regimes have been similarly disastrous from the viewpoint of social justice for youth. Crisis justice for youth stands in stark contrast to the 'bad old days' of the overreaching welfare model: "The minimalism of the 'Justice' model has justified the neglect of offenders and their problems that is far from benign ... the State has washed its hands of responsibility for anything other than punishing deviants" (Hudson, 1987: xi).

As we have argued, while conducted in liberal form the justice-model discourse reflects law and order ideology at a practical level. The critiques and autocritiques point out numerous paradoxes: its co-optability; that only in a welfarist context can it be benign; that the welfare model requires a dispersal of control (possibly less statism) while the justice model's neoclassical agenda requires a strong, centralized state monopolizing the definitions of harm and the schedules of correction; that far from decon-centrating discretionary power away from the hands of professionals it has reconcentrated it in a more corporatist juvenile justice system (Pratt, 1989), overseen now by juridical professionals rather than welfare ones. Ironically, this latter point has been documented by a stern critic of welfarism: "It is in fact much more the case that rather than welfare having distorted the administration of justice, judicial take-overs have emascu-lated the provision of welfare by obliterating the separation between the assistantial and the penal" (Donzelot, 1979: 109).

The source of the paradoxical and harmful features of the justice model has been located firmly in its liberal genesis rather than in its essence as a manifestation of the 'post-liberal' society (Bottoms, 1983). Liberal ide-ology capitulated to the Right in the face of the fiscal and ideological crises, rationalizing this by arguing: "If the state could not be trusted to do good and if doing good anyway had ambiguous results, then we should at least let the system be fair, justice, open and safe from abuse" (Cohen, 1985: 245). Within this context, Cohen urges a detailed examination of the more general features of liberalism. Hudson's (1987) substantial critique of the justice model begins to do this. Following Clarke (1978), Hudson high-lights the individualizing and abstracting process of the justice model. While the welfare model (as distinguished from the treatment model) claimed to locate delinquency in its social and familial context, the justice model abstracts act from agent (Hudson, 1987: 167). In this way it abandons the integrity of the individual by privileging events (the crime) over individuals: hence the focus on the principles of 'commission of an offence' and 'familial autonomy and responsibility.' Hudson argues that this is the antithesis of liberalism, which theoretically privileges the integrity of the individual (1987: 167). The ideological work of the justice model is to abstract youth crime from its wider context, which includes unemployment, poverty, homelessness, and the commodification of cul-ture. She concludes that conceding due-process rights to youth as indi-viduals in a legal system inherently biased on the basis of class, race, and gender, in a society in which youth are immiserated by chronic structured inequalities, is an empty gesture (see also Clarke, 1985). It would be empty even if the rights could be invoked through adequate provision of legal representation. Cutbacks in legal aid only serve to illustrate in an imme-diate way the limits of the liberal imagination and its easy acceptance of formalistic and symbolic notions of equality, individualism, and justice.

READING OFFICIAL DISCOURSE
Taking Ideology Seriously
One goal of a political economy of justice discourse is to expose the form and means whereby ideologies are explicitly and clandestinely inserted

into the discourses of lawmaking and law-applying. When we speak of discourses in this context we are talking about well-defined chains or clusters of interconnecting propositions (Hall, 1982: 10) making up complex philosophies about causal explanations for crime, about human nature, or about the way society, the economy, or the juvenile justice system ought to be organized, for example. Each ideological discourse contains ideas and words linked together in a way that triggers deliberate associations (see Milovanovic, Chapter 8). For example, justice-model proponents link *individual accountability — due process — determinate sentences* with *justice* in a positive association. Left-liberal and civil libertarians link *discretionary arbitrariness — indeterminacy treatment-as-punishment — state overreach* with *welfare* in a negative association. The law and order lobby links *indiscipline — youth crime* with *welfare or retribution — individual deterrence — discipline* and *— the family* with *social order*, and so on. Within this context, debates juxtaposing 'welfare' and 'justice' are: "part of an ideological struggle to break one ideological chain and replace it with another" (Hall, 1982: 10).

In these debates, which are amplified, reproduced, and disseminated through the media, texts of official discourse (such as Hansard), ministers' press releases, and judicial decisions, we can detect attempts to break the associations of the dominant ideology and establish new ones. Ideas and assumptions are not permanently chained together. The flexibility and taken-for-grantedness of liberal ideas, coupled with the efficiency of dominant players in breaking, co-opting, and conflating chains of ideas, have contributed to the initial repudiation of the notion of 'welfare' and given impetus to the 'back to justice' movement. A shared vocabulary, but one with different inflections of meaning, underlies the co-optation of the justice model by the Right.

As Laclau (1977: 103) observed for periods of ideological crisis such as the present one, a crisis of confidence in the automatic reproduction of the system (in this case the system of Keynesian Welfarism) exists. As a result, ideological contradictions become exacerbated, which contributes to a dissolution of the unity of the dominant ideological discourse. At such a moment: "Each one of the actors in struggle will try and re-constitute a system of narration as a vehicle which disarticulates the ideological discourses of opposing forces" (Laclau, 1977: 103). Therefore, debates surrounding the production of official texts such as laws deserve more attention as an ideal medium for observing this process.

Some Methodological Considerations

The present task is made somewhat difficult by the fact that little has been written about how to analyse the processes through which discourses are articulated, disarticulated, or co-opted in particular concrete settings (Goodrich, 1986). Sumner (1979) offers perhaps the most substantial discussion of competing approaches.[1] He dismisses speculative criticism or speculative polemics as subjective, qualitative, and unsystematic. In this mode, the analyst's discourse is juxtaposed against that of the object text, so that the discourse the analyst disagrees with is then deemed to be ideological. We recognize that while our method is subjective, qualitative, and not particularly systematic, it is contextualized: The analyst's ideology is explicit and the attempt is made to unpackage clandestine ideological discourses as well as to focus upon explicit discourses and their meanings.

Prediction and hindsight allow us to address the vexed question of the relationship between words, ideology, and action. What do the people who manage social control say about what they ought to do or are doing? Cohen reminds us: "These are not just ordinary people but politicians, reformers, social workers, psychiatrists, researchers, official committee members, professionals of all sorts" (1985: 101). How should we read the texts they produce? Liberal humanist traditions of literary criticism use a method whereby the text is interpreted by taking the author's intentions seriously. In contrast, a Marxist methodology of criticism tends to be one in which discerning stated intent is less important than decoding, demystifying, and unmasking deeper reality (Cohen, 1985: 107). This chapter clearly straddles both traditions.

Burton and Carlen (1979) alert us to the ideological purposes that official documents serve as texts *per se* as well as the purposes served by the production of such texts in the process of ideological transformation. Specifically, official texts provide a justificatory framework of political importance by attempting to institutionalize discourses of coercion in order to thereby secure public acceptance of coercion. Thus the production of official discourse can be understood as a system of 'intellectual collusion' between the judiciary, politicians, intelligentsia, lay people, and state functionaries. Burton and Carlen argue that official texts are:

> the realization of power in the creation of a distinct object that is fashioned from the discourses of law, epistemology, social science and commonsense. The object functions via its attempts (successful and unsuccessful, and always unfinished) to repair the fractured image of the self-acclaimed, essentially just characterization of the state's repressive and ideological apparatuses. (1979: 34)

In the introduction we presented the Declaration of Principle in the YOA as a text and illustrated its concrete reflection of the principles in the justice model as a discourse. In the following section we will sample texts that record the production of the YOA. In this examination we will expose for analysis chains of ideas, theorizing about the ideological conditions for their privileging or discarding.

DISGORGING THE DISCOURSES

The passages selected below are illustrative only. We are not attempting to quantify the appearance of specific categories of discourse. Rather, we will demonstrate the relevance and usage of the concepts 'moral panic,' 'individualism,' and 'familialism,' which appear in social-scientific investigation as central to the new establishment ideology and the justice model as a reflection of ideological formation. These interrelated conceptual categories emerge in the dialogue of the producers of the YOA in neatly scripted chains of discourse. By offering samples of dialogue we can show students of policy development and lawmaking both the importance of theory and of taking ideology seriously.

Moral Panic:
Legitimating Coercion

> Societies appear to be subject every now and then to periods of moral panic. A condition episode, person or groups of persons emerge to become defined as a threat to societal values and interests; its nature is presented in stylized and stereotypical fashion by mass-media; the moral barricades are manned by editors, bishops, politicians and other right-thinking people; social accredited experts pronounce their diagnoses and solutions; ways of coping are evolved or more often resorted to: the condition then disappears, submerges or deteriorates and becomes more visible. (Cohen, 1972: 28)

In 1961, the federal Department of Justice produced a *Report on Correctional Planning*, which anticipated that the consequences of the postwar 'baby-boom' would be a youth-crime problem that the *Juvenile Delinquents Act* would be inadequate to 'solve.' This fear explains part of the early impetus to replace the JDA's welfare model with something tougher. Many other factors flowing out of the fiscal and ideological crisis of the 1970s reinforced this trend. One of these was the 'spill-over' effect of the American fear of crime (Hall et al., 1978: 12), American labels, and American solutions, all of which naturalized the 'get tough' posture of the Canadian law and order lobby. Like their British counterparts (Hall et al., 1978: 26), Canadians have been increasingly encouraged or forced to subscribe to visions of the U.S. as potential future. During the 1970s and 1980s, U.S. models were transplanted out of context into Canada without much critical examination (Ratner, 1986). The justice model is simply one example.

This fear of crime and youth as a new dangerous class emerged as distinct themes in the debates of the Justice and Legal Affairs Committee. We have categorized this as the 'moral panic' discourse. It surfaces repeatedly during debates about the appropriate age of criminal accountability under the YOA. The analysis and proposal for change advanced by the law and order lobby reveal that this lobby wished to generate a respectable fear about the rise of youth crime. Their own perceptions were fed largely by their reading of developments within the United States 'as present and future' rather than by the Canadian experience in either statistical or perceptual terms (West, 1984: 57).

Pearson (1983: 2) reminds us of the repeated rediscovery of the overrepresentation of young people in criminal statistics, which can serve to spur us into discussions about an unprecedented deluge of crime and immorality "while gazing fondly back to the recently and dearly departed past." He points out that, by contrast, the "historical journey ... reveals a seamless tapestry of fears and complaints about the deteriorated present" (208). Thus the ideological work accomplished by conjuring up a 'respectable fear' is to legitimate the necessity of strategies that are more coercive than those of the past and which would have been politically impossible previously.

The following exchange of dialogue about the age of criminal accountability illustrates the centrality of the *moral panic* discourse in the production of the YOA:

Mr Kilgour: You mentioned, Superintendent Alexander, a change in the nature of juvenile crime. Can you give us some profile if you like, or sketch, based on your experience? I think it is something which concerns all of us. I mean the mild juvenile offender compared with — and I hate to use the term — the 'hard core' violent juvenile offender. Can you tell us, from your experience, what percentage of people that come into court now under our present Juvenile Delinquents Act would you say were violent or destructively violent in a 'hard' sense?

Sup Alexander: There are statistics available, but I do not have them with me, precisely. It is one of those things we missed in trying to frame this. However, I would suggest that 15 to 20 per cent are in the violent category; that is, robberies, purse snatchers, bank robberies, murders, rapes and the like.

Mr Kilgour: Well, I take it that the core of what you are saying is that some of those sections do not winnow out these 15 per cent effectively enough? Am I wrong in that? Is that not really the basis of some of your concerns; that this 15 per cent — let us call them hawks, if you like, of the juvenile offenders — are not being dealt with firmly enough? Is that part of your concern?

Sup Alexander: I would suggest that they are not being dealt with firmly enough under the present juvenile court system. In our province, of course, when we speak of juveniles we talk of under 16. The number of those, with an increase ... let us say the seriousness of their behaviour escalates the older they get. I perhaps should say to you that there was a time back in the early evolution of this bill when I would have argued for an upper age of 18, because I felt that the 14 to 18-year age group was really quite an easy identifiable age grouping in the population. They seemed to do things for the same reasons and the same way and did not seem to have any notion of the serious consequences of what they were doing.

As the years went by, the offences normally associated with that group shifted back until we began to see that kind of behaviour exhibited by the 12 to 16-year-olds. And I would suggest, I do not know where it is going to stop.

Mr Kilgour: How concerned are you — I do not think you mentioned it — with the idea that the 13-year-old mild offenders, if we pass the bill as it is, might be in close contact with 17-year-old hard-core offenders? Is that a major concern?

Sup Alexander:	It is indeed. I think it is a very serious concern. I know the concern has been expressed about the 16 or 17-year-old associating with adult criminals and I would suggest it is just as serious a concern that the 11, 12 or 13-year-old would be associating with a 17-year-old who is a confirmed criminal.
Mr Kilgour:	And you would use the term that some of those people of 17 are confirmed criminals?
Sup Alexander:	I certainly would, sir, without equivocation.
Mr Kilgour:	I have a Gallup poll — I am sure you all saw it — recently saying that one of four Canadians was a victim of a Criminal Code offence in the last year, according to Gallup. They mention things like homes broken into, money or property stolen, home, car, property vandalized, other crime. Can you give us again — it is a judgemental thing — what percentage of homes broken into in Toronto, where you are, would you say are done by people under the age of 18?
Sup Alexander:	75 per cent. And that may be conservative.
SOURCE:	Justice and Legal Affairs Committee, *Minutes*, Ottawa, Issue 64.17, 1982.

This dialogue is between two protagonists of 'law and order': Kilgour is a former crown prosecutor and Alberta Progressive Conservative MP while Superintendent Alexander represented the 60,000-strong Canadian Police Association and Association of Chiefs of Police. Alexander and Kilgour clearly link the *youth crime problem — hard core criminals — the increasing youthfulness of offenders — and the absence of firmness of the welfare-based youth-court system under the JDA*. Both speakers illustrate the ideological function of statistics in this *moral panic* discourse: "Statistics whether crime rates or opinion polls have an ideological function: they appear to ground free-floating and controvertable impressions in the hard and incontrovertible soil of numbers" (Hall, 1978: 51).

The justice model reflects a compromise of ideologies forced by the crisis: Hence we call it *'crisis justice.'* It reveals the convergence of the liberal and the moral authoritarian right using law and order rhetoric. Robert Kaplan — the Liberal solicitor-general — represents the former, while Kilgour represents the latter. The law and order lobby's discourse of moral panic links *youth as a new dangerous class — accountability — deterrence* and *punishment*:

Mr Kilgour:	The second reason is that it seems at least to me and, I think, to members on this side, self-evident that young people are maturing more quickly now than in earlier years. All provinces with the exception of Newfoundland licence 16-year-olds to operate the patently most lethal weapon of all, the motor vehicle. It seems to us, Mr Chairman, that if these licensed 16 and 17-year-olds are recognised as responsible for driving cars, Parliament might reasonably exact a similar standard for young people here.

I am also informed, Mr Chairman, that in many jurisdictions you can leave home at 16 and be eligible for social assistance. Most 16-year-olds across Canada are in their last years of high school and some of them are in junior colleges or technical institutions. We believe on this side that most 16-year-olds know a serious crime from a youthful misdemeanour or frolic. It goes without saying that we have to be arbitrary here, and this party opts for giving a reasonable measure of responsibility to young people at 16 rather than at 18...

The Canadian Centre for Justice Statistics indicates that in federal institutions there were during the calendar year 1979 a total of only 80 16 and 17-year-olds held in all adult federal correctional institutions. Nine of these were 16, and the rest regard 'juve' as a sort of bad cold, and these people are going to be less likely, we believe, to abstain from serious crime if they know there is at least a possibility that an all-out court will do something more than tell them to be good boys and girls.

The impression appears to be pretty well set — and I assure you I did not see the video tape before any of you did tonight, and you heard what one of the young fellows said on that —

Mr Kaplan: The young experts.

Mr Kilgour: Fair enough. The impression appears to be amongst teenagers that the present juvenile court is a pretty innocuous affair. I think this is the case across Canada. The Young Offenders Act, Mr Minister, of which you are so proud, will have to go a long way to erase this long-standing impression.

So, I simply say that the crime realities of the 1980s are sufficiently serious, Mr Chairman, that society, old, young and middle-aged, needs protection from the very serious sort of crime that is taking place these days, and on this basis [I] move[s] the amendment that I mentioned before. Thank you.

The Chair: I think the minister has comments, and then I have Mrs Hervieux-Payette and Mr Fennell.

Mr Kaplan: Mr Chairman, as Mr Kilgour conceded — not too generously but, nevertheless forthrightly — we are attempting with this legislation to toughen the kiddie-court image of the juvenile court and to make it a place where a mature young person will be punished and held accountable to society for what he has done. I expect that this change in philosophy will go a long way to repairing the image of the kiddie-court and making it a place where justice is administered, and that those young people who were indicating that the kiddie-court could not really control them and they did not have to get serious until they faced up to an adult jurisdiction will, if the courts develop the way we intend them to develop, be given something to think about when they appear before that youth court.

SOURCE: Justice and Legal Affairs Committee, *Minutes,* Ottawa, Issue 67-31 (23.3.82).

Individualism, Familialism, and the Mystification and Dispersal of Coercion

Most if not all twentieth century economic and social thought reflected this compromise between natural rights individualism, utilitarianism, property rights and human rights, liberalism and welfarism, capital and labour — a compromise which became increasingly embedded in economic policy (which in turn created new economic contradictions which inspired the revival of monetarism and neo-liberal economics after 1979. (O'Connor, 1984: 201).

The YOA debates illustrate the struggle to reach the compromise described by O'Connor. The ideological work of promoting crisis justice is burdened with a legacy of social thought that includes the ideology of liberal welfarism and Keynesian collectivist consensus. Both of these schools of thinking represent the mystificatory reconciliation of antagonism between the autonomous individual and the state through a social contract presupposing democratic participation (Offe, 1985: 274). Liberalism's emphasis on individual autonomy derives from a presumption that individual conduct is based upon free will and rationality, especially in the marketplace. In conflict with this assumption, however, is liberalism's commitment to formal egalitarianism, which cannot be reconciled with the Darwinist social order created by subservience to the egotistical free market. Thus liberals rely on a discourse of modified altruism to manage this conflict: Unequals are formally equalized by rhetorical fictions such as 'equality of opportunity' and 'equality before and under the law.' At the same time, liberals make a formal distinction between the public/market domain and the private/domestic domain. In conservative thought individual autonomy is sacrificed to familial autonomy, while in liberal and social-democratic thought the relative worth of individual versus familial autonomy is judged pragmatically. In either case, the antagonism between the individual and the state becomes an antagonism between the family and the state. Liberal welfare states attempted to resolve this dilemma by co-opting and transforming the 'private' patriarchal family into a core meditating unit for state/individual transactions. New establishment ideologues (Lasch, 1977; Donzelot, 1979; Gilder, 1981; Mount, 1984) have seized upon this. Provoked no doubt by liberal welfare concessions to liberal feminism, they have charged both women and the state with weakening the private patriarchal family system (Barrett and McIntosh, 1982: Pupo, 1988), which serves the minimalist state as a 'haven from a heartless world' and as a key site for the maintenance of discipline and surveillance (Zaretsky, 1982; Currie, 1986) of women, youth, and men. Discourses highlighting these ideological tenets are found in the debates of the Justice and Legal Affairs Committee as antagonisms between the primacy of the individual versus the state; individual rights versus protection of society; between the acknowledgement of social or collective culpability versus individual accountability; and between the primacy of familial responsibility versus individual accountability.

A central problem for liberal discourse as it attempts to accommodate the pushes from social-democratic Keynesian collectivists, law and order authoritarians, and civil libertarians was the appropriate location of the individual in the calculus of blame. This problem was particularly acute because of the resilience of a tradition of treatment and welfare, which the YOA is attempting to displace. This tradition acknowledged some collective responsibility for the problems facing youth, including youth crime. At the same time, civil libertarians wanted to privilege individuals in order to bestow rights to due process upon each one of them, while authoritarians schemed to privilege the protection of society by deterrence based on retribution against the individual and increased familial responsibility.

Individualism:
The Mystification of Coercion

During debates, Svend Robinson (MP, Burnaby) — one of the New Democratic Party's few avowedly socialist MP's — questioned the protection of society as being antagonistic to the individual:

Mr Robinson: Mr Chairman, I would like to turn to another area in dealing with this legislation. It is the other area that is, perhaps, the most contentious, at least from my perspective, and that is the question of the underlying philosophy of this legislation. The minister will know that in 1970 his predecessor, Mr Goyer, introduced Bill C-192, which met with tremendous public outcry, and in fact was allowed to die — I do not believe it was ever referred to committee. The suggestion was that the legislation was effectively a criminal code for children. I suggest to you that the underlying philosophy of this particular bill, Bill C-61, is no different, that in fact this also is basically a pint-sized criminal code in Canada for children.

I am wondering if you could indicate, Mr Minister, through you Mr Chairman, how the philosophy of this legislation, with its new thrust on responsibility — which indeed is important — how the underlying philosophy of this legislation differs from that of Bill C-192, if at all.

Mr Kaplan: I refer you to the statement of philosophy. I agree with you that from the present legislation this bill moves more in the direction of responsibility. To call it pint-sized criminal code, though, is to ignore a lot of the provisions that are contained in the bill, of which you are aware as I, which provide alternatives to incarceration and opportunities for increased direction and treatment to be given, the provisions for predisposition reports, for continual reviews by the court. These are extra rights and extra remedies that are available under the Criminal Code.

Mr Robinson: Mr Chairman, what is it, though, that — I am referring now to an editorial from the *Toronto Star* headed "Don't Treat Kids as Criminals". In that, Tom Sterritt, who has been working in this area for a considerable length of time, acknowledged the fact that it is no longer the protection of society that is to be paramount in dealing with this legislation. What evidence does the minister have that the new philosophy of this legislation is, in fact, going to increase the protection of society?

Mr Kaplan: It recognizes the responsibility of the offender in a way that has not been done. I indicated that in my opening statement.

Mr Robinson: How is this going to increase the protection of society?

Mr Kaplan: It provides for penalties to be imposed on young persons and for findings of criminality against them, subject to their greater degree of dependency and their maturity.

Mr Robinson: But there are penalties now. How is this new hardline thrust in this legislation going to increase the protection of society? What is the evidence that, in fact, this change in philosophy is going to achieve that objective?

Mr Kaplan: It really leaves the courts to do the job that you are asking about. What is provided here is that the needs and well-being of the juvenile is only one of the considerations; the rights of society and the responsibility of the juvenile to society are also to be given weight. Now how will that be developed in particular cases will be the answer to your question.

In the past, the courts had no mandate to look at the protection of society. Their mandate was to look to the needs and well-being of the young person. They will continue to have that responsibility. So that I do not think it is fair to say we have moved fully from a treatment model to a responsibility-only model, but we have moved to a model, where there is a better balance between the protection of society and the needs and interests of the young person. I do not think I can give a more complete answer than that.

Source: Justice and Legal Affairs Committee, *Minutes*, Ottawa, Issue 61:6, 1982.

In this dialogue, the discourse of collectivism/welfarism is responded to by Solicitor-General Kaplan in the formulation of the justice-model compromise. Hence the notion of 'balance' is used to ease the transition from a treatment (conflated with welfare) model to the justice model. The punitive outcome of increased individual accountability is presented as mitigated by the notion of 'extra' rights, that is, the normal rights of adults. Despite all of the minister's caveats, the law and order lobby are reassured that the 'protection of society' is the primary goal of the proposed legislation.

Within this context, Robinson attempted to disarticulate the *deterrence rights — individual accountability discourse* by affirming the *youth crime — social conditions* and *collective responsibility for prevention and care* linkages:

Mr Robinson: If I can just conclude on this point, Mr Chairman. What this bill totally neglects in my view to do is to acknowledge our responsibility collectively, society's responsibility for the conditions which ultimately lead to conditions of juvenile delinquency. And I wonder whether the minister is prepared to agree that in this new change of philosophy, a change which in fact was not recommended by the committee commissioned by his predecessor, Mr Allmand, Young Persons in Conflict with the Law, the YPICLE report, what we are doing is effectively sweeping our responsibility, society's responsibility, for these conditions under the carpet.

I would specifically like to ask the minister what action his government intends to take to deal with the conditions which have been identified by the Senate report, Child at Risk, for example, which showed that such things as the question of child abuse, the stresses on single parent families, violence on television, and poverty, particularly among single parent families, intra-uterine abuse, care and natal problems, the failure to detect dietary and learning disabilities — all these are the kinds of conditions that lead to young people coming in conflict with the law. Is the government doing to deal with those underlying conditions as opposed to bringing in a bill which effectively, as I say, is a mini criminal code for children? What are you doing to deal with those documented causes of young people coming into conflict with the law? Those are issues that should be dealt with elsewhere and that are being dealt with elsewhere.

SOURCE: Justice and Legal Affairs Committee, *Minutes*, Ottawa, Issue 61:22, 1982.

In reaction Kaplan disarticulated social conditions from collective responsibility for youth crime by extracting the legal apparatus from the discourse. He did this by making a suggestion that he presumed would be universally heard as absurd: namely, to *find against society* in court:

Mr Kaplan: I think merely to hear the catalogue of those social problems indicates that it would not be appropriate to give the court jurisdiction to make findings in relation to them. I take it that you would be suggesting that a court should be able to make a finding against the society, and against the conditions which might have led a child or young person into delinquency. My view is that the courtroom is not a place for that kind of hearing. It is not a place where society, provincial or federal governments should come to define its programs for prenatal care and so on. That would take the court very far from dealing with questions of responsibility, and it would take a judge, frankly, beyond an area of competence within the judicial system.

Mr Robinson: But what is the minister sold on doing to deal with

	these problems?
An Hon. Member:	Your time is over. Sorry.
Mr Kaplan:	The Solicitor General is part of a government in which other ministers, together with myself, are addressing all of those problems. To tell you what the government is proposing and is planning in the way of programs to promote a healthful childhood, to promote a healthful maternity period, to assist in the development of a wholesale social structure, I think really goes beyond the consideration of a young offenders act. So many of the government's programs are directed to this area and many of them were recognised in the Child at Risk study.
	I am not saying that these programs are perfect and the children are totally responsible for the troubles that befall them, even for the problems that are the result of their own behaviour, and every society has an obligation to try to see its young people develop in a helpful way, with opportunity and all the rest of it. But I am not prepared to admit that those are issues that should be dealt with in the juvenile justice system. Those issues that should be dealt with elsewhere and that are being dealt with elsewhere.
SOURCE:	Justice and Legal Affairs Committee, *Minutes*, Ottawa, Issue 61:22-3, 1982.

At the same time, the government's commitment to social safety-net programs was affirmed by the discourse.

The Saskatchewan NDP government also targeted the absence of sufficient acknowledgement of the community's collective responsibility. Its evidence reads:

> The preamble contains statements identifying the young person's and the parent's responsibilities respecting a young person's conflict with the law. No direct reference is made to the community's responsibilities.

> As the preamble stands, the issue of criminal activity focuses on the young person being totally responsible for his behaviour. Unquestionably, society has a part to play in this situation.

RECOMMENDATION:

> THAT THE PREAMBLE CONTAIN A STATEMENT IDENTIFYING THE COMMUNITY'S RESPONSIBILITY TO PREVENT AND ERADI-CATE CRIME.

Duane Lingenfelter (Saskatchewan NDP Minister of Social Services) Submission, Justice and Legal Affairs Committee, *Minutes*, Ottawa, Issue 63A:86 (23/2/82).

Nonetheless, Saskatchewan also emerged as one of the provinces critical of the three-year maximum sentence proposed under the YOA, advocating instead a harsher five-year maximum. Collective responsibility can clearly run parallel with an *individual accountability-deterrence by punishment* discourse:

Mr Robinson: On a point of order, Mr Chairman. Could the minister indicate which critics recommended this increased sentence?

Mr Kaplan: I have had a number of letters, from provincial governments and from other sources, and I am not prepared to make them public. But I think some of them were also sent to members of the committee, so you would know of them as well. The Saskatchewan brief, for example, asked for five years maximum for violent crimes. So this is a recognition that three years will make the juvenile court system more attractive to provinces.

SOURCE: Justice and Legal Affairs Committee, *Minutes*, Ottawa, Issue 61:23, 1982.

The explicit rationale for a five-year maximum was to make the YOA 'more attractive' to individual provinces by making it 'more attractive' to crown prosecutors: Essentially, this meant attractive to the law and order lobby.

FAMILIALISM AND THE DISPERSAL OF COERCION

The moral authoritarian discourse linking *youth crime-state intervention — 'extra' due process* with *the weakening of the family* also emerged in the critiques of the draft Declaration of Principle. Benno Friesen, a PC Member of Parliament, led the argument for 'familial responsibility' while Solicitor-General Kaplan defended the privileging of the individual as the unit for blame essential to the justice model:

The Chair: Okay. I will give the floor to Mr Friesen right now.

Mr Friesen: Thank you.

Mr Chairman, if Mr Robinson and Mr Allmand are correct in choosing 18 as the year, then surely the focus is — and ought to be — on the recognition that, up until age 18, the people we are talking about are considered juveniles of one dimension or another.

With that in mind then, I would like to look at the 'Declaration of Principle' which you have in Clause 3 (1) of the bill and point out that it has paragraphs (a) through (g). First, paragraph (a) deals with the young people, their accountability and their responsibility; paragraph (b) talks about requiring supervision, discipline and control; paragraph (c) talks about measures other than judicial proceedings; paragraph (d) deals with the Canadian Bill of Rights; paragraph (e) deals with the application of this act; paragraph (f) deals with the right of young persons to be informed in every instance; and, finally paragraph (g) — oh, as an afterthought: young people have parents.

Now, is that not a strong message on the part of the department and the government that the accountability of parents and the place of the home in the life of juveniles really comes last on the list? It seems to me that there is a very subtle but very dominant message being given to society here regarding the view of the government as it sees the relationship of young people and their place in society. It is a strong message.

Mr Minister, I would suggest to you that if you really want to place the focus where it ought to be, just the very beginning of that, paragraph (a) ought to be the accountability of parents, the responsibility of parents to establish an atmosphere of mutual respect in the home, and that they are accountable for the behaviour of their children, number one. Then, if that breaks down, then maybe all of those other things fall into place. But, sir, I would suggest that you are telling society, in very strong terms here, that the home is last on the list. I would like to have your reaction to that...

Mr Kaplan: I believe the young person's own responsibility should be first. I do not think it is a good idea to send a message to young people that their parents are responsible for their behaviour, particularly not when they are between the ages of 12 and 18. I believe we can look to them, more under this law than in the past to be responsible for their own behaviour. Perhaps to put parents ahead, if the priority is viewed as being ordinance, would be the wrong message to send young people; but I certainly agree with you that parents have a considerable responsibility to raise their children to be honest.

Mr Friesen: Well done, sir.

Mr Kaplan: I would not want to put too much weight on the order as you get down past (a), (b) and (c) and so on. Now, if there is a strong feeling about paragraph (g), it could be moved up behind (d), (e) or (f) or something, but I certainly do not think it would be a good message to young people to put it first.

Mr Friesen: Sir, with all due respect, you say that the focus of the bill is on the responsibility of young people for their behaviour. I suggest to you that the focus of this section is on the rights that they enjoy rather than the responsibilities they have to society.

SOURCE: Justice and Legal Affairs Committee, *Minutes,* Ottawa, Issue 61-28-29, 1982.

In his response to Friesen, the Solicitor-General advanced the compromise (the justice model) by claiming that the YOA would 'balance' competing interests. He universalized consent to the coercive potential of the YOA by appealing to the rationality of reform to promote the protection of society:

Mr Kaplan: I think it is a balance of both.

It was a difficult balance to achieve because in the past we have had a much more doctrinaire idea of how to handle crime, and it has not worked. Now, I think society as a whole tends to recognize it is a more complicated problem than to say it is totally the child's fault, totally the parent's fault, that the only interest to be served is that of society. These past ideological positions have always failed us. You can challenge the order in which these ideas are put forward but I am glad to see you are not challenging the ideas themselves.

We are attempting to get a balance which will give a judge, a sensible judge, the opportunity to fight crime in an appropriate way with the delinquent before him.

Mr Friesen: But, sir is it not possible that if you make the young people exclusively accountable for their behaviour then the irresponsible parent, under the present provisions, can act as a cover for those young people, as long as they have all of the protections, the protections that age or the juvenile age gives them. For example, a case in point. Where the police continuously apprehend a young fellow age 15 in my community to send out the kind of legal message that you are doing in the statement of principles. I think you owe it to society to correct this, unless the government has it in mind that the home is the last priority on the list and unless that is what you want to convey.

SOURCE: Justice and Legal Affairs Committee, *Minutes*, Ottawa, Issue 61-29, 1982.

In the continuation of the debate about the extent to which familial responsibility has been or ought to be subordinated to individual accountability, Mr Friesen spoke about the ideological work of the text and the paramount position of the family:

Mr Friesen: The fact is that all literature, and certainly law, has two levels of communication. There is the immediate textual statement, and then there is the implicit communication that we convey by such things as sequence and order which implies certain priorities. That is the message that I want to leave with you today sir. When we write good law we are sending, really, two messages, and I would like us to be careful that we convey both of them accurately to the young people who are going to be affected by this legislation.

Sir, the priority that I think our society would like us to keep in mind is that the home is central to all good order in our society and, in order to preserve the home, parents ought to have paramount consideration. I think the law should recognize that. I do not think the government is deliberately overlooking that in the legislation as it stated it. I think it may have been a drafting oversight, and I am not casting any aspersions on the government for this. However, I think it is clear that here a simple textual rearrangement can clarify the message and keep before society the more wholesome and constructive priority and focus first of all on the paramountcy of the home. Then, possibly, if the home has failed and all its resources have failed, then other support systems in society, and particularly, in this case, the judicial system, must take over. But the home is the first line of defence; and I would like to underscore that.

Hon. Members: Hear, hear.

SOURCE: Justice and Legal Affairs Committee, *Minutes*, Ottawa Issue 69-8, 1982.

Though Kaplan straddled individualism and familialism, in response his discourse retained fidelity to the individual accountability principle:

Mr. Kaplan: Very briefly, I have considered the amendment and I understand the point you are making, but I prefer the first priority being given to the responsibility of the young person. After all, if the home has failed the young offender badly, if he comes from a family of criminals or from a negligent family, he still is responsible for what he does; and the whole philosophy of this bill, in comparison with the act which it is to replace, is the increasing emphasis on the individual and his direct and personal responsibility and accountability for his offences; and I therefore think it is a distortion to put that principle first. I think the individual's responsibility should come first, because that is what the fact of this bill is. A bad family is no defence, although I certainly agree with the philosophic position you have taken. But it just strikes me from the point of view of the priority of these principles that the first should be the responsibility of the individual. As I said, that is the main thrust of the legislation.

SOURCE: Justice and Legal Affairs Committee, *Minutes*, Ottawa, Issue 69-8, 1982.

Further snippets of this dialogue on the ordering of clauses in the draft Declaration of Principle reveal how moral authoritarians deployed accusations of statism and anarchy and promoted the universality of the home as a paramount organic unit of social organization as a way of disarticulating the individual accountability discourse. Also explicit in Friesen's remarks is the expectation that the family will become part of the crime-control process by being included as 'supporting' and 'reporting' in the Youth Court:

Mr Friesen: Well, sir, then, by keeping the sequence as you have it in the legislation now, are you not focusing on a kind of statism in society rather than on the paramountcy of the home?

Mr Kaplan: I do not know how on earth you could draw that conclusion. I am focusing on the paramountcy of the individual. It is the opposite of the paramountcy of the state.

Mr Friesen: Sir, there is, with respect, no coherence to a position on the paramountcy of the individual if that individual is not related to the most important organic unit in our society, the home, and it is good and right that we focus on the responsibility of the individual. I do not deny that principle. But responsibility has always been the context of human relationships. You are absolutely —

Mr Kaplan: I am not saying the family should be left out. I am just saying that criminal responsibility addresses, in all of our concepts, the individual wrong-doer, and to put forward the family first would imply that having a bad family is an excuse.

Mr Friesen: But are you not in effect arguing with me when later on in the legislation you call for notice to be given to the family, to the parents, to be in a supporting — at least a reporting, if not supporting, situation within the court?

Mr Kaplan: We are certainly not talking about a very big difference between us. I recognize the paramountcy of the family as an influence in an individual's life. But I come back to the main principle of the criminal law: the responsibility of the individual for what he has done. To hide the individual behind family considerations is misleading, I think.

I do not have anything more to say on this. You are wanting to wind around what I have said, so that you can go out and say the Liberals are against the family. We are not against the family but, in criminal law, the individual is the most important entity. That is not an existentialist point of view, that is a religious point of view, if you like. It is a spiritual point of view.

Mr Friesen: Certainly I do not deny that.

Mr Kaplan: It is an affirmation of faith in individuality.

Mr Friesen: I do not deny that that is true, but that is not the only true aspect of it.

Mr Kaplan: I think it is the most important one.

Mr Friesen: I think you could find sociologists who have no particular religious belief, and would also believe that the family is the most important influence. , It is not exclusively a religious belief.

Mr Kaplan: Well then, why are we holding individuals accountable? Why? Because they are the central unit in the society; the individual.

Mr Friesen: The individual is the central unit?

Mr Kaplan: Yes.

Mr Friesen: Sir, then we are on the threshold of anarchy!

SOURCE: Justice and Legal Affairs Committee, *Minutes*, Ottawa, Issue 69:8-11, 1982.

The familialist discourse linking the moral authoritarian and law and order authoritarians chains together *deterrence — the family as responsible — control of youth crime:*

Mr Kilgour: What about this question of Section 22 of the Juvenile Delinquents Act holding parents responsible in certain cases for, I guess, damages, fines, this sort of thing? You are concerned, I note, that this is going to be taken out of the proposed bill. Do you feel with your experience, that it is a good thing? I can guess that you do, but how strongly do you feel about holding some parents responsible for the acts of some children found delinquent?

Supt Alexander: I think often the way children act is more of a reflection of how closely their parents supervise them than anything else. I rather think we would get some better parenting, if you like, in the form of supervision and discipline, if their wallets were in jeopardy. Now, that would satisfy in some cases, I am sure. In others, no; there would be no sense to that at all.

Mr Kilgour: So you would like Section 22 of the present JDA left essentially as it is? Would that be a fair way of putting your position?

Supt Alexander: No, not necessarily. What we were suggesting was that in the philosophies outlined in Clause 3 in the bill they speak about parental responsibility for supervision and so on, but we do not see it carried through in the bill; and we are merely suggesting that the sentencing section would seem to lend itself to that kind of involvement of parents, but we do not see it there in any form - not necessarily in the form of being responsible for money and payment of damages or whatever. It was in the form of general comment more than...

SOURCE: Justice and Legal Affairs Committee, *Minutes*, Ottawa, Issue 64:19, 1982.

The logical extension of the authoritarian familialism was to link *deterrence — the family as culpable — control of youth crime* in a discourse that would justify making bad parenting by commission or omission a criminal offence:

Mr Friesen: Well, it is easy to see from Mr Robinson that he tends to lose his lucidity when he gets involved with his ideology. He says he is not willing to entertain any such notion 'unless' I would suggest that he has to entertain such a notion if we introduce it. So I am willing to move, and then I will speak to it, that Clause 20 of Bill C-61 be amended by (a) striking out line 44 on page 26 and substituting the following:

Parent or guardian jointly liable with child.

(2) Where a young person is adjudged to have been guilty of an offence and the court is of the opinion that the case would be best met by the imposition of a fine, damages and costs, whether with or without restitution or any other action, the court shall, it satisfied that the parent or guardian has conducted to the commission of the offence by neglecting to exercise due care or supervision of the young person or otherwise, order that the young person and the parent or guardian of the young person are jointly or severally liable to pay the fine, damages or costs awarded.

SOURCE: Justice and Legal Affairs Committee, *Minutes*, Ottawa, Issue 72:28, 1982.

CONCLUSIONS

> If we assume law is no more than a mystifying and pompous way in which class power is registered we need not waste our labour studying its history and forms. (Thompson, 1981: 136)

The pursuit of human justice requires the practice of idealism. Idealism defined in the context of the present movement of the current ideological crisis draws heavily on liberal thought and liberal-inspired institutions and processes. Discomfort with notions that 'the medium' may well be 'the message' or that 'with the technology comes the ideology' has paralysed much of the practice of left idealism.

The YOA epitomizes crisis justice. Nonetheless, perhaps it offers the potential for minimal reforms. Can the principles of the welfare model be recaptured? Can collective caring arise from the principles of least restrictive alternatives, limitations on intervention, familial autonomy? Can we engage in a politics of social rights as well as legal rights based on the principles of the right to counsel, and the visibility and accountability of decision-making? Can fairness and a more restitutive rather than retributive social reaction to youth crime be promoted by the principles of determinacy and proportionality? Do such principles harbour squeaks of hope for the reaffirmation of the 'Rule of Law' and 'Social Justice' ?

Detailed empirical work, test-case advocacy, participatory practice, and education are needed to disarticulate the discourses of the new establishment ideology. A continual quest for the decentralization of authority and resistance to hierarchical ascriptive categorizing and power are required. The paradox to be understood is that at both the personal and political levels liberal thought encodes our practice and theory, simultaneously hampering them and concretizing them whenever we engage with the state. However, the limits of liberal ideology for progressive transformatory change must not blind us to its value in defending social justice.

This chapter has addressed a few of these issues. We had a modest aim, which was to study the interrelationship between *ideology — words — law — action* by exposing some of the more obvious chains of assumptions and their ideological pedigrees. In the final analysis, the crisis justice enshrined in the YOA demonstrates "the terrible power over human lives of ideological abstractions" (Berlin, 1981: 193).

NOTES

1. Ericson, Baranek and Chan (1987) discuss methods of textual analysis for examining the production of deviance in the print media. They alert us to the relationship between the *process* and the *product of textual production*. Their methodological prescriptions include both content analysis and the ethnography of the relations of (news) production. This chapter makes no claims to having employed either of these methods, although we feel that our contribution offers a suggestive agenda for a more holistic methodology.

Part Two

THE JUDICIARY: LAW FINDING

Chapter Five

Wildlife, Domestic Animals, and the Dene Aboriginal Rights Claim
Michael Asch

Negotiations over the "wildlife" clauses in aboriginal land-claims agreements have been particularly contentious. In this chapter, to explore the nature of the issues involved, Michael Asch examines the wildlife section of the James Bay Agreement. While this agreement provides some benefits to aboriginals, the final outcome is negotiations biased towards control of wildlife by the state. Asch traces this bias to definitions whereby binary opposition is posited between two fundamental categories of non-human animals: "wildlife" and "domesticates." In Canadian law, "domesticated" animals are held by private individuals while the right to own any wild animal or fish is not recognized until capture. In effect, animals in their wild state are "owned" by the Crown, which acts as ultimate manager. From this it follows that whereas persons who own what are defined as "domesticated animals" can dispose of their property as they see fit, without regard to season or bag limits, and can obtain compensation when this property is damaged or destroyed, a person who hunts "wildlife" can do none of these things. Asch contrasts these conceptualizations to Dene notions.

At first glance it appears that the Dene hunt wildlife because they do not own domesticated animals — in that they do not "manipulate animals to such an extent that genetic changes have occurred resulting in new races of species." However, closer examination reveals that the term "wildlife" may not be an appropriate way to describe the animals that the Dene hunt. Through an examination of recorded statements by Dene leaders and other ethnographic evidence, Asch reconstructs core concepts of wildlife agreements from the Dene perspective. From these sources it is clear that the Dene do not see these animals as "wild" or as "wildlife" in the dictionary sense and that they have been forced to accept a paradigm that is external to their worldview; within this paradigm they must negotiate guarantees

Michael Asch is Professor in Anthropology at the University of Alberta

that they see as already rightfully theirs. Furthermore, because conservation of the species for the common good is given priority over Native hunting rights, the popular conception is that the government has been generous — if not overly generous — in its limited concessions. Recognizing and exposing this bias in the settlement of aboriginal rights, Asch asks whether or not aboriginal conceptualizations cannot be accommodated within a new paradigm. To determine whether a new paradigm can be forged, Asch explores historical legal materials and finds it is possible to argue that the original intent of royal proclamations reserving certain "Hunting Grounds" for Indians was to treat these grounds as enclosures, imparting exclusive right of the aboriginal nations to the animals on those lands. Furthermore, it is also possible to argue that the animals used by the Dene are what Europeans considered to be "domesticates" and that only animals peripheral to their subsistence are properly "wildlife." In this way a paradigm can indeed be forged, supported by legal jurisprudence and moving closer to advancing the interests of aboriginal people.

INTRODUCTION

In the period since 1973 the Canadian state has entered into negotiations with various aboriginal nations in regard to outstanding aboriginal rights claims. These negotiations pertain both to political rights and to matters concerning 'property' and 'compensation.'[1] For most aboriginal nations, discussions on the political matters have been limited to a series of four constitutional conferences, which ended in 1987 with no tangible results. For the Dene, Metis, Inuvialuit, and Inuit of the Northwest Territories, however, as I have discussed elsewhere (Asch 1984), another set of negotiations is taking place that may lead to some political rights being entrenched in the constitutions of the two province-like jurisdictions that will replace the present Northwest Territories. Of interest here is the resolution of a number of claims that concern 'property' and 'compensation.' Among these are the *James Bay Agreement* with the Cree and Inuit of Quebec and the *COPE Agreement* with the Inuvialuit of the Western Arctic. The claims of the Dene and Metis of the Mackenzie River Valley are among those on the so-called front-burner for government, and this chapter focuses on one aspect of their claim in particular.

Specifically, I will examine one particular clause that appears in all so-called 'land claims agreements' — the wildlife agreement. Within this clause certain specific harvesting rights for the aboriginal party are codified. However, I will argue that the clauses are oriented in a manner that renders them somewhat suspect with respect to aboriginal concepts. In particular, I will ask if the term *'wildlife'* is appropriate to describe the animals as they are used by the aboriginal party. I do so in part because I believe it is necessary to discover a more appropriate way to describe such sections of claims agreements if Canadian aboriginal nations are to obtain a just resolution to their claims. I do so also because I expect that government representatives may well argue with respect to *'wildlife,'* as they have with respect to *'self-government,'* that aboriginal notions are too vague to be taken seriously. Further, they may also argue that these concepts are so different from Euro-Canadian ones that they form a fundamental cultural gulf that cannot be bridged without undermining the general ideological framework of the Canadian law.

Confidentiality precludes the possibility of using the 'wildlife' section as it appears in the Dene-Metis proposed agreement, something I would have preferred to do. However, with some exceptions, the clauses in all agreements and proposed agreements are similar. Therefore, for convenience, I have chosen to use the *James Bay Agreement*, which appears in a published document (*James Bay Agreement*, 1976: 359-391). Because I am not relating this discussion to the James Bay Cree or Inuit but rather choosing their agreement as a 'typical' case, I shall refer to it throughout the following discussion as the 'standard' wildlife agreement.

THE STANDARD AGREEMENT

The "Wildlife" section in the *James Bay Agreement* (1976) begins with a number of definitions (359-361). *'Wildlife,'* for example, "means all populations of wild fauna in the Territory (the Territory being the area within the claim)." *'Fauna'* are defined as all mammals, fish, and birds; *'sport hunting'* and *'sport fishing'* are used to describe hunting and fishing by non-Natives; *'Native Party'* is defined as those aboriginal peoples who are signatories to the agreement; and *'harvesting'* means hunting, fishing, and trapping by aboriginal people.

In reading the term *'harvesting'* one is struck by the inclusion of a proviso that permits hunting, fishing, and trapping *"except species from time to time completely protected to ensure the continued existence of that species or a population thereof"* (361: emphasis added). This idea is further echoed in the definition of the word *'conservation'* which is said to mean:

> the pursuit of the optimum natural productivity of all living resources and the protection of the ecological systems of the Territory so as to protect endangered species and to ensure primarily the continuance of the traditional pursuits of the Native people, and secondarily the satisfaction of the needs of non-Native people for sport hunting and fishing. (361)

At the same time, the Conservation Section of the agreement states that "The Hunting, Fishing and Trapping Regime established by and in accordance with this Section shall be subject to the principle of conservation" (361).

The agreement (367-75) calls for a Co-ordination Committee, which is "an expert body made up of Native and government members." Its purpose is to "review, manage, and in certain cases, supervise and regulate the Hunting, Fishing and Trapping Regime established by and in accordance with the provisions" of the agreement. There are twelve persons on this committee, with the membership divided so that the Cree, Inuit, government of Quebec, and government of Canada each get three members. Voting on this committee (with some technical exceptions concerning jurisdiction) is by a "one person – one vote" method, with the chair getting a second and deciding vote in the case of a tie. The chair alternates yearly between the government side and the Native side, rotating among the four parties so that each gets a turn to chair every fourth year. This body sets the regulations and administers the law.[2] Although it operates by delegated authority from the relevant minister of the Crown, it does not have much practical authority. However, it must follow the basic philosophy of the agreement and hence, among other matters, the definitions of *'wildlife,' 'harvesting,'* and *'conservation.'*

The agreement calls for some important guarantees for Native hunters. In the first place, contrary to liberal-democratic practice, Native people are defined as a special kind of user — *'Native Party'* — which is differentiated from other kinds of users, who are called *'sportsmen.'* Second, there are practical guarantees in terms of Native rights. These include the right to trade and conduct commerce in all byproducts of the animals they hunt and trap; the right to hunt without a licence; and, on a portion of their traditional lands, the exclusive right to hunt and trap (359-91). The agreement also secures measures to assist aboriginal people in financing hunting and trapping. Finally, provision is made to ensure that Native harvesting needs are met before the harvesting needs of non-Natives. Called 'priority for Native harvesting,' this principle stipulates that Native people are guaranteed levels of harvesting equal to the present levels of harvesting of all species in the Territory. To this end, the Native party is to be given preference over non-Natives in hunting and trapping. Again, however, this right is subject to the specific proviso *"in conformity with the principle of conservation and where game populations permit."*

In summary, the standard wildlife agreement provides tangible benefits to aboriginal signatories that provide real advantages for them over non-Native hunters. However, these guarantees and benefits are limited by an agreement to an overarching concern about conservation of species and the maintenance of game populations, a concern that is ultimately under the authority of the state. Finally, the *Inuvialuit Agreement* (1984: 25) makes explicit that "Nothing in this Section gives the [Native party] a proprietory interest in any wildlife."

The Philosophy of the Written Version of the Standard Agreement

The written version of the wildlife agreement closely follows Euro-Canadian cultural values and hence those of the government side in the negotiations. To illustrate this, it is useful to begin by examining how the concept *'wildlife'* is defined in Euro-Canadian dictionaries. According to *Webster's* (1966:2616), *'wildlife'* means "living things that are neither human nor domesticated; especially, the mammals, birds and fishes that are hunted by man for sport or food." It is pointed out that the term *'wildlife'* is analogous at some level to *'game,'* a word that *Webster's* denotes as "animals under pursuit or taken in hunting" (or) "animals considered worthy of pursuit by sportsmen; especially wild animals taken for sport or food." Although it is not made explicit, I presume that wildlife and game live in the *'wilderness,'* which is defined as "a tract or region uncultivated and uninhabited by human beings." The term *'wildlife'* is opposed in

Webster's Dictionary to the word *'domesticate,'* which is in turn defined as "adapted to life in intimate association with and to the advantage of man, usually by modifying growth and traits through the provision of food ... and selective breeding." According to Webster's, therefore, a binary opposition exists between two fundamental categories of non-human animals: *'wildlife'* and *'domesticates.'*

Curiously, the word *'wildlife'* does not appear in *The Oxford Dictionary.* Nonetheless, a similar opposition does exist when one begins with the word *'wild.'* According to *Oxford* (1976), among the definitions of *'wild'* the first is "of an animal: living in a state of nature; not tame, *not domesticated* " (emphasis added). References to this usage go back to 725 A.D. Also included are such associated meanings as: "produced or yielded by wild animals or plants; produced naturally without cultivation; sometimes having the characteristic (usually inferior) quality of such productions"; and "of a place or region: uncultivated or uninhabited; hence waste, desert, desolate" (that is, a wilderness); and "of persons (or their attributes): uncivilized, savage; uncultured, rude; also, not accepting, or resisting the constituted government."

An obverse can again be found in the word *'domestic.'* Here, among other terms, are "of or pertaining to one's own country or nation; not foreign, internal, inland, 'home,'"; and, more particularly, "of animals: living under the care of man, in or near his habitations; tame, not wild." This term goes back at least to the early seventeenth entury. These usages, it should be noted, closely follow those found in *Johnson's Dictionary.* Thus, in *The Oxford Dictionary* as in *Webster's,* there is a binary opposition between the concept *'wildlife'* and the concept *'domesticate'* when referring to animals. In my view, this opposition provides an important component for the ideological basis of the wildlife agreement.

A matter of some crucial import not expressed in dictionary definitions is the question of ownership. In law, *'domesticated'* animals are held by private individuals. However, the situation is different with respect to *'wildlife.'* As Peter Usher (1984: 401) argues: "Canadian law does not recognize the right of ownership in any wild animal or fish until it is captured. These resources are therefore called common property resources, and their management and regulation is the responsibility of the state on behalf of its citizens. Common property is thus, in effect, state property."

In this way, animals in their wild state are considered to be 'owned' by the Crown in contemporary Canadian law (Usher, 1984: 397; McCandless, 1985; also see Gumbert, 1984, for Australia). Given the dual nature of Canadian sovereignty, in some cases the Crown pertains to the prerogatives of the federal government, while in others it refers to a provincial government.

Although the Crown owns the wild animals, it does not act as though it were private owner and hoard hunting to itself. Rather, it acts as ultimate manager in that it issues licences to hunt; legislates on such matters as legal seasons to capture game animals and bag limits; and takes responsibility to ensure the preservation of species. Given that Canada is a liberal-democracy with an elected government, the Crown (following the wishes of the government) makes sure that, in acting as legal custodian for wildlife, it operates to ensure the widest possible access for all hunters without regard to race, religion, or any other discriminatory matters. Thus, its actions create the presumption that wild animals are a common property resource that it manages for the common good, defined as 'the good of the majority.'

In terms of ownership, then, wildlife differs from domesticated animals in Euro-Canadian ideology on one important point: A private individual can own domesticated animals but, until they have been captured, not wildlife. From this it follows that persons who own what are defined as domesticated animals, within some bounds, can dispose of their property as they see fit without regard to season or bag limits, and they can obtain compensation when their property is damaged or destroyed. A person who hunts wildlife can do none of these things, because the state, not the individual, owns the animals until they have been legally harvested. In short, there appears to be an homology between Euro-Canadian ideas about wildlife and the terms of the standard agreement itself. The question is whether the homology can be extended to the aboriginal side.

The Dene Idea of Ownership of Animals

If we begin with the terms 'wildlife' and 'domesticate' as they have been defined in the dictionaries, at first it seems that because they do not have any domestic animals, except for dogs, which are never used for food,[3] the Dene must hunt wildlife. Furthermore, the Dene do not have 'domestication' in the classical anthropological sense, because they do not manipulate animals "to such an extent that genetic changes have occurred resulting in new races of species" (Bender, 1975:1). Indeed, as would be appropriate if the animals on the land were conceptualized as 'wildlife,' the Dene commonly state that "No one can own an animal that has not been captured."

The Dene also accept a view that captured animals become the property of particular individuals and/or groups. This would again appear to reinforce the notion that Dene conceptualizations of animals on their land replicates the Euro-Canadian notion of 'wildlife.' However, although there are parallels, the Dene concept is not identical because the terms for claiming ownership are sometimes at variance with how Euro-Canadians assert a property right. This point can be illustrated by an example of a particular dispute over the ownership of a moose involving two senior males from the community of Wrigley. These men had been partners for years and on this occasion were on a long, cold, and relatively unsuccessful foray. One morning a moose appeared in a spot that was particularly advantageous to one of the hunters. Although he dispatched the moose and claimed ownership, the other individual disagreed. His partner claimed ownership to the animal because he had dreamed that the moose would appear at that particular place and time and would be shot by the other. While the dispute remained unresolved, the meat was shared between the families of the two men. This incident, as well as other reports by ethnographers with respect to trapped animals, indicates that there is a transformation between animals before and after they have been harvested that the Dene use to identify particular owners once an animal has been captured. It also indicates that an animal may be 'owned' before it has been physically captured.

Closer examination of other data further reveals that the idea of *'wildlife'* may not be an appropriate way to describe Dene concepts of the animals they hunt. Although the Dene say that "No one can own an animal that has not been captured," this does not mean that the animal is unowned. What is meant can be better understood by examining analogies used by Dene when describing their land and the animals on it. For example, it is common for Dene to make an analogy between their land and a *'bank,'* as illustrated by Chief J. Charlie of Fort McPherson when he stated, "The delta is the bank to the trappers and hunters" (Asch et al., 1976). Similarly, Chief Kodakin of Fort Franklin described Great Bear Lake as 'a store house': "The whole lake is like a deep freeze for Fort Franklin. Our ancestors have used it as a deep freeze and we will use it as a deep freeze for the future children." These comments give the impression that the Dene see their land as a repository for the animal and plant life they rely on and, further, that this repository is owned by them. This approach differs greatly from the idea of *'wildlife'* living in a *'wilderness.'* It is rather reminiscent of Steward's discussion of territories (Steward, 1955:135).

However, we can go further. While it is true that there are few recorded statements that explicitly link Dene notions of ownership directly to the animal populations on their land, two were made in the process of collecting information for the Dene Mapping Study in which information from Dogrib Chiefs lay out the proposition rather clearly. The first, by Louis Moosenose of Lac La Matre, argues, "This land was given to us to make our living for food, clothing and income…. The land was given to us to look after it and the land was supposed to be protected. The land, the water, and the animals are here for us to make a living on it, and it's not to play with" (Watkins, 1977: 22). The second is an unequivocal statement by Amen Tailbone of Rae Lakes:

> The animals is our food, the land is our everything and the water is our drink so the land is ours to keep as long as the sun is shining. The game wardens should not give hunting licenses to their friends, because they do not kill animals for food, they kill animals for sports. The land, the water, and the animals are not here to play with. (Watkins, 1977: 220)

From these statements it is clear that the Dene do not see these animals as *'wild'* or as *'wildlife'* in the sense of a dictionary definition. Rather, it is clear that although Dene will often say that animals in the wild belong to 'no one,' what they mean is that they do not belong to any one individual before capture. In the first instance, these animals belong to the Dene as a whole ("the animals is our food"). In large part the ownership of such uncaptured animals derives from the fact that they dwell, not in a wilderness, but on Dene land. A moral sense of ownership is drawn from the fact that, unlike sports hunters, rather than 'play with' the animals, they use them for food. In short, it would seem as though the Dene perceive of themselves as owning the uncaptured animals on their land not as individuals but as a collective.

In this way, despite initial impressions, Dene conceptualizations of the animals on their lands come closer to what the Euro-Canadians call 'domesticate' than to 'wildlife.' That is, the Dene see those animals as "adapted to life in intimate association with and to the advantage of man." The boundaries of the land within which 'intimate association' exists may be enormous by Euro-Canadian standards, but it is still an intimate association. Indeed, this is invariably the case when the vast landscape is transformed into small worksites through the practice of setting camps, capturing game, and preparing meat. Furthermore, the Dene conceive that they own wildlife on their lands collectively, even before it is captured. It would follow that in all respects, save the manipulation of the gene pool, the Dene relate to the animal populations they hunt as domesticates rather than wildlife.

The Wildlife Agreements:
An Evaluation of Ideology

There are profound differences between how the Dene view the animals covered within what is called the wildlife agreement and the ideology of the agreement itself. Most striking is the fact that the agreement defines the animals as 'wildlife' and hence suggests that they are not owned by the aboriginal people, but by the state. Given this orientation, as acknowledged owner and manager of these animals, the state must see itself as having made major concessions to aboriginal interests because — despite its liberal-democratic mandate to work for the good of the majority — the state has acknowledged that a particular segment of the population has specific rights to these animals. In as much as the general public subscribes to this view, they most likely see the government as being generous — if not overgenerous — and thus would certainly not be amenable to the idea that aboriginal people could garner more rights. Indeed, in the North this type of conflict is now developing as the non-Native-dominated hunters and trappers associations are organizing to prevent realization of even the small degree of special status provided in the standard wildlife agreement. Justification for doing so is made by appealing to the philosophy that wildlife is truly a common property resource.

At the same time, however, we must look at the issue from the aboriginal perspective. From their point of view, although aboriginals have obtained some concessions, they have had to accept a paradigm that is external to their ideology, all the while seeking ways within this paradigm to obtain some of the rights and guarantees they already see as rightly theirs. This is no mean feat and bears a cost. Specifically, the aboriginal parties have had to give ground on fundamental points. They have had to accept that what they hunt is 'wildlife' — a common property resource that they do not own and one that, because it is a common property resource, must be conserved so that the preservation of the species comes before their hunting rights. Finally, they have conceded the rights of an owner to manage, cull, and conserve their property without interference from the state and to obtain compensation for potential loss. It is on this basis that the Dene are unwilling to accept the government or any agent other than the Dene themselves as the ultimate authority with respect to management, seasonality, bag limits, conservation, or other matters respecting the animals on Dene land.

On balance, it would appear that despite the particular concessions made to aboriginal interests, the standard wildlife agreement is biased in favour of the government side because, above all else, it is framed within a Euro-Canadian conceptual framework. This particular framework is of advantage to the state because by definition it grants the state ownership and hence ultimate control over the animals within the Dene claim. At the same time, the use of the term *'wildlife'* to identify these animals denies the Dene or any other aboriginal party proprietary claims over them.

TOWARDS AN ALTERNATIVE

The wildlife agreement is framed within an opposition between *'wildlife'* and *'domesticate,'* which derives expressly from the cognitive organization of the descendants of the colonists. From this perspective, it is clear that the animals hunted by Dene are not *'domesticates'* as ethnocentrically understood, and hence those animals must be *'wildlife.'* On the other hand, for the Dene who do not have *'domesticates'* in the Euro-Canadian sense, the opposition is not appropriate. Rather, the evidence indicates that they see the animals as belonging to a category that one might label 'owned wildlife' or 'genetically unmanipulated domesticates.' As the terms of the standard agreement suggest, it is the framework of the descendants of the colonists that has taken precedence in the negotiations. This has not gone unnoticed and there have been some attempts to accommodate aboriginal concepts of ownership within such agreements. The possibilities that have been advanced are worth exploring here.

The most highly developed alternative advanced to date is that of 'profit à prendre.' This notion, which derives from English common law, means "not simply the right to hunt and fish, nor even the whole right to do so in the area of the grant, but also the right to enjoy the fruit (or 'profit') of these resources, which is in principle measurable and predictable" (Usher, 1984: 411). As Usher suggests, implementation of this arrangement would have significant benefits over the present system, because it would indicate that the aboriginal people have an interest in wildlife even before it has been harvested. A second and somewhat weaker solution is for the Dene to declare that, for the purposes of hunting, the claim area is to be considered a private ranch. This would provide aboriginal peoples with the exclusive right to hunt but, unlike the 'profit à prendre' position, it would not guarantee them the right to profit materially from their act and to receive compensation if they were unsuccessful.

These solutions — especially 'profit à prendre' — offer practical answers that would accommodate some of the concerns of the aboriginal people without challenging the basic paradigm within which the standard agreements are formulated. However, such solutions are inherently less satisfying than ones that incorporate Dene notions of ownership within the paradigm. A first step in creating such a framework is to determine whether there are parallels within Euro-Canadian legal thought to the Dene ideas that wildlife is owned prior to capture.

Wildlife and Canadian Law

The contemporary Canadian concept of ownership in wildlife is of recent vintage. McCandless (1985:18-20) argues that control by the state for purposes of conservation did not become a driving force of legal philosophy until the decimation of the buffalo in the latter part of the nineteenth century. He points out that:

> Reforms made in the nineteenth century provided concepts of limited access; that is, all men (with a license) may hunt some of the time. This has been the principle behind North American Game laws ever since. By selling licenses, the government acts both as game keeper and vendor of hunting rights and makes no distinction between those who hunt for pleasure and those who hunt for food. (1985: 21)

However, we gain no parallels to the Dene case from an examination of the earlier period of Canadian law because until the latter part of the nineteenth century, the colonial population acted as though wildlife were owned by no one, including the Crown. Thus, as McCandless argues:

> The early immigrants to North America would have resisted any attempts by colonial administrators to deny them access to land and wildlife. The promise of abundant wild meat had a wide appeal to those driven from the land by enclosure or the effects of the Industrial Revolution. An added inducement lay in the promise of economic gain based on wildlife such as the traffic in furs, hides, and meat. The immigrants hunted without restriction as to harvests and shooting seasons, for such restrictions would have conflicted with the expansionist philosophy of the age as well as with economic activity. (1985: 13)

Thus, within this context and with few exceptions,[4] the state did not assert its legal standing to regulate hunting through the passage of any relevant laws although given such prerogative under English law. It is clear, therefore, that were we to limit our discussion to concepts about wildlife as they developed in Canada, we would find no conceptual parallel to the situation where what is currently called *'wildlife'* could be owned prior to capture. Rather, we have an orientation that moves from a chaotic, unregulated regime in which wildlife is not considered to be owned prior to its capture to one in which wildlife belongs to the state until taken and is to be managed by the state as a common property resource.

Wildlife:
Some Perspectives from English Law

A different picture emerges when we examine the history of English game laws concerning wildlife. Although in the twentieth century game laws reflect universalistic and conservationist values found in the Canadian concept of Crown control (*Wild Creatures and Forest Laws Act*, 1971), before 1066 the Roman view that "Wild animals belonged to no one until they were killed or captured" may well have prevailed (McCandless, 1985: 2). During the period from 1066 to at least 1831, two regimes emerged, each containing analogues to the concept of the ownership of wildlife described for the Dene.

The first regime began with the Conquest in 1066 and the claim by William the Conqueror to all of England including "all forested and unoccupied areas" (McCandless, 1985: 3). William and his successors were extremely fond of hunting and to that end set aside vast tracts of land as sporting preserves "within which no person might hunt without his permission" (Munche, 1981: 9). According to Munche, during this period the king had two prerogatives: "to hunt wherever he pleased and to take such measures for the preservation of the game as he thought fit" (1981: 11). Thus, the Shelburne manuscript concerning a royal enclosure struck in the eighteenth century stated:

> The Forests in England are of very ancient date. Hunting was the great passion and amusement of the first savage and illiterate ages of this Country; and the power of the Crown, especially in the times immediately subsequent to the Conquest, not being under any certain limitation it was perhaps more freely exercised on this than any other subject. (Cross, 1928: 37)

In short, according to Munche (1981: 10) this was the period when legal theory maintained "that the Crown claimed that all the game in England was the property of the king." In particular, this meant the personal property of the king. Thus we have a circumstance where uncaptured wildlife was privately owned, albeit by the sovereign.[5]

The second period begins in 1671 and lasts until at least 1831. With the *Game Act* of 1671, the Crown "ceased to be source of sporting privilege" (Munche, 1981: 14). While it did not explicitly deny the king's personal rights, the *Game Act* provided legitimacy for hunting and by granting similar rights to the gentry, gave them responsibility for preserving game equal to that of the king. Of specific interest is the treatment of *'wildlife'* within these acts. According to Munche (1981: 3-5), *'game'* (which we might equate with *'wildlife'*) was limited to hares, partridges, pheasants, and moor fowl. Such animals as deer, rabbit, wild ducks, foxes, otters, or badgers were not considered *'game'* in the same sense. For animals such as badgers, otters, and foxes this was because they were considered 'vermin.' Since their destruction was considered beneficial to the community, they could be hunted by anyone. These animals could easily fit within the contemporary definition of *wildlife*. However, the case is different with respect to deer and rabbit. These animals, which would be properly classified as *'wildlife'* under contemporary Canadian law, were not considered so during the period from 1671 to 1831 (Munche, 1981: 4). The particular reason for this with respect to deer was the practice of 'enclosure' as a system whereby "wild animals were confined to a specific area where they were bred and nourished until the landowner permitted them to be hunted and killed" (Munche, 1981: 4). Due to enclosure, Munche (1981: 5) suggests that deer became seen as a type of private property that was entitled to legal protection as such. Thus we find that in the period from 1671 to 1831, a private individual who was not the sovereign could own what we would call *'wildlife'* prior to its capture.

DISCUSSION AND CONCLUSIONS

It is not my intention to argue that there is a direct parallel between English notions of sovereign ownership or rights of private individuals respecting enclosed wildlife and Dene concepts. However, the use of parallels from English law can clarify the nature of Dene claims regarding wildlife.

With respect to the issue of sovereign ownership, Canadian aboriginal people see themselves as retaining political rights of self-determination despite the assertion of Canadian sovereignty. They see these rights as being exercised through political accommodation within Canada. There has been a tendency to see these rights as exclusively political and hence pertaining only to such matters as constitutional guarantees with respect to self-government. However, these rights are not limited exclusively to matters of self-government. Aboriginal leaders often assert that their political rights relate equally to economic matters, which include property. Discussion of rights, such as aboriginal title, is reminiscent not of 'free simple' title, but of parallels to the situation of kings prior to 1671 with respect to *wildlife*, for example. However, instead of the sovereign being an individual, it is a collective: an aboriginal collective. Thus, Clem Chartier argues: "What we feel is that aboriginal title or aboriginal right is the right to collective ownership of land, water, resources, both renewable and non-renewable" (in Asch, 1984: 28). In this circumstance, *'wildlife'* would be considered a resource collectively owned, as it is, for example, by the Dene. Hence, any agreement that defined *wildlife* as a 'common property resource' to be controlled by the state for the benefit of Canadians as a whole — even if it were to include special provisions for aboriginal hunting and management — would be something of a reduction from the underlying philosophy of that title.

The notion that wildlife can be privately owned before capture, as found in English law between 1671 and 1831, also bears on this discussion. Of course, if one places exclusive emphasis on the idea that the animals in deer parks became property because, by being 'bred and nourished,' they became 'semi-domesticated,' there would appear to be no parallel to the Dene case because, despite the management that takes place to ensure harvests, the animals the Dene collect are not 'semi-domesticated.' However, when one focuses on the issue of known boundaries as being the defining characteristics for ownership, a different picture emerges. As in the English use of deer parks and enclosures, the Dene have ranges within which they routinely hunt. These territories run the gamut from the national boundaries of the Dene as a whole to the ranges of the local bands. It should be noted that these local bands are defined in Dene languages not on the basis of descent, but rather on the basis of location: that is, for example, 'the people of Willow Lake.' In this view, a place like Willow Lake would be seen as a bounded area within which a certain collective of Dene hunt, fish, and trap; and under normal conditions, they do so exclusively. In this sense, it is analogous to an enclosure. Similarly, there is a bounding of ranges between Dene bands when it comes to following migratory animals so that, for example, the people of Fort McPherson will track one caribou herd while the people from the neighbouring community of Arctic Red River will track another. However, this is not to suggest that the local bands 'own' the animals exclusively, because in a more general sense (as the citations from the Dogribs indicate), the animals are considered to 'belong' to the Dene as a whole. Thus it is reasonable to consider the entire territory of the Dene to be like an enclosure.

To draw this parallel to a conclusion, this was perhaps the view taken by the English themselves. One must remember that the *Royal Proclamation* of 1763 was during a period in which deer and other enclosed animals were considered private property. The *Royal Proclamation* stated:

> And whereas it is just and reasonable, and essential to our Interest, and the Security of our colonies, that the several Nations or Tribes of Indians with whom We are connected, and who live under our Protection, should not be molested or disturbed in the Possession of such Parts of Our Dominions and Territories as, not having been ceded to or purchased by Us, are reserved to them, or any of them, as the Hunting Grounds.

Given this context, it is reasonable to consider that the concept 'hunting grounds' in the *Royal Proclamation* was similar to the idea of 'enclosure,' and hence that the intent of the *Proclamation* was to confirm the exclusive right of the aboriginal nations to the animals on those lands. However, this is a matter that will require further discussion.

Finally, there is at least one more way to model the idea of these animals as *wildlife* used by the Dene. This is to describe the animals as analogous to what Euro-Canadians call '*domesticates.*' This view would argue that, like domesticates in Euro-Canadian society, (1) the animals the Dene hunt are essential for their subsistence; (2) that the Dene have the same kind of intimate knowledge of these animals as we ascribe to *domesticates*; and (3) that they consider that they 'own' them. To call these animals '*domesticates*' is to suggest that the category '*wildlife*' would be relegated in Dene society, as it is in Euro-Canadian, to animals that are peripheral for subsistence.[6]

In conclusion, concepts such as 'profit à prendre,' wildlife on a ranch, ownership of enclosed animals, and sovereign ownership, and the reshaping of the term *domesticate* have been advanced as possible means for the state and the Canadian public to accommodate Dene ideas about the animals essential to their lives without doing conceptual violence to existing Euro-Canadian ones. Clearly, the difficulty that the Dene face in negotiating recognition of their proprietary interest does not arise out of a fundamental cultural gulf between Dene and Euro-Canadian concepts that simply cannot be bridged. Rather, the essential difficulty lies in a lack of political will on the part of the Canadian government to use the tools already available to provide a resolution to aboriginal rights claims with respect to *wildlife* on terms more consonant with the perceptions and interests of the Dene and, I suspect, of many other aboriginal nations.

The text for this chapter was completed in 1988. A different version, bearing the name "Wildlife: Defining the Animals the Dene Hunt and the Settlement of Aboriginal Rights Claims," was published in Canadian Public Policy *, 15 (2): 205-219, 1989. Both of these versions appeared prior to the 1990 Sparrow decision (1990, 70 D.L.R. [4th] 385 [S.C.C.]). This decision clearly defined fishing as an existing Aboriginal right and thus protected under the Constitution Act, 1982. The analysis developed in this chapter seems consistent with the findings of the Sparrow decision. (For a detailed discussion of this decision, see Asch and Macklem, 1991).*

NOTES

1. It is necessary at this point to clarify usage of the terms *'property'* and *'ownership'* in relationship to the animals the Dene hunt, fish, and trap. While many writers prefer the concepts *'management'* and *'custodianship,'* I find these terms insufficient. While *ownership* implies the right to dispose of one's own property as one sees fit, *management* connotes something less than full ownership rights of property. Further, although this notion of property is culturally specific to Euro-Canadian (and other) societies, the Dene usage implies that ownership of property in animals entails the responsibility to ensure that the animal population as a whole flourishes while in the possession of the owner.

2. The clause in the *James Bay Agreement* is generous in comparison to other agreements where the chair (who is a fifth member) can ultimately be selected by government.

3. Because the Dene do not easily discuss their concepts of ownership respecting animals, there is very little verbal evidence to explicitly verify the discussion here. The sources of my information are limited primarily to observations, both personal and by one of my students, reports by other fieldworkers, and statements made especially during the course of the Berger Commission hearings into the Mackenzie Valley pipeline. Because the *James Bay Agreement* is used as the standard agreement, it would have been ideal to include comparable information on the Cree collected by researchers under my supervision. However, it has become clear to me that the Dene and Cree are not as culturally parallel as I had once thought, so it is difficult to provide easy parallels. For this reason, I have chosen to restrict my discussion to the Dene, where I feel more comfortable in translating impressions into words.

4. One exception here is the *Royal Proclamation* of 1763 in which the king reserved certain hunting grounds to Indians.

5. During this period the ritualized aspects of hunting bore some resem-

blance to practices found in other cultures, including the Dene. According to McCandless: "Persons received cuts according to their status, so the chief huntsman received the muzzle, tongue, ears, sweet guts (sweet breads), and testicles, the foresters took the shoulders, the hound master the hide ... while the chief Huntsmen or Master of the Hunt would apportion the remainder according to his own or custom's choosing. Even the braves had a piece reserved for them, the *os corbin*, while the all-important dogs were fed the entrails with even more ceremony and horn blowing" (1985: 7)

6. In this view, the concept of '*wildlife*' might well exist in foraging economies as well as in those with domesticates; however, it would represent a residual category implying that the animals so named are not important to subsistence and/or not considered property. In this view, the animals that were the focus of subsistence in any society would be termed '*domesticate.*' The problem is that this reasoning negates an important fact in history: the rise of what we might call true domestication. Therefore, another term is necessary to describe the situation among foragers. Needless to say, this term would not be '*wildlife.*'

That anthropologists have spent little time on this issue is not surprising. True domestication (as defined by genetic manipulation) stands out in the historical record as a major incident in human history and, as such, most studies within the evolutionary paradigm have focused on understanding that fact. However, in doing so anthropologists leave themselves with a very poorly developed model of how foragers relate to the animals they harvest, especially from the perspective of property. This model, I would venture, in many ways replicates the ethnocentric folk category "wildlife found in western society." As a result, anthropology can neither provide guidance to those who would attempt a more reasonable term than '*wildlife*' upon which to base claims agreements nor develop a sophisticated model to explain the emergence of true domestication.

Chapter Six

Due Process in Saskatchewan's Uranium Inquiries

Jim Harding

Using the quasi-legal proceedings of public inquiries as a case study, this chapter analyses how legal practices and discourse obscure the misadministration of justice. In his study of the Cluff Lake Uranium Hearings, Jim Harding argues that given the scope of the impact — especially of the potential harmfulness — of uranium mining, it would be reasonable to expect high standards of proof during the establishment of the "facts of the case." In actuality, however, the inquiry was conducted with a standard of proof less than that required during criminal and civil proceedings. This seems even more contradictory when one considers the importance given to the "expert witness." In his analysis of transcripts, Harding explicates how the ideology of scientism surrounding the establishment of proof "beyond a reasonable doubt" masks contradictions within the process of inquiry. "The whole truth" becomes replaced by "the facts of the case," which are dislocated from context so that "truth" is ripped from law. Harding argues that when applied to public inquiry, procedures of case law "manipulate and edit the raw material of the witnesses' perceptions of an incident into not so much an exhaustively accurate version of what happened as one which is advantageous to one side." A witness who says what a panelist anticipates because of shared underlying epistemological and ideological premises — in this case about science, technology, and economic growth — is bound to be seen as more believable, hence more factual.

Given that the stated mandate of the inquiry was to determine the concerns and viewpoints of the public at large, Harding also assesses evaluations of the adequacy of the hearings. When he compares the themes generated by the panel's questions to the attitudes of local participants, he finds a discrepancy between the views of participants and the recommendations of the panel. Although the evidence suggests that the final recommendation of the inquiry was the result of panelists' pro-nuclear attitudes, Judge E.D. Bayda concluded that all except the "committed" (in this case, those opposed to uranium development) would find the

Jim Harding is Professor in Human Justice at the University of Regina

inquiry to be adequate. In the final analysis, therefore, Harding challenges the existence of "due process" when it comes to public hearings.

INTRODUCTION:
The Administration of Social and Ecological Justice

The 'administration of justice' is commonly considered to be a matter of criminal justice. In Canada, with one of the highest incarceration rates in the world, criminal justice certainly needs radical rethinking. In Saskatchewan, with the highest incarceration rate of indigenous people in the country, such rethinking and reformulating should also be initiated (Havemann et al., 1985). There are, however, other significant ways that the administration of justice and injustice influences the quality of people's lives in a capitalist society such as Canada. For example, managing the politics of acid rain currently has the attention of Ottawa and Washington bureaucrats and of the media, illustrating how the construction of energy megaprojects by private and crown corporations has profound social and environmental impacts in all regions of the country. Due to the expansion of uranium mining megaprojects, Saskatchewan is now the focus of growing international attention. As of 1983, Saskatchewan production of uranium was greater than that of Northern Ontario, and as of 1984 Canada became the world's leading producer of uranium.

Saskatchewan's location in a continental economy makes its uranium highly attractive to the nuclear industry in the United States. As in the mid-1970s, when the NDP government expanded uranium mining in the North, Saskatchewan is again being referred to as the 'Saudi Arabia of Uranium.' But this is not due to the expansion of demand for nuclear electricity, as predicted by past public inquiries. In fact, Saskatchewan and Canada have become the top producers in the world primarily because production was reduced by 58 per cent in the United States from 1978-84. Actual production in Saskatchewan has not increased substantially since 1978. With the glut in the uranium market, the failure of the commercial industry to grow at the rates predicted by proponents, and Reagan's move to free trade in commodity markets, the marketing of Saskatchewan's higher-grade uranium ore is becoming interlocked with the U.S. nuclear industry. Because the commercial and military systems are integrated in the United States, we are becoming more and more complicit in the nuclear arms race to Armageddon despite the fact that proponents of uranium mining prefer to keep the discussion in a more parochial context. Some believe that the expansion of uranium mines in this province will ultimately benefit indigenous people in the north and thus reduce some of the problems leading to their overincarceration in Saskatchewan's jails. Some, like myself, believe that uranium mining — with its capital intensiveness and potential for long-term environmental contamination — will aggravate socioeconomic problems and lead to the expansion of even more crude and cruel law and order approaches. One thing is clear: The link between the issues and realities of criminal justice and social justice is on Saskatchewan's political agenda. With the growing links to the U.S.

nuclear industry, the issues of ecological justice and human survival must now be at the top of our political and policy agenda.

Sociolegal Studies of Justice

There have been attempts to make decisions about uranium and other megaprojects more accountable (or at least to appear to be more account-able) through the use of public inquiries. In the late 1970s Saskatchewan was the scene of the most intense series of provincial and federal inquiries on uranium mining and refining in all of Canada.

Given the significance of uranium mining in Saskatchewan, research on this topic has an added relevance. Criminologically-inspired research could be undertaken on both the inquiry process and the uranium industry as 'crimes against humanity.' Such an investigation could be profitably grounded within the tradition of sociolegal studies that place lawmaking and law enforcement in the context of a social-science knowledge of the state and civil society. Because an important record about the expansion of uranium mining exists in the transcripts of Saskatchewan inquiries, they provide a unique database for such study. Furthermore, the government was both the administrator of the public inquiries and a proponent through its uranium-mining crown corporation, the SMDC. This adds several vital dimensions to a critical study of the administration of social and ecological justice. Finally, because the inquiry proceedings were quasi-legal, this sociolegal research can be grounded in the growing and challenging body of knowledge about legal rules and processes.

This chapter begins with some theoretical issues concerning the administration of justice based in sociolegal studies of the legal system. It then turns to the database constructed through content analysis of the Cluff Lake Board of Inquiry (CLBI) as one test of the impartiality of these inquiries. Finally, I will compare Judge E.D. Bayda's own analysis of the public inquiry process, which he headed, to the conclusions of a more independent and thorough assessment cognizant of the issues implied by the existing system of justice.

THEORETICAL BEGINNINGS:
Demystifying 'Beyond Reasonable Doubt'
The Impact of Powerful Language

The focus on the impartiality and/or expertise that assumedly guides legal procedures ignores the subtle and not so subtle ways in which the social position and style of presentation of court witnesses influence judgments. As recent research shows, these influences can also operate in a public inquiry. This work includes sociolinguistic research conducted on what is referred to as 'powerful' versus 'powerless' speech styles in the courtroom. Based on previous studies suggesting that women use powerless speech styles and men use powerful ones, researchers had both male and female actors read powerless and powerful language based on actual court transcripts of female witnesses. These tapes were then played to partici-pant jurors in the experiment. As predicted, the results illustrated "that the style in which testimony is delivered strongly affects how favorably the witness is perceived, and by implication suggests that these sorts of differences may play a consequential role in the legal process itself" (O'Barr, 1982: 75).

As the researchers found, "The study of courtroom language has provided an opportunity for a specific consideration of the utility of distinguishing between normative and pragmatic rules in competitive arenas" (O'Barr, 1982: 118). This conclusion has far-reaching implications for beliefs about the administration of justice in the existing legal system.

Comparing Standards of Proof

The view in law that a decision must be 'beyond reasonable doubt' is clearly an affirmation of probability and not of certainty. It indicates that there is "no absolute standard in either criminal or civil cases" (Eggleston, 1978:108). Yet in the legal process the link between facts and inference is even more problematic than in scientific activities. This relates to the discussion about the interplay of pragmatic and normative rules. As Eggleston argues: "Since in most cases where the facts are disputed, the determination depends on which of the witnesses is believed, there is a tendency to carry this idea of belief over into the drawing of inferences from facts that are in evidence" (Eggleston, 1978:107).

An important question when we consider the administration of justice in the context of a public inquiry is the degree of probability required to draw an inference from the facts and beliefs in dispute. If a criminal court requires a higher standard of proof and greater degree of probability than a civil court, how should a public inquiry be treated? The general view is that proof needs to be clearer and stronger as the enormity of the crime increases. If the scope and scale of the impact of uranium mining are treated as a potential crime, what standard of proof should be required in an inquiry investigating the nuclear-fuel cycle — a discourse riddled with controversies about long-lived wastes and the proliferation of nuclear weapons? In actuality, a public inquiry tends to have a standard of proof that is less than the civil view of probability. Given that the mandate of the inquiry was to assess fact and related belief, it can be argued that 'reasonable doubt' should have led to the recommendation of a moratorium, which would have amounted to delaying belief. This argument is justified by the fact that support for a moratorium was actually the dominant position, endorsed by all major Native groups (Harding, 1988). Yet according to the proponents the gravity of Northern conditions made the hasty approval of the mine a moral imperative.

The final decision in a criminal or civil court, or in a public inquiry, should rest on "the weight of the evidence adduced by the parties in respect" to the question under discussion (Eggleston, 1978: 112). In all of these contexts the question will arise as to whether "the facts relied on to support the admission of evidence must be proved beyond reasonable doubt" (Eggleston, 1978: 112).

Disputes over the meaning and nature of 'beyond reasonable doubt' are often shown in the judgments of courts of appeal. For example, what is the role of 'fresh evidence' in reconsidering an earlier verdict? Generally, "If, as sometimes happens, it turns out in the end that the rejected evidence would have had a decisive influence on the result, it may be sought to reopen the case on the basis of the rejected evidence" (Eggleston, 1978: 114). In this situation, the life of one person may be affected by a past verdict. Thus it seems appropriate to ask what role 'fresh evidence,' such as on radiation standards, which came to light after or was not considered during the CLBI, should have in reconsidering a policy and technological projects that could have implications for thousands — perhaps millions — of people both now and in the future (Bertell, 1985).

The Advantage of the Expert

The example of radiation standards raises issues regarding the use of experts in establishing fact and in drawing inferences in legal contexts. Criminal and civil courts, like public inquiries, must decide when they "go outside the limits of common experience or general knowledge" (Eggleston, 1978: 119). Precedents established in criminal and civil courts pertaining to scientific, expert evidence have had a bearing on public inquiries. For example, the view that "in matters of science no other witnesses can be called" (Eggleston, 1978: 129) has reinforced normative beliefs that favour the evidence of outside experts, who are usually associated with the project under consideration, more than the citizenry who are to be directly affected. Yet, as Eggleston indicates: "To say that only men of science can give their opinion on matters of science does not involve the proposition that a man cannot be an expert unless he is a scientist" (Eggleston, 1978: 129).

The consequences of the exercise of normative rules in legal or quasi-legal judgments are, of course, more profound as the scale of change accelerates. Mass technological projects — such as the energy megaprojects which were expanding so quickly during the world throughout the 1970s — have created a new scale of impact. Technological, environmental, and social-impact fields of study have followed in the wake of these mass private and crown corporate projects, showing that, in particular, these massive projects influence the distribution of power and authority. As Kendal argues: "Technological change redraws the lines between the technologically competent, the obsolescent and the superfluous; it leads to re-divisions of labor and re-distributions of authority. Typically, technological behavior precedes the effort of scientific measurements as it is ready to take risks which knowledge at hand refuses to accept" (1980:9).

The Ideology of Scientism

Serious problems arise when a corporate, technological project such as a uranium mine is publicly reviewed in an inquiry. For one thing, the stated purpose of the review is to look at the 'facts of the case' in evaluating the proponent's Environmental Impact Assessment (EIA). Yet, by definition, most of the scientific facts are not available because public inquiries formulated to bring the relevant information together (if this information exists) have not occurred. Ironically, a crude ideology of science (for example, scientism) that gives the experts special authority and contradicts the self-critical activity of science is often used to shore up the proponent's viewpoint. If those controlling the inquiry procedures believe in a formalistic legal view of impartiality and expertise — which is most often the case — they are prone to accept this ideology and appeal to its authority as a basis of establishing fact and drawing inferences.

As David Suzuki has stated, knowledge of the problems and of the limitations of scientific discourse is typically quite dismal among the bureaucratic, legal, and political groups that steer corporate technological projects. Their espousal of the cult of the expert may say more about how they hide their own incompetence and unaccountability than about their understanding of scientific discourse on its limits. Several major problems result from the increasing reliance on scientific-expert witnesses in courts and inquiries. For one thing: "The ongoing fragmentation of scientific disciplines into sub-branches which close themselves off against each other in order to define themselves better creates problems of their own in the reception of scientific evidence" (Kendal, 1980: 79).

The pragmatic and normative rules influencing vital public decisions are typically not sensitive to these limits. This highlights the importance of developing a healthy scepticism about the whole paradigm within which the ideology of science is located, including scepticism regarding the supposedly unquestionable benefits of economic growth and the general belief that industrialization and so-called modernization are tantamount to unending, universal human progress and achievement. Unless the rules for assessing evidence are freed from such near-religious views, the reliance upon the scientific-expert witness could be deleterious to policy-making. As Kendal argues: "As scientific opinion is becoming more uncertain of itself and dependent on the technological systematizations and standardization of its measuring instruments, the obfuscation of issues becomes a common ploy in disputes involving the evidence of scientific experts" (Kendal, 1980: 81).

Because of these problems and the limits to expert witness, a number of writers argue that the procedures giving scientists particular rights (or privileges) to present evidence need fundamental rethinking. Kendal believes there should be "a reversal of the current practice in which the expert is permitted to give a continuous account and the layman is prevented from doing so. We suggest, further, that the same give and take which should obtain in the argument on the facts between counsel should also be practiced in expert testimony" (Kendal, 1980: 72).

Some might say this already occurs in the cross-examination of experts in public inquiries. However, due to the normative rules operating in such settings, proceedings result in the proponent and their rash of experts having a stylistic upper hand. Witnesses can be hired, prepared, and remunerated to fulfil the image of 'the expert' or to use more powerful and authoritative language than opponents, even opponent experts. This is the kind of hypothesis tested by the database from the CLBI.

Proof by Errors of Omission

The notion of 'beyond reasonable doubt' clearly hides many complex questions about reality and the search for truth. As Doreen McBarnet states: "The philosophical problem of how one reproduces 'reality' thus becomes a sociological one: how is it that in such a situation of ambiguity, conflict, subjectivity, fading or molded memories, the judges of the facts can so readily find themselves convinced beyond reasonable doubt?" (McBarnet, 1983: 12).

It seems fair to conclude that the notion 'beyond reasonable doubt' actually eludes careful inquiry into the contradictions of legal justice. This view is upheld by the fact that "English judges have now been advised it is safer not to try to define a reasonable doubt" (McBarnet, 1983:14-5). Several aspects of the actual process of establishing a case 'beyond reasonable doubt' show its fundamental inadequacies as a search for truth, whether in a criminal justice or public-policy context. For instance, the "concept of relevance transcends the problem of truth ... by allowing artificial boundaries to be drawn around unbounded reality, 'the whole truth' to be replaced by 'the facts of the case'" (McBarnet, 1983: 16). Furthermore, "adversary advocacy helps solve the philosophical problem of reproducing reality quite simply by not even attempting it" (McBarnet, 1983: 16). Finally, case law "is partial in both senses — partisan and incomplete" (McBarnet, 1983: 17).

An adversarial system rips facts from context and truth from law. Carrying the system into complex issues of public policy pertaining to science and technology simply exaggerates the inherent shortcomings. The limits of case law can apply to a public inquiry, since McBarnet argues: "Far from being the 'truth, the whole truth and nothing but the truth,' a case is a biased construct, manipulating and editing the raw material of the witnesses' perceptions of an incident into not so much an exhaustively accurate version of what happened as one which is advantageous to one side" (McBarnet, 1983:17).

Such a system of 'proof' clearly places form above content. A witness who says what a panelist anticipates because of shared underlying epistemological and ideological premises — for example, about science, technology, and economic growth — is bound to be seen as more believable, hence more factual in a public inquiry. The evidence can be further slanted through omission, allowing the stereotypic ethical posture that one is not lying or distorting the truth to be maintained.

In the court "the right of the advocate not just to question but to sum up — a right denied the witnesses themselves — allows still further editing, abstraction, and imputation of meaning to be imposed on what witnesses say" (McBarnet, 1983: 24). To the extent that this influence of legalistic 'reasoning' is brought into the public inquiry process it will have the same effect. Certainly the proponents, with expensive legal counsel present throughout formal hearings, are at a distinct advantage in constructing by cross-examination a case of facts that is in their interests.

There is, of course, irony in the fact that a standard of proof that is consciously constructed out of errors of omission should influence deliberations pertaining to questions of scientific discourse and technological impact. In these cases it is the unknowns, which will most likely be ignored by omission, that are so crucial. Clearly, philosophical rather than strictly legal criteria of proof would be appropriate in such cases. For:

> Both in its concepts and its form the legal system copes with the problems of proof and truth by redefining them. And the problem of how the judges of the facts can so readily find themselves convinced beyond reasonable doubt that a case is proved, is explained, in part, by the legal meaning attached to their task and the method by which they are presented with the information on which they must decide.... It is one thing to say the concept of the case obviates the philosophical problems of proof and truth; it is another to show how the prosecutor manages to construct a case in the face of all sorts of general principles which set limits on the methods by which evidence against the accused can be acquired and indeed exclude all kinds of information unfavorable to him. (McBarnet, 1983: 25)

We will now turn to an empirical evaluation of such intricate workings of partiality in the case of the Cluff Lake Board of Inquiry.

ASSESSING ATTITUDES OF THE CLUFF LAKE BOARD OF INQUIRY PANEL

The database created for the larger project is based on sampled participants from three uranium-related inquiries: the Cluff Lake Board of Inquiry (CLBI), The Corman Park Inquiry (Warman), and the Key Lake Board of Inquiry (KLBI). Approximately 5,000 pages of the 25,000 pages of transcripts from these inquiries were analysed, using over 200 attitude, theme, and other codes developed for the project. The methods are discussed in detail elsewhere (see Harding, 1986). This chapter will discuss findings from the CLCB as one means of analysing the administration of justice and injustice in the public inquiry process. The statements, questions, and interactions of all participants were coded, including those of panelists. The database, therefore, allows for a systematic assessment of the views of the panel members who made the final recommendations regarding uranium mining in the province. Specifically, these data on the CLBI panelists during its 23 local hearings show that, by far, the greatest number of attitude codes, 70 per cent, were conditionally supportive. Together with the facts that no unconditionally opposed attitudes were coded and that all panelists were coded as making unconditionally supportive attitudes, in view of the definitions used in the study the three panelists were categorized as unconditionally supportive of the Cluff Lake uranium mine.

The Impartiality of the Panel's Questions

Coders also recorded, when possible, attitudes that most closely described questions asked by members of the panel. Questions can be impartial in the sense that they are not answers. However, they can focus attention in some direction and away from other considerations. For example, a question about job benefits from uranium mining in the north is different than one about the prospects of environmental contamination. The way questions are framed, therefore, can indicate an attitude structure or worldview. This is not to say that the panel would be the only or main source of the implicit values and attitudes in their questions. It is possible for the panel to mirror the concerns of local people in their questions. An adequate interpretation of frequencies of *pro* and *con* attitude codes revealed in questions asked by panelists must compare these results to those of the participants with whom the panel is interacting and to the general attitudes of the inquiry participants.

With these qualifiers, the frequencies of attitudes associated with questions asked by the Cluff Lake panel at local hearings is quite suggestive. For example, as shown in Table 6-1, of the 105 questions from panel members, 45 per cent expressed pro-uranium sentiments. Six were unconditionally *pro*, 31 conditionally *pro*, and 11 reflected a positive view of the impact of the road to the mine. Of 105 such questions, 35 per cent expressed anti-uranium sentiments. Interestingly, these included 7 unconditionally opposed attitudes, as well as 21 conditionally opposed and 9 negative views of the impact of the road. Finally, of these 105 questions, only 19 per cent expressed support for a moratorium or were coded as neutral attitudes.

The interpretation of these findings is more challenging than those regarding the straightforward assertion of attitudes by the panel. The difference between *pro* and *con* attitudes is sufficiently small (11 per cent) that it might be explained by discrepancies in coding. Clearly, linking questions to attitude codes is more difficult and hence probably less reliable than simply coding attitude assertions. Of the 477 actual questions coded for panel members, only 105 — or 22 per cent — were linked to attitude codes. It remains to be analysed whether any of the remainder were attached to minor theme codes, since this could be another assessment of impartiality by panelists in the inquiry.

The above attitude results are highly general. The panel's questions were therefore analysed in terms of subcategories. For example, conditional *pro* and *con* attitudes included several codes dealing with economic and development issues, technology, and energy issues, and issues of nuclear weapons and war. The moratorium category included a general code, one dealing with guaranteed economic benefits, and another dealing with land rights. Several codes were also grouped under the neutral category. Finally, attitudes pertaining to transportation (impact of mining roads and airplane commuting of uranium workers) were separated for analysis.

These results were far more suggestive than the more general results. As shown in Table 6-2, there was a similar distribution of questions attached to *pro* and *con* attitudes dealing with the impact of roads, technological and ecological impact, and unconditional support or opposition. However, there were more than twice (21 to 9) the number of questions

TABLE 6-1: CLBI Panelists' Questions by Major Attitude Categories in Local Hearings

Attitude Category	Frequency	Per cent
Positive Roads	11	10.5
Negative Roads	9	8.6
Proponent	6	5.7
Conditional Proponent (CP)	31	29.5
Neutral	3	2.9
Moratorium	17	16.1
Conditional Opponent (CO)	21	20.0
Opponent	7	6.7
TOTAL	**105**	**100.0**

TABLE 6-2: CLBI Panelist's Questions by Attitude Subcategories in Local Hearings

Attitude Subcategory	Frequency	Per cent
Positive Roads	11	10.5
Negative Roads	9	8.5
Proponent	6	5.7
CP Economic Development	21	20.0
CP Technical/Ecological	10	9.5
Neutral	3	2.9
Moratorium Land Right	1	0.9
Moratorium North Benefits	13	12.3
Moratorium Support	3	2.9
CO Economic/Development	9	8.6
CO Technical/Ecological	9	8.6
CO Weapons	3	2.9
Opponents	7	6.7
TOTAL	**105**	**100.0**

TABLE 6-3: CLBI Chairman's Questions by Attitude Categories in Local Hearings

Attitude Category	Frequency	Per cent
Positive Roads	9	10.5
Negative Roads	8	9.4
Proponent	5	5.9
Conditional Proponent (CP)	23	27.1
Neutral	2	2.4
Moratorium	15	17.6
Conditional Opponent (CO)	17	20.0
Opponent	6	7.1
TOTAL	**85**	**100.0**

attached to economic development attitudes in support as compared to questions in opposition to the uranium mine. Consistent with this thrust, there were three times as many (13 to 4) questions attached to the moratorium code that stressed guaranteed economic benefits as there were questions attached to the general moratorium or to land rights. The latter results probably reflect the fact that the important issue of land rights was actually ruled out of the terms of reference of the inquiry — which merely illustrates how the partiality of the panel and/or government sponsor of the inquiry can be reinforced by pragmatic procedures.

Analysis of Individual Panelists

The roles of the three panelists in the CLBI local hearings were not really comparable. Judge Bayda's questions, for example, were responsible for 366 of 477 or 77 per cent of the total questions coded in the sample. He was also responsible for 81 per cent of the questions of the panel that were coded with attitudes. The other panelists, Drs Groome and McCallum, were respectively responsible for 79 and 32 questions, and 15 and 5 attitudes attached to questions. Although this reflects the role of the chair in the inquiry, it is nevertheless necessary to specifically analyse chairman Bayda's impartiality. As shown in Table 6-3, in total Bayda's questions were coded slightly more *pro* than *anti*-nuclear, with 44 per cent compared to 36 per cent of his questions depicted in that way. Seventeen, or 20 per cent, were coded with moratorium or neutral codes. As shown in Table 6-4, when the subcategories were analysed we found that the greater number of pro-nuclear questions were largely the result of twice as many pro-nuclear questions pertaining to economic growth and development, and most moratorium questions were linked to guaranteed economic benefits.

Only one of the other panelists appears to have contributed to the imbalance towards pro-nuclear attitudes in the questions asked. This other panelist, a university professor and member of the governing party at the time, asked 15 questions that were coded with attitudes. A full 9 of these, or 60 per cent of her questions, reflected a pro-nuclear attitude. Some 33 per cent reflected an anti-nuclear sentiment, and 13 per cent were coded as a moratorium attitude. As with Judge Bayda, the extent of pro-nuclear questions was largely the result of many more questions coded with a *pro* rather than *anti*-nuclear view of economic growth and development (5 compared to 1).

Comparisons to the Attitudes of Local Participants

These findings have to be carefully compared to other indicators of partiality among the CLBI panel. One interpretation is that the results reflect probing by panelists of the views of local participants. The interesting thing in this regard is that the apparent tendency of the chairman and one other panel member to lean towards pro-nuclear questions is the exact opposite of the general views of participants and speakers in these local hearings. Some 36 per cent of sampled participants, and 31 per cent of all speakers (including sampled participants) were either unconditionally or conditionally opposed to the uranium mine. This compares to 20 per cent of sampled participants and 17 per cent of all speakers who unconditionally or conditionally supported the mine.

Discrepancies between the overall attitudes implicit in the panel's attitudes and the attitudes of participants at the local hearings also vary according to the kinds of participants. For example, *none* of the sampled Native participants supported the Cluff Lake mine. Half of them supported a moratorium and one-quarter were in the neutral attitude category. Thus the discrepancy between northern Native people and the panel's attitudes and questions was huge. The same order of discrepancy existed between the panel and female participants sampled from the local hearings. For example, a full 55 per cent of sampled females opposed proceeding with the uranium mine. This compared to 30 per cent of sampled men. The main reason for this gender difference was that 20 per cent of women compared to 37 per cent of men supported a moratorium on the mine. Variations may still be found in the discrepancies between panelists and participants at different locations. In general, however, the interpretation that the panel's questions reflected the participants rather than their own beliefs does not stand up. It is far more parsimonious to interpret this as the result of the panelists' pro-nuclear attitudes, as coded in this study.

Major Themes of CLBI Panel

The database allows us to evaluate the impartiality and administration of justice in the CLBI panel in several other ways. In addition to the sampled participants and panelists being coded for 'attitudes,' they were coded in terms of the major and minor themes reflected in their statements. The major themes are shown in Table 6-5. A major theme code was used only when a general viewpoint was made or when several statements in total reflected such a general viewpoint. (These two kinds of major themes are not separated for this analysis.) Minor themes were used much more often to capture the specificity of the statements of participants and panelists. Major theme results can be treated as having more fundamental import in the structure of viewpoints.

The findings of the CLBI local hearings are quite noteworthy and somewhat unexpected. In total, 46 major themes were coded for the three panelists and two board staff who questioned local participants. All themes were pro-nuclear. This constitutes a cross-validation of the attitude coding, which also concluded that the panelists were all supportive of the expansion of uranium mining. All pro-nuclear major themes listed in Table 6-5, except one dealing with the provincial economy, were coded for the panel and staff.

The predominance among the panel of a theme claiming that the inquiry was fair and that the mine had not been prejudged suggests that an image of the inquiry as impartial was steadily affirmed at the local hearings. The fact that this major theme accounted for 21 of the 24 major theme codes of Judge Bayda is particularly noteworthy. It suggests that a

TABLE 6-4: CLBI Chairman's Questions by Attitude Subcategories in Local Hearings

Attitude Subcategory	Frequency	Per cent
Positive Roads	9	10.5
Negative Roads	8	9.5
Proponent	5	5.9
CP Economic Development	16	18.8
CP Technical/Ecological	7	8.1
Neutral	2	2.4
Moratorium Land Right	1	1.2
Moratorium North Benefits	12	14.1
Moratorium Support	2	2.4
CO Economic/Development	8	9.4
CO Technical/Ecological	6	7.1
CO Weapons	3	3.5
Opponents	6	7.1
TOTAL	**85**	**100.0**

TABLE 6-5: Pro-Nuclear Major Themes of CLBI Panel and Staff at Local Hearings

Major Theme	Bayda	Other Panelists	Staff	Total	Per cent
Inquiry	21	5	2	28	61
Energy	0	5	0	5	11
Regulatory	0	4	0	4	9
Technology	0	4	0	4	9
North	3	0	0	3	6
Science	0	2	0	2	4
Province	0	0	0	0	0
TOTAL	**24**	**20**	**2**	**46**	**100**

TABLE 6-6: Pro-Nuclear Major Themes of CLBI Panel and Staff at Local Hearings

Major Theme	Bayda	Other Panelists	Staff	Total	Per cent
Inquiry	.034590	.058569	.105263	.198422	51
Energy	0	.063291	0	.063291	16
Regulatory	0	.050633	0	.050633	13
Technology	0	.045911	0	.045911	12
Science	0	.025316	0	.025316	7
North	.004934	0	0	.004934	1
TOTAL	**.039524**	**.243720**	**.105263**	**.388507**	**100**

good part of his role as chairman was to convince people that his board was fair and impartial. Whether these statements occurred more often in northern, rural, or urban hearings remains to be analysed.

A more accurate analysis of major themes links the number of themes to the number of transcript pages used up by a panelist. Table 6-6 shows major themes divided by the number of pages of transcripts for different people. This standardized analysis suggests that in relative and not absolute terms the board's staff and panelists other than Bayda were even more assertive about the independence of the inquiry than was the board chairman. Bayda, however, tended to specialize in this role. This also suggests the emphasis on the inquiry's fairness was not quite as predominant as indicated by the analysis of frequencies alone in Table 6-5. It also suggests that, other than the pro-nuclear theme on the provincial economy, which had no codes at all, the view that uranium mining would develop the North was the least emphasized pro-nuclear major theme. It remains to be seen if this viewpoint was more often expressed at the Northern hearings.

JUDGE BAYDA'S IDEOLOGY OF PUBLIC INQUIRIES

Justice Edward Bayda, who headed the CLBI, succinctly stated his views on public inquiries at a Canadian conference on nuclear policy held in November 1978 (1980-81: 3-12). The address provides his evaluation of the 'adequacy' of the CLBI and a statement of his ideological orientation to the underlying disputes about rules, participation, and power. Rather than inferring his and the panel's role in the CLBI from our database alone, it is worth reconsidering the interpretations of the panel's partiality based on Bayda's own views about the inquiry he headed. Bayda raised the overriding question: "Is the public inquiry process as generally envisioned by the appropriate federal and provincial statutory provisions adequate for assessing major nuclear facilities?" (Bayda, 1980-81: 3).

The judge began by declaring — not arguing — that "A public inquiry concerning a nuclear facility should practically always be a statutory tribunal of inquiry and not a Royal Commission" (1980-81: 3). A more independent and thorough evaluation, however, came to a very different conclusion:

> The holding of a classical public local inquiry has now fallen into disrepute in those cases where the construction of the 'public works' in question is an important feature of some controversial national policy, and not merely a matter of local concern. That is especially the case where the 'works' entail a new, or particularly complex, technology whose long-term consequences are not readily or completely foreseeable — and even more especially where, as is often the case, the proponent is either government itself or someone with close links to the government. (Sieghart, 1979: 8)

Bayda's 'Elements' of an Inquiry

Bayda's approach was not so much to analyse the inquiry process but rather to state what he considered to be eleven characteristic 'elements' of an inquiry. The fact that he did not expand such a formal analysis into a substantive one suggests that he did not distinguish between the ideology and reality of an inquiry. His writings during 1978 suggest that he was largely unaware of the substantive issues about the administration of justice in the public inquiry process. In these writings he affirmed a reified view of the 'rules' of the inquiry, one ignoring the normative influences. Rather than acknowledging that such problems exist, Bayda simply listed as a 'characteristic element' that "The rules are framed to be impartial in substance and application" (1980-81: 4). Despite this claim, however, there was scepticism about the impartiality of the process. Rulings about the length of the CLBI and about the scheduling of the hearings were in dispute from the start.

There are many dialogues within the transcripts that illustrate disputes over the partiality of the rules of the CLBI. Here is but one example:

The Chair: Just one minute, Mr._____. Who was that who interrupted in that way? Well, would you speak up, please?

Speaker 1: No.

The Chair: What is your name?

Speaker 1: I don't have a name.

The Chair: Pardon?

Speaker 1: I don't have a name.

The Chair: Are you ashamed of it?

Speaker 1: No, I'm not ashamed of it. You should be ashamed of it, because the working class can't be here because of these afternoon hearings, because you have no respect for people that work.

The Chair: What is your name?

Speaker 1: I don't have a name.

The Chair: All right, that's fine. You can remain anonymous and quiet, and if you don't remain quiet, we have a way of dealing with you.

Speaker 1: You have a way of dealing with everybody, don't you? It's easy to deal with people, that's why you hold hearings in the afternoon when most people can't be here.

The Chair: This is cutting into the non-nuclear time. Now, I have a decision to make. I'm going to adjourn the hearings right now and we shall cut out this cross-examination. I appeal to some of the non-nuclear people to see what they can do with this man.

Speaker 2: Why are you putting it on the non-nuclear people?

The Chair: There's nothing I can do. I have no way of ...

Speaker 1: I represent Amok, if that's what you like. I represent Amok.

The Chair: I have no way of conducting this hearing.

Speaker 1: I like Amok, they're great, give lots of work to people. They don't exploit anybody.

The Chair: Will you allow us to continue?

Speaker 1: Go ahead.

(Bayda, 1978b: 7764-5).

From this dialogue a dispute over the timing of the CLBI formal hearings is clear. Whereas the proponent hired participants to monitor and intervene in daytime sessions, participation by the wider public — whose consultation was supposed to be the purpose of the inquiry — was seriously limited. Bayda would most likely disagree, because he accepted the notion of dichotomy between the formal and local hearings, as illustrated by one of his elements of a public inquiry: "Resort is had to formal hearings only when dealing with experts or scientific evidence. Resort is had to informal or local hearings when dealing with *non-expert evidence* or comments from the public" (Bayda, 1980-81: 4, emphasis added).

This does not mean that formal hearings exclude working people. Rather, this shows that Bayda accepted the advantage of the expert as a basic tenet of the inquiry process. Bayda also believed that these formal hearings, structured so the experts could speak about the more substantive issues, were to be "conducted in a manner analogous to court proceedings" (Bayda, 1980-81: 4) — which meant that many of the general issues about standards of proof would be examined in the context of the CLBI. Though the investigative roles are not identical to the courtroom, it is important to determine whether the generic problem of adversary/advocacy remained.

Bayda ends his 'description' of the elements of a public inquiry with the statement:

> Adequacy is not an absolute and thus cannot be assessed or tested objectively. Rather it is a relative and must be assessed and tested subjectively. Only after adding up the results of these subjective tests does one arrive at a conclusion respecting adequacy. It is a process which is akin, I believe, to the logician's process of inductive reasoning. (Bayda, 1980-81: 5)

This statement warrants attention, because it reflects an underlying epistemological orientation to knowledge and truth. While nothing is absolute, this does not stop us from devising objective methods that others can utilize. There are legal origins for the notion of 'subjective test' as a means to assess intent. Bayda's dichotomy of absolute and objective versus relative and subjective, however, goes well beyond this and reflects a fundamental confusion about issues of science and methodology. Such confusion is not atypical and has profound implications when legally trained people are standing in judgment of issues involving scientific discourse and technological systems. One implication, especially when the rules themselves give the expert special status, is that a formalistic ideology of science, which will obscure issues, is more likely to be accepted.

By implication Bayda was linking inductive reason to the relative and subjective. In his scheme deductive reason would be linked to the so-called absolute and objective. This dichotomy, however, flies in the face of the general theory of methodology. Induction involves working from observations which, one would hope, are linked to objective, replicable methods. Deduction involves working with propositions, which ideally will complement such observations. There is, of course, a continual dispute as to which approach has the greatest potential for advancing knowledge. There are advantages to a more dialectical approach to logic, one that sees an interplay based on what some have called an adductive logic. This study of the CLBI and other inquiries has inductive, deductive, and adductive aspects.

Bayda's relegation of the evaluation of the adequacy of the public inquiry to a 'subjective test' ignores the fact that the inquiry has left artifacts (for example, transcripts) that can be studied. Furthermore, researchers can later determine participants' assessments of the adequacy of the inquiry, with the added experience of retrospection and outcome. This research has been done in a follow-up study of inquiry participants (Harding et al., 1987). Both the artifacts and research can add an objective dimension to the discussion of adequacy.

Bayda's Interest Groups in the Inquiry

Bayda's 'seven classes of persons' in the public inquiry reflect similar limitations. His list includes: legislators, experts, non-experts, members of the passive or disinterested public, commissioners, the committed, and the proponent. Once again the dichotomy of 'expert' and 'non-expert' is posed as a fundamental distinction. Even members of the disinterested public are characterized as 'non-experts.' Furthermore, the expert's role is specified as 'thorough examination' whereas the non-expert's role is seen as 'participation' (Bayda, 1980-81: 8). Equally significant was Bayda's separation of the 'committed' — those who 'desire to convert the public' — from 'the proponent.' The proponent, interestingly, was given a certain objective status, being defined simply as "the builder of the proposed facility" (Bayda, 1980-81: 5). This depiction could not help but bias how Bayda heard and assessed evidence. Though Bayda described his category of 'committed' in impartial terms — for example, to theoretically include people on 'either side of the issue' — in fact, the proponent represented one side and the 'committed' primarily represented those in opposition to the project. Once again, a seemingly unbiased formal language reveals itself to be inherently normative once tested substantively. With this somewhat hidden but substantial bias it is not surprising that Bayda's 'subjective test' led him to conclude that all except the committed (that is, the opponents) would judge his public inquiry to be adequate.

Bayda concluded that for the legislator the public inquiry "is an excellent fact finder" that can deal "if necessary, with social and moral trends and opinions as well." Furthermore, it could "marshal" facts and present "them in appropriate sequence" (Bayda, 1980-81: 6). His view thus reinforces the underlying belief that the world can be separated into 'facts' and 'opinions' as well as 'experts' and 'non-experts.' In addition, as is typical in the courtroom, the vital philosophical and sociological issues as to how the 'facts' get 'marshalled' in certain ways is not even broached as an issue.

There is also a political aspect to Bayda's 'subjective test' for the legislators. According to Bayda, the legislator "must satisfy the constituents that he has provided the right answer. That is, he must be perceived to have provided the right answer" (Bayda, 1980-81: 5). Thus it appears that Bayda was not interested in how the appearance of truth or fairness cannot necessarily be taken as proof of truth or fairness. He went so far as to put this issue of 'perception' in the context of technological religion:

> It must be remembered that a legislator's constituency comprises a number of segments. One such segment undoubtedly has faith in experts. Technology has spawned complexity. Complexity has in turn spawned the ubiquitous expert. What better way is there to hear the story of experts than by having them relate it publicly, officially, and under scrutiny? What better way is there to create an instant 'expert' than to appoint someone to a Board of Inquiry to hear the story of experts? What better way is there to satisfy that segment of the legislator's constituency which requires that certain public questions be publicly scrutinized and satisfied by an expert's examination? (Bayda, 1980-81: 6)

This argument ceases to be proof of the adequacy of an inquiry once the underlying abstract faith in experts, which Bayda obviously holds, is itself open for examination.

With special status in the inquiry it is not surprising that the expert will see the inquiry as adequate. As Bayda says, the expert gets "a captive as well as quasi-captive audience for the propagation of his or her views." The expert gets a "pipeline to the public" (Bayda, 1980-81:7). Somehow this 'propagation' of 'facts' and the mystique of the expert are not tainted with the problem of being committed.

According to Bayda, the non-expert will also subjectively support the inquiry, because he or she will "establish if but a modicum of credibility for views expressed" (Bayda, 1980-81: 8). The disinterested non-expert members of the public, according to Bayda, will therefore also judge the inquiry as adequate. They are, for example, "given an opportunity to hear and examine, objectively all sides of the question" (Bayda, 1980-81: 9). Just what Bayda means by reintroducing a notion of 'objectivity' is not clear. What is clear is that he has forgotten his fundamental distinction between local and formal hearings, or the issue raised about working people not being able to attend the daytime sessions.

Bayda has the least to say about whether he, as chairman, would be suited to a 'subjectivity test.' In asking why commissioners would consider the public inquiry adequate, he says: "The inquiry process is a useful tool that assists them to properly and conscientiously arrive at their conclusion and to discharge the heavy onus which they bear" (Bayda, 1980-81: 9). Thus Bayda obviously believed that he had fulfilled his role 'properly and conscientiously' and that nothing more needed to be said.

Bayda then considered the 'committed.' Here, for the first and last time the elusive 'subjective test' concluded that the inquiry was inadequate. Because "an inquiry as the term itself connotes involves a process of asking, probing and listening" to the extent that the committed's aim "encompasses a need to convert vast numbers of the general public to his or her cause the inquiry process is woefully inadequate" (Bayda, 1980-81:

9). In contrast, the proponent does not deserve the motivational analysis of the 'committed.' According to this 'subjective test' the proponent's interests are simply to be 'treated fairly,' to have 'appropriate improvements' in the proposal, a 'reasonably quick decision,' and 'knowing where he stands.' He concluded that the proponent found the inquiry adequate for his purposes. Bayda denies that a social or economic interest, such as profit, would guide the proponent's behaviour.

We can see, therefore, that as a 'subjective test,' this procedure is merely the test of a self-conscious ideology that rules out vital problems by definition. This leaves us only to wonder about Bayda's motivation. As he himself stated:

> It is highly questionable whether it is adequate from the standpoint of the committed member of a public interest group. It is, however, adequate from the standpoint of the legislator, the expert, the non-expert who has an active interest, the member of the general public who has a passive but nevertheless real interest, the commissioner who is conducting the inquiry, and the proponent (Bayda, 1980-81: 10).

In this way, the 'committed' — which means those not committed to the project — are seen to stand apart from the rest by being dissatisfied with public inquiries. In the final analysis, this simply reinforces the liberal pluralist ideology that sees one big happy family threatened by a small minority of irrationals. However, Bayda added a few qualifications to his rather inefficient restatement of pluralist-cum-authoritarian liberalism. One qualification was an appeal to an ideology of professionalism (that is, to the impartial expert) to explain away all the issues of partiality that clearly remain after his 'subjective test.' He rejected the notion that the commitments and biases of panelists enter into the public inquiry:

> His or her professionalism and practised virtues of prudence, justice, temperance and fortitude (if that is the kind of person you have chosen) will enable him or her quite readily to put his biases concerning the subject matter to one side and to bring impartiality to the inquiry. Shelving biases and dealing impartially is not a phenomenon in our society; it is common-place. (Bayda, 1980-81: 10)

Such a person is himself or herself an expert — either in the judiciary, science and technology, or in "humanity and ordinary human experiences" (Bayda, 1980-81: 10). We find ourselves back, full circle, to a "disinterested investigation of the facts pertinent to the subject" (Bayda, 1980-81: 11), as though this was all self-evident. We are back at the objective experts even though we started from a position where objectivity was impossible. With this clear ideological orientation, based largely on denial rather than on analysis of normative and other issues pertaining to inquiries, it is amazing that Bayda can end by saying "that both sides of the issue" must be "properly represented and presented" (Bayda, 1980-81: 11).

Finally, the systematic bias shown in Bayda's analysis of the adequacy of his inquiry was apparent in the *Final Report* of the CLBI. For starters, the preface outlines Bayda's view of the opponents and proponents:

> Who are the opponents and who are the proponents? On the world level, opponents include some pre-eminent scientists although in fairness one should add that most are not nuclear scientists. They include existing organizations such as church groups and also groups especially established to combat the spread of nuclear energy. We do not know the composition of those groups outside Saskatchewan. Within Saskatchewan, the average opponent who appeared at the formal and southern local hearings before us would be under 30 years of age, with some recent university training, articulate, intelligent, sincere, idealistic, and who is a political activist and is committed to his view of human betterment. To be sure, not all fit each part of this description; in fact, some do not even remotely resemble the average. They are, however, the exceptions. The proponents, on their side, count most of the pre-eminent nuclear scientists in the world as well as many in other fields. We do not know the profile of the average proponent outside Saskatchewan. Within the province, and judging by those who appeared before us at the southern local hearings (at which they were in the minority), the proponents were older than the opponents, appeared to be established in their respective fields of endeavor, and practical in their approach. The proponents also include those persons who work in the various segments of the nuclear industry, both in the governmental and the private sectors. (Bayda, 1978: 2)

Let me end by asking: Is this not merely a description of the powerless and powerful styles of presenting evidence?

This chapter appeared initially in D. Currie and B. MacLean, eds., The Administration of Justice. *Saskatoon: Social Research Unit, University of Saskatchewan, 1986.*

Chapter Seven

"Sociologically Speaking": Law, Sexuality, and Social Change
Didi Herman

Historically, legal discourse affirms the apparent naturalness of the heterosexual family, contributing to the invisibility of the social processes that privilege heterosexuality. For this reason, litigation has been, and continues to be, a significant site of discursive and ideological struggle for gay men and lesbian women. In this chapter, Didi Herman explores a number of issues that surround this struggle. Asserting that the naturalization of heterosexuality in law and the invisibility of this process of naturalization are the result, in part, of the delegitimation of knowledge that challenges the 'truth' of law, Herman raises a number of important questions. For example, how resistant is legal discourse to external sources of knowledge? What is the relationship between meaning and truth in law? How does liberalism constitute sexual identities? In an attempt to begin to answer these questions, Herman examines aspects of the Mossop case.

After attending the funeral of his homosexual partner's father, Brian Mossop, a federal employee, applied to have his absence from work considered as 'bereavement leave' under the collective agreement. When this was denied, Mossop laid a complaint under the Canadian Human Rights Act, alleging that the collective agreement violated the 'family status' prohibited ground of discrimination of the act. The adjudicator for the Human Rights Tribunal found discrimination and subsequently ordered compensation and redress. Specifically, she concluded that Mossop lived in a 'familial relation.' When this decision was appealed, establishing the legal meaning of 'family' became an important point of jurisdictional struggle between the Tribunal and the Court of Appeal. Above all else, Mossop fundamentally challenged traditional definitions by bringing sociological feminist knowledge into the courtroom.

The Tribunal began by establishing that there is no consensus or standard definition for the constantly evolving notion of 'family.' Noting that the law does not always reflect how people live, and that simply because a relationship has not

Didi Herman is a Postgraduate Student at the University of Warwick

been heretofore recognized in law does not mean that it should not now be, the Tribunal adjudicator minimized the relevance of current legal provisions specifically based on opposite-sexed relations. The Court of Appeal, on the other hand, did not find the meaning of family so uncertain, unclear, and equivocal that it cannot be defined. In particular, the 'sociological approach' was argued to have missed the essence of the concept. The Court brought to the fore what it claimed was the real issue: sexual orientation. This strategy, in the final analysis, acted to maintain the status quo, all-the-while obscuring how alternative discourses embodying oppositional ideologies are structured out of the legal process.

INTRODUCTION

In June 1990, the Federal Court of Appeal reversed the findings of a Canadian Human Rights Tribunal in the case of *A.G.* v *Mossop*.[1] Both the decisions of the Tribunal and of the Federal Court have been the subjects of intense conflict and comment — not only within the confines of legal academe, but also throughout many sectors of society generally. In fact, the litigation itself has been and continues to be a significant site of discursive and ideological struggle for many people.[2] Mossop is, first and foremost, a piece of 'gay rights' litigation. It has been taken up as such by lesbian and gay communities, as well as by Canadian human rights organizations; it has been opposed as such by diverse religious and political forces.[3] This chapter highlights certain aspects of this struggle and comments upon possible implications of the decisions themselves.

A discussion of the legal arguments and a reading of the legal texts connected to the case, using various approaches to the study of law, particularly 'law and ideology'[4] and 'discourse theory,'[5] can reveal some of the politics embedded in law. The 'struggle' is the one between two forums of adjudication, the Human Rights Tribunal (HRT) and the Federal Court of Appeal (FCA). The analysis, I hope, will raise and begin to provide answers to some questions central to feminist legal theory. For example, how resistant is legal discourse to external sources of knowledge? What is the relationship between meaning and truth in law? How does legal liberalism constitute sexual identities? How are lesbian and gay rights claims subjugated to the imperatives of a capitalist economy? And, ultimately, what are the implications of this particular piece of litigation for a feminist theory of heterosexuality?[6]

BACKGROUND

The process of deciding which elements of a situation constitute the 'facts of the case' is itself an ideological one. The 'version' I report here is taken from the sections of the Tribunal and Appeal decisions described as "circumstances giving rise to the complaint" and "the factual context" respectively.

Brian Mossop worked for the federal government (Treasury Board) as a translator. As a federal civil servant his employment conditions were regulated by both a collective agreement and the *Canadian Human Rights Act*.[7] In the spring of 1985, the father of Mossop's partner died. Mossop attended the funeral and subsequently applied to have his absence from work considered as 'bereavement leave' under the collective agreement, specifically stating that his lover was male. The application was denied by the employer on the grounds that his relationship did not fall within the category covered by the bereavement leave provision. With the support of his union, Mossop filed a grievance, which was rejected. He then laid a complaint under the *Canadian Human Rights Act*, which the Human Rights Tribunal at first instance adjudicated. The complaint alleged that the collective agreement violated the 'family status' prohibited ground of discrimination in section 3 (1) of the *Act*.

Significantly, the Federal Court of Appeal reordered the 'Facts' as presented by the Tribunal judgment. In the Tribunal judgment, the reader is told that Mossop's lover is male in the seventh paragraph (2.3). It is not until the third page of the decision that one learns of the details of the relationship (for example, that they owned a house jointly) (para 2.13). In contrast, in the FCA decision Marceau J. informs us in the third paragraph of his judgment that Mossop lived in a "homosexual relationship," at which point he also gives details of the partnership. Marceau does not refer to the two men as lovers; he does state that they "represented themselves as lovers" (664). These initial statements both anticipate the subsequent analysis and signal each forum's articulation of the complaint. For the Human Rights Tribunal, Mossop is a federal employee first, a gay man second. For the Federal Court of Appeal, this is reversed.

MOSSOP'S ARGUMENT

The crux of Mossop's argument was that the collective agreement contravened the *Human Rights Act* on the ground of 'family status.' The agreement provided bereavement leave for 'immediate family,' including common-law couples of the 'opposite sex' (although not necessarily married), mothers- and fathers-in-law, etc. Mossop argued that this definition, and the resulting exclusion of same-sexed families, constituted discrimination under the 'family status' ground in the *Canadian Human Rights Act*.[8] His case depended upon the acceptance of his relationship with his partner being defined as 'family' for purposes of the *Act*. The main evidence supporting this contention was the testimony of sociologist Margrit Eichler, who maintained that there was no one definition of family, that some general characteristics of families could be delineated (such as co-habitation, sharing in domestic arrangements, presence of emotional and sexual reliance, joint ownerships) and that it was better to describe relations as 'familial' than as 'family.'[9] Her conclusion, based on Mossop and his partner exhibiting most of these characteristics, was that Mossop lived in a 'familial relationship.'

The adjudicator for the Human Rights Tribunal, M. E. Atcheson, adopted this view to support her finding of discrimination and her subsequent compensation and redress order. And this perspective on family became a significant site of struggle between the Tribunal and the Court of Appeal, both in terms of its form — as 'sociology' — and in its content. I will turn to this aspect of the case shortly; first I will draw out a related theme of the judgments, the formal or technical battles between the two forums.

WHO KNOWS LAW BEST ?
Issues of Jurisdiction and Statutory Interpretation

The decisions of the Tribunal and Court of Appeal in *Mossop* reflect the historical tension between these two forums of adjudication — human rights tribunals and the courts. Issues of jurisdiction and approach to statutory interpretation overlay other elements in the case, and both forums manipulate formal questions towards their substantive ends. It is thus important to view the extent to which the Court of Appeal discredits the 'sociology' of the Tribunal, as related to the judicial attack on the Tribunal's credibility generally.

Atcheson takes pains at the outset of her decision to establish the Tribunal's authority. While this is not unusual, the text seems particularly defensive, as if she anticipates judicial undermining. She notes that the authority of the Tribunal to "interpret family status" was "unchallenged" by counsel for the attorney-general, and the adjudicator quotes extensively from judgments supporting tribunal jurisdiction (paras 4.3; 4.10).

In contrast, in the Federal Court of Appeal Marceau attempts to minimize the ability of tribunals to deal properly with matters of law.[10] He distinguishes them from labour arbitration panels, which are protected from certain aspects of judicial review by a 'privity clause' limiting the jurisdiction of the courts (671). However, his dominant strategy of discreditation involves a more subtle use of language. He speaks about the Tribunal as one might of an impulsive, perhaps irresponsible, child. Marceau calls Atcheson's findings "precipitous" (669), and he laments her "quick conclusions" (671) arrived at with "no analysis" (670).

The Court's *coup de grâce* is its explicit accusation that the Tribunal missed the point. According to Marceau, the Tribunal was unable to "recognize" the "fundamental foundations" of the complaint, which were, he tells us, not about "family" at all, but about "spousal status" and, more "fundamentally," "sexual orientation" (675-6). Thus, Marceau invokes the spectre of homosexuality (previously signalled in his opening paragraphs), which he obviously feels Atcheson too neatly avoided.

A further point of conflict between the two forums concerns rules of statutory interpretation. The Tribunal quotes at length from judgments extolling the virtues of a liberal interpretation (see paras 4.14; 4.15; 4.16; 4.48). The Court, on the other hand, argues that the *Act* should be interpreted strictly, with reference to the intent of the drafters and the pre-eminence of parliamentary authority (672-3; 675; 677-8; and, Stone's concurring reasons, 679).

Marceau employs a number of other 'tricks of the trade,' such as reaching negative findings on 'secondary issues.' For example, despite Atcheson's quotations from Mossop's own testimony, Marceau chooses to ignore this evidence of emotional harm to the complainant and finds there was none. Another 'secondary issue' is his finding that bereavement leave was not an 'employment opportunity' under the *Act* (670); unfortunately for him, he cannot decide the case on this basis because no one made this argument.[11] The process by which judges define certain issues as 'secondary' is one that has political implications. On the one hand, this process constitutes — as I have argued — a 'trick' whereby judges, usually through simple assertion, tell us what is more and less significant about a case. In this way, issues that might muddle their substantive agenda are pushed to the margins. On the other hand, this methodological device is also a political tool. For example, the finding on 'harm' reveals the Court's minimization of personal experience as a source of judicial knowledge.[12] Marceau also distinguishes human rights codes from the *Charter of Rights and Freedoms*. The effects of the *Charter*, he argues, are contained by Section 1, which, by allowing legislation to be saved despite its contravention of *Charter* provisions, operates as a mechanism of restraint (677). The Court also invokes the 'slippery slope' spectre. A familiar friend of conservatives, this notion is employed by Marceau to suggest that, if the Tribunal is correct, employees could claim the bereavement leave benefit to attend any old funeral (674).[13]

These jurisdictional and interpretive debates permeate the two primary anatogisms of the decisions: how legal meanings are discovered and, related to this, the distinction between 'law' and 'sociology.'

Meaning and Truth in Law

The concept in need of definition in *Mossop* is 'family.' The Tribunal begins by establishing a lack of "standard definition" and "consensus" with respect to the "evolving" concept of family (paras 4.7; 4.5). Atcheson searches for sources of meaning, and she finds that the parliamentary record is of little assistance because the justice minister responsible at the time simply commented on what the concept "should mean, or might mean, as opposed to what it did mean" (para 4.56). Her response to the attorney-general's argument that "the" meaning was "generally understood" is that counsel adduced no evidence to support this contention and, further, that general understandings may be discriminatory and therefore not a valid source of meaning (para 4.59). Atcheson also notes that law does not always reflect how people live, and that simply because a relationship has not been heretofore recognized in law does not mean it should not be now (para 4.61). She thereby minimizes the relevance of current legal provisions specifically based on 'opposite sex' relations (para 4.61). The Tribunal adjudicator concludes that the term 'family status' is not "clear and unambiguous." Dictionary definitions, she adds, may be reasonably consistent but they are broad and allow for non-marital and non-biological relations (para 4.63). The Tribunal need not select "the all-inclusive meaning" but, rather, "a" "reasonable" meaning, one that "*best accords with the Act* " (para 4.67, emphasis in original).

Atcheson's final act of interpretation in this process is to find that the term 'reasonable' is itself fluid, "impossible of measurement" (para 4.70).

She then puts aside any formal 'test of reasonableness':

> As a practical matter, the Tribunal agrees with the Complainant that terms should not be confined to their historical roots, but must be tested in today's world, against an understanding of how people are living and how language reflects reality. Dr Eichler's evidence, as well as that of the Complainant, was helpful in making these assessments. Value judgments should play no part in this process because they may operate to favour a view of the world as it might be preferred over the world as it is. (para 4.70)[14]

How then, does the Court of Appeal respond to this view of meaning? According to Marceau:

> There is no doubt that the courts, in giving effect to the provisions of human rights legislation, should act as liberally and as 'bravely' as possible, bearing in mind that are [sic] often at stake are the interest of 'unpopular' groups which must be defended from majoritarian opinions. But I believe that if the courts were to adopt, in interpreting human rights acts, a "living-tree" approach towards discerning new grounds of discrimination for proscription, or re-defining past meanings given to existing grounds, they would step outside the scope of their constitutional responsibilities and usurp the function of parliament. (673)

"Family," Marceau continues, does not have a meaning "so uncertain, unclear and equivocal" that it cannot be defined (673). The word signifies a "basic concept" that has "always been" (673). Non-biological formations have been rendered "normal" through marriage and other legal mechanisms, but these do not affect the "core meaning" of the word (673). Other meanings are described as "peripheral," "residual" "analogical uses" (673).

Family, according to Marceau, is not a "fluid term." As noted, he maintains that the 'sociological approach' has missed the "essence of the concept" (675). There is a "generally understood meaning to the word 'family' " (675). This last point is legitimated through the judicial strategy of 'commonsense knowledge.' Phrases such as "generally seen," "no one would want," or "generally understood" are employed to persuade the reader of the 'normalcy' of the judge's views (673-5). This contrasts sharply with the Tribunal's explicit critique of such understandings as potentially discriminatory. The Court then concludes its discussion of the meaning of 'family status,' turning its attention to the "real issue underlying the complaint," sexual orientation (675).[15] The Court disposes of the 'real issue' by finding that although sexual orientation might be an analogous ground under Section 15, the *Charter* cannot be used as a "legislative amendment machine" to be read into human rights legislation (676).[16] Only parliament can legislate the inclusion of sexual orientation in the *Canadian Human Rights Act* (675-8).

How these texts constitute their subjects is also of interest. For the Tribunal, the subject of the complaint began and ended with the meaning of 'family.' The question to be decided was whether or not Mossop and his partner constituted a 'family.' If so, they were clearly being discriminated against on 'family status' grounds as their "kind of family" (as Marceau later put it) was being denied a benefit given to others. Once having determined that they were a family "sociologically speaking," there was little else to adjudicate (other than to diffuse the arguments of the attorney-general). The Tribunal is clearly not concerned with 'homosexuality' per se, but only its manifestation in a category called 'same-sex couple.' In fact, the entire Tribunal judgment functions to render sexuality itself invisible.

The judges of the Federal Court of Appeal refuse to allow this line of argumentation. Their subject is indeed 'the homosexual,' who according to their interpretation is the 'real issue' missed by the Tribunal. Marceau insists that it is 'sexual orientation' that lies at the root of the complaint; his strategy of conservative judicial constraint allows him to maintain the status quo of exclusion.[17]

THE 'SOCIOLOGY OF LAW' ?

One of the first steps taken by the Tribunal adjudicator in her decision is to establish the authority of the 'expert witness,' Margrit Eichler, upon whose testimony the judgment rests. While the 'expert's' qualifications are often briefly reviewed in reasons for judgment, in this case Eichler's academic and professional history is detailed. The reader is informed not only that Eichler holds a doctorate in sociology and is a 'full' professor at the Ontario Institute for Studies in Education, but also that she holds two cross-appointments, has received "numerous research and development grants," and "has published extensively." We also learn that she has written the only existing textbook of 'families' in Canada and that she provides consultation services to a host of public and private bodies (para 4.4).

The Tribunal then reiterates Eichler's perspective on family. Atcheson refers to her model as the 'functional approach' (para 4.18). At one point, the adjudicator notes that counsel for the attorney-general has urged her to "not consider a sociological approach to meaning, but only the plain meaning itself" (para 4.26). However, Atcheson attempts throughout the decision to underscore the *compatibility* of law and sociology: "The evidence of Dr Eichler was that the term does not have one definition for all purposes. Sociology and law appear to be similar in this regard" (para 4.65).

The Federal Court of Appeal, on the other hand, makes every effort to distance law from sociology. "Status," Marceau comments, is a "legal concept" — implying that it is not a sociological one (674). The "functional definition given by the sociological approach" is not "acceptable." Marceau misunderstands the sociology he is criticizing, arguing that the "functional approach" has simply taken "some attributes usually ascribed to families" as being "the essence of the concept itself being signified." Eichler, of course, had specifically maintained that family could not be reduced to the notion of an essence. At times, the Court of Appeal is quite derisive. Although the Tribunal had decided that Mossop and his lover constitute "sociologically speaking a sort of family," Marceau argued that *no* approach "other than the legal one" could lead to a proper understanding of what is meant by the phrase 'family status' (674). This is because law is science, sociology is "ad hoc" (674). Marceau refers to Eichler not as ar. 'expert witness,' but as "the expert sociologist" (676).

One of the most significant aspects of law's power is its claim to Truth, the ways in which "law sets itself above other knowledges" (Smart, 1989). Through deconstruction of law as 'Truth' Smart reveals the process by which certain knowledges are either translated into *legal* knowledge or excluded altogether. In the process, law claims to stand "outside the social order," able to reflect and offer objective comment upon the world before it (Smart, 1989).[18] While courts will often acknowledge the range of views contained 'out there,' they nevertheless see their task as one of choosing 'the right' answer for the question posed by the particular piece of litigation before them. The resources they draw upon in this truth-seeking mission reveal the process by which certain knowledge sources are validated, others excluded. External knowledges that *are* considered will be subject to a process of legalization that can serve to render them pale imitations of themselves.

An illustration of this process can be found in a U.S. case decided a few years ago, which became the subject of extensive feminist debate. In the case of *E.E.O.C. (Equal Employment Opportunity Commission)* v *Sears, Roebuck & Co.*,[19] the question of feminist history as knowledge was put before the courts. Here two feminist historians appeared as 'expert witnesses,' for opposing sides. Rosalind Rosenberg, testifying for the employer, argued that women internalized the 'cult of domesticity' and thus did not share men's aspiration to sales positions associated with high commissions. Alice Kessler-Harris testified for the Equal Employment Opportunity Commission that women have always performed non-traditional labour but are kept from higher paying positions because of institutional discrimination.[20] It was not the result of this case (which favoured the employer), however, that occasioned feminist (and other) comment, so much as it was the role played by each expert witness, as well as that of 'women's history' itself in such cases.

The 'Expert' Witness

Alice Kessler-Harris has documented her experience as a witness for the Commission (see Kessler-Harris, 1987). Her article is primarily a defence of her theoretical position; however, it is also a fascinating account of a feminist 'expert witness' at trial. Kessler-Harris describes how she was asked by the Commission to testify because Sears had a feminist historian appearing for its side, and she notes how becoming involved in an adversarial process distorts the craft that historians practise (1987: 42, 52). She further reflects on how difficult it was to present a "nuanced historical argument" in court:

> One intuits the difference between working in a library and participating in a courtroom drama, but until one has experienced it, the disjunction between the two remains abstract. Accustomed to developing the subtle

distinctions of an argument, to negotiating about fine points of interpretation, the historian quickly discovers that these skills must be abandoned in
testifying. Maintaining a position is as important as the position taken.
Consistency is not merely a virtue but evidence of one's expertise.... I got
my first taste of the clear distinction made by the legal profession between
learning the truth and constructing a case; between understanding and
persuading. And there, I also learned for the first time, that precisely what
I as a historian cared most about would surely destroy my testimony if I
pursued it. My job, I was told, was to answer all questions, but to provide
no more information than was demanded.... Any attempt I made to
introduce controversy, disagreement and analysis merely revealed that
history was an uncertain tool and invalidated both its findings and my
conclusions.... I found myself constructing a rebuttal in which subtlety and
nuance were omitted, and in which evidence was marshalled to make a
point while complexities and exceptions vanished from sight. (1987:61; see
also 55)

Kessler-Harris expresses "surprise" at how the lawyer for Sears often did
not challenge the substance of her testimony but, rather, the language in
which it was phrased — a tactic that often resulted in her comments being
presented as absurd or extreme. The structure of 'yes' or 'no' answers also
complicated her testimony: "I was nevertheless astonished at how easy it
was, within the yes or no format demanded by the court, to agree with
statements simply because I could not deny them, not because they
represented my understanding of the issues involved" (1987: 64). Here
one can see how feminist discourse is structured out of litigation at the
hearing stage. Only judges have authority and 'expertise' to inquire into
shades of meaning: Witnesses must simply make bald, uncomplicated
statements. What, then, did the judges in this case do with the feminist
historical testimony before them as 'evidence'?

There were two decisions in *Sears*, the first at Illinois District Court, the
second at the Court of Appeals. In the initial judgment, the District Court
judge issued an 89-page decision in favour of the employer, Sears Roebuck
and Company. The bulk of the ruling condemns the E.E.O.C.'s statistical
evidence and lack of direct-witness testimony of discrimination. Under a
section entitled "Other Evidence of Interest," the judge devotes four
paragraphs and three footnotes to the court appearances of the feminist
historians (1314-15).

In the District Court judge's words, Kessler-Harris's testimony consisted of "bald assertions" with "little persuasive authority" (1314, fn 63).
Kessler-Harris and two other E.E.O.C. witnesses are accused of making
"sweeping generalizations" from "isolated examples," focusing on "small
groups of unusual women" (1314). The judge acknowledges that "some"
women have always worked in non-traditional fields, but states that this
is not at issue because the case at hand is concerned with the history and
practices of the Sears company.[21] Rosenberg, on the other hand, gave
"convincing" testimony with "reasonable conclusions" (1315). While
discussion of Rosenberg's testimony takes up no more than one paragraph
of the decision, the District Court judge clearly uses her conclusions to

attack the basis of the E.E.O.C.'s statistical evidence:

> In conclusion, E.E.O.C.'s statistical analyses are dependent upon the crucial arbitrary assumption that men and women are equally interested in commission sales at Sears.... The E.E.O.C. has provided nothing more than unsupported generalizations by expert witnesses with no knowledge of Sears to support that assumption.... All the evidence presented by Sears indicates that men are at least two times more interested in commission selling than women. (1315)

It is in these four paragraphs, then, that the judge lays the foundation for the attack on E.E.O.C.'s statistics; however, he does so casually, barely giving consideration to the actual evidence submitted by *either* historian. He certainly does not begin to engage in the discussion about women's agency and the problematizing of 'interests' that animated the resulting feminist debate.[22] The actual space given to their comments indicates the relative insignificance the judge attaches to this evidence, compared to other evidence. Yet the historians' evidence was not inconsequential; Rosenberg's testimony gave the judge an extra tool he could use to chisel away at the E.E.O.C.'s case.

In the Circuit Court of Appeal decision neither historian is mentioned by name, nor is their testimony referred to in any explicit way. In one paragraph (of the 58-page majority judgment), the 7th Circuit Court of Appeal affirms the District Court's view of women's interests (321). The 'experts' that really concern the Court of Appeal are the statisticians: Their testimony receives plenty of consideration. The one dissenting voice argues that the notion that women were never "interested" in commission sales jobs is unpersuasive, although the judge never refers to the evidence given by Kessler-Harris directly (360-2).

It is interesting, then, that the judgments in this case, which occasioned so much feminist comment and distress, for the most part ignored both the appearance of the historians and the primary intellectual debate they were engaged in. This 'invisibility' of feminist discourse and presence is one way in which the legal process excludes other voices at the final stage of judgment. Not only was Kessler-Harris's historical scholarship rendered absurd at the hearing stage, but the courts hardly cared about it anyway. Many feminists became enraged at the *Sears* process and result, yet the roles of *both* historians (*vis à vis* the decision) were minimal. In *Sears* one can see a range of issues relevant to *Mossop*, including the validity of knowledge outside law, the role of feminist 'experts' in litigation, and the subversion by law and legal process of feminist discourse. All in all, it is clear that feminists take the law more seriously than the law takes them.

In Canada a similar pattern emerges in a recent 'lesbian rights' case, *Karen Andrews v Ontario (Minister of Health)*.[23] In support of the lesbian complainant, a number of affidavits were filed. Three of these were from sociologists: Margrit Eichler (a familiar participant); Marianna Valverde; and Barry Adam (the latter two also being active in lesbian and gay theorization and politics). Margrit Eichler was called upon to testify, as she was in *Mossop*. Her experience in cross-examination must have been remarkably similar to that of Kessler-Harris in *Sears*. The 'nuances' of her approach were structured out of the testimony, her 'yes' and 'no' answers indicating agreement with statements by counsel for the attorney-general because — as Kessler-Harris put it — she could not deny them, not because they represented her understanding of the issues involved. What, then, became of Eichler's testimony? In his Ontario Supreme Court reasons for decision in *Karen Andrews*, McRae J. neglected to mention that the evidence by Eichler had been presented, let alone give it consideration. Instead, he consulted a number of dictionaries and a few legal precedents.[24] Eichler's entire participation is rendered completely invisible in the reported decision.[25] In *Mossop*, the Federal Court attacks her testimony head-on. Marceau also cites a number of cases, as courts are supposed to do, but does not actually rely upon any of them at all (see, for example, 671-2). Thus, the 'legal' sources called upon by the courts provide little guidance to them; as repositories of knowledge these precedents appear to fail miserably. Yet, despite this, other discourses are at best ignored, at worst derided — the effect in either case being exclusion.

By examining the various characteristics of legal discourse as represented in *Mossop*, as well as in the *Sears* and *Karen Andrews* cases, and in highlighting certain aspects of 'legal method,' the diverse techniques that have historically constituted 'legal reasoning,' we can see that this method incorporates devices that enable and facilitate accompanying substantive analyses. Its form, consisting of a series of (constrained) choices, is thus political. The legal discourse validates and excludes knowledge, and the process through which legal Truth is sought entrenches the 'power of law' (Smart, 1989). Still, this is an arena of struggle: In *Mossop*, two forums adopt very different approaches.

As we shall see, an ideological analysis of law maintains that legal discourse is not autonomous from the social relations that produce it. The dominant ideologies of legal discourse will be those that are dominant in the social formation.[26] Thus, 'subjects,' 'knowledge,' 'truth,' and so on are constituted by both the distinctive features of 'law as discourse' and the ideologies embedded within and transmitted by this discourse.

IDEOLOGIES
Liberal Ideology

By liberalism, I mean to describe a political ideology that is also, at times, a social theory. As manifested in legal discourse, liberalism contains a number of elementary principles, the most significant of which for our purposes are equality (as embodied by 'rights'), neutrality, and the supremacy of capitalist market relations (Dworkin, 1984; Sagoff, 1983; MacNeil, 1989; Sandel, 1982, 1984). The liberal model of society is a pluralist one, in which interest groups attempt to realize their goals under the auspices of a neutral state that interferes as little as possible, but will do so when necessary. Judges are 'neutral arbiters' who facilitate market freedom and individual protection (from majoritarian domination) through a value-free adjudication process.

In *Mossop*, Tribunal adjudicator Acheson's dilemma is that of the progressive liberal. She is faced with a case in which the 'law as it is' does not 'go the way' that she wants (see Kennedy, 1987). She must, therefore, develop a strategy that allows her to ignore the range of prior cases and legislative provisions that clearly do *not* help Brian Mossop. In the process, she articulates a broad liberal ideology that allows her to override and trivialize what has heretofore stood as 'precedent' on the issue of homosexuality. There is really no basis 'in law' for her decision — she must actively create new law *and rely on other sources of knowledge* to support her finding of discrimination.

The Tribunal sees its task as one of performing 'value-free' adjudication, not imposing any conception of 'the good life' upon litigants (para 4.70; see Dworkin, 1984). The Tribunal's society is a pluralist one, in which the role of adjudicators is to protect the minority from 'majoritarian' authority. No one group should have the power to impose its morality on another, all people are equal and are due equal rights and benefits.[27] Here the 'same sex couple' is *equal to* or *the same as* the heterosexual couple. Heterosexuality remains unchallenged, represented instead as the unproblematic norm. This approach has been extensively explored as the 'sameness/difference' debate in feminist legal theory.[28] The Tribunal adopts a 'same as' approach to counter the usual 'different than' analysis exhibited in earlier cases on sexual orientation (see Herman, 1990: 793-5). At the same time as excluding this conservative ideology, an oppositional feminist analysis of sexuality is precluded, one that would posit *heterosexuality* as the problematic and could insist on the radical politics of lesbianism.[29] These 'sameness' principles are what have animated Canadian liberal human rights law in recent years. However, these same principles have not yet been extended to the legal treatment of homosexuality. It is this failure of law, both judge-made and statutory (with some exceptions), that compels the Tribunal to rely on the insights of sociology. Legal liberalism does not go its way on this one.

Two other recent cases, on similar themes, also exhibit some of these elements of liberal ideology. The Trial Division of the Federal Court declared in *Veysey* that sexual orientation was an analogous ground under section 15 of the *Charter*.[30] Sexual orientation, the Court stated, fulfilled the requirements of *Andrews* v *Law Society (B.C.)* [31] in that both immutability and a history of prejudice were present (79). Echoing the *Mossop* Tribunal views, Dube J. argued that: "The purpose of these proceedings is not to pass moral judgment on sexual orientation, but to decide whether or not the rights of the applicant have been violated under s.15 of the *Charter* (79).

The separation of 'law' and 'morality' is made abundantly clear. Additionally, the Court refers on more than one occasion to Veysey's relationship with his partner being "his most supportive relationship" (75, 79). Dube J. goes on to find the discrimination unjustifiable under section 1, always assuming 'equality' between heterosexual and homosexual relationships, never mentioning the reasons why policies are 'heterosexuals only,' reasons consistently invoked by conservative judges.

The British Columbia Supreme Court judgment in *Brown* reveals a similar ideological approach.[32] Although the plaintiffs were denied relief, Coultas J.'s sympathy with them and his implicit condemnation of the moralistic conservatism of the Social Credit government are apparent:

> The history of western civilisation records that from biblical times to our own, homosexuals have been subjected to discrimination because of their sexual orientation. As with other forms of discrimination, it is unjust for it fails to take into account individual merit, character or accomplishment. The form and extent of it is uglier, the cry more shrill since the onset of AIDS. I accept that those who suffer HIV or AIDS, often very ill, are discriminated against and persecuted in various subtle ways, and some not so subtle at all. (309)

The comments of the B.C. health minister are characterized as "unnecessary, inflammatory, and reflecting ignorance of the disease that one would not expect" (311). Coultas J.'s concluding comments perhaps exemplify the best that liberal law has to offer: "I have found that the funding policy does not contravene the law. Nevertheless, I recognize that AIDS is one of the great tragedies of our age. It behoves those in private life and in government, whose actions affect the well-being of those suffering the disease to act decently, fairly, compassionately" (322). Coultas J. gives the impression here of someone who feels their hands are tied by the wording and existing interpretations of the *Charter*. His decision is thus more clearly an example of how judges are constrained than is the Tribunal ruling in *Mossop*, in which Atcheson virtually ignores the law that does not go her way.

The initial decisions in *Mossop*, *Veysey*, and *Brown* all reveal liberalism as their dominant ideology. Interestingly, in *Brown* the gay plaintiff's claims were rejected, in *Veysey* the decision was affirmed on administrative law grounds by the Federal Court of Appeal, and in *Mossop* a favourable decision was overturned by the same court. In no case did the litigants ultimately win on the 'merits' of the case they argued.

Conservative Ideology

The ideological bias of the *Mossop* Federal Court decision is not as easily discernible. The Court is primarily concerned with 'debunking' sociology (not in itself an endeavour free of ideology) and finding (and disposing of) the 'real issue.' Yet in his discussion of the relationship between the *Charter* and human rights legislation, Marceau J.'s politics come to the fore.

In the FCA's discussion of how section 15 cannot be read into human rights enactments, Marceau clearly expresses himself as a protector of the private sector:

> For one thing, human rights codes impact on areas of the private sector of economic life which are not readily seen to fall within the scope of the *Charter*. It may well be that the legislators who entrenched the *Charter* were willing to impose a more demanding standard of conduct on themselves and on the executive than they would have decided to impose on the population at large ... the *Charter* [does not] purport to restructure the

global juristic background against which all private ordering takes place. (676)

First, either this point is simply one of principle, having no bearing on the case at hand, or Marceau has completely lost track of what he is doing. The *Canadian Human Rights Act*, which is, after all, the statute being considered here, applies to the federal government as employer; it has nothing to do with the private sector (as other codes do). The FCA is protecting the freedom of private economic ordering in a case that has nothing *directly* to do with this. The Court is, therefore, engaging in a rhetorical strategy to persuade other courts dealing with codes that *do* apply to the private sector to follow its lead. However, the rhetorical use of this argument suggests that it is applicable to the case at hand.

Second, it must be kept in mind that what we know about Marceau's political ideology up to this point can only be discerned from his use of classically conservative interpretive techniques (such as 'strict construction' and 'original intent'); by how he constitutes the 'facts' and the 'real issue'; and by his less-than-subtle affirmation of the naturalness of traditional family forms (and heterosexuality). His economic philosophy could fit either classical liberal or conservative ideology.

Some of the points Marceau J. might have liked to make, but refrained from so doing, were made by McCrae J. in *Karen Andrews*. McCrae J. based his findings that a 'homosexual partner' could not be a 'spouse' on the 'fact' that homosexuals were unable to marry and procreate (193).[33] In his section 1 analysis (which he went through despite finding no analogous ground and no discrimination), he argued that the government's definition of 'spouse' was related to the important objective of "establishing and maintaining traditional families" (194). In *Mossop*, Marceau J. is never quite this explicit, although these views are certainly implied within his search for the meaning of 'family.'

Summary

What, then, does conservative law have to say about lesbian and gay existence and the role of law? It would seem that it is the conservative approach that most clearly reveals the role of law as envisaged by Marxist instrumentalists. For Marceau and McCrae, the law must maintain the status quo, it must not be used as a weapon of social change, and it must reflect the values and morals of patriarchal capitalism. These judges exhibit a 'small-minded' worldview, and they claim this view as representative of the 'common folks' common sense.' They avail themselves of various conservative judicial techniques to underpin their decisions.

What do liberal ideologies say about lesbians, gays, and the law? On the one hand, the initial judgments in the three cases signal an increased willingness on the part of legal decision-makers to approach 'sexual orientation' liberally and not to impose conservative moralism. Law must be value-neutral, and all people are deserving of respect and equality. On the other hand, *Brown* reveals the limits to *Charter* litigation with respect to achieving real improvements in the lives of people with AIDS, despite the liberal discourse. *Mossop* reveals the temporality of a legal victory, and *Veysey* also does not go a long way towards inspiring optimism.

CONCLUSIONS

I want to conclude by commenting on the possible implications of *Mossop* and other recent lesbian and gay rights cases for feminist theories of heterosexuality. It would seem to be extremely difficult to problematize heterosexuality within both legal discourse and dominant legal ideologies. On the one hand, the characteristics of legal discourse render it relatively impervious to external sources of knowledge. Not only is feminist theory itself marginalized, but so is experiential testimony, which is, in itself, a central epistemological basis of much feminist theory. Law's search for a fixed 'Truth' similarly serves to uncomplicate meaning, obscuring both how meanings are chosen and how these choices legitimize gender relations of power. However, I have also shown that this is an arena of struggle; non-legal discourses do make incursions into legal territory from time to time.[34]

On the level of ideology, the ideologies dominant in legal discourse are ones that fail to respond to feminist concerns. Neither conservative nor liberal ideologies problematize masculinity, patriarchal relations, or heterosexuality. Ultimately, recent cases in this area tell us that there is a discursive struggle going on between liberals and conservatives, that lower-level forums are likely to be more liberal,[35] and that both direct benefits and symbolic gains are few and far between. What is also apparent is how *alternative* discourses, embodying *oppositional* ideologies, are structured out of the legal process. There is no room for arguing a radical politics of sexuality, the choices are liberal or conservative only, and radical discourse will be subverted and altered beyond recognition. In the process, oppositional ideologies — ones that question male domination, heterosexuality, capitalism, and so on — will also be left to picket signs on the courthouse steps.

Perhaps this analysis of law is overly pessimistic. Many might argue, among other things, that the few tangible benefits gained are important first steps, that lesbian and gay rights litigation is partially responsible for prompting statutory initiatives such as those currently being proposed in Ontario, and that, through legal struggle, lesbian and gay communities are politicized and strengthened. Elsewhere, I have explored some of these issues with respect to the concept of rights (Herman, 1990). Here I have examined the discourses and ideologies within several legal texts to show that judicial process does not treat all knowledge equally but, rather, privileges certain ways of understanding social relations above others. However, legal texts are not homogeneous and I hope to have revealed the tensions that exist at different points in this process. Thus, while certain judges and courts articulate conservative ideologies and the pre-eminence of legal discourse, other approaches use external discourses within a liberal attempt to make law more responsive to humanitarian values. Nevertheless, even this liberal approach has its limitations. Finally, I have offered a tentative assessment of some of the possible implications of this analysis for feminist theory. I hope that through such a process, we can deepen our understanding of the relationship between law, sexuality, and social change.

Reprinted with permission from The Journal of Human Justice, *Vol. 2, No. 2 (Spring) 1991. The chapter is part of a larger work in progress exploring the relationship between the Canadian lesbian and gay rights movement, feminism, and law. I would like to thank Davina Cooper, Marlee Kline, and Carol Smart for their helpful comments on an earlier draft.*

NOTES

1. The Tribunal decision is indexed as *Mossop* v *Department of Secretary of State et al.* (1989) 89 C.L.L.C. 16, 041. Further references to this decision will be by paragraph number in the text. The Appeal decision is indexed as *Canada (A.G.)* v *Mossop* (1990), 71 DLR (4th) 661. Further references to this decision will be by page number in the text.

2. For example, submissions were made on behalf of the attorney-general from The Salvation Army, Focus on the Family Association Canada, Realwomen, the Pentecostal Assemblies of Canada, and the Evangelical Fellowship of Canada. Representations in support of Brian Mossop came from the Canadian Rights and Liberties Federation, Equality for Gays and Lesbians Everywhere, the National Association of Women and the Law, the Canadian Disability Rights Council, and the National Action Committee on the Status of Women.

3. Intervenors, *supra*, note 2.

4. By 'law and ideology' approach, I mean those analyses of law that explain the role of law in terms of its ideological function in society; the ways in which law both legitimates and reproduces status quo social relations. I have been influenced in this area by a number of writers, including Sumner, 1979; Hunt, 1985; Hirst, 1979; Gavigan, 1988; Mandel, 1989; Glasbeek and Mandel, 1984; Cain, 1983; Kairys (ed.), 1982; Sugarman (ed.), 1983.

5. By 'discourse theory' I mean approaches to the study of law that derive from the work of Michel Foucault. See Smart, 1989, 1990; Eisenstein, 1988; Williams, 1988; Hutchinson, 1988; Farmer, 1987; De Michel, 1983; Hunt, 1990. A number of writers have also offered Derridean analyses. See Williams, 1988; Balkin, 1987; Dalton, 1985; Hoy, 1985.

6. See, for example, the work of Adrienne Rich, Catharine MacKinnon, and Gayle Rubin. See also Herman, 1990. There are many points within the litigation process that could be analysed in this way; this chapter concentrates primarily on the final (legal) product: decisions themselves.

7. *Canadian Human Rights Act*, R. S. C. 1985, c. H-6 [hereinafter *Act*]. Mossop's union was the Canadian Union of Professional and Technical Employees (CUPTE).

8. Obviously, this statement of the case is very bare and does little justice to the actual experiences of Mossop during the years that ensued between the death of his partner's father and the Tribunal decision.

9. Her testimony in this regard repeated that of her appearance in the *Karen*

Andrews litigation. See *Andrews* v *Ontario (Ministry of Health)*, [1988] 49 D.L.R. (4th) 584 (Ont. H.C.) [hereinafter *Karen Andrews*, cited to C.L.L.C.] [Affadavit of Margrit Eichler].

10. His was the main appeal judgment in a unanimous decision. Pratte J. wrote a short concurring judgment. Note that Marceau J. was the lone dissenting voice in *Schaap and Lagace* v *Canadian Armed Forces* (1989), 95 N. R. 132. That case found that a non-married heterosexual couple had been discriminated against on the grounds of 'marital status' when refused an apartment on an army base. The majority argued that human rights legislation was not to be read so as to further and protect the institution of marriage; only Marceau dissented.

11. Marceau has certainly ensured that the attorney-general will make it in the future. The finding that bereavement leave is not an employment opportunity under the *Act* leads to the result that the *Act* would not apply in this case at all; Mossop would have no human rights remedy. By developing this point that, on his own admission, no one argued, Marceau even more clearly reveals his own bias.

12. I will return to this point in my concluding remarks.

13. In *Karen Andrews, supra,* note 9, counsel for the attorney-general invoked the 'slippery slope' in his cross-examination of Margrit Eichler. See Herman, 1990: 798. The work of Peter Goodrich (1984, 1986) has been helpful for this analysis.

14. Interestingly, Atcheson seems to be implying that the new forms of family are the 'is' and old forms the moralist's 'should be.'

15. Note how this phraseology implies that both Mossop and Atcheson either missed or avoided the 'real issue,' or, more sinisterly, deliberately attempted to obscure it.

16. Marceau J. acknowledges that the attorney-general is not disputing sexual orientation as an analogous ground after *Veysey* v *Canada (Comm. Corr. Serv.)*, (1990) 109 NR 300 (F. C. A.) and *Brown* v *B. C. (Min. of Health)*, (1990) 66 D.L.R. (4th) 444. The initial decision in *Veysey* [1990] 1 F. C. 321 and the judge's approach in *Brown* bear considerable similarities to the *Mossop* Tribunal decision. The three texts are all examples of the increasing deployment of liberal discourse in the area of 'sexual orientation.' I return to this in the final section of the paper.

17. I do not want to suggest that these strategies are the conscious, instrumentalist manipulations of the judiciary intent on furthering a homophobic agenda. They may be this in certain cases, but they do not have to be this. Rather, the traditions and culture of law, the various techniques and approaches embedded in legal discourse themselves have some autonomy. The discourse itself is more than what individual judges are able to make of it. See also Bakan,1990, 1991; Coombe, 1989b; Hutchinson, 1989.

18. See also Farmer, 1987; Goodrich, 1984; Williams, 1988.

19. *E.E.O.C.* v *Sears, Roebuck and Company*, 628 F Supp. 1264 (N. D. Ill. 1986), aff'd. 839 F. 2d 302 (7th Circuit 1988).

20. Here, I am only interested in one particular aspect of this case and will therefore not provide a detailed description of the issues. See the following for information and comment: Kessler-Harris, 1987; Scott, 1988a, 1988b; Milkman, 1986. See also Wiener, 1985 and Sternhell, 1986. For a different perspective (one that supports Rosenberg's intervention) see

Haskell and Levinson, 1988.

21. It is the relative 'truth' of this statement that made Kessler-Harris's testimony appear absurd, because she was forced into arguing 'either/or.' See Scott, 1988a.

22. That is, how are women's 'interests' constructed? What role do women play in this process? Do women passively internalize sexist ideologies of 'womanhood' or is the construction of interests a site of struggle? See *supra*, note 20.

23. *Supra*, note 9.

24. And what did most of these precedential pearls of valid wisdom consist of? Nothing more, or less, than the magical Section 1 Incantations from *Oakes* and *Edward Books. Regina v Oakes* (1986), 26 D. L. R. (4th) 200 (S. C. C.); *Edwards Books and Art Ltd. et al. v The Queen* (1986), 35 D. L. R. (4th) 1 (S. C. C.). McCrae simply reproduces large chunks of text from these Supreme Court of Canada decisions without any real application or analysis. He goes through the Section 1 exercise despite having made a finding of no discrimination.

25. As is the evidence submitted by Valverde and Adams.

26. *Supra*, note 4.

27. See use of words and phrases like "harmony" (para 4.47) and "equal opportunity" (para 4.49). The Tribunal also expresses the liberal view that values "should play no part" in the adjudication process (para 4.70).

28. For a discussion of the relationship between this dichotomy and liberal law, see West, 1988 and Finley, 1989.

29. The Tribunal also endorses a kind of poststructuralist view of meaning. The adjudicator engages in a kind of deconstruction of the concept 'family,' finding, at the end of the day, that the word 'family' has no inner core of meaning. One 'True' meaning cannot be revealed and adjudicatory forums must simply look at social relations to determine the range of *possible* meanings. It would seem obvious that this approach is certainly incompatible with the conservative fixity of the Federal Court; however, it clearly facilitates the liberal ideology of the Tribunal.

30. *Supra*, note 16. This case involved a gay male prisoner who argued that his lover's exclusion from the prison-policy definition of 'family' (for the purposes of private family visiting) was discriminatory. In other words, he was not arguing that his relationship constituted a 'family' under the definition; he acknowledged that it did not. He argued, rather, that the definition and policy were discriminatory on grounds of sexual orientation. The Trial Division agreed, and the Federal Court of Appeal upheld the ruling on other grounds (improper use of administrative discretion).

31. [1989] 1 S.C.R. 143.

32. *Supra*, note 16. This case involved a gay man with HIV infection who argued that the B.C. government's refusal to offer free AZT was contrary to sections 15 and 7 of the *Charter* on grounds of 'physical handicap' (enumerated ground) and sexual orientation (by analogy). While finding that sexual orientation was an analogous ground, Coultas J. ruled that discrimination had not been proved under section 15 and that section 7 could not apply to cases where benefits were being sought (as opposed to where 'liberty' had been imperilled).

33. Actually, Marceau in *Mossop* does imply he holds this view when discuss-

ing the meaning of 'spouse': see p. 675 regarding creation of "new family units."

34. Law can both resist and accommodate this challenge, extending its own colonization of external discourse at the same time (Smart, 1989).

35. This is happening for various reasons, including more women and 'minorities' on the bench, less need for compromise (that is, often only one decision-maker), and the possible role of appellate courts as having a different role regarding legitimation and reproduction.

Chapter Eight

Subjectivity and Reality Construction in Law
Dragan Milovanovic

Discourse analysis is being increasingly used by social scientists as a way of revealing the assumptions behind the construction of both social reality and the individual subject. In particular, discourse analysis presents the enlightenment view of a stable, coherent human subject existing prior to its social constitution as fictitious. Instead, postmodern writers argue that both objects and subjects of investigation are the effects, and not the causes, of inquiry. Drawing upon semiotics and other methods of literary criticism, language and texts are explored for their previously neglected role in the creation of the subject. This exploration is especially important in revealing how both compliant and subversive subjects are created. It thus provides a deeper and more revolutionary understanding of how repressive social orders are reconstituted and resisted than that provided by deterministic readings of Marx.

In what follows, Dragan Milovanovic extends the insights provided by semiotics to an analysis of law as discourse. He begins by explaining the notion of the decentred subject, drawing upon Lacan's revision of Freud's early work on the ego. Fundamentally, this approach provides a way of understanding how the subject takes up temporary residence in personal pronouns of language and text, which stand for the 'presence of an absence.' The way in which this occurs is determined by a number of intrapsychic and discursive processes, which together make a "quintrivium."

In the humanities, literature and cinema offer good examples of how different, competing subject positions are opened to the reader/viewer. Legal scholars are beginning to find analyses of the ways in which these subject positions are assumed by readers/viewers useful for understanding adjudicatory proceedings in which jurors are being offered contradictory and competing accounts of "what happened?" Just as the film director attempts to manipulate a filmic discourse, so do

Dragan Milovanovic is Associate Professor in Criminal Justice at Northeastern Illinois University

lawyers before the court attempt to construct a story: the prosecutor of guilt and culpability, the defence counsellor of innocence or diminished culpability. Story-telling in the courtroom is limited, however, by a number of discursive and non-discursive factors: the juridico-linguistic co-ordination system; legally constructed definitions of words; accepted methods of narration; unequal access to the specialized skills through which story-telling takes place; and the formal context of the court. Alternative — potentially subversive — story-telling is quickly repressed or discounted. Milovanovic concludes, however, that this understanding of how hegemony is reconstituted also tells us how domination might be resisted and subverted when we refuse subject positions supportive of the status quo and construct alternative, revolutionary subjects.

INTRODUCTION

Discourse analysis has become a critical tool of inquiry in the social sciences. It is especially valuable in deciphering the underlying assumptions behind reality construction processes as well as the metaphysical assumptions of the subject. In this chapter we would like to specify some alternative lines of inquiry of how subjectivity is constructed in cinematic and literary texts and show how these alternatives shed light on the creation of the legal subject (the reasonable man/woman in law) as well as the recreation of dominant understandings of reality in law during adjudicatory practices.

DECENTRING THE SUBJECT

The notion of the individual, a self-transparent, determining, and fully conscious being, so dear to Western metaphysics, has recently been challenged by the postmodernist's notion of the decentred subject. Created through the processes about which it speaks, the subject is no longer given *a priori* existence, outside language and text. Drawing inspiration from Lacan's revisionism of Freud's early work, the notion of the decentred subject offers an alternative way of seeing subjectivity. Here we want to briefly lay out Lacan's notion of the subject, his idea of speech production, and integrate this idea into our notion of the 'quintrivium' as a specification of how speech and subjectivity are created. We will then apply this to cinematic and literary texts in providing an alternative method of conceptualizing the legal subject and justice-rendering in the courts.

Lacan has provided his notion of the subject in the form of "Schema L," which can be depicted as:

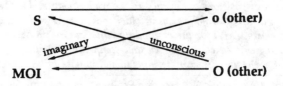

Briefly, the subject is said to be stretched out over all four corners of this schema (Lacan, 1977: 194; see also Ragland-Sullivan, 1986:2-67). The Other (*L'Autre*) stands for the unconscious, the locus of signifiers that "slumber in anticipation." The small "o" represents the internalized conception of the other, an object of desire. The "moi," or the ego, is the illusory conception of self; it provides an illusory conception of unity, control, and stability. Finally, the "S" is the grammatical "I" of discourse. It is a signifier; when mobilized it acts as a "shifter," a personal pronoun, standing for a presence of an absence (Benveniste, 1971: 67, 218, 226-227). The "I" represents the subject that resides below the surface of awareness (Lacan, 1977, 1981). Hence, two subjects exist along two planes (unconscious and conscious): the subject of the discourses' production, the speaking subject (*sujet de l'énonciation*); and the subject of speech (*sujet de l'énoncé*), the grammatical "I" of utterances.

Lacan's model is an intra- and intersubjective model of the subject, as indicated by the two diagonals. The diagonal that connects the "S" with the Other is an unconscious dimension. The Other is seen as the locus of desire, signifiers ("letters"), and a discourse — "the unconscious is structured like a language" (Lacan, 1981: 149) — organized by metaphor and metonymy (see the introductory chapter of this book). The "I" of discourse is always subject to the determinants originating from the Other. For Lacan it is language that speaks the subject. The diagonal that runs from the "moi," the ego (or more specifically, the ideal ego), to the "other" is the imaginary axis. The moi can be conceived of as a locus of imaginary identifications with the other by and through which its own subjectivity is constituted. It is characterized both by narcissism (it holds out the possibility of fulfilment), and aggressivity (the subject recognizes that the other is never identical to it but is the source of pleasure; the subject desires the desire of the other, Lacan repeatedly says). Again, the subject ultimately exists everywhere on this "Schema L" and nowhere in particular.

Lacan's subject is situated in three orders: the order of the Real, which represents lived experience beyond any possibility of accurate conceptualization; the Symbolic Order, the sphere of language (again, see the book's introduction) and culture; and the order of the Imaginary, the sphere where illusory constructs of objects of desire are created. These three orders act together to produce speech and the subject. Lacan's more dynamic rendition of the subject is portrayed in his "Graphs of Desire." Here Lacan maintains that the subject periodically perceives gaps, felt lacks, or a lack-in-being (*mangue-à-être*) to which it responds by mobilizing desire for closure. In other words, confronted by a lack in the Other a search follows for objects of desire (*objets petit à*) that promise to give completeness (*plenitude*). The Imaginary Order provides specular images and promises of completeness (*jouissance*). The Symbolic Order provides key signifiers that hold the promise of giving form and expression to desire. These signifiers, "slumbering in anticipation" in the Other, are further organized by the effects of metaphor and metonymy at the unconscious level, and by paradigm and syntagm at the the conscious level of discourse production.[1] "Suture" is the process by which gaps are "stitched" over — "a conjuncture of the imaginary and symbolic" (Lacan, 1981: 118) — that provides coherence and relative stability in discursive production (Lacan, 1981: 117-119; Heath, 1981: 76-112; Silverman, 1983: 194-236; Smith, P., 1988: 75-77). In the Lacanian schema the subject begins to fade ("aphanisis") from the scene as form is given to desire.[2] The subject disappears in his or her objects of desire, desire becomes embodied, is given a representative in the form of a signifier (see also Smith, P., 1988: 75-77). Speech production thus entails the anticipatory dimension by which, with the completion of a word, the next is anticipated and this in turn leads to the anticipation of the next word and so on. But it is only with the punctuation that a reflective glance (a retrograde) takes place, giving the whole utterance meaning (Lacan, 1977: 303-304). Specific words only take on value in their relation to the whole discursive chain.

Applying this to legal discourse, we envision several discourses in existence, organized by the paradigmatic and syntagmatic semiotic axes that provide material (signifiers, legally constituted words) out of which meaning is constructed. Creating narratively coherent stories in the courtroom, then, has everything to do with mastering the syntax as well as the legally constituted lexical storehouse (signifiers) (see Jackson, 1988; Milovanovic, 1986).

Elsewhere we have extended the Lacanian framework by situating it within the quintrivium (Milovanovic, 1991b). This quintrivium, which is a holistic specification of how speech and therefore subjectivity is produced, is composed of: the domain of desire where the psychic apparatus is mobilized when a perception of a *mangue-à-être* arises; the discursive plane (organized by paradigm and syntagm; the sphere responsible for producing coherent narrative constructions on the conscious plane); the referential plane (the unconscious plane organized by metaphor or condensation and metonymy or displacements); the pragmatic context (spatiotemporal locations and their determinants); and the plane of diverse linguistic co-ordinate systems (discourses) and the available positions within which an "I" can take up temporary residence in speech production (discursive subject-positions). We view speech production as being determined by the quintrivium. In the context of the quintrivium, Lacan provides an exact specification of how desire is embodied in signifiers (words), which eventually are organized on the discursive plane by syntax and the available lexical storehouse. In this formulation, the subject is unstable, always subject to the unconscious effects of the referential plane where desire seeks fuller expression. The subject, in the Lacanian framework, can be better conceptualized as a "speaking" subject.

THE SPOKEN SUBJECT

The psychoanalytic semiotic perspective has offered us the idea of two subjects: the subject of speech (*le sujet de l'énoncé*) and the speaking subject (*le sujet de l'énonciation*). The former is the grammatical "I" of discourse; the latter is the more hidden producer of the discursive chain. Benveniste

(1971) has well argued how the subject of speech, the grammatical "I," acts as a "shifter": as a personal pronoun, or signifier, it takes on value as it acquires a place in discursive chains:

> *I* refers to the act of individual discourse in which it is pronounced, and by this it designates the speaker.... language puts forth "empty" forms which each speaker, in the exercise of discourse, appropriates to himself and which he relates to his "person," at the same time defining himself as *I* and a partner as *you*.... *I* signifies "the person who is uttering the present instance of the discourse containing *I*."... *I* can only be identified by the instance of discourse that contains it and by that alone. (1971: 226, 227, 218)

The "I" of grammatical structures, however, can also be conceptualized as a presence of an absence. The actual producer of the speech, the speaking subject, remains unconscious; this is the sphere of desire and the referential plane of the quintrivium. During conversation, the speaking subject identifies with the grammatical "I" of speech while recognizing the "you" (the other), the person with whom he or she is speaking (Benveniste, 1971: 67, 218; Silverman, 1983: 196-200). During the reading of literature or the viewing of cinema, however, only identification takes place; the "you" remains more hidden (the locus of discursive production remains opaque). As Benveniste tells us, "The subject makes use of the act of speech and discourse in order to 'represent himself' to himself as he wishes to see himself and as he calls upon the 'other' to observe him" (1971: 67). In other words, we are in the realm of imaginary identifications. The other (the "you") acts as a mirror by which the "I" can take on more concrete form. In viewing film and in reading literature, however, this "other" is absent. Consider this statement by Williamson:

> What the advertisement clearly does is thus to signify, to represent to us, the *object* of desire. Since that object *is the self*, this means that, while ensnaring/creating the subject through his or her exchange of signs, the advertisement is actually feeding off that subject's own desire for coherence and meaning in him or her self. This is as it were the supply of power that drives the whole ad motor, and must be recognized as such. (1987: 60)

Literature and cinema offer subject positions (fictional and non-fictional characters) with which to identify. Hence, suggested is yet a third subject, the "spoken subject" (Silverman, 1983: 46-52, 198-200). The spoken subject is that subject that is constituted by way of her or his identification with, on the one hand, the subject of speech, and on the other, the characters presented in literature or film (Silverman, 1983: 47). Put another way, literary and cinematic texts offer subject positions with which to identify (for example, those of protagonists, heroes, villains, victims, and so forth). By identifying with these others, the viewer or reader constitutes him/herself with the guise of a coherent and stable subject ("Yes, I am the one who sees it as the character sees it"). The viewer or reader, in other words, identifies with the subject of discourse (cinematic, literary) and thereby inserts her/himself as a filled-in "I" of speech, creating meaning out of the unfolding narrative. As Silverman says, "The cinematic text constitutes the viewer's subjectivity for him or her, it engages the viewer in a discursive exchange during which he or she is spoken as subject" (1983: 48).

Focusing strictly on everyday conversation, this notion of the spoken subject has been given further force by Pecheux (1982: 155-162), in his notion of the "good subject"; by Althusser (1971), in his idea of "interpellation"; and, more recently, by Deleuze and Guattari (1987) in their notion of the "doubling of the subject" (see also Bogue, 1989: 141-144). In each case, an interplay of imaginary and symbolic transactions takes place with the person identifying, in imagination, with a fictional character (the subject of speech) and simultaneously assuming a discursive subject-position within a particular discourse that defines it (see also Silverman, 1983: 219). Lacan has referred to this as "suture"; it is the essential process by which speech production can take place at all. The spoken subject, then, can be seen as the result of this process: The identification with fictional (imaginary) characters allows a stabilization of a subject that can find its place in meaning production (see also Smith, P., 1988: 75-77). The person situating herself within a discursive subject-position can then avail herself of the constituted signifiers in order to give form and expression to her desire. The paradigmatic and syntagmatic semiotic axes will then be the co-ordinates of discursive production (the utterance, speech).

Visée

To better conceptualize how the "what happened?" in adjudicatory proceedings is discursively constructed we draw from cinematic theory, which posits the idea of a *"visée de conscience"* (Metz, 1982: 104, 138, 141, 143, n 6). A visée can be conceptualized as an orientation of consciousness, an increased tension of consciousness towards something. For example, Metz has described a "filmic visée" (1982: 104; 138-142). This visée "is marked by a general tendency to lower wakefulness ... a step in the direction of sleep and dreaming" (106-107); we could envision a continuum here: from a dream visée, to a daydreaming visée, to the filmic visée. It is during this state, the filmic visée, that the subject may slide towards unconscious mechanisms (the sphere of the referential plane, organized by metaphor and metonymy) stopping short of hallucinations in constructing meaning. Here a more liberated flow of desire in the form of images flows in a dynamic manner.

The film director Sergei Eisenstein has explained how he orchestrated a desired imagery that would be conjured up by the viewing audience, a notion referred to as "montage" (1975: 3-12; 30-36; see also MacCabe, 1985: 41-42). As Eisenstein states:

> Before the inner vision, before the perception of the creator [for our purposes below, lawyers], hovers a given image, emotionally embodying his theme. The task that confronts him is to transform this image into a few basic *partial representations* which, in their combination and juxtaposition, shall evoke in the consciousness and feelings of the spectator, reader, or auditor [for our purposes below, jurors], that same initial general image

which originally hovered before the creative artists [for our purposes, opposing lawyers attempting to create a narratively coherent version of the "what happened?" favourable to their respective side]. (1975: 30-31; emphasis in the original)

Just as the film director attempts to manipulate a sequence of shots (a filmic discourse if you will) in producing a coherent story, so too, does the lawyer before the court attempt to construct a story that captures the "what happened?" Stories can be envisioned as organizational devices for presenting plausible renditions of events. Lawyers, therefore, appear before the court in heightened visées; more specifically a visée either of an advocacy or a prosecutorial form. Jurors, too, enter discursive subject-positions in which they don a particular visée, an "attributional visée." Much like film directors, lawyers attempt to construct stories that evoke particular imageries from jurors (*montage*); the prosecutor, the imagery of guilt and culpability; in a similar way, the defence counsellor of innocence or diminished culpability.

Jurors, situating themselves within a particular discursive subject-position (as jurors), donning a particular visée (an attributional visée), find themselves at the intersection of Imaginary and Symbolic transactions. At the imaginary level, jurors develop identifications with an ego-ideal, the "reasonable man/woman in law," in rendering judgments. The Symbolic Order provides a distinct discourse, the legal discourse (we have referred to it as a "linguistic co-ordinate system"), which becomes the co-ordinating milieu within which coherent narratives are constructed.

Lawyers, whether prosecutorial- or defence-oriented, attempt to create a spoken subject, a juror who will identify with the rendition of the "what happened?" that he or she is creating before the juror's eyes. The viewer/listener/reader — here the juror — becomes a spoken subject at the point where they "experience the dynamic process of the emergence and assembly of the image just as it was experienced by the author [here the author being the prosecutor or the defence counsellor]" (Eisenstein, 1975: 32). For their part, jurors see contradictory versions of the "what happened?" Faced with gaps, inconsistencies, contrarieties, they attempt to suture; that is, they find themselves in the intersection of the interplay of the imaginary and symbolic in creating a complete story of "what happened?" *Jouissance* is experienced at that point where the juror creates a complete, coherent, and plausible narrative form of the "what happened?"

Story constructions, however, can be seen as limited by the discourse in use (the juridico-linguistic co-ordinate system), the available constituted signifiers (legally constructed definitions of words), the accepted method for narrative construction (during appeals, deductive logic and syllogistic reasoning), the unequal access to linguistic skills (a defendant purchases juridico-linguistic skills), and the context (the formalism of the courts). Alternative constructions of the "what happened?" — such as political renditions — are quickly repressed by either outright denial or, ironically, by activists themselves before the court who must remain within the quintrivium of the court (the latter is a specification of the notion of hegemony). Elsewhere we have elaborated on this process of the dialectics of struggle (Milovanovic, 1988a; Milovanovic and Thomas, 1989; Bannister and Milovanovic, 1990; Henry and Milovanovic, 1991). What is perpetuated is a form of "symbolic violence" (Bourdieu, 1987: 85; Lecercle, 1990) whereby dominant understandings are continuously reconstructed and other more politically or contextually oriented renditions of the "what happened?" are denied.

WRITERLY AND READERLY TEXTS:
Towards a Replacement Discourse

Here we will elaborate on the construction and deconstruction of the subject in textual productions, drawing out the implications for the development of a replacement discourse reflecting the decentred nature of subjectivity. Central to this discussion is the work of Barthes, who has offered us two ways of reading the classic text (see Barthes, 1974; Silverman, 1983: 237-283; MacCabe, 1985). He refers to these ways as "readerly" and "writerly" texts. Although he applies his analysis to the literary text, similar to Silverman (1983) we see the relevance of Barthes's work in reading the cinematic text, as well as in everyday conversation.

The readerly approach reproduces the classic text's ideals. The organizing principles of this reading (and viewing) are foremost non-contradiction. The reader/viewer is encouraged to accept privileged signifiers and their assumed signifieds (meaning). The underlying sphere of production of the text is hidden; therefore its connectedness to political-economic determinants remains opaque. The reader/viewer is encouraged to identify with the subjects (actors) in the film or literature, who, in the end, will agree to be spoken by and through them. The classic text offers the reader/viewer an opportunity to identify with the unfolding plot and hence to conjure up appropriate signifiers that will suture gaps encountered. The Imaginary and Symbolic Orders are thereby constitutive. Key orientations revolve around the idea of structure and production. The classic text, therefore, offers a "pleasurable dependence" (Silverman, 1983: 245) whereby the reader/viewer is promised the possibility of coherence and thereby closure and *jouissance*. A readerly approach produces subjects who reconstitute dominant understandings of reality, as well as the illusion of the centred subjects who are in control, reflective, and conscious of their activities.

In contrast, the writerly approach to reading the classic text is subversive. It encourages "an infinite play of signification; in it there can be no transcendental signified, only provisional ones which function in turn as signifiers" (Silverman, 1983: 246). The possibility of definitive closure is denied. Rather than the orienting principles of structure and product, the writerly approach focuses on process and "segmentation" (Silverman, 1983: 247). By segmentation, Silverman means the deconstruction of the structure of the classic text and the revelations of the underlying hidden voices that are its products. The notion of suture is challenged. Reading/

viewing proceeds in the reverse direction to uncover hidden and repressed voices, constructions, and understandings of reality. The reader or viewer is not encouraged to assume permanent discursive subject-positions in which they can take up temporary residence. Instead, displacements are encouraged: "the writerly project 'dis-places' the reader or viewer, alienates him or her from the all-too-familiar subject-positions of the existing cultural regime" (Silverman, 1983: 248-249). Rather than being spoken, the reader or viewer is called upon to actively deconstruct and reconstruct the Symbolic Order (249). Rather than an endless reconstruction of the given social order, as in the readerly approach, the writerly approach demands transcendence.

Now let us briefly examine the text itself rather than the approach to reading it. Here Deleuze and Guattari identify "major" and "minor" literatures (1986: 16-19, 28; 1987; Bogue, 1989: 119-120, 147-149; Lecercle, 1990: 241-243). By a major literature they refer to restrictive and static usage of linguistic variation. This conforms to the classic text, which offers preconstructed discursive subject-positions within which an identifactory "I" can take up residence in constructing pre-established meaning. The passive playing out of the dictates of discursive subject-positions produces, in the end, the spoken subject. A minor literature, however, is revolutionary; it destabilizes meaning and therefore potentially offers alternative understandings. It is characterized by an emphasis on "deterritorialization"; political, contextualized readings; and collective enunciations. By deterritorialization, Deleuze and Guattari mean that conventional content is deconstructed, placed in "continuous variation," and reconstructed in novel ways.[3] This approach has much in common with Silverman's notion of "segmentation," as well as with the chaotic pathways of the flow of desire captured by Deleuze and Guattari's idea of the "rhizome" (1987: 6-9, 12-15, 21-25; see also Bogue, 1989: 107). The referential plane of our quintrivium knows not the dictates of the discursive plane of paradigm and syntagm. It is only in the discursive plane that desire is manipulated into appropriate forms of expression. The rhizome, however, can be pictured as essentially chaotic, having multiple entry-points and exits, denying rigid structuration.[4]

We are now in a position to diagram the intersections of the major (the classic text) and minor literature and the two methods of reading or viewing them (Table 8-1). Briefly, we conceptualize a readerly approach to the classic text (major literature) producing and reproducing conventional understandings of reality (reification). Its metaphysics is Newtonian with an underlying Euclidean geometry (three-dimensional space). It is a linear reading of texts (cinematic, literary, legal) wherein the notion of the self-determining individual is worshipped. The subject is interpellated or spoken as it assumes preconstructed discursive subject-positions within dominant linguistic co-ordinate systems. The organizing tropes of paradigm and syntagm, and the always already available circumscribed signifiers assure material from which reality, the "what happened?" is constructed. The subject, too, by assuming these positions, and by giving form

TABLE 8-1: Reading / Viewing The Text

	MAJOR LITERATURE (CLASSIC TEXT)	MINOR LITERATURE (SUBVERSIVE TEXT)
READERLY TEXT	Spoken (interpellated) subject	Alienated subject
	Reification	Passive conversion
	Structure: production suture, linearity, passivity	Instilling politically correct views
	Newtonian metaphysics and Euclidean geometry	Constitutive methodology
	Hegemony	
WRITERLY TEXT	Oppositional subject	Revolutionary subject
	React / negate (Hegel)	Dis-identification
	Segmentation	Active negation (Nietzche) geneology
	Exhuming the marginalized voices	Chaos theory with rhizome, fractals, iteration, attractors, libido, "will to power"
	Relativity theory with quantum mechanics, uncertainty	Orderly disorder
	Dialectics of struggle	Replacement discourse
	Reversal of hierarchies	

to his or her desire with the available signifiers, while identifying with an offered image of plenitude, is assured the possibility of gaining mastery and control of the existential gaps continuously confronted through the process of suture. The subject is offered moments of illusory assurance that she or he is determining, stable, and in control. Hegemony is thus assured as even the exploited actively participate in the construction of an oppressive order all the while giving themselves the appearance of subjects in control.

In contrast, a readerly approach to minor literature produces moments of dissonance as gaps are confronted, or when a discourse is encountered that provides contrarieties to accepted wisdom that would otherwise anchor subjectivity. The range of predictable results is from alienation, on the one hand, to a passive conversion, on the other. Alternatively, an imposition might be sought; for example, we see in the contemporary U.S. scene the growing movement to instil "correct political views" on college campuses. Elsewhere we have argued that the field of criminology is most often engaged in a constitutive science manufacturing texts of lawbreakers, giving these scripts form and sustenance, finding or constituting the subject it needs (Henry and Milovanovic, 1991).

A writerly approach to major literature is oppositional. In the Hegelian formulation, it is an attempt to affirm a positive value by "negating a negation" (Milovanovic, 1991a) through the active deconstruction (segmentation) of hierarchies and exhuming of repressed or denied voices (Giroux, 1988). Although it assumes relativity and rejects foundational truths, in the attempt to "reverse hierarchies" the oppositional subject does just that. Remaining within a framework of hierarchy and opposition, would-be reformers often inadvertently reconstitute the forms of domination (Milovanovic, 1991a; Henry and Milovanovic, 1991). This paradox is captured by the notion of the dialectics of struggle (see also Bannister and Milovanovic, 1990; Milovanovic and Thomas, 1989).

Finally, a writerly approach to reading or viewing minor literature produces the revolutionary subject. The subject dis-identifies with the lure of discursive subject-positions and signifiers readily available for story construction (Pecheux, 1982: 158-59, 162-63; MacCabe, 1985: 108-109, 111n 13). The revolutionary subject actively negates (Nietzsche) without at the same time falling prey to reconstituting forms of domination or hierarchy. Rather than linear historical development,[5] the Nietzschean and Foucaldian idea of "genealogy" is a central guiding ideal (see Love, 1986). Here chaos theory (Hayles, 1990; Serres, 1982; Deleuze and Guattari, 1987), with its notion of rhizomatic pathways behind expression of desire, offers a liberating reading of the text. Central to this reading are emerging concepts from the chaos paradigm: iteration;[6] fractals;[7] uncertainty in the specification of original conditions;[8] non-linearity;[9] attractors;[10] phase-space;[11] and orderly disorder[12] (Briggs and Peat, 1989; Hayles, 1990; Young, 1990, 1991). With a writerly reading of a minor literature complexity, multiplicity, variability, chance, contrarieties, spontaneous discoveries, and discontinuities are celebrated. A replacement discourse, offering a multiplicity of "lines of continuous variation" and a diversity of forms for the embodiment of desire, once constituted and stabilized, would offer loose discursive subject-positions that present a sensitizing orientation to discursive production.

The call for the revolutionary subject is a call for a transpraxis (Henry and Milovanovic, 1991; Milovanovic, 1991a). Transpraxis moves beyond the simple and inherently conservative attempt to create new values through the "negation of a negation," implying an active negation that transcends existent forms and begins the movement towards what Nietzsche called the "overman" and what Marx referred to as the communist wo/man. Here value is created by an active affirmation (Milovanovic, 1991a: 222-224). Within transpraxis, multiplicity, chance, becoming, spontaneous developments, and a subject that gives multiple forms to her/his desire are acknowledged. The most promising inquiry for writerly readings and viewings of minor literature is critical feminism (see Grosz, 1990). Although a diversity of views, often hotly debated, exist that build on Lacan, critical feminism offers novel lines of inquiry in gender construction, especially around the issue of essentialism, and hence provides a better understanding of the relation between subjectivity and structure (see especially, Moi, 1985; Cixous, 1981; Irigaray, 1985; Kristeva, 1984). The wherewithal of a replacement discourse is central to these examinations.

CONCLUSION

Subjectivity and reality construction in law, then, can be fruitfully understood by a discourse analysis rooted in the post-Frankfurt, postmodern approach. The reading of literature and law, and the viewing of cinema, all provide instances in which subjects are created. Within reading and viewing, hegemonic groups strive to assure the existence of mechanisms by which the spoken subject continues to be produced. Paradoxically, oppositional subjects often inadvertently reconstitute forms of domination by reproducing hierarchy and opposition in their discursive attempts to valorize alternative, repressed values and meanings. In contrast, this chapter highlights the need to create a revolutionary, not simply oppositional, subject. What will be needed is the institutionalization of a minor literature, which then offers a discourse composed of signifiers that are multi-accentuated (Volosinov, 1986); that resonates with the accentuations of multiple various and understandings (Deleuze and Guattari, 1986, 1987); that provides discursive subject-positions within which an "I" can take up momentary residence without these positions unilaterally dominating and subjecting experience to premature closure; that, finally, provides chaotic (rhizomatic) pathways along which desire may seek expression in ever creative ways. The revolution has just begun!

NOTES

1. The complex interconnections between the metaphor/metonymy semiotic axis and paradigm/syntagm semiotic axis are the subject of my book in progress, 1991b.

2. Lacan has conceptualized this process in his algorithm $S \lozenge a$, read, slashed subject, chisel (*"losange"* or stamp), *objet petit à*.

3. According to Deleuze and Guattari (1986) the writings of Kafka and Beckett are exemplifications.

4. The work of Serres (1982) best exemplifies its application to the novel.

5. As in Hegel's notion of the Absolute Spirit, and Newton's deterministic metaphysics.

6. "Iteration" refers to the use of formulae that take their result as input for new computations. This notion of looping feedbacks is intrinsic to textual production and can be conceived as one specification of the Nietzschean "eternal return."

7. Signifiers do not assume stable meaning from one iteration to the next, but can be seen in terms of fractional dimensions, occupying fractions of semantic space.

8. Small differences can, after a number of iterations, contribute disproportionate effects in final outcomes.

9. Phenomena do not progress in linear fashion but are subject to the uncertainties in initial conditions. The notion of genealogy offered by Nietzsche and Foucault have strong affinities with this notion of non-linearity.

10. Non-linear dynamics produce predictable regions or "fractal basins"; in other words, predictable regions or patterns of activity are produced without the possibility of any specific prediction of an instance. An attractor is a location towards which dynamic systems tend.

11. "Phase-space" refers to a methodology of mapping non-linear dynamics and the patterning of their attractors.

12. "Orderly disorder" refers to the way in which both determinism and indeterminism can exist side by side.

Part Three

THE EXECUTIVE BRANCH: POLICING

The RCMP and Its Ancestors:
Over 100 Years of Willing Service
Lorne Brown

In 1984 the Canadian Security Intelligence Service replaced the RCMP Security Service, which had been found to be in contempt of law and a danger to civil liberties. Four years later, however, the new service faced similar allegations of spying on non-violent and legal organizations. In its activities, CSIS has been prying into the private lives of a great many Canadians and has signed a number of provincial agreements that would give it access to confidential hospital, medical, telephone, and personnel records. To justify these practices, CSIS staff interpreted the terms "foreign influenced" and "subversive" in a manner that allowed them to see their mandate in terms of controlling public opinion. Rejecting the view that these problems merely reflect the misconduct of a few overzealous individuals, Lorne Brown documents the continuity between the newly created CSIS and its ancestors. While the new agency recruited a majority of its members from former members of the RCMP as well as from other police agencies, Brown rejects this as an explanation for current problems. Instead, he documents the history of national policing in Canada, exploring the role that the RCMP has played in managing political dissent and economic unrest.

Brown's historical examination of the RCMP reveals that from its inception, the force was developed as an agency for social control on behalf of dominant class interests at least as much as it was an institution devoted to law enforcement in the conventional sense. Overall, there has been a remarkably consistent pattern in activities from the early days of the North West Mounted Police to the RCMP of the 1980s. In his overview Brown documents how the force was executing Indian rebels in Saskatchewan after 1885, spying on Indian organizations throughout Canada in the 1970s, and arresting Innu protestors in Labrador in 1989; the force was breaking strikes for the CPR in 1883 and among Newfoundland wood workers in 1959: they spied on pacifists in the 1920s and the peace

Lorne Brown is Professor in Political Science at the University of Regina

movement in the 1960s. While the North West Mounted Police performed useful functions for the British Empire, the modern RCMP has played a similar role for the American Empire since 1945. The RCMP was spying upon and sometimes harassing communists, social democrats, labour militants, and dissident intellectuals from the 1920s into the 1970s.

Despite this range of activities, Brown points out that in their entire history the RCMP has never apprehended a single important foreign spy. Similarly, although there have been violent conspiracies against the state by organizations like the FLQ, instances of this sort have been very few in Canada. Most RCMP activity outside of normal police functions has been directed at combatting those people who sought basic changes in either the class structure or the conventional political arrangements. These people were regarded as enemies of the state regardless of their mode of dissent. In this way, the excesses committed by the RCMP during the 1970s that became the focus of public attention and royal inquiries were not a result of the force temporarily running amok. Rather, they were in keeping with the Mounted Police traditions built up over their one hundred years of service. From this perspective, Brown concludes by raising the question uniformly neglected by previous "critical" investigations into police wrongdoing: "service to whom?"

INTRODUCTION

"CSIS defends spying on legitimate groups to identify 'subversion.'"
(Geoffrey York, *The Globe and Mail*, headline, July 30, 1988)

The Globe and Mail headline refers to a front-page story describing the activities of the Canadian Security Intelligence Service. Perhaps ironically, CSIS was created in 1984 to replace the old RCMP Security Services, which had been described by a Royal Commission to have been incredibly sophisticated, contemptuous of the law, and dangerous to the civil liberties of Canadians. CSIS, by comparison, was supposed to be more unsophisticated, have more respect for civil liberties, and confine themselves to combatting foreign spies, terrorists, and those planning violent or illegal activities against the state. As the headline implies, after four years of existence, CSIS was admitting to spying on non-violent and perfectly legal organizations. It was only because of a court case that Joseph Dagenais, director-general of information management of CSIS and director-general of countersubversion (1984 to 1986) lifted the veil of secrecy in an affidavit sworn before the Federal Court of Canada. Without a shred of evidence, the affidavit claimed that foreign-influenced subversives had infiltrated 'broad based political movements' in Canada as a means of putting pressure on the Canadian government. These 'subversives' were supposedly "attempting to exploit volatile issues" by using movements to "confuse perception (and) sway opinion."

What alarmed many Canadians was not only the admitted spying on legitimate political movements, but also the reasoning of CSIS. In particular, CSIS staff were using the terms 'foreign influenced' and 'subversive' in an extremely subjective manner and interpreting their mandate to include the control of public opinion. Critics of the status quo were their main enemy, regardless of how those critics pursued their objectives.

CSIS has been very active in spying into the private lives of a great many Canadians. They have signed agreements with all provinces except Quebec that would give them access to provincial files (*The Leader-Post*, Sept. 3, 1988). While in most cases the details have never been made public, if the Manitoba agreement is any indication, the scope is far-reaching. It includes confidential hospital, medical, telephone, and personnel records. In 1986 the federal government requested CSIS to carry out security screenings of 74,500 public servants and contract employees (*The Globe and Mail*, Nov. 12, 1987). As though there was not already sufficient snooping, in 1985 CSIS Director Darcy Finn admitted that intelligence agents of some 'friendly' foreign governments are sometimes given permission to carry on activities in Canada (*The Globe and Mail*, Jan. 15, 1985). CSIS refused to say whether this might include foreign agents infiltrating political parties or groups.

If much of the above reminds people of the recent history of the RCMP and their Security Service, this is not surprising. In the first year of their existence, 95 per cent of the staff came directly to CSIS from the RCMP Security Service. Some of these would later return to the RCMP, but by 1987 83 per cent of CSIS staff were still former members of the force and many new recruits had come from other police forces (*The Globe and Mail*, July 3, 1987). The new agency was exhibiting such a pro-police bias in recruiting, and interpreting its intelligence role in such a way, that it would only be a slight exaggeration to describe CSIS as the old RCMP Security Service with a new name. Clearly, Canadians who are concerned about what to expect from CSIS in the future are well advised to examine the historical role of the RCMP and its predecessors. This chapter is a contribution towards that examination.

CONTEMPORARY DILEMMAS

One of the major scandals besetting Canadian governments in the 1970s arose from revelations concerning massive violations of the civil liberties of Canadians by the RCMP. Over a period of years the efforts of civil liberties associations, labour, Native, and academic groups, opposition politicians, and the press, along with leaks from within the RCMP themselves brought to light an array of unsavory activities that had hitherto been hidden from the general public. By the time most of the facts were out in the open, after years of prying and prodding, it had become public knowledge that the RCMP Security Service had committed the following assaults on the civil liberties of Canadians:

1. spying upon, and in some cases attempting to disrupt, the Parti Québécois, the Waffle caucus of the NDP, the trade union movement, several Native associations, the National Farmers Union, and a host of minor parties and groups on the left of the political spectrum;
2. drawing up a black list of civil servants and potential civil servants who were alleged to be security risks, though the individuals concerned had

    broken no laws;

3. bugging telephone conversations between lawyers and their clients;
4. illegally entering the office of the Parti Québécois in 1973 and stealing and copying the party membership lists;
5. breaking into the office of a left-wing press agency, the Agence de Presse Libre du Québec (APLQ), and stealing files and documents;
6. illegally opening mail over many years;
7. spying upon and keeping files on cabinet ministers, civil servants, and MPs;
8. maintaining a network of paid informants in the Post Office and the civil service;
9. burning down a barn, stealing dynamite from a construction site, and destroying files that RCMP agents had themselves stolen;
10. acting as provocateurs by counselling political dissidents to commit acts of violence;
11. bugging the office of the Quebec Common Front of trade unions in 1972 and turning the information over to the provincial government with whom the unions were negotiating a new contract for state employees.[1]

Many of these activities were not only a denial of people's civil liberties but also obvious violations of the *Criminal Code*. And the list is by no means exhaustive, as official government commissions would soon reveal. The scandals surrounding the force became one of the most extensively covered news items of 1977. By then official commissions and inquiries had been mounted by four different provincial governments to inquire into charges of wrongdoing by the RCMP.[2] The parliamentary opposition, much of the press, and many important provincial politicians were demanding that the Trudeau government of the day put a stop to such activities.

The response of the RCMP to this public outcry was to deny and cover up as much as possible. Where denial was impossible — as in the case of the APLQ break-in and burglary — the tactic was to claim that these were isolated instances of officers being overzealous in carrying out their duties and did not represent the general policy of the security service. Their political superiors in the federal government at first took an extremely hard line in defence of the force. Prime Minister Trudeau defended the fact that the RCMP might find it necessary, under some circumstances, to break the law in defence of 'national security.' He also asserted that the problem of illegality could be resolved if Parliament would "make such types of surveillance permissible by the RCMP or by whatever security agency you have" (Brown and Brown, 1978). Trudeau and Solicitor-General Francis Fox at first rejected the idea of a public enquiry on the grounds that the ensuing revelations might become a threat to 'national security.'

Trudeau and his colleagues had to change their strategy after the PQ government of Quebec appointed the Keable Commission to investigate the circumstances surrounding the APLQ break-in and related matters. By now it was clear that the Quebec commission and the press would succeed in ferreting out much of the damaging information that the RCMP and the federal authorities had been attempting to hide. To take control of the situation, the Trudeau government appointed, by an Order-in-Council on July 6, 1977, the Commission of Inquiry Concerning Certain Activities of the Royal Canadian Mounted Police. The Commission was chaired by Mr Justice D.C. McDonald and would be popularly known as the McDonald Commission.

Over the next four years the McDonald Commission would conduct the most exhaustive inquiry ever undertaken by a body of this nature into the security affairs of the RCMP. By August 1981 it had made three reports amounting to more than 2,000 pages in length. The reports demonstrated that the clandestine activities of the RCMP were much more extensive than had previously been suspected by the public and even more widespread than most critics had alleged. The RCMP Security Service was censured for callousness towards civil liberties, dishonest and manipulative relations with their political superiors and the public, widespread illegal activities, and an appalling lack of sophistication. Many of their activities were deemed to be an unacceptable threat to the right to dissent in a democratic society.

The McDonald Commission made scores of recommendations designed to place more limits on police power and safeguard the rights of Canadians. The most important called for legislation to remove the security service from what was deemed to be the inappropriate jurisdiction of the RCMP and establish a new civilian agency governed by legislative guidelines and political directives that would make security operations more sophisticated (and hence more effective) and less of a threat to the political rights of 'legitimate' dissenters. Many of these recommendations, particularly the ones stipulating the necessity for safeguards, were resisted vociferously by the security establishment in Ottawa. Nonetheless, they did lead to the creation of the Canadian Security Intelligence Service (CSIS) by the Trudeau government in 1984.

While the creation of the CSIS and the legislative framework surrounding it were portrayed by the government and much of the media as inaugurating, among other things, a new era of respect for civil liberties in this country, that remains to be seen. There have been some disturbing signs that the changes may turn out to have been more cosmetic than substantive.[3] What is important for our study is that the RCMP was for the first time stripped of some of its power and some of its significant functions despite tremendous resistance from the top officers of the force and their numerous and often powerful supporters among the political and bureaucratic elites, as well as the general population. Despite complaints about its activities over many years the RCMP had been an almost sacrosanct institution, which governments and politicians had been reluctant to confront, even in those rare instances when they were inclined to do so.

An earlier commission, the Royal Commission on Security (popularly known as the Mackenzie Commission) had been appointed by the Pearson government in 1966 after a public uproar about violation of civil liberties. It reported to the Trudeau government in 1968. Mackenzie and his colleagues had taken a much more narrow and more conservative approach than would the McDonald Commission more than a decade later, but even it recognized that the RCMP was an inappropriate body to be in charge of the security service. It recommended "the establishment of a new civilian non-police agency to perform the functions of a security service in Canada" (Mackenzie, 1969; McDonald, 1981a, 1981b). The senior management of the RCMP put up a ferocious fight against even publishing an abridged version of the Mackenzie Report let alone implementing it. The Trudeau government of that day compromised by leaving the security agency under RCMP auspices but with guidelines intended to make the security intelligence function "increasingly separate in structure and civilian in nature" (McDonald, 1981a, 1981b). Thirteen years later the McDonald Commission would chide the RCMP for failing to implement the new guidelines and making no serious effort to do so (McDonald, 1981a, 1981b).

Why did the Trudeau government move to divest the RCMP of the national security function after 1981 when it had been unwilling or unable to do so after 1968? Part of the answer lies in the changing balance of forces and the increasing political consciousness that had developed in the intervening years. The years from about the mid-1960s to the end of the 1970s witnessed an intense drive for political and social change in this country. Trade unions were expanding in membership and becoming more militant. The extensive strike wave of the mid-1960s, the general strike of the Quebec Common Front in 1972, and the one-day general strike across Canada (accompanied by massive street demonstrations) against wage controls in 1976 were indicative of increasing class conflict. Students, farmers, and women were also on the move during these years. Farmer and student demonstrations and occasional occupations were most evident in the late 1960s and early 1970s. Native organizations also became better organized and more militant and, like farmers and students, Native people often engaged in demonstrations and occupations.

There were indications throughout Canada that the general population was moving slightly to the left, and a committed minority were organizing for fundamental social change. In the early 1970s the NDP were to govern three provinces simultaneously for the first time in history. And the rise of the Waffle movement within the federal NDP meant that the socialist wing of the party was better organized and stronger than ever before. The tying together of the struggle for socialism and Canadian independence from the United States held a potentially potent appeal for many people, which proved to be worrisome to the ruling sectors of this country, particularly the guardians of official ideology in the RCMP Security Service. In the late 1970s there also arose to the left of the NDP a number of Marxist and Marxist-Leninist groups and minor parties that were representative of a radicalization among a small, but for a time growing, minority of the population.[4]

However, it was an independence movement in Quebec dedicated to fundamentally changing the very basis of Confederation that worried Canadian ruling circles most of all. The decade of the 1970s had been preceded by the so-called 'Quiet Revolution' of the early 1960s and the formation of the Parti Québécois (PQ) in 1967. This latter event brought the question of political independence into the mainstream of Quebec politics for the first time. Over the next decade the issue of independence would be a dominant part of the political debate in Quebec, and the national question would often overlap with an intense class struggle. There would be unprecedented ideological turmoil within the labour movement and among youth and significant sectors of the intelligentsia and the new 'technocratic' elite.

The decade would begin with the October Crisis and the use of the War Measures Act in 1970.[5] The ensuing years would witness the general strike of 1972, the election of the first PQ government in 1976, and the 'sovereignty association' referendum of 1980 — to name only three of the most important events in ten years of constant change and incessant struggle. The Trudeau regime governed during all these years (except for the short-lived Joe Clark government of 1979-80) and became almost obsessed with what it perceived as a threatening situation in Quebec. The activities of the RCMP Security Service in the province, which would get the force into so much trouble before the decade was out, reflected this obsession.

The struggle for social and political change by broad sectors of the population in both English Canada and Quebec was viewed with dismay by the security establishment in Ottawa. The size of the Security Service was greatly expanded during these years and its members intervened in mass struggle as both intelligence gatherers and protagonists on a scale that was more intrusive and more extensive than at any time since the depths of the Cold War. The extent and the degree were such that, by the mid-1970s, the 'tip of the iceberg' was clearly visible. As the revelations reached scandalous proportions by 1977, Trudeau and his ministers were forced to act to satisfy public opinion, stymie their critics, and prepare the political ground for a more sophisticated and effective security service. The McDonald Commission became the instrument that would play a crucial role in satisfying all of these needs, although its investigations were more thorough and some of its recommendations more far-reaching than the Trudeau government had bargained for.

Opposition MPs, much of the mainstream media, prominent figures in the legal community, and elements within the Liberal Party leadership and the bureaucratic elite had been among those pressuring the federal government to both restrain the RCMP and modernize the security establishment. What neither these groups nor much of the public realized, admitted, or cared to investigate — and what the McDonald Commission did not really address — was that the role played by the RCMP in the 1970s was consistent in its essentials with the functions the force had always performed since it was founded as the North West Mounted Police in 1873. The top officers of the RCMP, and usually their political masters as well, had always understood the role they were expected to play within the class structure, political system, and ideological framework of the Canadian political economy.

As in previous decades, during the 1970s combatting espionage by unfriendly foreign powers and preventing violent internal conspiracies against the state were part of the rationale for the Security Service.

However, these functions represented only one part of the political work of the force. Much of its effort was expended in controlling class conflict and combatting those workers, farmers, national minorities, and political groups and individuals who were attempting to promote either revolutionary or radical change or, in some cases, even significant reforms that threatened the status quo. And this was generally true regardless of whether or not the people promoting social and political change were employing non-violent and perfectly legal means.

By the early 1970s the forces promoting social and political change represented such a significantly broad cross-section of the population that the RCMP felt compelled to cast its net extremely wide. The force mounted spying missions and in some cases illegal actions against popular reformist parties, such as the PQ and the NDP. However, as it attempted to disrupt the mainstream trade unions and these activities could no longer be adequately covered up, the force found it had bitten off more than it could chew. The ensuing public outcry demanded that these activities be halted and that there be a serious investigation of the contemporary role of the RCMP as an institution. The Cold War mentality may still have been alive and well in the minds of the security establishment, but the majority of the population had long since outgrown it. Canadians were no longer willing to tolerate such obvious abuses of police power. But few realized that the RCMP had always engaged in such activities — though previously its work had usually been directed against a narrower cross-section of the population and operated with somewhat less visibility.

HISTORICAL ROOTS
Dominion Police
An examination of the antecedents of the modern RCMP reveals that the force had been designed to be and was developed as an agency for social control on behalf of dominant class interests at least as much as it was an institution devoted to enforcing the law in the conventional way that people usually view that role. Under the *BNA Act*, which created the Dominion of Canada in 1867, the *Criminal Code* was placed in federal legislative jurisdiction but the enforcement of law, both federal and provincial, was the responsibility of the provinces. Thus, in 1867 each province established a provincial police force responsible to the provincial attorney-general or equivalent minister. New provinces did likewise as they entered Confederation. Before 1873 the only police force under federal control (aside from military police and certain customs officials) was the Dominion Police, which operated under a much narrower jurisdiction than its provincial counterparts. The Dominion Police acted as a secret police (equivalent to the contemporary security service) on behalf of the federal authorities. They also performed such functions as guarding federal government facilities, protecting federal politicians and officials and enforcing laws and carrying out investigations that involved contact with the officials of foreign governments and, hence, would have been considered inappropriate for provincial policemen. Because of the divi-

sion of responsibility under the constitution there was not considered to be the need for any additional policing role for the federal government.

This was to change after 1869 when Canada acquired Rupert's Land from the Hudson's Bay Company. Comprising what would today be the Prairie provinces, the Northwest Territories, the Yukon, and parts of northern Ontario and Quebec, the new territory was to be administered directly by Ottawa in a colonial manner with no pretense of allowing either representative or responsible government. Gaining control of this territory as well as bringing British Columbia into the new Dominion of Canada had been one of the important reasons for Confederation. The central Canadian politicians of the 1860s were tied closely to banks, railways, and other financial, transportation, and manufacturing interests, and the new federal state created in 1867 very much reflected these interests.[6] This growing bourgeoisie required raw materials and markets, business for the railways and shipping interests, and expanded opportunities for investment and speculation. The strategy of this powerful combination of businessmen and politicians involved settling the Prairies with a large population of farmers and workers. They would produce the agricultural and resource products that could be bought, sold, transported, processed, and financed by the Central Canadian business class and its collaborators in Britain and the United States. The settlers could also provide markets for both manufactured and primary products, and the building of an entirely new economic infrastructure on the Prairies would lead to an expansion of the entire Canadian economy. There would be lucrative opportunities for speculation in resources, agricultural land, and urban real estate. The project would destroy the economy and way of life of the Indian inhabitants of this vast territory and require that the Aboriginal title to most of the land be extinguished.

When the federal government made plans for the administration of its new acquisition it planned to police the territory with a centrally controlled military-style police force based on the Royal Irish Constabulary and modelled on the way the British policed both Ireland and India (Horrall, 1972). But the inhabitants of Rupert's Land were not consulted about the British-Canadian agreements and they — particularly the Metis in the Red River vicinity — objected strenuously to being transferred from one authority to another with no say in the matter. The Metis took up arms under the leadership of Louis Riel and compelled the federal government to negotiate the terms of transfer to Canadian sovereignty. The result was the *Manitoba Act* of 1870, creating the Province of Manitoba. The new province would control its own police force.

The province of Manitoba created in 1870 was much smaller than it is today, and the rest of the North West, including present-day Saskatchewan, Alberta, and most of Manitoba, remained under direct federal government control as a non-self-governing region known as the North West Territories. Because it soon proved impractical to police the territory with the regular armed forces, the way was paved for the founding of the North West Mounted Police (NWMP).

The North West Mounted Police

Until recently the official mythology surrounding the NWMP was that they were founded in response to the 1873 Cypress Hills Massacre, when American whiskey traders murdered a party of Indians. This was true only in the sense that the massacre hastened the organization and dispatch of the force. The federal government officially sanctioned the establishment of the North West Mounted Police in 1872, with the intention of not sending them into the field until at least 1874, but they moved more quickly from fear of general disorder and perhaps even an Indian war sparked by events like the Cypress Hills Massacre. But the force was not founded primarily to protect Indians from whiskey traders and white outlaws. It was formed to control the Metis and Indians, to ensure that the situation would be conducive to the construction of the CPR, large-scale white settlement, and attendant economic developments (Horrall, 1972; Morgan, 1970).

It was for this reason that the NWMP was designed for both a military role and more conventional policing functions. Like its premature predecessors of 1870 it was modelled after the Royal Irish Constabulary as a force destined for the occupation and control of a colony. Most of the top officers and many of the rank and file came directly from military careers. This would continue in later years and, in fact, the majority of Commissioners since the founding of the force have either come directly from a military career or received prior military training (Brown and Brown, 1978). The military style of organization and leadership would permanently influence both the ideology of the force and its use by governments.

Not only was the force organized along military lines, but the *North West Mounted Police Act* of 1873 also gave it sweeping powers not accorded to the police forces of the provinces. The *Act* provided for magistrates and justices of the peace and stipulated that these positions be filled by members of the force. In fact there were many instances in the first few years when the same police officers arrested, prosecuted, judged, and jailed an accused and when there was no appeal procedure (Ward, 1966). That these practices would be considered appropriate by the leaders of the force and the governments of the day indicates the official outlook towards the rights of the citizenry in the North West. They occasioned considerable criticism throughout the region and were described by the *Prince Albert Times* of March 21, 1884, as "monstrous, extraordinary, abnormal and utterly unconstitutional" (Ward, 1966). The practices were gradually discontinued after much public protest.

The NWMP dealt with Metis and Indian people more than with anyone else during its first few years, establishing a pattern that has continued to this day. The force was involved with others in the negotiation of the treaties that ultimately extinguished the Aboriginal title to most of the land and confined Indians to reservations. While the Mounted Police did not make this policy, the force was one of the main instruments in carrying it out. One of its responsibilities was moving the Indians to reserves and keeping them there.

Relations between the NWMP and the various Indian nations varied considerably over the first few years but deteriorated severely during and after the Saskatchewan Rebellion of 1885. The police had not been the cause of the rebellion and had, in fact, repeatedly warned the federal government that unrest and well-founded grievances could lead to an uprising if concessions were not forthcoming. When the government ignored these and other warnings, a rebellion indeed broke out. The NWMP participated, along with regular military forces, in suppressing it.

In the aftermath of the rebellion the Mounted Police had primary responsibility for apprehending and meting out punishment to the participants. About fifty Metis and Indians, including Big Bear and Poundmaker, were sentenced to penitentiary terms. Louis Riel and eight Indian leaders were executed. Ikta, Little Bear, Wandering Spirit, Round-the-Sky, Miserable Man, Bad Arrow, Man-Without-Blood, and Iron Body were publicly hanged at the NWMP stockade in Battleford. Bands from nearby reserves were 'encouraged' to witness the executions "as it was held that such a tragic spectacle would be an emphatic deterrent against a repetition of such offences" (Turner, 1950). The description of the execution in John Peter Turner's official history of the North West Mounted Police illustrates the police concept of justice and their view of the Indian customs of the day:[7]

> The scaffold, which stood in the open square within the Mounted Police stockade, consisted of a platform about ten feet high and twenty feet long supported by posts at the corners and two higher posts on either side of the centre with a stout crossbeam between. Beneath this was a trap surrounded by a railing. Two full divisions of the Mounted Police, 'D' and 'K', and 'A' Battery — the regulars from Eastern Canada — about 350 men in all — formed a hollow square surrounding the scaffold. At a respectable distance, the assembled crowd had a complete and uninterrupted view. As the hour drew near, weird chanting arose from the direction of the Indian camp, and as one by one the condemned were conducted from the barracks the impressive dirge grew louder. Among those about to die there was little evidence of mental agitation; several joked openly or chatted casually. The shackles they had worn were removed but their arms were pinioned. Each walked between and was preceded and followed by Mounted Police constables. They were soon on the scaffold, each beneath a dangling rope. But before the eight ropes were adjusted and black caps drawn over eight shaven heads, all were told they could speak for ten minutes. Only Ikta and Little Bear availed themselves of the privilege, both shouting defiance. Others uttered a few high pitched war cries or sang their weird lamentations. Wandering Spirit was completely resigned and undemonstrative. Then Hodson spoke, silence fell and the bolt was drawn.
>
> All died instantly. The bodies were hurried away in rough pine boxes and committed to a common grave on the hillside below the barracks.
>
> The days of the scalping knives and war clubs were definitely of the past.

The authorities meted out punishment to Native people suspected of having supported the rebellion regardless of whether they had been tried for specific offences. Many Metis houses were looted and burned by troops. The government withheld annuities from Indian bands who had supported the rebellion and confiscated their horses and guns. Greater efforts were made to restrict Indians to the reserves and the sale of ammunition for hunting purposes was strictly regulated. The NWMP was responsible for carrying out most of these punitive measures. It was an inauspicious beginning to over one hundred years of very unhappy relations between the Mounted Police and Native people in this country.

By 1885 the Mounted Police had also begun what would become over one hundred years of a very strained relationship with organized labour and a cozy one with corporate capital. The force actively protected the CPR against interference from Indians and sided with railway management against their employees. The rapid construction of the railway was the main reason for an increase in the force from 300 to 500 men in 1882 and they were soon breaking strikes for the CPR and other employers. The NWMP helped to smash two strikes in 1883 — one a strike of CPR engineers accompanied by a company lockout of many of the other railway employees. The employers won both strikes with the crucial help of Mounted Police officers who arrested union activists, intimidated strikers, and protected strikebreakers (Fitzpatrick, 1921; Turner, 1950; Morgan, 1970). In the case of the CPR strike, police officers even filled in by driving trains when there was a shortage of scabs (Fitzpatrick, 1921; *Regina Leader*, Dec. 23, 1883). In the NWMP Annual Report for 1883 Commissioner A.G. Irvine reported on the strike activities with great pride in the role played by the force. "I shall only add that the prompt and I trust effectual, quelling of what at one time appeared to be a universal railway strike is — a matter of the utmost congratulation" (Morgan, 1970). The same Annual Report quoted with pride a letter of commendation from CPR Superintendent Egan to Commissioner Irvine. "The services of your men during recent trouble among a certain class of our employees prevented destruction to property and preserved obedience to law and order in a manner highly commendable" (Morgan, 1970).

As CPR construction proceeded into British Columbia, the NWMP and not the B.C. provincial police was given jurisdiction over a ten-mile belt on either side of the railway. This land had been declared by the federal government to be under the *Act for the Preservation of Peace on Public Works*, an act that dated back to the 1850s when troops and police were often used to break strikes on railways and canals in Upper and Lower Canada. The Mounties were soon busy enforcing 'labour peace' among CPR construction workers in B.C. One episode involved a strike of several hundred workers who had not been paid by their contractors for three months on a construction site known as the Beaver in the Rocky Mountains. Superintendent Sam Steele was instrumental in leading a contingent of police officers who broke this strike by protecting scabs and arresting the strike leaders. Steele would boast about this accomplishment for years afterwards. "The strike had collapsed, the roughs of the Beaver, having had a lesson, were quiet. I was much pleased and so were all the contractors, Mr. Ross [engineer in charge] especially" (Steele, 1914).

From the early 1880s until the turn of the century NWMP leaders were busy consolidating and expanding the force. They were also cementing what would become for them an extremely useful relationship with the CPR and related corporate interests, as well as the federal state and the established order in general. The fate of the force was very much tied to that of the CPR and the federal strategy for Western development. What was good for the CPR was often also good for the Mounted Police and vice versa, as was evident in the various labour disputes. Being highly regarded by the CPR, which had tremendous influence with the federal government, the NWMP remained in good standing during a period when it was being criticized by the public for corruption and high-handedness (Brown and Brown, 1978; Morgan, 1970; Ward, 1966).

The NWMP and the CPR together often gained stature with the government from the same events. The Saskatchewan Rebellion could not have happened at a more opportune time for the CPR. The company was then engaged in attempting to both sell more bonds in London and persuade the Canadian government to provide yet more handouts. Neither enterprise looked hopeful before the outbreak of the rebellion. Seeing the opportunity to promote the railway, the CPR generously offered free transportation for troops and equipment, and subsequently much was made of the fact that troop movements to the North West would have been delayed for several weeks without the railway. In the final analysis, the CPR got more money from the taxpayers and successfully floated its bonds in London. The NWMP also gained from the aftermath of the rebellion. The force was increased from five hundred to a thousand men because of its increased activity and the fact that, with the Indians now confined to reservations and the CPR nearing completion, increased settlement and economic expansion were expected to follow.

The NWMP did not become less but rather more military in structure after its first few years as a force.[8] One might have thought that the opposite should have occurred as the West gradually changed from a frontier society to a region of stable agricultural settlement and growing towns and cities. But the leading officers, most with previous military experience, preferred to maintain and enhance the military structure and tradition. These officers saw themselves as heading more than a regional police force. Both ambitious and ideological, they viewed the force as a projection of the power of the Canadian state and the British Empire and hence the guardian of the established order.

Leaders and members of the force were quick to seize the opportunity to serve the Canadian state, the British Empire, and the CPR with the outbreak of the Boer War at the turn of the century. The Canadian government sent a contingent to fight with the British in South Africa. One of the regiments was raised and paid for by Donald A. Smith, the CPR railway magnate who had driven in 'the last spike' in 1885.[9] Smith was one of the richest and most powerful men in Canada as well as being a man of considerable significance in Britain: He had been Governor of the Hudson's Bay Company, chief shareholder and president of the Bank of Montreal, and one of the largest shareholders of the CPR. Smith became Canadian High Commissioner to London and was elevated to the peerage as Lord Strathcona and Mount Royal. The regiment would be known as Strathcona's Horse and was commanded by Colonel Sam Steele (formerly Superintendent Steele of Beaver fame) of the NWMP. Many of the other officers and men were also from the force. Mounted Police Commissioner L.W. Herchmer was given command of another regiment that also consisted of many members of the force.

Their connection to events around the Boer War helped to enhance and cement a relationship that NWMP leaders had been cultivating for three decades. Henceforth people like Lord Strathcona and his powerful friends in the corporate world would be virtual patrons of the Mounted Police and operated on a first-name basis with many of the leading personalities of the force. The British would also recognize the service to the Empire, and in 1904 the name North West Mounted Police was changed to Royal North West Mounted Police (RNWMP). The increased public profile also contributed to the legend that the top officers had been attempting to construct around themselves since the inception of the force. They were attempting to become an institution so identified with the state and the country that a patriotic citizenry would find it difficult to seriously question their authority.

The Royal North West Mounted Police

As Western settlement boomed in the years up to 1914, the RNWMP increased in prestige and continued to expand. In 1905 Alberta and Saskatchewan achieved provincial status but decided at first to retain the Mounties in the capacity of provincial police rather than establishing their own forces. Leading up to and during World War I both the Mounted Police in the West and the Dominion Police throughout the country were kept extra busy in view of the social unrest that was accompanying the rapid industrialization that was further escalated by the war effort.

During the war itself the force assisted in the internment of thousands of 'enemy aliens' (immigrants from countries then at war with the British Empire) and investigated, intimidated, and sometimes arrested socialists, pacifists, and trade unionists who were opposed to the war. The RNWMP also worked with the Dominion Police and other forces in enforcing a vast array of sweeping regulations under the *War Measures Act* and applying the *Military Service Act* of 1917, which imposed military conscription and made it illegal to oppose its implementation by word or deed. During 1917 and the first three months of 1918, 3,895 people were arrested on charges connected with anticonscriptionist activity (Brown and Brown, 1978; Lipton, 1968). During this period Commissioner A.B. Perry constructed a network of plainclothes detectives and undercover men who would become part of the Security and Intelligence (S and I) branch, which would constitute Canada's main secret police in later years.

While the RNWMP was busy with new tasks during these years its future was called into question towards the end of the war. Saskatchewan and Alberta had by then established their own police forces, and many Mounted Police personnel had joined the regular armed forces for service overseas — often as officers in the provost corps. In 1918 a special squadron of the RNWMP was also sent to Siberia to fight with the counterrevolutionary forces in the Russian Civil War as part of the allied intervention. Some Mounties had also been loaned to the Dominion Police for use in Central Canada. By 1918 there were only a little over three hundred Mounties still on active duty with the force in Canada — little more than it had begun with in 1874. There was talk in official circles about disbanding the Mounted Police after the war. Many people failed to see the need for a semimilitary mounted police force under federal auspices during peacetime given that the entire country except for the sparsely settled Yukon and North West Territories had achieved provincial status. Most thought that policing could be handled sufficiently by the Dominion Police and provincial forces. Now that frontier conditions no longer existed, they viewed the RNWMP as increasingly anachronistic.

The future of the force would be assured by the tremendous outburst of social, industrial, and political unrest that followed the war. Agrarian and working-class unrest would be reflected on the parliamentary front by the rise of new political vehicles like the National Progressive Party and the Independent Labour Party (ILP) of J.S. Woodsworth. On the industrial front, class conflict reached new heights with a national wave of strikes unprecedented in size and militancy and the formation of radical union movements like the One Big Union (OBU). All of this unrest and turmoil reflected the Canadian version of the intense class conflict that was sweeping the entire capitalist world in the aftermath of World War I. This conflict and the influence of the Bolshevik Revolution provided the catalysts for a revolutionary upsurge. In Canada this upsurge took the organizational form of first the OBU and later the Communist Party of Canada, which was founded in 1921.

The pivotal event of these years was the Winnipeg General Strike of 1919.[10] It was the first extended general strike in Canadian history and was accompanied by sporadic sympathetic strikes and support actions throughout the country. While the main issue involved the right to collective bargaining in Winnipeg, the strike also reflected general unrest and was closely followed by working-class activists throughout the country. The implications were nationwide in scope. The general strike was viewed as a national showdown between capital and labour. The federal government and state apparatus led the forces of capital in close collaboration with provincial and local politicians and the employers in Winnipeg and elsewhere. They were determined to smash the strike as matter of principle and as a demonstration to the working class that the strategy of a general strike was futile.

The federal government made sweeping amendments to the *Immigration Act* and the *Criminal Code*, also proposing, along with local authorities, to use force against the strikers. But both levels of government and the business community were given a severe scare when the forces they usually employed in these types of situations proved to be unreliable. The Winnipeg city police at first went out on strike in sympathy with the trade union movement. Later the local police went back at the request of the Strike Committee, after making it clear that their role would be to keep order and that they would not be used as strikebreakers. Subsequently most of them were fired and replaced by 'specials' recruited by the employer-sponsored Citizens Committee. The majority of returned soldiers also favoured the strikers. The rank and file of the regular army, many just returned from overseas, threw a real scare into the authorities. For instance, when the 27th Battalion (a local unit) arrived back in Winnipeg hardly any of them would volunteer for strike duty. They were promptly disbanded and General Ketchen, Commanding Officer in Winnipeg, recruited volunteers for militia units instead, knowing that only men opposed to the strike would volunteer.

The one regular armed force the authorities could rely upon without question was the RNWMP. The force arranged to demobilize a squadron of Mounted Police returning from overseas in Winnipeg to be placed at the disposal of Commissioner Perry, and the Mounties played a crucial role in smashing the strike. They arrested the strike leaders and, along with the 'specials,' broke up demonstrations of strikers and returned soldiers. On June 21 they broke up the last big demonstration of returned soldiers by riding through crowds swinging baseball bats and firing volleys into the crowds from their revolvers. Two people were killed and dozens injured. The city was put under military control, and the strike had collapsed by June 25.

One immediate aftermath of the Winnipeg General Strike was a guaranteed future for the Mounted Police (Brown and Brown, 1978). Once again they had demonstrated in a very convincing fashion their value to the established order. The authorities were not long in showing their gratitude. The authorized strength of the force had been set at 1,200 in December 1918, but suddenly increased to 2,500 in July 1919. By September its strength had been built up to 1,600. In November a new federal act provided for the absorption of the Dominion Police into the RNWMP and a change of name to the Royal Canadian Mounted Police (RCMP). As the new name implied, the force would now be the main federal police force throughout the country. The new regime took effect on February 1, 1920.

The Royal Canadian Mounted Police

The military structure of the old force was kept intact in the new RCMP, and it was clear from the comments of ministers and top RCMP officers that one of its main functions was to control class conflict and suppress industrial or political disturbances. In his comments on the RCMP Annual Report for 1920, N.W. Rowell, the minister responsible for the force, made it clear that he regarded the Mounties as an important adjunct to the military power of the state. Rowell, noting that the force had been increased to 74 officers and 1,734 NCOs and constables, added, "I think that so soon as the militia is definitely re-organized and put upon a sound basis and the Permanent Force is put in shape — the strength of the Mounted Police can be decreased" (*Canadian Annual Review*, 1920). In his Annual Report for 1919 Commissioner Perry put considerable emphasis on the political-military character of the force. He noted that one of its duties had been "generally to aid and assist the civil power in the preservation of law and order wherever the Government of Canada may direct." Perry mentioned that the federal government had taken pains to withdraw the Mounted Police squadrons from Europe and Siberia as quickly as possible so as to increase their strength in Canada. He thought there were now sufficient personnel to meet any emergencies and "to supervise the mining and industrial areas, to watch the settlements of enemy nationality and foreigners whose sentiments might be disloyal and attitudes antagonistic." Perry lamented the unrest that he said was reflected by strikers with a 'sinister purpose' and upon which 'seditious conspiracies' were allegedly thriving. The report noted that several people had been convicted for possessing prohibited literature, "but there is a flood of pernicious and mischievous literature not on the prohibited list. Under the cloak of freedom of thought and speech, this literature is being spread for the avowed purpose of overthrowing democratic government and destroying the foundations of civilization." Perry's report also boasted about the role of the force in defeating the Winnipeg General Strike.

The unrest that so alarmed Commissioner Perry and so many state officials abated somewhat in 1920 but remained a continuing feature in some regions of the country until at least 1923. The RCMP was to play a role of some sort in most areas of unrest and industrial conflict over the next two decades. Its structure and ideology made it by far the most suitable police force for suppressing civil disorder and particularly for breaking strikes. Most members were recruited from rural districts where trade unions were virtually unknown. They were recruited while young and then trained in a military manner in barracks away from the influences of a modern urban society. When training was complete and recruits entered the force, they were moved frequently from place to place and hence could not easily put down roots in any one locality. Thus there developed a distance between Mounted Police officers and the public. Perhaps most importantly, a force of RCMP officers could be assembled from distant points, used against workers in a strike situation, and then removed from the scene of the conflict: They did not have to live with the consequences on a day-to-day basis afterwards. This approach contrasted sharply with that of a typical city police force. In a city the rank and file of a local force would be recruited mainly from the working class and might very well have relatives, acquaintances, or friends who were trade union members and would therefore be involved in strikes from time to time. Further, the children of policemen would go to the same schools as the children of trade unionists. All in all, although city police were sometimes used as strikebreakers, they were seldom regarded as being so consistently reliable as their RCMP counterparts.

The RCMP role in breaking strikes and dispersing political and unemployment demonstrations was most marked in the 1930s, a decade of intense conflict — but it also reflects the earlier activities of the nine-teenth century and the continued 'strike duty' by the force in the 1980s. In fact, the RCMP has played such an important role in class conflict that it may have inadvertently increased the class and political consciousness of Canadian working people. Its role has frequently been commented upon by labour historians and students of industrial relations. In his 1968 study of labour unrest for the federal Task Force on Labour Relations, Professor Stuart Jamieson asserts that RCMP activities helped to develop a distrust for the federal government among trade unionists:

> The RCMP has thus become a highly pervasive force in Canadian society. Its presence has been felt with enough force to tip the scales of battle in hundreds of strikes and labour demonstrations. The particular image of the RCMP and the federal government itself, which this situation has generated in the eyes of many in the ranks of organized labour, in all probability has had a profound effect on the climate of labour relations in this country. (Jamieson, 1968)

From the time it was organized in 1920 the RCMP grew rapidly so that it soon dwarfed its predecessor in size, scope, and power. In the early 1930s several provinces were in such dire financial straits that they disbanded their police forces and contracted with the RCMP to act as provincial police. This was the beginning of a process that would eventually see the RCMP act not only as a federal force but also as provincial police (every-where except Ontario, Quebec, and Newfoundland) and often municipal police as well. Canada thus developed a more highly centralized and powerful federal police force than the United States or most other coun-tries with a federal constitution.

The federal government was not averse to using this centralized police power during periods of crisis. It prepared for years of crises in 1931 by appointing Major-General James H. MacBrien as the new RCMP Commis-sioner. A former Chief of the General Staff of the regular army, MacBrien brought with him a reputation for being 'trigger happy' in his reaction to strikes and industrial unrest. He expanded the RCMP by nearly a thou-sand men during his first year of office and made the force more military in character. Over the next few years there would be plenty of action, during which the federal government was not always sensitive to constitutional niceties in dealing with those provinces where the RCMP acted as provincial police and were thus supposedly responsible to the provincial attorneys-general. Thus the Bennett government used the RCMP to stop the On-to-Ottawa trek in Regina in 1935 against the wishes and in violation of the constitutional prerogatives of the Saskatchewan government (Brown, 1987).

When the RCMP was founded in 1920 it already had a security service, because it had taken over many of the functions formerly performed by the old Dominion Police. The force later absorbed the remainder of the old federal secret police as well. Under the RCMP the new agency would be known as the Security and Intelligence (S and I) branch, becoming in later years the Special Branch and eventually the Security Service (SS), which was to become the centre of so much public controversy in the 1970s.

Canada's 'SS': Security Service

The pattern of operation established by the S and I in the 1920s would change very little over more than fifty years except that the branch would be much more active during periods of intense economic and political controversy — such as the 1930s and 1970s — and periods of international tension that affected domestic politics — such as the Cold War period from the late 1940s to the early 1960s. In the early 1920s the security police were most active in spying upon, infiltrating, intimidating, and disrupting radical trade unions like the OBU and radical political organizations like the Communist Party of Canada (CPC). In its trade union activities the S and I worked closely with the main body of the RCMP. Sometimes S and I employed people on contract, and sometimes it employed private detective firms such as Pinkerton's Detective Agency, which was notorious for thuggery and acts of espionage against trade unions (Brown and Brown, 1978). As in the 1970s, the force did not confine its attention to unions or political groups that could be considered revolutionary or even particularly radical. Pacifists, social democrats, labour reformers, critical intellectuals, and progressive clergymen received their share of attention. J.S. Woodsworth, devout pacifist and leader of the Independent Labour Party, revealed some of these activities in a speech to the House of Commons in 1922. He complained that trade unionists and reformers were being subjected to constant surveillance and harassment and provided some examples from his personal experience:

> I remember a few instances particularly. Before I threw myself into the labour movement I could hardly credit this kind of thing. I remember addressing one night a meeting of labour people, and the next morning an officer of the Mounted Police came to my home and asked me to go to his office. You speak about this as a civil police force. Well, when I entered the office I found everything exactly as though it were a military tribunal. There was an effort made to persuade or intimidate me into either retracting my statements or pledging myself not to make similar statements to the people. I was trying to plead for decency and good order in this country, and to prevent the occasions of strife which are so frequently occurring. I remember speaking at a little town in southern Saskatchewan. The local clergyman was chairman of the meeting, and everything was conducted in perfectly good order. But the next day after I left, the local clergyman was subjected to all kinds of indignities at the hands of the local Mounted Police officer. The clergyman happened to have been born in England. He had to tell the Mounted Police officer when he came over to this country, whether he had any connections with the Reds, and Labour, and all the rest of it. A few days later I happened to be addressing a class in political economy at the University of Saskatchewan, and the Mounted Police tried to discover what was going on inside the class room. (House of Commons, *Debates*, April 4, 1922)

During the years 1930 to 1935 the RCMP security forces were perhaps busier than at any time before or since. The unrest occasioned by the

Depression coincided with what was perhaps the most authoritarian government in Canadian history, under Prime Minister R.B. Bennett. Bennett promised to use the 'iron hand of ruthlessness' against what he perceived to be the enemies of the established order. The RCMP were to be his shock troops. The force would play a major role in infiltrating and disrupting farm and labour organizations, radical political groups, and ethnic associations. The Communist Party was declared illegal under Section 98 of the *Criminal Code* and many of its leaders and activists imprisoned.[11] Several thousand people were arrested over these five years for their activities in strikes, demonstrations, and political movements. The *Canadian Labour Defender* counted 720 arrests and 155 convictions for political offences in 1931 alone (Buhay, 1932; Brown and Brown, 1978).

The people victimized most of all were immigrants. Under the *Immigration Act* a person who had been in Canada less than five years could be deported if he or she became a 'public charge' — in other words, was on public relief. The *Act* also provided that anyone not born in Canada could be deported, regardless of length of residence, for advocating the overthrow by force of constituted authority "or by word or act creating or attempting to create riot or public disorder in Canada." Immigrants scheduled for deportation also had few rights before the courts and in many cases could be deported with no hearing in open court whatsoever. Many thousands were deported for being public charges and hundreds for political offences (Roberts, 1988). Many of the Communists and other radicals deported for political reasons were sent to countries governed by military or fascist dictatorships where they would be almost guaranteed imprisonment or worse upon arrival (Brown and Brown, 1978; Roberts, 1988). The increased magnitude of deportations during these years becomes clear in the statistics: For the six years from 1930 to 1935 inclusive, 28,097 immigrants were deported from Canada, in contrast to 10,923 for the six years from 1924 to 1929 inclusive (Roberts, 1988). The RCMP played a major role in many of these deportation proceedings, as it would continue to do over the years. Eventually the security branch would play a significant role in who should be allowed into Canada as well (Whitaker, 1987).

The work of the Security and Intelligence branch abated considerably after the defeat of the Bennett government in 1935 and as the depression lifted slightly in the last years of the decade. It would be busier during World War II investigating and sometimes arresting for internment Nazis and Fascists and their sympathizers. The force also kept a close eye on pacifists and other dissidents who opposed or were critical of the war effort. In the first two years, before the Soviet Union became allies in the war effort, the RCMP also participated in the surveillance and internment of Communists and related radicals who were opposed to the war. It was this work which RCMP Commissioner S.T. Wood appeared to enjoy most. In an article entitled "Tools for Treachery," which appeared in the *RCMP Quarterly* of April, 1941, Commissioner Wood informed Canadians that combatting domestic Nazis and Fascists was not the main problem for the force and the government. "Many may be surprised to hear that it is not the Nazi nor the Fascist but the radical who constitutes our most troublesome problem" (Wood, 1941). Wood then proceeded with an attack on those Communists and on trade unionists, civil rights associations, pacifists, newspaper editors, and Members of Parliament who were alleged to be "greatly encouraging the subversive elements by attacking the Defence Regulations." These regulations were passed under the authority of the *War Measures Act* and often grossly abused by government officials, particularly the RCMP. The exigencies of the war had placed tremendous power in the hands of the police, and Wood must have resented those who would interfere with his opportunity to settle old scores.[12] Within two months of this article the Soviets were in the war and the RCMP was in the unenviable position of having to treat their old enemies as allies. Even so, many Communists were not released from internment until the fall of 1942 — more than a year after the Communist Party had come out in full support of the war effort.[13]

In the post-World War II period the RCMP would soon get the opportunity to concentrate once again on hounding the radical left. By 1946 the Cold War had begun in earnest and was escalated in Canada with the so-called 'Gouzenko revelations' concerning a Soviet spy ring in this country.[14] This was followed by the appointment of a Royal Commission with sweeping authority under the *War Measures Act* and the use of the draconian procedures sanctioned by the *Official Secrets Act*. Spy trials followed and were accompanied by a sensational and hysterical campaign orchestrated by the government and the media. The Cold War had been launched with a vengeance in Canada, and the political psychology that resulted would inhibit public debate into at least the early 1960s.

The Cold War atmosphere that the publicity surrounding the Gouzenko revelations had helped to create was intensified with the outbreak of the Korean War in 1950. The RCMP security branch was thus enabled to operate within a climate of fear. Many of its targets were very similar to those of the past. It continued to hound the Communist Party even though, like its counterparts in most other Western countries, the CPC was undergoing a rapid decline in size and influence throughout the 1950s.

As in the past, the RCMP net was cast much beyond those organizations and individuals that a reasonable person would consider revolutionary or particularly radical. Security checks became widespread throughout the civil service, government agencies, and many private corporations that had defence contracts with the government. The RCMP carried out the investigations of such people and built up dossiers that could affect their careers. Much of the information was based on hearsay, rumour, and interrogation of neighbours and acquaintances. The people being investigated were seldom informed of the fact and had no right to see their dossiers if they did discover their existence. Government officials would peruse the RCMP reports and then decide on the fate of the employees concerned. There was no appeal to any outside authority, and people could be denied promotion, demoted, or fired with no explanation.

Trade unions continued to be the object of RCMP attention. The force placed considerable emphasis on destroying what remained of the already declining influence of Communist Party supporters in the trade union movement. The most notorious example of this was the government and RCMP collaboration with U.S. gangster Hal Banks and his Seafarers' International Union (SIU) to destroy the Canadian Seamen's Union (CSU).[15]

In the years after World War II the RCMP increased its influence with Canadian immigration officials in helping to determine which immigrants should be deported and, far more important in this period, which prospective immigrants should be allowed into the country in the first place. During these years RCMP and immigration officials screened prospective immigrants more thoroughly and on a much greater scale than in any previous period in our history. And they consistently applied a double standard — right-wing immigrants were generally welcome and leftists unwelcome, with Communists being barred altogether (Whitaker, 1987). Thus former Nazis and their collaborators often had an easier time entering Canada than leftists who had been their victims in occupied Europe. The same criteria applied to temporary visitors. People were sometimes denied entry to Canada when they wished merely to attend conferences or accept speaking engagements (Whitaker, 1987).

The policies of immigration officials and the RCMP reflected long-standing political biases and the conservative climate of the time. But they were also a reflection of Canada's role in the Cold War as a junior partner in military alliances such as NATO and NORAD. The force, like its predecessors, remained the guardian of the established order. However, by this time the United States had replaced Britain as the most important arbiter of that order on the international scene. The ideological gurus of the Canadian state apparatus had now completed the long process of transforming their ultimate allegiance from London to Washington, and it followed from this that what was good for the United States was good for Canada.

Recent scholarship has demonstrated the continuing influence of the Cold War on immigration and general intelligence and security policy into the late 1980s (Littleton, 1986; Whitaker, 1987). Littleton and Whitaker depict a secret and powerful security and intelligence establishment, which to some extent usurped policy-making from the civil authorities and displayed a frightening contempt for the liberal-democratic process. Whitaker demonstrates that a secret 'state within a state' has developed in the administration of immigration policy and that this has happened under the guise of protecting 'national security.' Littleton demonstrates the ambiguity surrounding the loyalties of the personnel who determine policy for the overall security and intelligence apparatus. These people are torn between loyalty to their mentors in the CIA and the international security establishment and their immediate political superiors in the government of Canada.

While the leadership of the RCMP and the security community would increasingly reveal their dual allegiance over the years, it was already becoming evident by the early 1950s. The Canadian peace movement was harassed throughout the 1950s mainly because many in the movement were critical of Canadian participation in NATO and NORAD and because most peace activists were from time to time critical of U.S. foreign and military policy, particularly U.S. nuclear strategy. This was interpreted as giving aid and comfort to the Communists, while many in the RCMP and elsewhere considered it unpatriotic for Canadians to criticize the United States. The force recruited informers within peace organizations, who invariably took pictures at peace demonstrations for the purpose of identifying participants (Brown and Brown, 1978). Sometimes they would later visit the homes of demonstrators to question them about their political views and warn them to dissociate themselves from the peace movement. As a result it took courage to even attend a peace demonstration throughout much of the 1950s.

The policy of federal government officials harassing Canadians for opposing U.S. foreign policy reached such heights that it came close to costing Dr James Endicott his life.[16] Endicott travelled to southern China on behalf of the Canadian Peace Congress in 1952 to investigate charges that the U.S. military had been practising germ warfare during the Korean War. He then toured Canada arguing that the charges were true (Whitaker, 1987; Endicott, 1980). Endicott was vilified by the Canadian establishment to the point where the federal Cabinet held lengthy discussions about whether to prosecute him for treason. They finally decided against it, partly because of the severity of the penalty, which was death, and partly because the Americans were reluctant to publicly testify that they had not used germ warfare. Reg Whitaker has perhaps best expressed the absurdity of this situation in his book, *Double Standard*. "Canadians were thus spared the irony of a Canadian being tried for treason in a Canadian court for statements made not against Canada but against the United States" (Whitaker, 1987).

The political psychology resulting from the Cold War began to decline slightly in the early 1960s. This led to a more critical atmosphere in the universities, an intellectual ferment in the population as a whole, and the expansion of the peace movement. In this period the peace movement in Canada tended to be led by the Campaign for Nuclear Disarmament (CND) and the Combined Universities Campaign for Nuclear Disarmament (CUCND), which adopted many of their ideas from the nuclear disarmament movement led by Bertrand Russell in Britain. They concentrated on opposition to Canadian acquisition of nuclear weapons and the stationing of such weapons on Canadian soil. These people, like their predecessors of the 1950s, were generally opposed to U.S. foreign policy and critical of what they viewed as Canadian subservience to that policy. Their tactics included petitions to government, mass demonstrations, and the sporadic use of the type of civil disobedience coming into vogue at this time in the British peace movement and the civil rights campaign led by Martin Luther King in the United States. While the peace movement would become very broad in scope it tended to be most influential among students and youth. These were the very early years of the ferment among youth throughout much of North America and Europe, which would lead to the rise of the New Left in the later 1960s.

The growing influence of the peace movement was regarded by right-wing pro-American circles in Canada as a subversive threat, and the RCMP responded accordingly. The Security and Intelligence branch was soon recruiting informers and placing spies within organizations like the CUCND and generally harassing peace activists, just as it had done in the previous decade. What was different this time was that public criticism of these tactics developed quickly and vociferously. This in itself was evidence that the Cold War political psychology was waning.

What really got the RCMP into trouble was its practice of sending agents onto university campuses to recruit informers among faculty, staff, and students. Seeing this as an obvious threat to academic freedom, the Canadian Association of University Teachers (CAUT) and the National Federation of Canadian University Students (NFCUS) complained publicly to the government, receiving support from a variety of trade unions, civil liberties groups, women's organizations, opposition MPs, and even some daily newspapers. The initial responses of the RCMP and the government were the same as they would be later during the bigger scandals of the 1970s. For as long as possible, they denied that such activities were taking place. When this was no longer feasible, they then attempted to justify them (Brown and Brown, 1978). RCMP Commissioner C.W. Harvison claimed that the charges were communist-inspired and implied that they were part of an international communist conspiracy hatched in Prague. He claimed that only security personnel were capable of distinguishing between the mere radical or dissenter and the 'subversive conspirators.' When the facts could no longer be denied Harvison exhibited novel reasoning on the proper role for a police force in a liberal democracy: "University students are naturally curious. At this age one finds a great deal of idealism and a strong sense of social morality. There are certain abuses in our system which the student may think communism will cure, if he gets only one side of the picture" (*The Gateway*, March 27, 1963; House of Commons, *Debates*, May 31, 1963).

Political conditions had already changed enough in Canada that governments could no longer sustain this stance and were forced to at least appear to be taking corrective measures to reign in the RCMP. In 1963 the Pearson government responded to public pressure by issuing guidelines to the effect that the force should discontinue 'fishing expeditions' on university campuses and cease to investigate people at such institutions except in the course of normal law-enforcement duties or where individuals required security clearance because they had applied to particular positions. They also instructed the RCMP to cease making public statements on controversial political issues.

In spite of these governmental assurances, RCMP spying and interference continued on campuses, as it did elsewhere, and considerable evidence also surfaced that in some of this work the force collaborated with private right-wing organizations and individuals (House of Commons, *Debates*, November 28, 1963; CAUT *Bulletin*, December 1967; Brown and Brown, 1978; McDonald, 1981). The controversy surrounding these and related situations finally prompted the Pearson government to appoint the Royal Commission on Security (Mackenzie Commission) by an Order-in-Council of November 16, 1966.[17]

The Mackenzie Commission was prohibited by its terms of reference from holding public hearings and could only hear *in camera* witnesses. It was manipulated by members of the RCMP in such a manner that the later McDonald report felt compelled to comment adversely on the matter. The Mackenzie Commission did show sufficient independence to call for a civilian security agency separate from the RCMP. But aside from this major recommendation — which the federal government did not act upon — the Mackenzie Report was extremely conservative in its recommendations. The report recommended security checks and fingerprinting of every federal government employee rather than just those in sensitive positions (Mackenzie, 1969; Sawatsky, 1980). The report also recommended that the security service have more influence in determining who got security clearance for jobs within the civil service.

What was disturbing about the Mackenzie Report was not just its callousness towards individual rights in some of the specific recommendations but its philosophical approach to the role of a security service in a liberal democracy. It saw this role as being much broader than protecting the state from foreign spies or foreign and domestic espionage and violent or illegal conspiracies. In the commission's view, the secret police should combat communist groups no matter how legal their methods, and the police should also play a role in moulding public opinion:

> The forms of Communist subversive activity in Canada are varied, ranging from efforts to develop front organizations to attempts to *subvert individuals* in government, mass media, the universities, the trade unions, emigre and ethnic groups and political parties. Such activities are assisted by the fact that the Communists are able to *exploit and exaggerate existing elements of social unrest and dissent concerned with a variety of appealing causes.* Some facets of their operations are worthy of special mention. First, activities in universities and trade unions appear at present to be of special significance. Half the population is under twenty-five and activities in universities will have a considerable effect *on the national climate of opinion in future years.* (Mackenzie, 1969; emphasis added).

The Mackenzie Report also emphasized that the interests of Canada and the United States in the security field were virtually identical.[18] Immigration was particularly an area in which Canada owed it to the United States to allow only politically correct people into this country lest they pollute our great neighbour as well as ourselves. It was clear from the Mackenzie Report that the ideologists of the Cold War were alive and well — and that not all of them were in the RCMP.

The years after the Mackenzie Report would see the RCMP Security Service expand its activities enormously, and nearly all of these additional activities would involve combatting domestic unrest. The scandals that arose would eventually lead to the McDonald Commission and the beginning of the end for the leading role of the RCMP in the security field. The force would, of course, continue strike duties when called upon and carry on as the main federal police force and a provincial force in eight of the ten provinces.

CONCLUSION

There has been a remarkably consistent pattern in Mounted Police activities from the early days of the North West Mounted Police to the RCMP of the 1980s. The force was executing Indian rebels in Saskatchewan after 1885, spying on Indian organizations throughout Canada in the 1970s, and arresting Innu protestors in Labrador in 1989. It was breaking strikes for the CPR in 1883 and among Newfoundland wood workers in 1959. It was spying upon pacifists in the 1920s and the peace movement in the 1960s. The North West Mounted Police performed useful functions for the British Empire for two decades after 1900 and the modern RCMP has played a similar role for the American Empire since 1945. The RCMP were spying upon and sometimes harassing communists, social democrats, labour militants, and dissident intellectuals in the 1920s and doing the same thing among those same groups in the 1970s. Along the way ethnic minorities, radical farmers, and Quebec nationalists did not always escape their attention.

In its entire history the RCMP has never apprehended a single important foreign spy, although it did pick off a few very minor practitioners of the art. Its apprehensions of violent domestic conspirators have been few and far between. In fact, though there have been violent conspiracies against the state by organizations such as the FLQ, instances of this sort have been very few in Canada. Most RCMP activity outside of normal police functions has been directed at combatting people who sought basic changes in either the class structure or the conventional political arrangements in the country, or both. These people were often regarded as enemies of the state regardless of the methods they employed to achieve their aims.

The excesses committed by the RCMP during the 1970s were not a result of the force temporarily running amok. They were in keeping with the Mounted Police tradition of over one hundred years of willing service. But the question never seriously asked was 'service to whom?' The various government commissions probing the role of the force did not really examine this consistent historical pattern, and they did not ask this fundamental question. This is not surprising because, even if they had been so inclined, they had no mandate to do so. Very few of those reformist politicians and investigative journalists who combined with the critics to finally call the RCMP to account bothered to examine the consistent historical pattern or ask the fundamental question either. Most studiously refrained from doing so. That fundamental question seems to be beyond the pale for those who insist upon examining the role of the state and the institutional framework of our society within the boundaries established by the dominant liberal ideology.

NOTES

1. This list includes the activities that were generally known by 1977 *before* the McDonald Commission got down to work, and it was the furor around this activity that forced the government to act. The commissioner would unearth much more, including spying on the Quebec Liberal government and the federal Liberal caucus, writing false communiques urging the FLQ to take more violent action, and attempting to manipulate the press. It is not my intention to go into detail on those activities here. The richest sources of details on the period are the second and third reports of the McDonald Commission (1981). There have also been a number of books examining these details and their implications. The best is *The RCMP vs. the People* by T.A. Lee and E. Mann with Norman Penner (1979). Two useful accounts by journalists during these years are *Men in the Shadows* by John Sawatsky (1980) and *Nobody Said No* by Jeff Sallot (1979). *Crimes of the Secret Police* by Robert Dion (1982) is a useful account covering RCMP activities in Quebec.

2. The Keable Commission is mentioned in the text of this chapter. The Krever Commission was appointed by the Ontario government to inquire into improper use of confidential health information after complaints that the RCMP was using such information to disrupt left-wing groups and harass individuals. The Alberta government appointed the Laycraft Commission and New Brunswick the Hughes Commission to examine matters relating to the administration of justice and the RCMP.

3. The CSIS has already been involved in controversy involving infiltration of trade unions and left-wing associations.

4. A number of Marxist-Leninist groups and parties arose in the late 1970s and it appeared for a while that they might eclipse the traditional Communist Party of Canada as the main expression of the Marxist-Leninist tendency in Canada. The two most important were En Lutte/In Struggle and the Workers' Communist Party, both of which had most of their strength in Quebec. Both organizations disbanded in the early 1980s.

5. One of the most useful examinations of the October Crisis of 1970 is *Bleeding Hearts, Bleeding Country* by Denis Smith (1971).

6. The class connections between business, politics, and state strategy in the nineteenth century are a central theme of many of the economic histories of the period. Tom Naylor's *History of Canadian Business, 1867-1914* (1975), Vol. I, is a good example and *A History of Canadian Wealth* by Gustavas Myers (1972) is a useful muckraking account, originally published in 1914.

7. John Peter Turner wrote a multivolume official history of the Mounted Police that helped to provide an ideological frame of reference from which the force and its supporters could view their own history. Until the 1970s nearly all books on RCMP history, whether or not they were 'official' commissioned histories, carried an unabashedly pro-force point of view and were often examined by the office of the Commissioner before publication.

8. The military-style rules governing internal discipline in the force were tightened in the nineteenth century and again after the formation of the

RCMP — particularly by Major-General MacBrien when he became Commissioner in the 1930s. See *An Authorized History of the RCMP* by Lorne and Caroline Brown (1978).

9.   The practice of rich and powerful men financing military units of the national armed forces was common up to World War I. Timothy Eaton financed such a regiment during the war. During the Winnipeg General Strike the T. Eaton Company was also kind enough to donate horses for the use of the Police Specials.

10. The Winnipeg General Strike has been written about extensively. There is a short account of the strike in *Times of Trouble: Labour Unrest and Industrial Conflict in Canada, 1900-66* by Stuart Jamieson (1971) that puts the strike in the context of labour unrest throughout much of this century. Full-length accounts include *Confrontation at Winnipeg: Labour, Industrial Relations and the General Strike* by David J. Bercuson (1974) and *Winnipeg 1919: The Strikers' Own History of the Winnipeg General Strike* edited by Norman Penner (1973). For a brief account of the influence of the strike upon the fate of the RNWMP see *An Unauthorized History of the RCMP*.

11. Frank Scott, Professor and later Dean of Law at McGill University, pointed out at the time that the Communist Party may have been persecuted more in Canada than in any other liberal democracy during the early 1930s. See F.R. Scott, "The Trial of the Toronto Communists," in *Queen's Quarterly*, 1932.

12. S.T. Wood was well known for his anti-labour sentiments. He was Assistant Commissioner in charge of Saskatchewan when the On-to-Ottawa trek was stopped in Regina in 1935. Wood had been trained at the Royal Military College and was known to be 'trigger happy' in strike situations. He was a personal friend and great admirer of J. Edgar Hoover, long-time director of the FBI.

13. An interesting collection of first-hand accounts by left wingers who were interned in the 1940-42 period is contained in *Dangerous Patriots* by William and Kathleen Repka (1982). The most outrageous abuse of power during these years was, of course, the internment of Japanese Canadians. In fairness to the RCMP this was not their idea and, in fact, they reported that there was little danger of disloyalty among Japanese Canadians. In rounding up the Japanese for internment the RCMP was merely following the instructions of the Mackenzie King government, which was pandering to racist demagogues and greedy opportunists anxious to get their hands on property owned by Japanese Canadians. See *The Enemy That Never Was* by Ken Adachi (1974) and *A Man of Our Times* by Rolf Knight and Maya Koizumi (1976).

14. There has been considerable writing done concerning the influence of the Igor Gouzenko affair. One of the early books on how the Gouzenko case was used to manipulate public opinion and launch the Cold War in North America is *The Atom Spy Hoax* by William A. Reuben (1955). Two books that reveal how the trials and surrounding publicity affected those caught up in them are *Emma* by June Callwood (1984) and *The Strangest Dream* by Merrily Weisbord (1983). Reg Whitaker's *Double Standard* (1987) discusses the influence of the Gouzenko affair on the Cold War atmosphere, as does James Littleton in *Target Nation* (1986). John Sawatsky's *Gouzenko: The Untold Story* (1984) has many first-hand accounts by people who knew or worked with Gouzenko and is revealing about the man's motives.

Sawatsky's *Men in the Shadows* also includes a chapter entitled "The Gouzenko Defection."

15. The story of how the RCMP and several different governments related to Hal Banks, the Seafarers' International Union, and the Canadian Seamen's Union is mentioned in most labour histories of the period. Two recent books dealing specifically with the subject are *Against the Tide: The Story of the Canadian Seamen's Union* (1986) and William Kaplan's *Anything That Floats: Pat Sullivan, Hal Banks and the Seamen's Unions of Canada* (1987).

16. James Endicott had been born of Canadian missionary parents in China. He later became a United Church minister and missionary himself. Endicott supported the Chinese Revolution of 1949 and became an advocate of the new China and a controversial peace activist in Canada during the 1950s. The United Church succumbed to the Cold War hysteria and Endicott was expelled from the ministry in the 1950s; the United Church officially apologized and reinstated Endicott in the 1980s. Information concerning Endicott and the germ warfare charges, for which there is considerable circumstantial evidence, can be found in *James G. Endicott: Rebel Out of China* (1980) and Reg Whitaker's *Double Standard* (1987).

17. The Mackenzie Commission consisted of Maxwell Mackenzie (Chair), Yve Pratte, and M.J. Coldwell, former leader of the CCF. The RCMP feared the influence of Coldwell because of his social-democratic connections but he turned out to be the most conservative of the three commissioners. John Sawatsky points out that Coldwell "became the conservative anchor on the commission and often argued against some of the more liberal proposals of his two fellow commissioners" (*Men in the Shadows*, 1980). Reg Whitaker comments in *Double Standard* on the propensity of some American liberals and some Canadian social democrats to become more McCarthyist than McCarthy during the Cold War. Coldwell was apparently still fighting the Cold War in 1968.

18. Except for the new guidelines for a more civilian orientation to the Security Service, the Trudeau government did not make it clear whether it agreed or disagreed with most of the specific recommendations of the Mackenzie Report or with its philosophical thrust. The RCMP certainly agreed with the report's pro-American stance. The force harassed U.S. draft dodgers and deserters in Canada during the Vietnam War, even to the point of ignoring Canadian government guidelines. It was another case of its dual loyalty coming into play. In one case the RCMP picked up three U.S. deserters legally resident in British Columbia and illegally turned them over to U.S. military authorities at the B.C.-Washington border. For a discussion of this and similar cases, see *An Unauthorized History of the RCMP*.

Chapter Ten

In Defiance of the Law of the Land: Social Control and the Unemployed Movement in the Dirty Thirties in British Columbia

Louise Gorman Arkle / John McMullan

While Lorne Brown documents the history of Canadian policing as one of political "misadventure," Louise Gorman Arkle and John McMullan link policing to the political economy of the state in advanced capitalist society and explore the specific policing activities during the Great Depression within British Columbia. They see these activities as state management of the unemployed in response to the threat of a spreading political unrest directed against the capitalist system.

By January 1933, unemployment in Canada had reached 30.4 per cent. With an influx of unemployed workers into British Columbia, municipalities complained of being "overrun by beggars and panhandlers." The activities of the unemployed were closely monitored by the Vancouver city police, the railway police, and the Investigations Branch of the Vancouver Relief Department. Efforts were made to block the westward migration of the unemployed, who congregated on the outskirts of the city. While both the local and provincial governments were unable to provide financial or social assistance, the Communist Party of Canada organized the unemployed into a political force. As a result, the Vancouver chief of police identified the unemployed as "agitators desirous of fermenting trouble." In negotiations with Ottawa, a program of relief camps that would help to relocate the potential threat was initiated. Given the intolerable conditions that characterized these camps, however, it is not surprising that they fostered strikes and riots. During these strikes, the municipal, provincial, and Royal Canadian Mounted Police maintained a vigilant surveillance. A vivid illustration of police vigilance and intervention is provided by the "On to Ottawa Trek," when a peaceful

---

John McMullan is Professor in Sociology at St. Mary's University and Louise Gorman Arkle is an Instructor in Sociology at Okanagan College

demonstration was transformed into a riot, with a number of casualties and over one hundred arrests.

From this overview, Gorman and McMullan highlight how the militant, communist-led unemployed constituted a counterhegemonic force. Labelled as a threat to peace, order, and good government, this movement represented a crisis of authority. To lead to an understanding of the state's response, the authors explore how the state maintains social order by mediating between the interests of capital and the working class. A number of structural mechanisms ordinarily operate to maintain the appearance that the state is acting in the interests of the general public. Acting as "crisis manager," the state maintains a delicate balance between the needs of capital and the political demands of the working class, while concealing the class nature of the state and maintaining social calm. However, when a crisis occurs — such as during the Great Depression — these selective mechanisms fail and a crisis in the state's role as crisis manager develops. Ultimately, the state must stifle the demands of the working class, by direct repression if necessary. From this perspective, rather than being harbingers of public order, the police are revealed as instruments of surveillance and control over working-class politics and culture.

INTRODUCTION

A great deal has been written about the role of the state and economic crisis in the 'dirty thirties' in Canada, but little is known about specific state social-control operations during that period. This chapter is a detailed examination of social-control strategies as they affected the unemployment movement in British Columbia. It documents the rise and demise of this movement, the policing strategies and surveillance tactics of the government, the use of relief work camps to control the single, unemployed male population — especially the camps run by the Department of National Defence — the resistance to the camps, and the increased coercive response of the federal state to the unemployed worker's dissent, which culminated in the Regina Riot and the dismantling of relief camp schemes. It concludes with a discussion of state theory and social-justice politics under capitalism in crisis.

The chapter is also a contribution to state analysis in that it supports the utility of Claus Offe's thesis about the state as a crisis manager. By concentrating on this period, our case study confirms the importance of studying the *internal* selective mechanisms of state rule. We interpret our data within a multidimensional structural framework and conclude that by the mid-1930s the normal structural mechanisms of the state were in a condition of collapse. At the levels of organization, ideology, and administrative rules there was a 'crisis of crisis management.' Political rule moved into an exceptional phase and with it came a powerful repressive response.

THE GREAT DEPRESSION IN BRITISH COLUMBIA

The social and economic development of Canada has always been characterized by reliance upon resource exports; from the onset of the early fisheries through the decades of the fur and timber trades to the wheat economy, and including the current export of mineral resources, oil and gas, and hydroelectrical power. Early in the nineteenth century Britain established a mercantile system whereby colonial merchants monopolized exports for their home market and controlled the supply of manufactured goods entering Canada. To maintain this system of trade, artisans were banned from emigration to the Canadas and little in the way of a manufacturing base was encouraged in either Upper or Lower Canada (Willox, 1980: 40). These colonies became resource hinterlands dependent on the British imperial metropolis.

As industrialization in Britain displaced the position of British merchant capital, Canada turned to the rapidly developing United States for its supply of manufactured goods. With the *Reciprocity Treaty* of 1854, Canada's raw materials and U.S. manufactured goods crossed the 49th parallel at reduced tariff rates. The abrogation of this treaty in 1866, however, shifted the economic and political balance back into the British imperial orbit. To create a reliable financial climate that would support east-west trade in British North America, Canadian merchants and British financiers established a nation-state and shortly thereafter formulated a National Policy, with three objectives: the construction of a transcontinental railway to link the raw resources of the opening West to Montreal and the St. Lawrence Seaway; the promotion of immigration to the developing resource-rich West; and the erection of a tariff that suppressed the development of secondary industry in the West and forced the new settlers to depend upon the developing industrial heartland of Central Canada for manufactured goods. The tariff bolstered the trade monopoly of Eastern Canadian merchants and encouraged U.S. industrialists to invest directly by establishing factories in the burgeoning cities of Central Canada. Thus, the National Policy gave rise to uneven regional development in Canada, and the West was confirmed as an internal resource hinterland for Central Canadian and U.S. manufacturing bases.

The post-World War I settlement period witnessed the consolidation of U.S. economic power. Extensive growth was spawned by the expansion of the automobile industry, especially in related industries such as oil, rubber, glass, plastics, and synthetics. In turn these fed construction, service, leisure, and housing demands (Sweezy, 1980: 4). Western Canadian producers of raw materials seized this opportunity to supply the ever-expanding U.S. markets, and by the mid-1920s British Columbia had become heavily reliant upon the export of raw resources to feed the growing U.S. economy of the 'roaring twenties' (Phillips, 1982: 79). The advancing U.S. industries encouraged extensive mining of B.C. copper and lead resources, and throughout the first eight years of the decade production and prices consistently increased (*Budget Address*, B.C. Legislative Assembly, 1929: 50). Similarly, the volume of timber cut and high lumber prices made 1928 a bumper year in that industry (*Budget Address*, 1929: 76). The province's fishing industry, too, expanded as increased production was led by higher prices, resulting in a very profitable 1927-28 fiscal year. The general effect of the rapid development of the resource industries due to the expansion of the U.S. markets resulted in steady prosperity in all sectors of the B.C. economy during the 1920s and in high levels of employment (Fearon, 1979: 28; Struthers, 1983: 42).

This rapid economic expansion characterized by rising profits and technological advancement, however, contained a major structural weakness. While technological changes brought productivity to 94 per cent of the total capacity during the 1920s (Carlo, 1975: 174) and the economic surplus rose, economic expansion was not followed by an even distribution of profits. Industrial output increased by 43 per cent between 1919 and 1929, but wages increased by only 11 per cent (Erickson, 1972: 11; Taylor, 1983a: 174). Initially this profit was reinvested, but due to the lag between the appropriation of the economic surplus and its distribution, the surplus rose both absolutely and relatively. As the surplus increased, investment began to outpace consumption and investors started to draw back. Thus, profits were being withheld from recirculation for capital formation. Because the goods available were not being appropriated by the consumer at a rate equal to their production, profits were not being pumped into the economy and capital formation lagged (Heilbroner, 1980: 237). The surplus of consumer goods on the already bloated market led to a 50 per cent reduction in the production of consumer durables between 1929 and 1933 (Baran and Sweezy, 1966: 237). Similarly, over the same period the manufacture of producers' equipment fell by a staggering 75 per cent (Fearon, 1979: 35); as industrial production declined, unemployment rose. Indeed, even those who worked faced a 36 per cent drop in real income between 1929 and 1933. The purchasing power of the dollar plummeted (Fearon, 1979: 35).[1] Overproduction was combined with technological advancements that further displaced jobs and industries in the manufacturing sector while severely dislocating the agricultural sector. As farm equipment was automated and production was increased, many independent farmers lost their land and were forced into tenantry (Heilbroner, 1980: 144-6).

When the U.S. boom broke, the Western Canadian economy soon collapsed. Not only were Canadian farmers and industrial workers experiencing the same difficulties as their U.S. counterparts, but the profits and dividends produced in Canada were not being reinvested in the local economy; they were instead being drained from the region and divided between Canadian investors and U.S. parent companies. The resource hinterland economy of British Columbia was particularly vulnerable when its exports could not be absorbed by faltering U.S. industries. Between 1929 and 1933 the total value of production in B.C. fell 53 per cent (Conway, 1983: 101). By 1931 Canadian export of copper declined by 60 per cent and lead exports dropped 83 per cent (Lane, 1966: 4), and between 1929 and 1933 the value of B.C.'s timber production fell 62 per cent (Conway, 1983: 101). By 1933 pulp and paper sold for 40 per cent less than it had in 1929. Similarly, the 1931 price for B.C.'s fish was 45 per cent lower than in 1929, and between 1929 and 1933 B.C. fisheries experienced a 72 per cent drop in net monthly income (Conway, 1983: 99).

By 1933 the per capita income of British Columbia had fallen by 47 per cent from its 1929 level (Conway, 1983: 99; Lane, 1966: 4), and the per capita income of 1937 was only $240, compared to $595 in 1929 (Conway, 1983: 104). By June 1931 British Columbia had the highest unemployment level in Canada, with nearly 28 per cent of wage earners out of work. By January 1933, the level of unemployment had reached 30.4 per cent (Saunders, 1939: 16).

Responsibility for those left destitute belonged to the municipalities since British Columbia had delegated this duty to the cities and towns in the 1871 Municipal Act (Hill, 1951: 6; King, 1939: 77). Vancouver, however, was the only city with a relief department that assisted its residents and provided emergency funds for non-residents. The province also maintained a 'Destitute and Sick Fund' for those who lived outside municipal boundaries, but it was very poorly funded and administered (Lane, 1966; Lautard, 1965: 56).

The municipalities were soon unable to bear the increased relief burden and quickly petitioned the provincial government for financial aid. Between 1929 and 1931 the province's relief expenditures increased by 31.8 per cent (*Budget Address*, 1931: 30). During the 1928-29 fiscal year the provincial government was obliged to spend $555,034.73 on direct relief provisions. By December 1933 this contribution had risen to an unprecedented $9,979,826.13 (*Budget Address*, 1932: Schedule G; *Budget Address*, 1934: 9).

The increased demand for relief provisions was combined with severe decreases in provincial revenues, especially from primary resources. In 1927-28 provincial sales of timber leases, licences, and royalties amounted to $2,979,004.50, but fell to $1,956,751.84 in 1931-32 (*Budget Address*, 1930: 36; *Budget Address*, 1932: Schedule C). Timber sales for the province dropped from a value of $603,363.03 in 1928-29 to a value of $443,694.43 in 1931-32 (*Budget Address*, 1932: Schedule C; *Budget Address*, 1932: Schedule E1). Over the same period revenue from coke and coal taxation decreased from $210,559.69 to $138,969.76, and mineral taxation fell from $390,811.23 to a dismal $77,524.25 (*Budget Address*, 1932: Schedule C; *Budget Address*, 1934: Schedule E1).

The drastic drop in provincial revenue from primary resources and the exceptional increase in relief demands resulted in a 69 per cent increase in the province's gross debt between May 1928 and March 1934 (*Budget Address*, 1934: 4,9). By November 1933, $314,952.89 worth of cheques, mostly for unemployment relief, could not be forwarded because of lack of government funds (*Budget Address*, 1934: 6). British Columbia defaulted on its payments to the federal government and, by 1933, Ottawa was the province's only source of credit: The local state was in a major fiscal crisis situation (Struthers, 1983: 112-3).

THE EMERGENCE OF THE UNEMPLOYED MOVEMENT[2]

Those who relied solely upon the resource industries for their livelihood were most seriously affected by the Depression. They tended to be single men who travelled from job to job according to the availability of work, wages, and seasons (Brown, 1978: 191; Lane, 1966: 18; Cassidy, 1939: 177). These resource workers were a diverse group; some were Canadian-born, many were new immigrants, others were veterans of the Great War, and others were youths who had just joined the labour force.

Single men were ineligible for family assistance and municipal relief work programs. Furthermore, available casual employment was usually awarded only to those with dependents. In their search for work the single unemployed began to roam and 'ride the rods' across the country. Thousands of single unemployed men rode westward from the prairies, congregating in British Columbia. By February of 1931 the number of registered unemployed in the province had reached 67,128, and municipal officials began to complain of being "overrun by beggars and pan handlers" (Ormsby, 1958: 445). By 1932 as many as two hundred transients a day were arriving in Vancouver (VCA, Public Records, Mayor, Vol. 9, File: Relief 1, April 30, 1932, May 3, 1932).

Transients were highly mobile. Perceived as social outcasts, they were quickly subjected to social regulation and evicted from towns or arrested for vagrancy and theft.[3] City authorities also rooted them out of their jurisdictions and denied them residency and relief benefits. The government of British Columbia flatly refused responsibility for the single unemployed population. It changed the definition of transients eligible for social relief by manipulating residence rules and insisting that the poor be able to prove self-support from earnings for eight of twelve subsequent months (Cassidy, 1939: 179,190). The Vancouver City Council sought legal advice on whether it had the power to "prevent indigents from entering the province from the East" (VCA, Administrative History, Vol. 5: *City Council Minutes*, March 2, 1931). The Council even contemplated advertising in prairie newspapers to deter the unemployed from coming to the province (VCA, City Clerk's, Vol. 141, File: Relief July-December) but finally they lobbied the federal government to intervene.

The movement of the unemployed was monitored closely by local authorities. The Vancouver city police, the railway police, and the Investigations Branch of the Vancouver Relief Department kept records of the the number entering and leaving the city (VCA, Public Records, Mayor, Vol. 9, File: Relief 1, June 27, 1932). While B.C. had no legal authority to prevent entry to its province, it pressured federal authorities to allow the province to evict non-resident unemployed (Matthews, 1935, Vol. 8, No. 1: July 24, 1932, 167). The B.C. government protested to Prime Minister R.B. Bennett, and the railway police, the B.C. Provincial Police, and the RCMP blockaded the movement of workers coming into British Columbia. This effort limited the movement of transients in 1932, but the following autumn the westward migration reoccurred.

The poverty of the unemployed meant they could not afford rooming houses in the cities, and had to construct makeshift homes and small settlements. In Vancouver there were three main 'unemployed jungles' containing a variety of flimsy shelters and lean-tos. The shelters were built from scrap wood, cardboard boxes, packing barrels, scrap metal, and grain doors from rail cars (Matthews, 1931-34, Vol. 8, No. 1: 12). The number in each jungle fluctuated, but the larger housed about 450 men, and the others had a population of about 250 residents (VCA City Clerk's, Vol. 155, File: Relief Officer, 1931, July-Sept., Public Welfare and Relief Office Report, Sept. 3, 1931). No economic or social provisions were made for the men but charitable organizations, local fishers, and food packers provided basic food and clothing (Matthews, 1935, Vol. 8, No. 1: 11). They were not directly policed by the authorities but watches from the Vancouver Harbours Board monitored their activities (VCA, City Clerk's, Vol. 155, File: Relief Officer, 1931, July-Sept., Public Welfare and Relief Office, Report, Sept. 3, 1931).

In the summer of 1931 a case of typhoid and a death led to a medical investigation of the jungles. A report outlined the severity of sanitation and disease problems and led to the jungles being destroyed (VCA, City Clerk's, Vol. 155, File: Relief Officer, 1931, July-Sept., Public Welfare and Relief Office, Report, Sept. 3, 1931). The increased numbers and problems of the homeless were not met with an enlightened relief program, however. The city could not cope with the swelling demand for social assistance, the province offered no aid, and Ottawa would not accept direct responsibility.

In sharp contrast to the disinterest of the state, the Communist Party of Canada took an active interest in the single, homeless, unemployed men, organizing them into a political force. Numerous rallies and meetings were held. Petitions demanding work and wages for their members were sent to government authorities, weekly publications were distributed, and posters and pamphlets called for direct, mass action by the unemployed. Thousands of unemployed workers received widespread publicity during 'hunger marches' and through 'tin-canning.' Parades were led by banners with slogans calling for job-creation and relief provisions. Typically, a thousand men in Vancouver would assemble at a mass meeting, parade peacefully through the city with banners and the 'Red Flag,' and then march to government offices for an audience with an official. Repeatedly their demands were for work and wages (VCA, Public Records, Mayor, Vol. 9, File: Relief 1). Quickly, a cohesive politicized movement emerged that was viewed as a distinct threat to law and order.

SOCIAL CONTROL AND THE UNEMPLOYED

The tolerance and support afforded by the public were not shared by state authorities. The Vancouver police chief reported that the unemployed were "agitators [and] simply desirous of fermenting trouble" (B.C. Provincial Archives: correspondence from Vancouver Police Chief Constable to Mayor and Police Commission, January 21, 1931). Violent clashes between the police and unemployed became common as Mounted Police repeatedly broke up gatherings by using clubs and tear gas. The chief constable of the Vancouver police reported that mass demonstrations meant many hours of overtime work and hence necessitated an expansion of police personnel and power. A special police riot squad of 50 men and a temporary force of 47 men were formed to handle unemployment demonstrations (Matthews, 1935, Vol. 8, No. 1: 53). In addition, the B.C. provincial police and the RCMP monitored the unemployed. Together, the three police forces used over two hundred officers to control an unemployed demonstration during December, 1930 (VCA, City Records, Loc. 75, F1).

The police had more than visible force at their disposal; from the outset they infiltrated the movement and hired informants from the ranks. These undercover agents submitted detailed reports to the police and supplied a record of leaders, organizations, and political strategies, which formed an extensive file on the general organization of the unemployed and on the Communist Party of Canada.

The police were not the only state institution that repressed the unemployed. The civic authorities in Vancouver were also convinced that the demonstrations represented a serious threat. In the spring of 1932 they banned all hunger marches and tag days. Not surprisingly, increased police action led to more frequent arrests and the involvement of the military as a backup force (VCA, Public Records, Mayor, Vol. 8, File: Police Commission). Military style policing was bolstered by internal surveillance afforded by the Vancouver Relief Department through its detailed reports on all those who registered for relief. Five full-time investigators carried out 'intensive investigations' on relief recipients, which were shared with policing agencies (VCA, Public Records, Mayor, Vol. 9, File: Relief 1).

A further attempt to control the organization of the unemployed and the Communist Party was made by deporting 'undesirable aliens' who "did not appear likely to become good citizens" (Matthews, 1935, Vol. 8, No. 1: 53). The Vancouver Board of Police Commissioners recommended: "that the Immigration Act be amended ... and provision be made for the immediate deportation of such undesirable aliens ... and that the process of deportation be speeded up" (VCA, Public Records, Mayor, Vol. 8, File: Police 1932).

The city police and the metropolitan authorities also lobbied the provincial and federal governments. R.B. Bennett reluctantly recognized the scope of the problem and in 1931 the *Unemployment Relief Act* was passed. Some $20 million were earmarked to deal with the "temporary unemployment crisis" (Struthers, 1983: 47). Married men were given preference for work and civic relief. Later the same year the *Unemployment and Farm Relief Act* was passed to manage the problem of single unemployed men (Struthers, 1983: 48, 51).

British Columbia was quick to strike an agreement with the federal minister of labour to start a program of relief work camps. Premier Tolmie noted: "Immediately after negotiations with Ottawa ... it was decided to rush the men out of the cities in order to prevent, what the Chief of Police was afraid might happen, wholesale damage to property" (Tolmie, 1981, Box 9, File: 16: February 1, 1932).

By February 1932, B.C. operated 237 permanent and temporary work camps with a capacity for 35,122 men. A system of fines and the denial of relief ensured some enrolment in the camps. However, by March 1932, 55 per cent of these eligible men refused to go to what they termed 'slave camps' in remote areas of the province (Matthews, 1935, Vol. 8, No. 1: March 31, 1932). The relief workers complained about the low wages of 30 cents an hour, the poor food, insufficient clothing, and the harsh working conditions (*Vancouver Province*, letter to the editor, December 2, 1932; Matthews, 1935, Vol. 8, No. 1: 151).

Problems in the relief camps were compounded by patronage and high-cost overruns. By November 1931 British Columbia had spent most of its budget and requested an additional $6,677,000. Ottawa balked at further funding for what it termed excessive expenditures and forwarded only $3,250,000. The province refused to operate the camps on this budget. The premier ordered the work to cease, and for three months the men were given direct relief in the camps. Deterioration of intergovernmental relations worsened and in November the federal government instructed the Fordham Commission to take responsibility for the B.C. work camps. The commission closed some camps and reduced spending to a fixed rate of 40 cents per man per day in the operating camps. Despite these and other changes, the camps remained in turmoil and were shut down permanently in March 1933. Once again, hundreds of single, transient, unemployed men were required to survive on their own.

These attempts had not solved the problems created by high levels of unemployment. While federal, provincial, and municipal police tried to monitor the organized, militant unemployed, and while the provincial and federal governments made some effort to address the causes for unrest, the state was still unable to deal adequately with the social and political problems. The fiscal incapacity of the local and provincial governments to solve the problem, the lack of co-ordinated policy in the higher government institutions, the inability of the police to contain and suppress the unemployed movement, and public support for the unemployed together created a crisis that forced the Canadian state to take exceptional measures.

THE DEVELOPMENT OF THE NATIONAL DEFENCE RELIEF CAMP SCHEME

The establishment of a national relief work camp scheme had been much discussed in high political circles in Ottawa. Bennett regularly argued that such action was outside the federal government's jurisdiction (House of Commons, *Debates*, October 10, 1932: 50). Nevertheless, a proposal forwarded by Major-General A.G.L. McNaughton, Chief of the General Staff and a senior military advisor, provided a new initiative for the Bennett government.[4] McNaughton proposed a military scheme of relief camps. The unemployed were to be dealt with at the national level, but the federal government itself would not have to accept direct responsibility. Thus, in October 1932, Order in Council P.C. 2248 created the Department of

National Defence (DND) relief camp scheme.[5] Some $300,000 was allocated for the initial program. Subsequent Relief Acts in 1932, 1933, 1934, and 1935 continued the financing and 23 Orders in Council enacted the Ministry of National Defence to administer the scheme and allocate the funds. Major-General McNaughton assumed executive responsibility for the camps, and regional military headquarters were put in charge of their daily operations. Thus, thousands of civilian unemployed men came under the direct control of the national armed forces.

The alleviation of the unemployed problem was the official reason justifying the establishment of the national program. A second reason was "The preservation of the morale of the youth of Canada by keeping them in such physical and mental health that they would be re-employable when the economic conditions improved and they could be absorbed by industry" (LeFresne, 1961: 17). In addition to the fear of demoralization and loss of work discipline was the spectre of social revolution led by the communist, militant unemployed. McNaughton stated: "By taking the men out of ... the cities ... we were removing the active elements on which the 'Red' agitators could play.... If we had not taken this preventative work and did not continue ... it was only a matter of time until we had to resort to arms to maintain order" (McNaughton Papers, cited in Eayrs, 1964: 129, Struthers 1983: 99).

Enrolment in a Department of National Defence relief camp was voluntary, but any single, homeless, medically fit, unemployed male British subject was expected to register at a Canadian Employment and Welfare Office. Shelter, clothing, food, medical and dental care, and a tobacco ration were provided for the inmates. The men were expected to work an eight-hour day for five and one half days per week. An allowance of 20 cents per day was provided, while cooks and junior supervisory staff received more, according to their tasks. Because the scheme was an emergency project, the twenty cents was termed an allowance, not a wage. Furthermore, the DND scheme was exempt from the provisions of federal legislation, and the unemployed men were not covered by Workmen's Compensation Board regulations, minimum wage legislation, or any social benefits programs.[6] The scheme operated by Order in Council and policies and regulations were established by the Department of National Defence without reference to parliament (LeFresne, 1961: 65).

The men were sheltered in wood and tarpaper bunkhouses heated by coal or wood stoves and equipped with electric, coal oil, or gasoline lighting — whichever was most economical. Hot showers were provided and supplies were sent from the department's Central Ordinance Depot in Ottawa and distributed through military headquarters. Economy was a primary objective and every possible cost-saving measure was taken. No recreational facilities were provided, although sports equipment, reading materials, radios, and playing cards were supplied by local technical schools, when available.

By June 1933, the national relief camp program included British Columbia. Some of the earlier camps built by the B.C. government were utilized by the DND. The 101 camps in B.C. housed one-third of the national relief camp population (Cassidy, 1939: 18, Eayrs, 1964: 137). The men in these 'royal 20 centres' — as they were aptly called — worked primarily on road construction projects. The worksites were situated in remote regions of the province. One relief camp member recalled: "You come in broke, work all winter and still you are broke. It looks like they want to keep us bums all our lives" (quoted in Struthers, 1983: 100). The work was repetitive, manual, and fatiguing (Liversedge, 1973: 35). The most labour-intensive methods were used to avoid expenditures on machinery and maximize the number of man-days (Swettenham, 1968: 7). As one relief camp worker observed: "You had the crazy situation of a $3,000 bulldozer and a steam roller sitting by the side of the road while 50 men went at the dirt and rock with shovels and picks" (quoted in Broadfoot, 1973: 97). The camps were also designed to restrict competition for jobs. In McNaughton's words they served the "function of removing the single men from the urban labour market and thus reserving existing jobs for married men with dependents" (McNaughton Papers, cited in Struthers, 1983: 98).

The conditions in the camps were reflected in the inmates' work performance. The average nationwide efficiency of relief camp workers was about 35 per cent of that of ordinary labour employed at prevailing rates (Cassidy, 1939: 185). Most of the B.C. camps were below the national average, and one B.C. camp reported the lowest efficiency, at 20 per cent of the standard level (LeFresne, 1961: 180).

The inefficiency of the workers in B.C. relief camps was an indicator of a more general demoralization. Isolation and boredom fuelled many grievances, and complaints about medical services, food, and military rules were legion. The MacDonald Commission investigating B.C.'s DND camps found that the food was substandard and that complaints were warranted (MacDonald, McHattie and Branden, 1935: 9-10). Other committees reported that the DND administration did not seem to know that "food for the mind is as important as food for the body and that healthy recreation in addition to the daily work is so essential" (Correspondence to McNeely, Chairman, Vancouver Council of Social Agencies from Carey, Chairman, Wilson, Vice-Chairman and Committee: March 9, 1934; in VCA, City Clerk's, Vol. 166). Discontent was furthered by the fact that many inmates were politically disenfranchised since they had not lived in the camps long enough to establish the residency requirements for voting rights.

The climate in B.C. posed further problems. In many camps housing conditions were inadequate for the snow and freezing temperatures, while the firewood was frequently too wet to provide basic heat (Salmo B.C. Project 24, March 12, 1935; cited in LeFresne, 1961: 105-6). The clothing situation also caused alarm; not only was it 'used,' temporary clothing, it also carried the DND imprint, reminding relief workers that they were, in fact, inmates of the state.

While the DND allowed complaints, these had to be voiced by

individuals and forwarded to the camp foreman, the group superintendent, or district headquarters (LeFresne, 1961: 99). DND rules stipulated
that "camp grievance committees or other organizations of like character
will not be permitted, nor will complaints by groups, either verbally or in
writing be entertained" (LeFresne, 1961: 99). Although grievances were
many, inmates hesitated to present them to the camp foreman, because he
had the authority to dismiss them 'for cause' and could report the inmates
as 'Red agitators' (Woods, 1985, interview). Despite many prohibitions,
inmates managed to publish their grievances through the press, taking
their cause to politicians, charitable groups, and the public at large (Le-
Fresne, 1961: 105; Matthews, 1935, Vol. 8, No. 3, April 17 and May 18, 1935).

As the grievances mounted, the inmates began to perceive themselves
as unwanted dependents of an uncaring state, shut in remote camps so
their demands for work and wages would be silenced. One relief worker
noted: "In the relief camps of the Thirties we weren't treated as humans.
We weren't treated as animals either, and I've always thought we were just
statistics written into some big ledger in Ottawa.... But it was the monot-
ony, the jail of it all. It *was* jail you know" (quoted in Broadfoot, 1973: 97).

RESISTANCE AND COERCION

The discontent of the unemployed in the relief camps was organized by the
Workers' Unity League (WUL) in the form of the Relief Camp Workers'
Union (RCWU). Strikes and riots were frequent in many of the camps
(VCA, City Clerk's, Vol. 195, File: Provincial Government, 1935, Jan.-Dec.;
Matthews, 1935b, Vol. 8, No. 3: Feb. 11, 1935). The first general strike of the
RCWU involved 1,200 to 1,500 men from 40 camps. The unemployed
strikers had four demands: a five-day workweek with a seven-hour day
and wages of 40 cents an hour; a compensation program for injuries
sustained on the job; the removal of the camps from the control of the
Department of National Defence; and the right to vote in provincial and
federal elections (Sheils and Swanky, 1977: 80). After several weeks of
demonstrations in Vancouver the unemployed strikers received some
concessions from B.C.'s Premier Pattullo. He recommended to Ottawa
that a commission of inquiry investigate the relief camps, and he allowed
the unemployed blacklisted by the DND to collect relief in Vancouver
(Howard, 1974: 11). After the men gained these concessions, the strike was
called off and they returned to the camps.

During the strike in Vancouver, as during those in the camps, the
municipal, provincial, and RCMP maintained a vigilant surveillance. The
police forces, in conjunction with the DND, the railway police, and
government bodies, had designed plans to allow the police to arrest any
who were expelled from or left the relief camps on vagrancy charges
(Provincial Archives, GR 429, Box 21, 1934). Furthermore, many camp
foremen operated as informers, notifying the police about suspicious
visitors, meetings, strikes, and other irregularities. Railway authorities
were enjoined to enforce the *Railways Act* to contain the movement of
transient unemployed men in B.C. (Provincial Archives, GR 429, Box 21,

File: 1, June 6, 1934, July 13, 1934; Provincial Archives, GR 429, Files: 1,2,3,4). Police spies posed as relief camp inmates and informed on the activities in the camps, on the 'Reds,' and on future plans of action.

On April 2, 1935, the second general strike of the relief workers occurred. The strikers drafted seven demands, once again pressing for work and wages and opposing the military control of the camps. Despite some arrests, the removal of the men from the camps was relatively orderly, although in Vancouver the mayor claimed that the strikers were "a disturbing element and a menace to peace, order and good government" (VCA, City Records, Loc. 33, B6, File: 1935 Strike Situation). Nevertheless, the unemployed received widespread support, reflected in the thousands of dollars collected on tag days.

As in the first major strike, the unemployed demonstrated in and about department stores. While the almost daily report of informers and police infiltrators forewarned the police, politicians, and businesses about demonstrations, this did not stave off confrontations (VCA, City Records, Loc. 33, B6, File: Strike Situation, April 26, 1935; Constable's Report to Chief). The Hudson's Bay Company was the site of one major conflict; as one group of parading camp workers addressed demands to the public, they were charged by the police (VCA, City Records, Loc. 33 B6, File: Strike Situation, April 25, 1935). Strikers and police were injured, unemployed camp workers were arrested, and merchandise and property were damaged.

Although a delegation of 12 relief camp strikers obtained an audience with the mayor, he refused to grant money to the strikers and had ten of them arrested for vagrancy. He then made his way to Victory Square, where he read the riot act to the unemployed (Howard, 1974: 25), claiming:

> It is now perfectly clear that Vancouver is being victimized by an organized attempt to capitalize, for revolutionary purposes, on the conditions of the depression which do not exist. From information supplied to me, there is a definite organization of Communistic activities which are centering on calling of a general strike in Vancouver. (Cited in *Vancouver News Herald*, Matthews, 1935b, Vol. 8, No. 3: April 24, 1935)

The crowd was dispersed by two hundred mounted and foot police drawn from three police forces (Sheils and Swanky, 1977: 90). However, the unemployed strikers remained active in Vancouver. Six weeks later approximately five hundred men occupied the City Museum for 24 hours. In response to a banner draped from the window asking "When do we eat?" the crowds supplied food. Eventually the city was pressured into providing the strikers with two meals per day for six days on the condition that they leave the museum (Howard, 1974: 30, Liversedge, 1973: 80).

At best, short-term temporary victories could be won. No level of the state was prepared to negotiate seriously with the strikers and the unemployed. At worst they were ignored or arrested. On May 29, Arthur Evans, an active leader of the unemployed, suggested that the men put their demands before the federal authorities. The "On to Ottawa Trek" commenced and on June 3 and 4 one thousand single, unemployed relief camp inmates left Vancouver. Despite attempts by Calgary city officials to have the RCMP stop the men at the B.C.-Alberta border, the size and support for the unemployed cause increased. By June 14 the trekkers arrived in Regina, where they met considerable state coercion.

On June 8, Prime Minister Bennett told the House of Commons that he would not prevent the men from marching to Ottawa unless he received complaints from local authorities (Matthews, 1935, Vol. 8, No. 3: June 8, 1935). This turned out to be a hollow promise. The trek was stopped by the federal cabinet in a decision made without consultation or agreement of local governments (*Regina Riot Inquiry*, cited in Liversedge, 1973: 178; Sheils and Swanky, 1977: 119).

The federal police forces were immediately strengthened by 125 officers. Railway officials sent at least eight extra officers to enforce the *Railways Act* (Sheils and Swanky, 1977: 154).[7] The unemployed were under constant surveillance and finally were put under guard in the Regina Exhibition grounds (Matthews, 1935, Vol. 8, No. 3: June 12, 1935).

On June 17, the federal minister of agriculture, the minister of railways, and the leaders of the trek met. The federal government agreed to finance a delegation to Ottawa where the demands of the strikers and unemployed would be presented to the government. On June 22 the delegation met with Bennett and his cabinet. The meeting was short, heated, and ultimately unproductive. Bennett claimed: "The present movement of these men toward Ottawa ... is an organized effort to effect the overthrow of the constituted authority, in defiance of the law of the land, on the part of several communistic societies in Canada" (Matthews, 1935, Vol. 8, No. 3: June 24, 1935). On June 25, relief to the trekkers in Regina was cut off and it was made illegal to donate money to the strikers. The RCMP arrested those who tried to leave the city. The federal police gathered information about the leaders of the movement to substantiate arrest warrants, which had been already issued.

On July 1, 1935, a meeting of 3,000 trekkers and townspeople was held in the city square (Sheils and Swanky, 1977: 180, 184). At this point the RCMP and the Regina city police arrested eight trek leaders under the authority of Section 98 of the *Criminal Code*. Three vans transporting 75 officers and a mounted troop of 38 policemen were armed with batons, steel helmets, and side arms. The trucks contained ammunition rounds and gas grenades. In addition, about 20 to 25 plainclothes officers armed with batons infiltrated the crowd. After surrounding three sides of the square with police vans, the officers charged the meeting. The crowd retaliated by using sticks, throwing stones, and employing makeshift weapons. The skirmish rapidly became a riot, spreading out into the city streets. The day ended tragically with the death of an undercover police officer and the hospitalization of at least 40 trekkers for gunshot wounds (Liversedge, 1973: 116). Over one hundred arrests were made (Report in the Regina press, cited in Liversedge, 1973: 183-4, 195).

When the riot ended, most of the trekkers returned to the stadium. Armed RCMP officers surrounded it and erected a barbed wire fence. No one was permitted to enter the grounds' building, and men were allowed to leave only in pairs. The next day an agreement was reached by which the trekkers were offered railway tickets to anywhere in Canada and the injured were given medical treatment. Some 700 to 800 unemployed went to Vancouver, most of them registering to re-enter the relief camps. Shortly thereafter the federal government began to reconsider and then to dismantle the relief camp scheme. The final closure of the camps, a year later, spelled the end of the DND program.

UNDERSTANDING STATE AND JUSTICE UNDER CAPITALISM

The DND relief camp scheme served a purpose beyond providing work discipline. The unemployed were a constant vocal reminder that the capitalist economy could not provide employment for all those who were willing to work. Indeed, this group passed suddenly from a state of political passivity to a level of organized activity that was clearly oppositional. The militant, communist-led unemployed constituted a counterhegemonic force and were viewed as a threat to peace, order, and good government (Gramsci, 1971: 210). Through the relief camp scheme the state undertook exceptional action to contain this crisis of authority. While the men were not legally obliged to become relief camp inmates, they were ineligible for relief provisions if they refused to go to the camps. Moreover, the efforts made by state authorities to keep the unemployed inside the camps confirm that the scheme was a control mechanism. To understand this broader social-control response it is necessary to analyse the role of the state more generally.[8]

The state is not self-financing. It relies upon the economy for most of its revenues, either through taxes or loans. Thus it is predisposed to bolster growth in the accumulation process. Yet at the same time it must maintain social order by mediating between the interests of capital and the political demands of the working class (Jessop, 1977: 370; O'Connor, 1973; Offe, 1975). The way the state ensures the domination of capital while maintaining social peace is best considered in light of Claus Offe's analysis of the internal mechanisms of the state during a crisis period. Offe argues that the structural mechanisms within the state system are composed of interrelated institutions that work to bolster the domination of the capitalist social order upon which they depend.

The first structural mechanism identified is the negative selective mechanism. On the levels of structure, ideology, process, and repression, the *negative* selective mechanism creates a "hierarchical filter system" to exclude issues that are contrary to capitalist interests. The *positive* selective mechanism operates to facilitate the promotion by the state of issues that have passed the filter of the first selective mechanism and so further the interests of capital. The third selective mechanism is a mystical one. It operates to impart the appearance that the state is acting in the general public interest, rather than for narrow sectoral interests. In this way, a degree of popular support for state actions is accorded and hegemony is achieved, in that political rule entails a large measure of consensus (Offe, 1975; Offe and Ronge, 1982).

According to Offe, the state functions as a 'crisis manager,' maintaining a delicate balance between the needs of capital and the political demands of the working class. In normal times these selective mechanisms conceal the class nature of the state and maintain a social calm. However, when a political or social crisis occurs, these selective mechanisms begin to collapse and a crisis in the state's role as crisis manager develops. In turn, the delicate mediation ability of the state is put in jeopardy.

The severe economic depression of the 1930s initiated just such a crisis of crisis management in the Canadian state. The fiscal crisis within the state meant that the state could not fulfil its obligation to capital by supporting the greatly enlarged surplus labour force. Additionally, the Canadian state could not satisfy the political demands of the unemployed segment of the working class. This came to pose a major challenge to capitalist law and order. The economic depression revealed the inability of the capitalist economy to maintain large segments of the working class and so created a conspicuous group of single, transient unemployed men. The Communist Party of Canada was at its strongest and was able to organize and unify the unemployed, creating a counterhegemonic force. In the historical and cultural context of the Great Depression, the Canadian state faced a crisis in its mediation between the political demands of the working class and the requirements of capital. The structural mechanisms of the state became ineffective.

The first negative selective mechanism that started to break down was at the level of structure. The inability of local governments to provide relief for the unemployed was a key indicator of the incapacity of the state to address the political demands of the unemployed segment of the working class. Previously the constitutional delegation of responsibility for the poor and destitute posed few problems, but the fiscal crisis laid bare the ineffectiveness of this structural legal framework. On the basis of the *BNA Act*, higher levels of government refused responsibility for the unemployed prior to the implementation of the DND scheme, during the relief camp strikes and on the Ottawa Trek. Intergovernmental disputes were considerable, jurisdictions and responsibilities were uncertain, and ambiguity and ambivalence meant that the state was incapable of effectively excluding working-class demands. The 1931 *Relief Act* revealed that limited, piecemeal reforms within the boundaries of the state structure did not adequately contain working-class demands. The DND plan for control of the single unemployed indicated that the structural limits imposed on state action by the demands of the unemployed had broken down. Through the relief scheme a federal institution accepted responsibility for a group outside its normal authority, and the national military took control of civilians who were under provincial and local jurisdiction, thus superseding existing state mandates.

The breakdown of the ideological level, which filters out anticapitalist demands from the political sphere by defining them as non-problems outside state action, is best illustrated by considering social-welfare ideals. While Canada's welfare policy was based on Elizabethan poor laws, it was not assumed that able-bodied men would be unemployed in the developing frontier economy. Extensive provision for the unemployed was not a matter of regular state involvement. The family and private charities were expected to make the necessary provisions. This ideology was embedded in the Canadian Constitution with only minimal care for the poor relegated to scattered local state institutions. But the higher levels of unemployment in the 1930s initiated widespread demands for extensive state assistance. This challenged the ideology of local private support. The *Relief Acts* of 1931, instituted within the structural boundaries of the times, were considered to be exceptional state actions intended to address only the temporary unemployment problem. Ultimately, however, the establishment of the DND camp scheme signalled the end of state reluctance to assume social responsibility for the destitute unemployed. The ideological negative selective mechanism surrounding welfare ideals was repudiated and state involvement through federal institutions and welfare institutions came to be defined as a prerequisite to capitalist social-order maintenance.

The third level of the negative selective mechanism involves rules that govern internal state decision-making or process. Offe notes that this decision-making relegates working-class demands to low priority for state attention. Prior to the DND camp scheme, the Canadian state sought to control the unemployed within the normal rules and procedures that governed their decision-making. However, the crisis created by the militant unemployed required immediate and unusual state action. The normal processes were bypassed and the perceived urgency of the situation created by this counterhegemonic movement required unusual responses. The DND relief camp scheme was rapidly introduced by an Order in Council and legitimated through a moral panic about peace, order, and good government in Canada. Contrary to usual state procedures on national policies, no studies or investigation teams were established. Instead the DND plan was drawn up within nineteen hours on an informal request from the prime minister. The usual democratic procedures that contained and limited working-class demands were insufficient to manage the threat posed by the unemployed.

Before the establishment of the DND relief camp scheme, considerable repression took place. A panoply of repressive laws, regulations, and police powers was unable to effectively control the radicalized, unemployed segment of the working class. In the context of the Great Depression, the coercive level of the negative selective mechanism of the Canadian state was overrun and outflanked by the power of the unemployed politicized segment of the working class. The DND relief camp scheme was implemented as a repressive carceral measure.

Despite this surveillance and containment, political opposition and mobilization continued. But the violent response exercised in Regina, the elimination of all relief provisions to the trekkers, the decapitation of the movement through the arrest of its leaders, and the outlawing of the unemployed movement as an illegal association all worked to break the back of the movement and stifle dissent.

The closure of the DND camps in 1936 marked the end of this social-control strategy. Assisted by government funds, the DNR and the DPR temporarily agreed to employ 10,000 camp workers, and B.C. established forestry and mining camps to employ a further 7,000 men.[9] Leaving the unemployed movement without leadership and in retreat, and with a gradual improvement in the economy, the state reconstituted its normal structural procedures to maintain the balance between capital and the working class. A recession in 1938 led to a temporary renewal of violence between the unemployed and state authorities. But coercive means to control dissent were exercised with strict adherence to jurisdictional authority and legal procedure. The provision of relief in 1938 was specified as a *temporary emergency* measure. The negative selective mechanism operated effectively. The demands of the unemployed were addressed, but only to the degree necessary for maintaining social peace.

The threat posed by the unemployed in 1938 was short-lived. The expanding economy of 1939 absorbed thousands of workers. But the struggle led by the unemployed did have an impact upon the state. The *Unemployment Insurance Act* of 1940 was an outcome of the struggle of the depression years. By 1940 Canada was at war, the economy was booming, and the radical politics of a large segment of the working class was still in the foreground. Indeed, the prospect of demobilization combined with the likely downturn of the war industries in the future were further incentives to establish a national program for "maintaining industrial peace" (*Labour Gazette*, July 1940: 683). The war economy provided the fiscal base for an unemployment insurance program. The passage of this legislation indicates that the Canadian state had recovered from the crisis of crisis management. While this policy change did benefit the working class, it was subject to the structural constraints of the capitalist state. The positive selective mechanisms ensured that the interests of capital were protected through this act. Specifically, by providing social assistance at a level far less appealing than the lowest level of employment, a surplus labour force was made available. In addition, the rules attached to the centralized state distribution of this social benefit allowed the state to maintain extensive surveillance and control over working-class politics and culture.

This article appeared earlier in Canadian Criminology Forum, *Vol. 8, 1987: 84-102 and is reprinted here with the kind permission of that journal.*

NOTES

1. Investors lost approximately $40 billion in the weeks following the great crash of the New York Stock Exchange of October 1929. Stockholders affected constituted only 8 per cent of the U.S. population and the stock market financed only 6 per cent of gross private investment (Fearon, 1979: 34).

2. Before and during the Great Depression, families, widowed mothers, the elderly, and single men who were residents of Vancouver were provided with a scattered variety of state provisions (Hill, 1951: 7; Lane, 1966: 5; Lautard, 1965: 65). Records do not show any establishment assistance for single women until the implementation of the DND relief camp scheme (see note 6). Transient single men were not eligible for assistance and they demonstrated the most active social resistance and were eventually singled out as a group for extensive state control. For an account of the role of women relative to the single, unemployed men, see Irene Howard, "The Mother's Council of Vancouver: Holding the Fort for the Unemployed, 1935-38," *B.C. Studies*, Nos. 69-70, (Spring-Summer 1986, pp.249-87.

3. In his study of crime in Vancouver during the Great Depression, Huzel finds that prosecutions and convictions in the 1930s for crime against property generally rose in the early 1930s, reaching an all-time peak in 1934 (1986: 211-48).

4. This account of the implementation and administration of the DND relief camp scheme is drawn primarily from LeFresne, 1961.

5. Orders in Council do not require parliamentary debate.

6. The federal government shared with the provinces half the cost for physically unfit homeless men and single homeless women in B.C. at a total cost of not more than 40 cents per person per day. This was discontinued in 1934. Chinese, Doukhobors, and aliens in B.C. were provided with direct relief of 15 cents per man per day for single men and 25 cents per man per day for married men. All pensions were deducted from the relief allowance (Cassidy, 1939: 182-183; Winch Papers: 4; Provincial Archives of B.C.: GR 429, Box 21 File 1, March 16, 1934).

7. The RCMP were acting under the authority of Orders in Council passed under the *Relief Measures Act*. However, the 1934 enactment had expired in March 1935, and no new law had passed to authorize such a blockade (Communication between the Saskatchewan attorney-general and the federal minister of justice, cited in Sheils and Swanky, 1977: 195, July 2, 1935).

8. This analysis of the capitalist state stems from arguments initially advanced by Miliband and Poulantzas, but we rely primarily on the work of Offe (1972, 1975, 1980, 1984). The instrumentalist and structuralist perspectives examine the effects of external influences on the state in identifying its capitalist character. The former focuses on the manipulation of state institutions by members of the ruling class, while the latter emphasizes the constraints imposed by capitalism that place limitation on the activities of the state system. Offe, however, argues that one must also examine the *internal* characteristics of the state to determine its capitalist character. According to him, an examination of the state is best undertaken during the period of intense class struggle. During a social crisis the internal structural mechanisms of the state collapse and its real bias is revealed, because it is ineffective in managing political demands from working class.

Neither the instrumentalist nor structuralist position pays adequate attention to the effect working class struggle has on the state. Due to the overwhelming manipulation of the state by the ruling elite, the instrumentalist perspective views the working class as fragmented and seldom able to articulate common demands. Structuralists also perceive the possibilities for conscious, collective action by the working class to be problematic, since actors are portrayed as "bearers of the objective functions" of the state. These two positions do not allow for a real dialectical relation between structure and action. In our view the interplay between the constraints on the capitalist state and the dynamic of working-class struggle is very important in an analysis of social-control policy. For these reasons we stress the value of Offe's work.

9. Approximately 600 relief camp workers joined the Mackenzie-Papineau Battalion in the Spanish War (Walsh, in Montero, 1979: 45).

Chapter Eleven

Casino Gambling and Organized Crime: Towards an Analysis of Police Discourses

Colin S. Campbell

Since the amendment of the Criminal Code in 1969, Canadians have witnessed the proliferation of legitimate gambling operations. But, as Colin Campbell notes, although decriminalization reflects the general liberalization of attitudes towards gambling, state regulation is paralleled by increased police involvement. Thus, while the legalization of gambling stands in direct contradistinction to the case of marijuana use, which has become a criminal offence, the effect remains similar: It has allowed policing agencies to expand their activities into the "moral" realm. This chapter examines how and why the relaxation of criminal prohibitions has the paradoxical effect of allowing policing agencies to play a larger role than they would have under a continued restrictive approach.

To explore how police have secured control over legalized gaming, Campbell overviews the discourse that accompanied the advent of licensed casino gambling in Canada. Specifically, he examines police discourse regarding both the threat of "organized crime" and the need for vigilant control over legal gambling operations. In the case of charity casino gambling, a number of police agency reports drew extensively upon U.S. literature on organized crime to perpetuate the belief that gambling activity contributes significantly to organized crime coffers, which are then used to underwrite other criminal enterprises. Campbell points out that no firm evidence has been provided to substantiate these claims. In fact, statistics indicate that contrary to RCMP assertions casino gambling is relatively free of internal theft or fraud. Furthermore, a number of public inquiries have failed to confirm police claims that organized criminal interests are associated with casino operations in Canada. Despite this lack of empirical support, however, the British

---

Colin Campbell is Assistant Professor in Sociology/Anthropology at the University of Windsor

Columbia Gaming Commission of 1987 placed particular emphasis upon the testimony of police forces and individual officers. It is not surprising, therefore, that the commission's recommendations included "the intent to cultivate a close supportive relationship with police throughout the Province."

Campbell notes that media sources have also tended to overemphasize the police accounts of organized crime's relationship to gambling activities. He maintains that a "signification spiral" results, amplifying the perception of threat. This occurs primarily through the association within the police and media discourses of "gambling" with "organized crime." In the final analysis, to the extent that police gaming specialists have acted as principal sources for media reports, the police have been able to establish a monopoly over the control of the bureaucracies that regulate legalized gaming. In general, a provincial willingness to license charitable gambling has expanded the market for police knowledge and expertise.

INTRODUCTION

Since the amendment of the *Criminal Code of Canada* in 1969, Canadians have witnessed the proliferation of legitimate gambling operations. This chapter examines a particular discourse[1] that has arisen in response to the advent of licensed casino gambling in Western Canada. Specifically, it examines police discourse regarding both the threat of 'organized crime' and the need for vigilant control over legal gambling enterprises. By examining the emergence of legalized casino gambling in the Western Canadian provinces, we can place in context the circumstances in which these jurisdictions have been willing to accommodate a once legally prohibited form of risk-taking; and we can observe a shifting category of crime. That is, as the activity of gambling went through a legal and perceptual transformation from 'criminal' to 'licensed and controlled,' there was a concomitant emergence of related peripheral concerns about organized crime — concerns actively promulgated by police agencies and by particular police agents. By examining existing police accounts and other official studies of gambling, we can see that police discourse has had important consequences for the regulation of gambling.

Against this backdrop, it is clear that the police discourse as "claims-making activities" (Spector and Kitsuse, 1977) in respect to gambling operations represents a variant of Becker's (1963) observations regarding the 'bureaucratic entrepreneurship' of the U.S. Federal Bureau of Narcotics. Becker's study of the U.S. Federal Bureau of Narcotics' campaign against marijuana during the 1930s reveals how a bureaucracy was able to increase its scope, prestige, and power (Pfohl, 1985: 307). By arguing that marijuana use led to addiction, sexual promiscuity, madness, and murder, the Bureau was successful in directing media and public attention towards marijuana's putative threat potential. In brief, by supporting the introduction of anti-marijuana legislation at both state and federal levels, the Bureau sought to extend and perpetuate its law enforcement mandate. The Bureau's efforts culminated in 1937 when the U.S. Congress passed the *Marijuana Tax Act* designed to stamp out use of the drug (Becker, 1963:

135). As Becker notes:

> While it is, of course, difficult to know what the motives of Bureau officials
> were, we need assume no more than that they perceived an area of
> wrongdoing that properly belonged in their jurisdiction and moved to put
> it there. The personal interest they satisfied in pressing for marijuana
> legislation was one common to many officials: the interest in successfully
> accomplishing the task one has been assigned and in acquiring the best
> tools with which to accomplish it. The Bureau's efforts took two forms:
> cooperating in the development of state legislation affecting the use of
> marijuana, and providing facts and figures for journalistic accounts of the
> problem. (Becker, 1963: 137)

With respect to gambling in Canada, somewhat in contradistinction to
the U.S. experience with marijuana, wherein increased restrictions fostered greater police involvement, the relaxation of criminal prohibitions
has allowed policing agencies to play a larger role than would a continued
restrictive approach.

LOTTERIES AND 'QUASI-LOTTERIES' IN CANADA

Although gambling in the form of pari-mutuel wagering has been permitted in Canada since 1910, an amendment in 1969 to the *Criminal Code of
Canada* marked the transformation of policy regarding various forms of
gambling from federal prohibition to provincial regulation. Intended to
permit both federal and provincial governments — as well as charitable
and religious organizations — to generate revenues by conducting games
of chance such as lotteries, the amendment resulted in a significant growth
in the amount of real dollars annually expended by Canadians on state-
operated or state-licensed gambling activities. Conservative estimates for
1988 place legal domestic gambling operations in excess of $4 billion.
Lotteries have become the most visible form of permitted gambling with
every province, the Yukon, and the Northwest Territories deriving significant annual revenues from the sale and distribution of such well-known
lottery games as *Lotto 6/49*. Additionally, particular provinces have seen
fit to license and regulate other gambling activities such as casinos, bingos,
and raffles.

In Canada it has become apparent that considerable uniformity exists
across the nation with respect to 'true' lotteries (such as, *Lotto 6/49, Super
Lotto, The Provincial*) which are conducted under the aegis of the Interprovincial Lottery Corporation. However, with respect to 'quasi-lotteries'
(that is, other forms of permitted gaming such as bingos, casinos, raffles),
extensive public-policy variations have occurred regarding the licensing
and regulation of such activities (Osborne and Campbell, 1988). The issues
addressed here focus on one type of quasi-lottery — casino gambling. In
Canada this form of gaming can be regarded as *charity casino gaming* or
public gaming, which stands in contrast to *commercial casino gaming*, which
is found in such U.S. jurisdictions as Las Vegas and Atlantic City, where
private-sector business interests are licensed to operate casino ventures
and appropriate profits from gaming revenues. Although revenues

derived from charity casino gaming are directed towards charitable purposes and are licensed by provincial governments for that expressed purpose, it does not follow that such casinos are innocuous, amateur operations. In some provinces private casino management companies have evolved, specializing in the operation of casino gambling on behalf of licensed charitable organizations. Such companies are owned by private business interests and provide their services to charitable organizations on the basis of negotiated fees. In addition to providing premises and casino equipment, such as blackjack tables and roulette wheels, the companies also provide technically trained workers who specialize as dealers/croupiers and conduct the table games on behalf of the licensed charity. Nonetheless, given that such casinos are licensed explicitly to generate revenues for charitable purposes, it is appropriate to refer to such casinos as constituting charity gaming.

The growth of charity casino gaming has occurred within the context of the expansion of state-conducted or state-licensed gaming in general. That is, the expansion of provincially regulated casino gambling has occurred alongside an overall expansion of state-operated lotteries in Canada. A complete accounting of the expansion of casino gambling within a particular jurisdiction must be cognizant of the general social, economic, political, and legal developments pertaining to the introduction and expansion of true lotteries. Similarly, the expansion of casino gaming has taken place alongside the expansion of quasi-lotteries in general. While a full exposition of the political and economic circumstances pertaining to the expansion of gambling and lotteries is beyond the scope of this discussion, it must be acknowledged that gambling activities have been particularly appealing to state authorities in Canada as a means of generating revenues for deserving non-profit organizations. Western Canadian provinces in particular have demonstrated a willingness to permit expanded levels of gambling activities in general and licensed casino gaming in particular.

Nowhere in Canada has the expansion of gambling been more evident than in the province of Alberta, which has been at the forefront of quasi-lottery gaming. Indeed, Alberta's experience with charity gaming has stood as a prototype for other jurisdictions. For example, in 1981, as part of a series of measures to implement stringent regulatory control over charitable gaming, Alberta created the Alberta Gaming Commission as the provincial authority for licensing and regulating charitable gaming operations. Since then other Canadian provinces, most notably British Columbia and Saskatchewan, have adopted similar regulatory structures and policies. Thus a cursory overview of the emergence of casino gaming in Alberta sheds light on important issues that have become salient in efforts to control gambling activities in other Canadian jurisdictions.

Legitimate casino-style games of chance such as blackjack and roulette first appeared in Western Canada in 1967 in conjunction with the Edmonton Exhibition and Klondike Days. Sections of the *Criminal Code of Canada* allowed certain exceptions to the general prohibitions of gambling, so that Western Canadian provinces had long been willing to tolerate various gambling games that appeared annually with travelling carnival mid-ways. Given this legacy of condoned gambling activity the introduction of casino-style games of chance at agricultural fairs in 1967 represented a seemingly innocuous increment (Campbell, 1981). Casino gaming in Edmonton was soon followed by the introduction of casino operations at fairs in Alberta, Saskatchewan, and Manitoba. In these other jurisdictions, a Calgary businessman with carnival-industry experience was instrumental in promoting the concept of casino gambling to the exhibition boards as a way of generating additional revenues. Acting as an agent for a travelling carnival midway company, Royal American Shows, he supplied the gaming tables and other gambling apparatus.

From 1967 until 1974, the only casino gaming permitted in Western Canada was at agricultural fairs. On occasion, 'Las Vegas' or 'Monte Carlo' nights were permitted in conjunction with philanthropic fundraising activities. In the fall of 1975, however, a significant transformation occurred. Following the advice of the Calgary businessman, a prominent Calgary charity used its influence to persuade the Alberta attorney-general's department to grant a short-term licence for a casino to generate funds. This represented the first effort to capitalize on the 1969 amend-ment to the *Criminal Code* permitting charitable or religious organizations to operate lottery schemes for fundraising purposes[2] (Campbell and Ponting, 1984: 145). This charity casino event proved to be a milestone in the evolution of casino gaming in Alberta and, indeed, in Canada. Specifi-cally, it alerted other charitable organizations to the fundraising potential of casino gaming activities.

In 1976 a rapid proliferation of organizations seeking to conduct fundraising activities within Alberta compelled the attorney-general to initiate a series of measures to license and oversee gaming events. The creation of a gaming control agency in Alberta came amid police fears that criminal interests were penetrating the growing casino industry (Campbell and Ponting, 1984: 145). During the previous summer, a task force made up of 130 personnel from the RCMP, Department of National Revenue investigators, and several Western Canadian municipal police forces had raided the carnival offices of Royal American Shows. As events were to transpire, Royal American Shows had been suspected of engaging in 'organized criminal activities,' including tax evasion, fraudulent underre-porting of revenues to exhibition boards, operating illegal carnival games, customs offences, and corruption of police and municipal officials, as well as skimming from exhibition casino operations (Laycraft, 1978). These suspicions were subsequently brought to light during a 1977 royal com-mission appointed by the province of Alberta to inquire into the alleged Royal American Shows wrongdoings. Testimony given during the in-quiry revealed that criminal intelligence data had led the RCMP to believe that the illegal activities of the carnival company fell within its interpreta-tion of organized crime and that Royal American Shows was connected with Mafia families in the United States.

As a result of public concern regarding the influence of criminal interests on an expanding charity casino industry, the government of

Alberta deemed it prudent to implement a stringent system of regulatory control under the auspices of the Gaming Control Section of the attorney-general. Appointed to head the Gaming Control Section was the former leader of the joint task force, who retired from the RCMP to accept the position. As the senior RCMP gaming specialist, the former staff sergeant was widely respected for his expertise in gambling control. Assigned to develop a regulatory system to oversee charitable gambling operations and to deter opportunities for criminal conduct, his major objective was to ensure the integrity of gaming for the purposes of generating charitable revenues. While in the employ of the Alberta government he had been much sought for his expert knowledge and advice on issues related to the regulation of gambling by numerous Canadian and U.S. authorities. Subsequently, this individual left the province of Alberta to assume a senior position as Director of Gaming Operations with the province of Manitoba.

The history of casino gaming and its legal control in Alberta illustrates many of the concerns and issues that have subsequently emerged in other Western Canadian provinces. Indeed, Alberta has since refined the regulatory model introduced in the late 1970s. Today Alberta's regulatory framework and strict policies are held in high regard by other jurisdictions both within and outside Canada. Consequently, as the provinces of Saskatchewan, Manitoba, and British Columbia have experienced similar concerns, each has taken measures to implement regulatory agencies to control charity casino gaming.

GAMBLING AND ORGANIZED CRIME
A Stigma

Justifiable or otherwise, in North America a stigma has been attached to gambling and gamblers. At least two images accompany this stigma. The first is that gamblers are lazy, undisciplined, and dishonest, and likely to acquire their wealth through the victimization of others (Cornell Law Project, 1977, cited in Dombrink, 1981:53). The second is the spectre of organized crime. As Skolnick (1979, 1978) points out, the legalization of a formerly prohibited activity such as gambling raises particularly vexing regulatory problems for the political authorities and controlling agencies. Most notably, the authorities are faced, on the one hand, with the contradiction of "implicitly justifying legalization on the grounds that the legalized activity isn't all that harmful," while, on the other hand, having to maintain a system of control which, to be effective, "must constantly point out the possibility of infiltration by organized crime, the usual possibility of defrauding consumers, and the dangers of tax evasion — declarations, that, willy-nilly, suggest that the now legalized activity maintains features of its formerly opprobrious self" (Skolnick, 1979: 63).

In providing an overview of illegal gambling in the United States, Rosecrance (1988: 88) convincingly argues that illegal gambling is "shrouded in misconception, mythology, and misinformation." Furthermore, he notes the existence of an established body of orthodoxy held and sustained by both law-enforcement authorities and policy-makers that, despite a lack of supporting empirical evidence and research, hinges on the belief that organized crime interests dominate illegal gambling activities. Rosecrance seriously challenges this orthodoxy. For example, he suggests that the lack of hard data results from two related factors: the relatively clandestine nature of illegal gambling and the bureaucratic nature of the data gathering that does occur. He argues:

> Information concerning the nature and dimensions of America's illegal gambling industry remains the exclusive property of impenetrable law enforcement bureaucracies, each with a particular vested interest in maintaining certain public perceptions of bookmaking and illegal numbers, and of illegal gaming and bingo and other games as well. (Christiansen, 1985, cited in Rosecrance, 1988: 91)

Rosecrance notes that the data underpinning this orthodoxy were originally gathered exclusively by official sources — gambling enforcement agencies. During numerous public hearings, presidential commissions, and inquiries held in the United States since the 1950s and looking into both organized crime and gambling, these data were presented by law-enforcement authorities. Little or no research was conducted independently of police sources. As the various inquiries submitted their final reports, in turn law-enforcement data became 'validated.'

A Monopoly of Knowledge

By the late nineteenth century various police agencies had begun to express concern about how the press was reporting crime trends (Maltz, 1977). In 1927 the International Association of the Chiefs of Police (IACP) formed a committee to study the potential for developing systematic crime reports. Funded by the Rockerfeller Foundation and composed of such personages as J. Edgar Hoover, Director of the FBI, the IACP was concerned that press reportage of crime topics was creating the impression "that police have failed in their task of protection and that all forms of crime are steadily mounting" (IACP, 1929: 16-7, cited in MacLean, 1988: 19). In their 1929 report on the need for uniform crime reporting, the IACP declared:

> In the absence of data on the subject irresponsible parties have often manufactured so-called 'crime waves' out of whole cloth to the discredit of police departments. ... The police alone are in a position to report extensively upon the volume of criminal acts and the great mass of offenders.... The police have the greatest stake in the game. (IACP, 1929: 16-7, cited in MacLean, 1988: 19)

In this light, the IACP has apparently been less concerned with the need to develop reliable and valid indicators of crime trends and more with developing a device for controlling public opinion about both police and crime (MacLean, 1988: 19). Adoption of uniform crime reporting, as advocated by the IACP, "would put police in control of information *vis a vis* the press ... [and] make everyone concerned about crime dependent upon them for the facts. In short, the adoption of uniform crime reporting based upon crimes known to the police was a method of transforming the police into experts of crime and policing phenomena" (MacLean, 1988: 19-20).

Within the context of the historical development of uniform crime reporting, police agencies were well aware of the potential that the control of crime statistics and their interpretation held for the manipulation of public opinion. In a similar manner, police control of secretive 'criminal intelligence' data has led to a corresponding control over media and public knowledge about the phenomenon of 'organized crime.' Echoing scholars such as Kitsuse and Cicourel (1963) and Reuter and Rubinstein (1982), Rosecrance questions the analytic ability of police agencies and their data. He is particularly sceptical of police ability to produce data opposed to the prevailing mythology regarding organized crime. Rosecrance maintains that enforcement agencies foster the mythology of organized crime's domination of illegal gambling in the self-interest of justifying both funding and expansion of gambling enforcement. Additionally, he notes that the existence of this mythology has a significant influence on policy decisions concerning legalization. That is, the argument is often brought to bear that since organized crime is generating such vast profits from illegal gambling, the state should 'get in on the action.' From a methodological perspective, the hegemony of the existing mythology emanating from law-enforcement sources makes this myth difficult to challenge, despite the fact that the historical stigma and moral opprobrium towards gambling has appreciably diminished.

Although gambling is viewed with considerable ambivalence in the eyes of most members of the public (Newman, 1975; Dombrink, 1981; Skolnick, 1988), Western Canadian provinces have been willing to license casino gambling activity in order to generate revenues for purposes broadly defined to be 'charitable' and thus in the public's interest. Discourses favouring the expansion of gambling have tended to be predominant.[3] Other discourses — such as those opposing gambling on religious, moral, or psychological grounds — have been less apparent in Canada in the face of the widespread liberalization of the laws pertaining to lotteries and quasi-lotteries. Indeed, increased levels of legal gaming are indicative of a weakening of moral constraints about gambling. Given the charitable, community benefits to which gaming revenues have been allocated, it would appear that the altruistic use of gambling proceeds has facilitated a perceptual transformation wherein the stigma associated with gambling has diminished in the wake of gambling's fundraising potential.

In identifying factors leading to social acceptance of forms of vice like gambling, Skolnick (1988) discusses such considerations as society's familiarity with the activity under question, the social status and conventionality of the lifestyle of its participants, the susceptibility of the young, the activity's potential for fostering dependency, the public visibility of the activity, the views of influential community leaders, and — what is most relevant to this discussion — the perceived controllability of the vice. As Skolnick points out, any activity deemed to be uncontrollable will be more likely to be regarded as undesirable (Skolnick, 1988: 25). With respect to gambling in Western Canada, the altruistic uses to which gambling proceeds have been allocated, in conjunction with an extensive police rhetoric proclaiming the necessity of stringent control, have facilitated the perceptual transformation of gambling's criminal status to a legalized activity. The moral worth of this activity has been measured by "the feature of raising money through a voluntary activity in lieu of taxation" (Skolnick, 1988: 18).

Canadian Police Agency Reports

In 1974 and 1979, the Co-ordinated Law Enforcement Unit (CLEU) of the Ministry of the Attorney-General in British Columbia prepared reports drawing extensively on U.S. literature on organized crime.[4] U.S. organized crime interests and their relationship to both illegal and legal forms of gambling figure prominently in these reports. Both subscribe to beliefs that gambling activity contributes significant amounts to organized crime coffers, which are then used to underwrite other criminal enterprises. For example, the 1974 report argues: "Most authorities consider gambling the bread and butter activity of organized crime. It is alleged to be a multi-billion dollar industry in the United States, where it provides huge profits to invest in drugs or legitimate businesses" (CLEU, 1974: 18). With specific regard to casinos in Western Canada, the 1974 CLEU report states that casinos "have been permitted in certain circumstances in the Prairie provinces. Royal Canadian Mounted Police gambling experts have studied them and found them ill-conceived and poorly run.... Other authorities are convinced that organized crime is involved in Prairie casino operations" (CLEU, 1974: 22).

In a similar vein, a 1984 overview of legalized gambling prepared by the Ministry of the Solicitor-General Canada, in response to a request by Senior Gaming Specialists of the RCMP, states: "Wherever casinos are found they are inseparable from organized criminal activities. Virtually, every study undertaken in the United States, Britain, Australia, and elsewhere points out that casino gaming, whether illegal or legal encourages organized crime activity" (Canada, Solicitor General, 1984: 16).

A confidential research paper prepared for the Gaming Specialist Understudy Program of the RCMP in 1984 forewarns that U.S. experiences with organized crime present a 'harbinger' for Canada (RCMP, 1984: 2). Drawing on the orthodox accounts of organized crime in the United States and on journalistic sources such as the CBC television series *Connections*, the report argues that "Illegal gambling and legalized gaming are out of control in the majority of Canadian jurisdictions" (RCMP, 1984: 13). The report further asserts: "Legalized gaming in Canada presents as great or greater a challenge to the police as does illegal gambling. The two have been inextricably intertwined in this country and many of the players are identical in both fields" (RCMP, 1984: 47).

In tracing the emergence of casinos at agricultural fairs in Western Canada, impervious to the lack of supporting evidence noted by the Laycraft Inquiry, the RCMP report nonetheless makes the unsubstantiated claim that "Theft by skimming of profits and the massive defrauding of exhibition boards, marked the birth of casinos in Canada" (RCMP, 1984: 19). In attempting to sustain the impression that theft and skimming had continued in casino operations, the 1984 report alleges, "Conspiracies to commit theft involving player-dealers, pitboss-dealers, bankers-games managers, *ad infinitum*, are occurring and few are ever reported to the police" (RCMP, 1984: 51). While charges have, on occasion, been laid against casino workers in Western Canadian casinos, no firm evidence is provided by the author of this report to support the claim that internal theft or collusion is widespread. In fact, recent statistics compiled by the Alberta Gaming Control Branch for the period 1978-87 indicate that contrary to RCMP assertions, casino gaming is relatively free of internal theft and fraud. Over the ten-year period, internal casino theft and fraud had led to the laying of charges against ten persons. This represents 7.4 per cent of all persons charged for various offences across all forms of licensed gambling (that is, including charitable bingos, raffles, and pull-ticket sales). According to Alberta Gaming Control Branch statistics, internal theft from casinos over the ten-year period totalled $16,375, an average of just over $1,600 per year (McCall, 1988: 23-7). Furthermore, the available evidence does not reveal that these offences were anything more than isolated thefts perpetrated by individuals acting alone. While charges have been laid against small groups of individuals, including casino personnel working in collaboration with players, nothing suggests that their activities were related to any kind of organized crime conspiracy.

A 1985 Calgary police report contends that the history of casinos in Alberta is indicative of the casinos' potential for conspiracy. The report states: "In 1974 [sic], new regulations and audit procedures introduced by [the newly appointed head] reportedly, increased the 'hold'[5] by 55%" (Calgary Police Service, 1985: 9).[6] It is not at all certain that this stated increase — whether an accurate figure or not — is attributable to the elimination of fraudulent behaviour. Any one or more of a number of factors may have contributed to the increased hold. For example, increased betting limits, longer hours of operation, faster-paced games (such as the introduction of face-up, no-hole card blackjack) and better trained dealers are all possible contributing factors. The conclusion that fraudulent behaviour was held in check with the introduction of new controls is therefore not fully warranted. Nonetheless, what is implicit in the report's discussion of the increase is that misappropriation was occurring and that proper financial controls apprehended the revenue leakage.

Canadian Public Inquiries

In the years that the Western Canadian provinces have seen fit to license quasi-lottery gaming, several public inquiries have been convened to address a variety of concerns pertaining to gaming operations and their control. Headed by Mr. Justice James Laycraft, a 1977 royal commission in Alberta failed to confirm police suspicions that organized criminal interests were engaged in defrauding exhibition casino operations.

Nonetheless, the attention directed towards casino gaming during the Royal American Shows scandal was sufficient to provoke the introduction of a stringent gaming control bureaucracy. In Manitoba a 1979 royal commission headed by Mr. Graeme Haig, Q.C. reported having heard the concerns of Winnipeg city police, the RCMP, and Alberta Gaming Control officials about the possibility of infiltration of organized crime into gambling activities. Well aware of the existing perceptions of the relationship between organized crime interests and casino gaming industries in the United States and Great Britain, Haig, nonetheless, concluded that:

> Concerns about criminal participation in Western Canadian gambling seems to be misplaced. So long as the various provinces continue to issue licenses only to charitable or religious organizations or organizations with such purposes to raise money to be used in furtherance of [their purposes] ... games and casinos will remain, for the criminal element, non-existent. (Haig, 1979: 142)

A subsequent inquiry conducted by Mr. Justice Gerald Jewers in 1983 investigated the role of private operators in gaming industries in Manitoba. With respect to casino operations, Jewers's inquiry concluded that licensed organizations were "well served by the private operators and games personnel who are apparently competent and whose fees are generally reasonable" (Jewers, 1983: 224). Finally, the attorney-general of British Columbia announced the formation of the British Columbia Gaming Commission in 1987. He requested the commission to undertake a series of specific tasks, including a comprehensive review of policies related to casino gaming. According to a Province of British Columbia news release, the attorney-general stated: "Government has a major concern with the growth of current casino activity in the Province.... It was pointed out by policing authorities in the Province that the major problem has been a lack of effective enforcement" (B.C. Gaming Commission, 1988: XVIII-5,6). In preparing its report, the B.C. Gaming Commission solicited and received extensive background information from various policing agencies in the province. In the submission made by the British Columbia Association of Chiefs of Police (BCACP), the following concerns were expressed:

> Gaming of necessity means that substantial amounts of cash will be present at premises where these activities take place. The opportunities for laundering money, internal theft, cheating and collusion are always present. In order to minimize these opportunities, it is essential that gaming is strictly controlled from the outset. It will be easier to prevent these problems by high profile monitoring, auditing and enforcement. (B.C. Gaming Commission, 1988: XVII-4)

In addition to the BCACP submission, the Gaming Commission heard from other police forces and individual officers. As well, the commission was privy to three secret reports prepared by the province's Co-ordinated Law Enforcement Unit dealing with casino gambling, carnivals, and private social club gaming in the province. In the commission's final report to the attorney-general, the police position on gambling was held to merit such attention that it was included as a separate chapter of the report.

Thus, amid numerous recommendations for greater regulatory control over the entire spectrum of charity gaming in the province, the commission noted:

> There is ongoing dialogue between the police and the [Public Gaming] Branch.... We value this liaison and advice we receive and we consider it extremely important in helping us structure policies, guidelines, terms and conditions, etc. which will ensure that organized criminals will not infiltrate the charity gaming industry.... We are in need of, and intend to cultivate a close supportive relationship with police throughout the Province. (B.C. Gaming Commission, 1988: XVII-1)

There is, then, a considerable contradiction in these reports. Police suspicions and allegations have not led to persuasive testimony being introduced at the judicial inquiries held in Western Canada. Nonetheless, even in the absence of hard evidence for either the presence or pervasiveness of organized crime, the inquiry reports consistently advocate the desirability of stringent regulatory controls in respect to charitable casino gambling. The alleged threat potential of organized crime would appear both to create and to justify the need for close regulatory scrutiny.

Police, Media, and Signification

As has been demonstrated in several studies of moral panics,[7] symbolic crusades,[8] and moral entrepreneurs[9] (Becker, 1963; Cohen, 1972; Gusfield, 1963; Hall et al., 1978; Voumvakis and Ericson, 1984), the news media have played major roles in arousing public attention to particular issues, and it can also be hypothesized here that the media have played an influential role in stimulating both public and governmental responses towards casino gaming issues. In this regard, it can further be hypothesized that the media have played a major role in Western Canadian jurisdictions in creating what Hall et al. (1978) have called 'signification spirals.'[10] That is, in respect to mugging in Great Britain, Hall et al. have noted that the wedding of the concepts 'youth,' 'violence,' 'race,' and 'crime' in media accounts of crime evoked extensive public fear and reaction. The outcome of the convergence of these concepts was the creation of the widespread perception that the established ways of British life were under attack by racial minority youths. With respect to gambling, media sources have tended to give considerable attention to 'police accounts' of organized crime's relationship to gambling activities. Through reliance on police spokespersons as authoritative sources for news items in respect to the issue of gambling, various media have contributed to the 'amplification of threat potential' (Hall et al., 1978: 223) allegedly posed by organized crime. Informed by the work of Cohen, Hall et al., and Voumvakis and Ericson, as well as by a preliminary review of news-media accounts, it is not unreasonable to suggest that police authorities have acted as 'primary definers,' that is, as key spokespersons who both identify and interpret the salient issues in respect to gambling activities. At this juncture, what is required is a more thorough explication of news accounts of gambling issues. Even in the absence of such analysis, though, some speculations may be tendered.

As observed by Hall et al., when the media rely on police sources: "Translation of official viewpoints into public idioms not only makes the former more 'available' to the uninitiated, it invests them with particular force and resonance, naturalizing them within the horizon of understandings of the various publics" (Hall et al., 1978: 61). Thus it can be contended that official accounts that maintain the vulnerability of casinos to penetration by organized crime are not only newsworthy, but that their utilization is fundamental in a signification spiral. Likewise, the association of the idea of casino gambling with organized crime is illustrative of the idea of the 'convergence' phenomenon found in the spiral process. That is, the association of the two notions (gambling and organized crime) converge in a manner similar to that observed by Hall et al. in regard to the concepts of 'youth' and 'violence.' In other words, the 'pairing' or 'dovetailing' of such concepts creates an entirely new perception of the issues believed to be at stake.[11]

To the extent that police gaming specialists have acted as principal sources for media reports, police can be hypothesized to have played a major role in bringing the issue of unregulated gambling and the threat of organized crime onto the political agenda of various provincial governments. In response to media accounts and mounting public concern, provincial political leaders and government agencies have been forced to turn to the police for expert advice on the appropriate policy responses. This was evident in the discussion of Canadian police agency reports and public inquiries. As further illustration it is helpful to recount a conversation with two Western Canadian RCMP senior gaming specialists, wherein one of the officers, while the other nodded his head in affirmation, stated: "We are not the anti-gambling squad. People tend to see us as anti-gambling. We are not anti-gambling. In fact, we have nothing against gambling as long as it is adequately licensed and controlled" (author's field notes).

These two police officers subsequently retired from the RCMP to accept positions with provincial gaming regulatory agencies. One of the officers was the author of several widely circulated RCMP reports on gambling[12] and was much consulted by various municipal, provincial, and federal authorities during his tenure with the RCMP for his expert knowledge as a gaming specialist. In addition to liaising with municipal police forces and provincial regulatory agencies, he also testified in camera before several provincial cabinets and before a 1985 Senate committee reviewing proposed amendments to sections of the Criminal Code of Canada dealing with gambling.[13]

CONCLUSIONS

In several respects, the various police reports' claims about gambling and organized crime are reminiscent of Becker's (1963) analysis of bureaucratic entrepreneurship by the Federal Bureau of Narcotics in the 1930s, when the Bureau actively undertook to have the Marijuana Tax Act passed to further its own bureaucratic interests. The Bureau's strategy took two forms. First, it co-operated willingly with numerous state legislatures in the development of sanctions against the use of marijuana. Secondly, the Bureau and particularly the Bureau's Director provided media sources with both numerous facts and figures purporting to document the growing use of marijuana and sensationalized details of horrendous crimes allegedly perpetrated by marijuana users. Becker notes that through such actions the Bureau successfully used the media to produce a desired objective, that is, to arouse public interest and concern. The concerns ultimately contributed to the willingness of political representatives to legislate stringent controls on marijuana and its possession. Western Canada's experiences with gambling would seem to indicate a variant of this theme. That is, rather than calling for increased proscription of gambling activities, Canadian police agencies have not decried the activity of gambling in any generic sense. Recognizing the economic and political attractiveness of state-generated gaming revenues, police agencies have been willing to accommodate increased amounts of state licensed gambling. The police are unequivocally concerned, though, that increased levels of gaming must be accompanied by increased levels of regulation.

With the increase in licensed gambling and a marked trend towards further decriminalization, the nature of the discourse originating from police sources marked a transition in the object of censure. That is, the discourse originating from police sources has not attended directly to the issue of gambling *per se*. The object of censure has been a related concern — that of *organized crime*. As McLaren and Lowman have noted in regard to prostitution: "Police generate their own discourses and appropriate elements of others to serve their own purposes.... They do so in a way that creates a variety of contradictions and conflicts within the control system" (McLaren and Lowman, 1988: 83). Nowhere is this more apparent than in regard to the control of charity casino gambling. Indeed, this is the very paradox identified by Skolnick (1979) earlier:

> To be effective, the controlling agency must point out the precariousness of the activity — the possibility of infiltration by organized crime, the unusual possibilities of consumer fraud — suggesting willy-nilly that the now-legalized activity maintains features of its formerly opprobrious self. How is the controlling agency supposed to maintain the rationale for strict control while justifying legislation on the grounds that the legalized activity isn't all that harmful? (Skolnick, 1979: 11)[14]

In the case of casino gambling in Western Canada, police agencies have not chosen to censure the increase of gambling activity in and of itself. Rather, the object of their attention and censure has been the issue of *organized crime*. The discourse of police agencies reveals the extent to which police have accommodated the decriminalization of gambling. It illustrates that police concerns rest with the need for regulatory control in order to exclude the alleged omnipresence of criminal elements. Discourses about the threat of organized crime have been taken seriously by political leaders and policy-makers. Thus, provincial governments have carefully sought to regulate legal gambling activities in the interest of sustaining the legitimacy of gambling as a vehicle for raising funds for charitable objectives. The extent to which police concerns have been expressed, attended to by the media, and, in turn, attended to by political authorities, is evident in the nature of the regulatory controls and bureaucracies implemented in the Western Canadian provinces. Those provinces have predominantly hired former RCMP officers to head and staff their regulatory agencies. Three of the four western provinces have recruited RCMP gaming specialists. Two of these former specialists came to command senior positions within their respective agencies. In addition to the police gaming specialists, provinces have generally deemed it desirable to recruit former police officers to their gaming investigation branches. As a retired RCMP officer remarked, "The legalization of provincial gambling has created a 'retirement Mecca' for former RCMP officers."

Vigilance against organized crime has also justified a series of intrusive surveillance measures in most Western Canadian provinces. For example, prospective casino employees are subjected to Canadian Police Information Centre (CPIC) checks. Individuals found to have criminal records or other 'undesirable pasts' are deemed unsuitable for hiring. Additionally, community-based charitable organizations seeking eligibility to conduct gambling fundraising activities are subject to a series of prelicensing checks to ensure their legitimacy. As well, licensed organizations are subject to extensive audits and follow-up investigations to ensure that generated funds have not been misused or misappropriated. In brief, the perceived need for vigilance about organized crime has been used to justify a series of net-widening measures through which state gaming regulatory agencies closely survey community-based charities. In Alberta, for example, in 1987 some 611 charitable organizations were licensed to conduct charity casino events (Alberta Gaming Commission, 1988), thus coming under the ambit of the provincial gaming regulatory agency.[15] In and of itself, such intrusion may appear to be relatively benign and innocuous. However, when conditions of licensing specify that regulatory agencies have access to minutes, financial statements, and virtually all business records of licensed charitable organizations, including files on the clients of particular charitable organizations, state intrusion is significant.

Where the issue of the control of gambling has become increasingly controversial is in regard to gambling operations on Native reserves. Recently, numerous Indian bands have introduced gambling operations such as bingos and casinos on their reservations. Catering primarily to a non-Indian clientele, gambling operations have been perceived by Native leaders to hold the potential for generating large amounts of much needed capital. Such gambling operations have additionally provided significant numbers of jobs for band members. Given Native sovereignty over tribal lands, as well as their historical autonomy from provincial authority, Native leaders have refused to seek provincial permission to operate their gambling enterprises. As a result, it has become increasingly problematic that provincial authorities have reacted strongly to unlicensed and un-regulated gambling operations on Native reserves. In several Canadian provinces, criminal charges have been laid against Native leaders for the operation of unlicensed gambling enterprises. Criminal intelligence reports gathered by both police and regulatory agency personnel in these jurisdictions have led to allegations that organized crime interests are attempting to infiltrate Native gaming industries. Hence, criminal charges have been justified on the grounds that unfettered gambling is conducive to penetration by organized crime interests and that licensing and control by provincial authorities is imperative if the integrity of gambling enterprises is to be ensured. While, once again, such regulatory measures may appear on the surface to be innocuous and well-intended, the issue of control by provincial authorities of gambling activities on Native lands represents a major intrusion in Native affairs and a major threat to Native autonomy. As a consequence, Native leaders in Canada as well as the United States have grown particularly sceptical and disdainful of measures to curtail their gambling. Indeed, Natives have come to view the putative threat of organized crime as little more than a red herring carefully constructed to usurp their endeavours to attain economic and political autonomy.

In summary, unlike the U.S. experience with marijuana wherein increased restrictions fostered greater police involvement, in Canada the relaxation of criminal prohibitions with respect to gambling has allowed policing agencies to play a larger role than in a continued restrictive approach. Given the experience of Western Canadian provinces, it would appear that police discourse about organized crime and the need for stringent control has resulted in the implementation of formidable regulatory systems and bureaucracies. These, in turn, have facilitated the relaxation of gambling prohibitions. By virtue of the translocation of policing personnel to regulatory agencies, the scope and influence of police authority have been extensively expanded. Indeed, provincial willingness to license charitable gambling has expanded 'the market' for police knowledge and expertise about organized crime and gambling regulation. In sum, police authorities have successfully exerted considerable influence and control over the direction and thrust of provincial policies towards gambling.

NOTES

1. By discourse I mean "the verbal or written articulations of a series of claims about the cause or character of a 'social problem,' claims which reflect values and assumptions rooted in wider political, social, economic, religious, cultural and discursive systems" (McLaren and Lowman, 1988).

2. Provinces have tended to interpret the phrase *lottery scheme* to include such games as bingo as well as casino games like blackjack and roulette.

3. Campbell and Ponting (1984) have documented how charitable organizations in Alberta were successful in having their funding needs met via the mechanism of gambling. In short, their analysis reveals how a *revenue-*

raising discourse favouring expansion became dominant.

4. See, for example, Co-ordinated Law Enforcement Unit, *Third Findings Report on Organized Crime in British Columbia* (1979), pp. 26-7.

5. The 'hold' is the dollar amount of a casino's winnings over a fixed period of time (day, week, year) expressed as a percentage of total revenues received at the gaming tables. It is generally used as a measure of how well the casino is doing relative to the volume of play or 'action' at the tables.

6. The Calgary Police Report would appear to be in error regarding the date of the introduction of the new regulations and procedures. That is, the appointment of the new head did not occur until the spring of 1976 and the introduction of the new regulations occurred after that date (Johnson, 1980: 15).

7. Cohen describes a moral panic: "A condition, episode, person or group of persons emerges to become defined as a threat to societal values and interests; its nature is presented in a stylized and stereotypical fashion by the mass media; the moral barricades are manned by editors, bishops, politicians and other right-thinking people; socially accredited experts pronounce their diagnoses and solutions; ways of coping are evolved or (more often) resorted to" (Cohen, 1972: 9).

8. Gusfield's (1963) study of prohibition laws reveals how, by mounting what he calls 'a symbolic crusade' against alcohol, rural, Protestant, middle-class Americans sought to protect their declining status and influence within the changing social landscape of the early twentieth-century United States.

9. Moral entrepreneurs can be defined as powerful individuals or groups of individuals who are successful in having their values, beliefs, and ideas translated into laws, public policy, or both.

10. According to Hall et al.: "The signification spiral is a way of signifying events which also intrinsically escalates their threat. The notion of a signification spiral is similar to that of an 'amplification spiral'. An amplification spiral suggests that reaction has the effect, under certain conditions, not of lessening but of increasing deviance" (1978: 223).

11. Of course, the concept *organized crime* is laden with considerable connotative baggage. That is, organized crime as extensively portrayed in both news and entertainment media conjures up a considerable array of images, including that of systematic violence. Even the Co-ordinated Law Enforcement Unit Initial Report on Organized Crime in B.C., October 1974, reproduces graphic crime-scene photographs of drug-related contract killings and the murder of a known loan shark.

12. For example, see RCMP (1984).

13. See, for example, *Proceedings*, Standing Senate Committee On Legal and Constitutional Affairs, 1st Session, 33rd Parliament, 1984-85, Issues 32 and 33, Dec. 11, 12, 13, 1985.

14. Skolnick presented this idea in 1978 and subsequently in 1979. Both sources are cited in this chapter.

15. The total of 611 represents only those charities conducting casinos. Even greater numbers of charitable organizations came under regulatory scrutiny by virtue of having sought bingo or raffle licensing.

Chapter Twelve

Women, Men, and Police: Losing the Fight against Wife Battery in Canada

Dawn H. Currie / Brian D. MacLean

Within a short period of time wife battery has been transformed from a private trouble for individual Canadian women into a public issue. Reflecting this transformation, Canada has been among the first of the advanced industrial nations to institute a nationwide policy encouraging the arrest of battering men. Here, Dawn Currie and Brian MacLean discuss the criminological debates that have accompanied this movement to criminalize wife assault. On the whole, the criminological community has supported the movement to redefine wife assault as a crime. But, while a number of women have welcomed the protection provided by police intervention and the opportunity to use the courts, this approach raises a number of dilemmas. For one thing, activists within the feminist community are beginning to decry the growing alliance between women and the state that results from the institutionalization of women's issues. From this perspective, the issue of wife battery poses a serious challenge to critical criminology, which is committed both to issues of justice for women and to a critique of a "law and order" approach to social problems. Currie and MacLean argue that while it may be true that the policing needs of women reflect a real need for protection of women from male violence, the satisfaction of this need has become equated with solving the problem. The redefinition of wife abuse as a crime redirects criminological research away from processes that underlie and perpetuate wife battery and towards its efficient management by policing and social-service agencies that do not fundamentally challenge the status quo. Thus it is not surprising that battered women have reported that mandatory arrest is an inappropriate response to their dilemma. The real challenge that violence against women poses for critical criminology is an explication of how radical demands become transformed into liberal responses.

Dawn Currie is Assistant Professor in Sociology at the University of British Columbia and Brian MacLean is a Criminologist in Vancouver

INTRODUCTION

When Margaret Mitchell (NDP, Vancouver) raised wife battery as a public concern in the House of Commons, laughter echoed throughout Parliament; but within five years Canada had adopted a nationwide policy that encouraged police to lay charges in wife-battering cases. This shifting of attitudes reflected in social policy is directly linked to the activities of two interest groups — women's organizations and academically trained professionals. While the notion of wife assault as a serious social issue did not exist prior to the late 1970s, today a diverse literature addresses the causes and extent of domestic violence as the basis for the development of programs of intervention. This chapter will look at the transformation of wife battery from a 'private trouble' to a 'public issue,' highlighting how attention was subsequently directed towards policing and criminal justice. Within this context, a number of writers are beginning to criticize the growing alliance between feminism and the state (see Burstyn, 1985; Strong-Boag, 1986; Snider, 1991). Snider (1991: 239), for example, is critical of how campaigns against violence against women have led to lobbying for new criminal offences, making arrests, charges, and convictions easier, and increasing punishment. As a feminist struggle for justice, the law and order agenda is defended on a number of grounds: Women only want the same kind of justice that has been given to other victims of crime; feminism is not responsible for the current form of *male* justice, it only asks for it to be applied consistently, against men; the use of criminal legislation against violence against women establishes the principle of women's dignity as a people by recognition of violence against them as a major crime; and, finally, although law will not diminish crimes and harsher sentencing will not alter the general picture, the use of law becomes an occasion for public debates, which increase cultural and political awareness of the issue (see Pitch, 1985: 43).

While we do not in any way want to downplay the reality of the victimization of women (see especially Jones, MacLean, and Young, 1986), here we are concerned about how current campaigns feed a call for *law and order* and about the challenge that wife battery poses for a critical criminology, at both the theoretical and political level. Specifically, while we agree that the policing needs of women reflect a real need, we believe that a *law and order* lobby represents the transformation of wife battery as a social issue into a criminological issue. This stands in direct contrast to initial feminist campaigns. Concomitant to this redefinition of wife battery as a crime, research and political practice become redirected away from processes that underlie and perpetuate wife battery and towards its efficient "management" by policing and other social-service agencies. Within this context, liberal activists demand more resources for an extension of current institutional responses. Although we agree with Straus (1976, 1980) and others that the practice of policing (and of social work, for that matter) is an unsatisfactory response because it represents an individualized and case-by-case response to a structural problem, the real problem is neither merely the *amount* nor the *level* of intervention. Rather, *police intervention is inadequate because it does not challenge the fundamental processes that perpetuate domestic violence.* Police intervention — like that of social-service agencies — has as its mandate reconstitution of patriarchal and bourgeois institutions and, within them, the secondary position of women. The challenge to critical criminology, therefore, involves an exploration of how radical demands become transformed into liberal responses that fail to consider the real rather than merely symbolic role of the police.

FROM THE PERSONAL TO THE POLITICAL
Documenting the Extent of Wife Battery

While writers do not agree upon the nature and causes of violence within families, most concur that its frequency has been historically underestimated. Before 1970, wife assault was an infrequently recorded category in either criminal justice or medical statistics. Because wife assault remained officially invisible, the view advanced by traditional social scientists and family practitioners — that the violence was restricted to unusual cases of pathological families — was generally accepted. For this reason, the documentation of the frequency of wife battery was a necessary feature of early campaigns to politicize domestic violence.

The underestimation of violence against wives is both a political and methodological issue. As a political issue, feminists in particular point out that women's definitions of themselves and their situation foster "self-blame" on the part of battered women, who then come to regard the violence as a "personal problem." Because battered wives see themselves as 'different' from other 'normal' married women, they internalize responsibility for family problems and, as a consequence, lose self-esteem and confidence (Dobash and Dobash, 1979; Swanson, 1985; Schechter, 1982). Walker (1979) in particular developed this line of argumentation into a 'theory' of learned helplessness which, paradoxically, fuelled an already apparent tendency in victim-precipitation approaches to blame women for their problems. In contrast to this individualism reminiscent of traditional criminology, Chalmers and Smith (1988) emphasize the physical, psychological, and social isolation of wives and highlight how the nuclear family and the organization of community responses contribute to the invisibility and privatization of domestic violence. To Chalmers and Smith, the provision of women-centred refuges represents one way to overcome the isolation of women on the individual level, which may in turn lead to further politicization by bringing battered women together.

Academics have pointed out, as a strictly methodological issue, the problems inherent in almost all the available information sources. Because wife-battery is (technically) a criminal offence, one obvious source of information is official records kept by agencies of criminal justice. But these data grossly underestimate domestic violence, leading some writers to conclude that they probably tell us more about the activities of the agencies than about domestic violence itself (Jones, MacLean, and Young, 1986). Other sources include hospital records and transition-house statistics, which also yield underestimates. Historically, physicians have been reluctant to classify presenting symptoms as evidence of abuse and, further, are unlikely to encourage self-disclosure (see Ahluwalia, 1987). Transition houses, on the other hand, draw upon a select clientele, often because of their funding mandate. MacLeod (1980) indicates that transition houses are forced to turn away working women and women without children. A third source of information about wife abuse is victimization surveys. Most researchers agree that these types of surveys provide more accurate estimates, particularly when they incorporate techniques to encourage disclosure (see Jones, MacLean, and Young, 1986). But they too are an imperfect measure.

Recognizing these limitations, it is nevertheless useful to examine the available estimates of wife battery in Canada. In a liberal estimate, *The Gazette* (Montreal) indicated that 750, 000 Canadian women were victims of family violence in 1985 (Feb. 4, 1987), while the Canadian Urban Victimization Survey (CUVS) more conservatively reported that 97,700 women were assaulted during 1982, with 23 per cent of these respondents victimized in their own homes. Of the cases uncovered by the CUVS, only 50 percent came to the attention of police (1985, Bulletin 4: 5). The primary reason victims gave for failing to contact the police was the belief that "The police couldn't do anything about it." While this reasoning reflects one reason why the 'real' extent of violence against women is difficult to measure, researchers since have emphasized the conservative nature of the CUVS (DeKeseredy and MacLean, 1991; MacLean, 1991).

Smith (1987a) notes that respondents were not asked directly if their husbands or ex-husbands had assaulted them. In attempting to correct this obvious source of bias, many researchers in Canada have adopted the "conflict tactics scale" (CTS) to measure the extent of physical victimization between family members. The CTS consists of 18 items measuring three different ways of dealing with interpersonal conflict: reasoning, verbal aggression, and physical violence. The items are categorized on a continuum from least to most severe, with the first ten items describing non-violent acts. The preamble to the scale encourages disclosure by reassuring respondents that "no matter how well couples get along, there are times when they disagree on major decisions" (see DeKeseredy and MacLean, 1990). Rates of violence gathered in this fashion range from 11 to 25 per cent of representative samples. In addition, DeKeseredy (1989) reports that 12 per cent of a convenience sample of male university students in Ontario reported using one of the violent tactics at least once in the twelve months before the survey.

While the estimates of violence against women by intimates based on the CTS have made a useful contribution to the limited data base, DeKeseredy and MacLean (1990: 19) indicate the political nature of what may appear to be 'objective' scientific procedures. Specifically, they note that CTS data misrepresent the social reality of male violence against women by de-emphasizing wife battery while overemphasizing the phenomenon of husband battery, creating the image of battery within the family as gender-neutral. By placing wife battery within a broad scope of 'family problems,' academic research thus has the potential to obstruct efforts to provide adequate shelters for battered women, supporting instead programs to rehabilitate violent 'families.'

While methodological debates about the actual frequency of violence against women by intimates are unlikely to be resolved for some time, most experts accept the claim that approximately one in four households are affected by violence (in Ahluwalia, 1987) and that one in ten women living in marriage or common-law unions are battered every year (MacLeod, 1980: 16). The Canadian Advisory Council on the Status of Women (CACSW) concludes: "Even if we 'guesstimate' that two out of three women report their battering to some official agency — a very conservative estimate according to front-line workers interviewed — this would mean that almost one million women in Canada may be battered each year" (MacLeod, 1987: 9). At the strictly empirical level, therefore, wife battery has been documented as a serious social problem for Canadian women.

THE POLITICIZATION OF WIFE BATTERY
The Legacy of Liberalism

While feminists emphasize that these estimates reflect the stark reality of male violence against women, they do not agree upon how this violence is related to women's oppression. For example, radicals like Brownmiller (1975) argue that male violence and women's fear of it play a primary *causal* role in women's secondary position, while writers like Clark and Lewis (1977) or the Schwendingers (1983) see it as an *effect* of the societal oppression of women and thus an indicator rather than cause of sexual inequality. While this means that long-term agendas are likely to differ, women's groups universally support the notion of 'shelters' for women seeking refuge from violent men and reform of its legal treatment. As in Britain and the United States, the provision of "safe houses" directly linked to community women's groups was the primary initial response to violence against wives. Usually run by volunteers operating on minimal budgets, these houses subsequently became the locus of considerable political and research activities. By the mid-1970s, a series of books documenting the experiences of women who use these services began to draw public attention to the plight of battered women. Reflecting links to the anti-rape movement of the time, a common theme of this early literature is violence as "a mechanism for female social control" (see Schechter, 1982). Pizzey (1974: 30) in particular drew attention to how the still common dictum that "a man's home is his castle" renders the family a dangerous place for women. In total, these works drew attention to women's economic and social dependency upon men within contemporary institutions. As a critique of current social-work practices that saw domestic violence as a problem of alcohol abuse and advocated family rehabilitation, within the women's liberation movement (WLM) wife battering was portrayed as a manifestation of women's specific domestic oppression, which cannot be justified or excused under *any* circumstances.

Together with the increased visibility of wife battery in the media, these kinds of critiques prompted traditional organizations — particularly universities — to recognize the need for research and the deployment of resources. However, once placed on the agenda of patriarchal institutions, discourses increasingly shifted away from discussions of 'wife abuse' towards the more objective and neutral-sounding notion of "family" or "domestic" violence.[1] At the same time, grassroots workers found themselves in direct confrontation with 'professionals' — feminist or otherwise. While this was to become a continuing source of strife still evident today (see Barnsley, 1985), strategies and programs of intervention became shaped along liberal social-scientific rather than 'radical'[2] feminist lines (see Ahluwalia, 1987). This means that at the individual level a *quasi*-medical approach prevails, favouring case-by-case 'diagnosis' and individualized 'treatment.' Although the issue of sexual inequality is included in the political forum, it is placed within the bourgeois framework of women's rights to protection and freedom from personal violence.[3] While raising a number of demands, this approach fostered an optimistic demand for reforms in the application of the existing criminal-justice apparatus (see Currie, 1990).

According to liberals, law is an important arena of feminist intervention because it both mirrors and shapes our culture, thereby not only reflecting but also contributing to the development of shared meanings and aspirations. From a liberal perspective the problem for women is that the law currently sanctions the differential authority wielded by men over women, and by husbands over wives in particular. Reflecting prescriptions about the proper roles for men and women within marriage, gender ideologies come to the forefront during the formulation and interpretation of law. While the origin of these ideologies is a neglected theoretical question within the liberal framework, writers document how law historically has sanctioned the abuse of wives by husbands. In her report for the CACSW, for example, MacLeod (1980: 27) points to the first known written laws, dating from 2500 BC, which proclaimed, "The name of any woman who verbally abused her husband was to be engraved on a brick which was then to be used to bash out her teeth." Continuing into the nineteenth century, when British law stated that "The husband had by law 'power and domination over his wife' and could 'beat her, but not in a cruel or violent manner,' " MacLeod identifies four legal themes: that men are considered to own their wives; that, conversely, women are expected to obey their husbands and conform to an ideal of self-denial; that men have a complete authority over their wives that is unquestioned within the home; and that women's place is in the family sphere. Because these are argued to represent outdated beliefs about what is proper behaviour in the family, reform of law became a key issue of liberal campaigns.

At the same time liberals link the oppression of women within families to the privatization of family life, which results in the law being unequally available to men and women. From a liberal perspective, social life is organized into two distinct spheres, each governed by a differing set of values and principles: the public sphere of economic or market relationships as opposed to the private sphere of personal or familial relations. Values associated with the public realm include individualism, competitiveness, and rational self-interest. The public sphere is the realm of the juridic individual. In contrast, the private sphere is seen as governed by co-operation, sharing, and self-sacrifice and is equated with personal relations. In industrialized societies, this 'public/private' dichotomy corresponds to divisions between the workplace and the family. The problem for women is that they have been historically relegated to the family sphere, where they remain tied to the activities and values associated with procreation and childcare, and where they are subjected to the authority of men as the economic and legal 'head' of the household. Because of this association with the natural rather than social order, women were mistakenly identified within classical social and political theory as being closer to Nature than Culture, an ideology justifying their exclusion from political life. While this division and opposition between public and private vis à vis men and women are upheld by law, the family was designated as an area in which the law has no legitimate authority to intervene. While liberals may disagree as to precisely where the line is to be drawn, they do not question that it exists (see Jaggar, 1983). In general, liberals agree that there is a private area of life that should be beyond the scope of legal government regulation.[4]

The history of liberal political theory is the provision of a philosophical rationale for the gradual enlargement of the public realm of juridic relations, an extension often equated with the 'equality' of women and their 'liberation' (see Currie, 1989). From about the middle of the nineteenth century onwards, political theory has included arguments by feminists that liberal principles should apply equally to women as they apply to men. Because women were historically marginal to the operation of law by virtue of their assignation to the private realm, campaigns to extend the public rights enjoyed by men to women were central to "First Wave" feminism.[5] Early reform efforts focused upon married women's right to own property, the repeal of legislation barring women from higher education and the professions, and the right for women to vote and run as political candidates. In this way, the First Wave established women's legal ability to function as men's equals in the public realm. By the 1960s this limited vision of equality was recognized as inadequate. Political activity associated with the "Second Wave" challenged the liberal legacy against intervention by the state in family life as upholding the authority of men over women in the private realm. Identifying this authority as a patriarchal anachronism, feminists lobbied for reform of family law and the criminal code regarding rape and assault. The latter struggles in particular made demands upon the Criminal Justice System (CJS).[6]

IDENTIFICATION OF THE LEGAL ISSUES
Framing the Public Discourse

Emphasis upon how the CJS might be instrumental in preventing wife assault is reflected in a number of briefs and reports prepared for the public as well as for parliamentarians. Of these documents, the CACSW reports (MacLeod, 1980, 1987) have been the most accessible and influential. Beginning from the premise that "one of the most important roles of the CJS is a symbolic one: it reflects and helps to promote emerging values," *Battered But Not Beaten* identifies the CJS as an important ally in the struggle against wife battering. The report details initiatives that would symbolize "what is beyond tolerance," including:

> a growing attention to the victims of crime; an ongoing attempt to make the *Criminal Code*, sentencing, and the criminal justice system generally more responsive to current social norms and problems; a search for more co-ordination among police, court, prison, and probation workers; and a growing interest in the preventive and even the "curative" role of the criminal justice system. (MacLeod, 1987: 78)

As the first national study of battered wives conducted in this country, MacLeod (1980) gathered information from 73 transition houses across Canada about barriers to effective help encountered by battered women and transition-house workers. Although provincial and local police departments were contacted — as well as provincial family court offices, offices of attorneys-general, provincial social-services offices, selected Children's Aid Society offices, and a few larger hospitals — in an attempt to gather statistical information, this work proved "virtually fruitless." Police data on assaults were not separated according to sex of the victim or offender, or by the relation between them. Further, none of the other services contacted collected statistics in any systematic way (1980: 8). A primary value of this first effort, therefore, rests upon its pioneering documentation of the case histories of battered women, which served to challenge prevalent myths about the pattern and causes of abuse. Highlighted in the report and reflected by the subtitle — *The Vicious Circle* — is the fact that one-third of the battered women who used the shelters returned to abusive partners, largely because "they had nowhere to go." MacLeod linked this to societal factors such as the labour force and "authority divisions built into our society," but also criticized responses to battering on the part of medical professionals, social-service agencies, and family/friends as inadequate. All these factors contributed to making transition houses the only alternative for women without independent resources who must escape abusive husbands. At the same time, these houses were forced to turn away one-third of the women who came to them because of overcrowding and as a result of funding regulations. This isolation of battered women was exacerbated by the legal response. As front-line workers, the police lacked clear guidelines on how to deal with wife-battery cases. As a result they frequently chose what MacLeod called "a common human retreat" — they denied that the situation existed or they simply avoided it as much as possible (1980: 37). MacLeod concluded that the weak sentencing and arrest policies that act to increase the powerlessness and hopelessness of women who have been battered can only be understood in the context of laws impacting on the family.

In a separate section on "Wife Battering and the Law," MacLeod noted that considerable variation existed in the criminal-justice response, partly due to the division of jurisdiction between the federal and provincial governments. She also highlighted the unsuitability of the options available to Canadian women at that time. At the federal level a battered woman could charge her husband with assault or apply for a peace bond under the *Criminal Code of Canada*, or she could divorce her husband on the grounds of physical cruelty under the *Divorce Act*. Under provincial legislation or civil law a battered woman could apply for an injunction or an *ex parte interim* order against the husband.[7] However, laws regarding injunctions were never intended primarily to cover domestic cases and are granted only in support of legal right. The wife's legal rights are frequently unclear and are complicated by her legal duty as wife to cohabit unless relieved of this obligation by the court. Thus a wife could exercise this right only if she accompanies her application for an injunction with an application for divorce or separation. MacLeod further noted that even when granted, "an injunction frequently amounts to little more than a legal scolding" (1980: 45). In contrast, an *ex parte* order is a short-term provincial order that can be granted by a judge either in or out of court and that takes force immediately because it does not require first finding and serving the husband and giving him notice. While this provides temporary protection for women in need of immediate relief, MacLeod noted that few police or lawyers inform women of this right. Two further options existed for women outside marriage: rape and civil suit.[8] Given the limitations in these options, MacLeod concludes:

> The rights of the wife who has been battered often stop at the doorstep of the matrimonial home. Stipulations which separate wife abuse from other forms of assault and rape muddy the role that judges, lawyers, and police can play and place the sanctity of the home above the protection of its occupants. Wives must be given the same rights as other citizens to call on the law for assistance and to expect true potential for action, when they feel the law is their only or best possible recourse. (1980: 47)

From this perspective, *The Vicious Circle* advocated an immediate plan of action for the protection of battered wives and their children, emphasizing the symbolic dimension of law as a deterrent and the rights of wives to legal protection and input into determination of the most appropriate line of action (1980: 64). The suggested legislative changes included: deleting of spousal immunity in rape cases; allowing spouses to sue each other; and requiring third parties who have knowledge of wife battering to report it (1980: 63). Along with reforms in legislation, the report also recommended changes in policies that determine how law is enforced, including the better co-ordination of support services, following through with arrests and sentencing when wives do press charges, and training the police to respond more appropriately in cases of domestic violence (1980: 64). As an immediate goal, MacLeod advocated "a clear, publicly advertised policy applying the same standards of non/arrest to family violence as to assault outside the family" (1980: 64). In closing, the report acknowledged that the long-range as opposed to the immediate prevention of wife battery requires at least three basic types of strategies: programs which help to promote the economic independence of women; education and training; and information collection and research (1980: 65). Some of its recommendations were subsequently adopted by the *World Conference Report to Review and Appraise the Achievements of the United Nations Decade for Women*.

Reflecting the sentiments of this report, feminists began to point out that according to the *Criminal Code of Canada*, no one has the 'right' to beat another person. Because the law does not modify this statement relative to the relationship of actors involved, a man beating his wife is committing a crime. As in other crimes, the police therefore have the clear mandate as well as the responsibility to respond quickly and to enforce the law "equally and without prejudice," using all the means at their disposal. In reality, the *Criminal Code* was not being applied as written. Most of the recommendations of the CACSW report were endorsed by, or similar to, those of other advocacy groups, such as the United Way, the Law Reform Commission of Canada, provincial associations of interval and transition houses, and women's groups. In a brief to the Parliamentary Committee on Health, Welfare and Social Affairs, the Vancouver Women's Research Centre highlighted how procedures of classifying and prioritizing calls for assistance from police by battered wives resulted in non-response in many cases and ineffective response in others. Supported by interviews with battered women, this brief condemned the fact that the most common response to a wife-assault call was non-arrest (see Women's Research Centre, 1982). While this failure can be linked to outright sexism on the part of law enforcers, the brief emphasizes that a major factor influencing the practice is the interpretation of "assault." In practice the crucial legal term, *"bodily harm,"* has come to mean "serious" or "severe" bodily harm, a determination involving considerable police discretion. Added to this is the question from the officer's perspective of whether wives will be likely to follow through once charges are laid, given that the attrition rate of these types of cases has been historically high. Police were reported as treating wife-abuse calls as crisis intervention rather than law enforcement. During police training, officers were instructed to defuse the situation, primarily by "giving both parties room" or by "walking the husband around the block" (Women's Research Centre, 1982: 12; see also Parnas, 1972, Brown, 1984).

In conclusion, the brief recommended a policy of mandatory arrest by police officers in cases where there is evidence of bodily harm and where the situation is likely to reoccur, *or* where there are any prior convictions for assault, any current restraining orders, peace bonds, or probation orders (Women's Research Centre, 1982: appendix I). In cases not covered by this policy, this brief recommended that police officers advise the woman of her rights to civil and criminal remedies, of legal aid offices, of transition-house services, and instruct her how and where to lay a charge. The proposed model further outlines recommendations for each stage of trial and sentencing, including mandatory minimum prison sentences in cases of bodily harm. The recommended sentences are 30 days for first offence, 90 for second offence, and 180 days for third offence with no conditional discharges. When bodily harm has not been established, the brief recommends minimum and graduated sentences ranging from fine and probation to imprisonment.

ACADEMIC COMPLICITY
Theories of Policing as Deterrence

While activists documented women's stories of violence and lobbied for reforms, academic research and writing on "domestic violence" mushroomed during the 1970s. Today a vast and diverse literature addresses the frequency, distribution, causes, and effects of interspousal violence (DeKeseredy and Hinch, 1991). Much of this research is policy-oriented and the bulk of it supports police intervention. Within the vast array of 'scientific' arguments used to support police intervention, exchange theory provides a particularly relevant example of academic support for the deterrence arguments forwarded by liberals.

Based upon behavioural psychology and economic theory, exchange theory analyses human activity in terms of reward and cost. From the standpoint of actors, social interaction is an exchange of resources in which each participant strives to reduce the 'costs' of interaction while maximizing the gain or 'profit.' This conceptualization leads Blau (1964), in particular, to argue that self-interest rather than moral norms is the necessary condition of exchange. Applying the theory to family dynamics, Goode (1971) identifies four major sets of resources that can be exchanged: economic variables; prestige or respect; force and its threat; and likability, attractiveness, friendship, or love. He argues that each of these resources can be acquired and expended and that each can be exchanged to some degree for each other. As a resource, force is argued to be primarily a deterrent: It stops others from doing something that those with force disapprove of. It can also be used to gain compliance, along with other rewards such as love, respect, or money. Goode argues that violence as a resource is invoked only when individuals lack other legitimate resources that are a basis for power. Most people do not willingly choose overt force when they have command of other means, because the costs of force are high, especially in the family where it may undermine the possibility of achieving goals other than mere conformity, such as affection and respect. Consequently, Goode proposes a general rule: "The greater the other resources an individual can command, the more force he *can* muster, the less he will actually deploy it in an *overt* manner" (1971: 628).

Due to this proposition that the relationship between power and the use of force is contingent upon what resources other than violence are available, researchers hypothesize that because husbands in working-class households adhere more to patriarchal norms than do those from the middle classes, the relationship between resources, power, and violence is indirectly correlated with the occupational status of the husband. Allen and Straus (1980), for example, argue that low-status men, lacking the monetary, prestige, and educational resources on which to base power, are more likely to compensate by using actual or threatened physical force as the basis for maintaining dominance in the family. They concluded that because instrumental violence is disapproved of by the middle class, its use by middle-class husbands is more 'costly.' More generally, a number of writers have predicted that although the long-run consequences of a more egalitarian society may lessen the frequency of violence against wives, the short-run consequences may be the opposite (see Straus, 1980; Kolb and Straus, 1974; Whitehurst, 1974). As women's income, prestige, and education as resources come to approximate those of their partners, men who retain outdated notions of patriarchal authority and control will be 'forced' to rely on physical resources.

While many of the hypothesized relationships between occupational status, wives' employment, and the use of violence have not been demonstrated empirically, the tenets of exchange theory have provided scientific arguments for the use of criminal-justice agencies by battered women. Supporting exchange theory, Humphreys and Humphreys (1985: 267), for example, argue that marital abuse exists because the 'costs' of the abuse are not strong enough to counteract the 'rewards.' They say the imposition of mandatory laws will create primary and secondary preventative methods for eliminating wife battering, because these laws will act as a deterrent. While the role of the traditional family and women's physical and economic inequality act to lower the 'costs' of physical coercion, laws that represent social disapproval of violence will address this imbalance so that the 'rewards' will no longer outweigh the 'costs.' From the perspective of exchange theory, therefore, the ability of women to invoke police intervention represents the redistribution of resources at a societal level. From both a social-scientific and commonsense perspective, the police are seen to represent a resource that can be legitimately used to redress the unequal distribution of both physical and social 'resources' within the gender relations of the family system.

TAKING ACTION
Accelerating Police Intervention

Reflecting the momentum that academic arguments gave to the call for police intervention, beginning in the late 1970s criminologists became involved in documenting and monitoring the policing of domestic violence. Not surprisingly, initial research universally testified to the failure of police to become involved in 'family' matters. While the reluctance on the part of women to disclose victimization contributes to problems in its measurement, a number of writers have pointed out that police practices further acted to cloak violence against wives. In Vancouver, for example, Dutton and Levens (1980: 213) reported that the Vancouver Police Department received on average 283 requests for domestic-crisis intervention a week during 1975. Of these calls, over one-third pertained to husband/wife disputes, in which the female was victim. In 45 per cent of such cases, the police responded with advice only (1980: 28). Burris and Jaffe (1983: 310) similarly noted that in a six-month period, the London (Ontario) police force arrested only 3 per cent of wife assaulters, although it advised 20 per cent of female victims to seek treatment and 60 per cent to lay charges. In general, research has indicated that the police view violence as a normal aspect of marital life and, as a consequence, that they see 'talking' with complainants or "cooling out the situation" as the most appropriate actions (see Brown, 1984; Parnas, 1972; Hanmer, 1989). This practice stands in direct contrast to the documented seriousness of the problem. For example, in an assessment of 58,532 domestic disputes reported to the Ohio police, Bell (1984) noted that the victims of violence were predominantly wives (71 per cent) who were injured or killed in 38 per cent of the cases in which criminal complaints were initiated, although the police arrested men in only 14 per cent of cases. Bell further noted that the police failed to make arrests in incidents in which they were legally justified to do so. Clearly, the unofficial response to domestic violence was one of avoidance and non-arrest. Bell calculated that the rate for non-arrest of assaultive husbands was seven times higher than the arrest rate. After police non-intervention was linked to underreporting and identified as a major obstacle to justice for women, however, both public and academic attention focused upon the problem of domestic violence as one of police inefficiency.

In assessing the dismal record of police action, researchers have associated a number of factors with police non-intervention. While Bell (1987) highlights the victim-offender relationship as a primary determinant of whether or not police are likely to take action once assault has been reported, Ferraro (1989: 176) notes that the overriding factor in police categorization of events is social class. In her study, wife battering among lower-income couples was generally not taken as seriously as battery in middle-class homes. In assessing the effect of police discretion, Berk and Loseke (1980-81) examined recorded incident characteristics for their impact on variation in police decisions. Situational variables found to be associated with positive arrest decisions included drinking by the male and the presence of a witness or children. The probability of arrest decreased when the woman herself requested assistance, presumably because her ability to do so was seen to indicate that she was not in immediate danger. Thus the police management of domestic disturbances does not necessarily centre upon consideration of 'proof' that the law has been violated but is determined by the nature of police-citizen encounters. Worden and Pollitz (1984) noted that while all arrest decisions depend upon situational cues, in domestic cases the salience of relevant factors differs according to the role orientations of individual officers. Those officers who adhere to a 'crime-control' model of policing may emphasize the law-enforcement aspect of domestic violence, while those who tend to see their job as 'assisting citizens' and 'keeping the peace' may prefer conflict resolution, which does not entail legal solutions. Thus they point out that arrest, by itself, is an ambiguous indicator of responsible policing.

While a concerned officer's determination to protect a victim may manifest itself in arrest, it can also take a number of other forms. In fact, arrest may simply be the easiest way for an officer to end a domestic dispute, and as an action it may not benefit the victim.

In total, a number of processes have been documented that explain the reluctance of police to lay assault charges: the absence of clearly defined policies regarding arrests and laying of charges; the lack of training by police personnel in handling domestic disputes; the lack of rewards for officers who rigorously pursue arrest or charges in domestic violence cases, as a consequence of their low priority; the fact that convictions are notoriously difficult to obtain for marital assault; the belief that domestic situations endanger police personnel;[9] beliefs by individual officers that wife abuse should remain within the private domain, that wives are legitimate victims, and that assault against a female partner is less serious than assault between strangers (see Burris and Jaffe, 1983; Buzawa, 1982; Dolon, Hendricks and Meagher, 1986). Thus a number of factors encourage police personnel to conclude that they do not have the mandate or the skills to intervene in marital conflict and that therefore calls should be screened out from 'real' police work. Missing from these criminological discussions of discretion as integral to police work, however, is recognition of the role of sexist attitudes on the part of individual officers. MacLeod (1980: 38), for example, draws attention to a well-publicized case in which an officer was quoted as saying, "If it had been my house, I would have beaten my wife for the condition it was in."[10]

At the same time as documenting the causes of non-intervention, writers have suggested that this inaction not only perpetuates domestic violence, but that it may also make the situation worse. Loving and Quirk (1982) point out that the reluctance of police to take a clear line of action once they are called to the scene suggests to husbands that they are immune to legal sanction. Russell (1982) adds that because police identify with the husband rather than the female victim, the societal effect of policing is to reinforce the patriarchal control of women (see also Hatty, 1989). On the other hand, Brown (1984) found that a positive police response can have the effect of enhancing the victim's self-image, thus encouraging her to mobilize the law in her own behalf. In assessing the far-reaching and serious implications of minimal intervention, Burris and Jaffe (1983) conclude that police inaction can exacerbate the victim's feeling of helplessness and thus perpetuate the cycle of violence; that other battered women in the community will be discouraged from requesting police assistance; that the police themselves become frustrated with repeated calls to the same residence; that the batterer believes he will not be held responsible for his actions; and that crown attorneys and judges do not treat cases seriously when victims initiate legal action, because they assume that the police would have intervened if the charge was warranted. It is not surprising, therefore, that surveys of battered women historically indicate high levels of dissatisfaction with police (see Zoomer, 1989; Chalmers and Smith, 1988; Jones, MacLean and Young, 1986).

Within this milieu of academic and public concern, the 1980s witnessed extensive innovations in approaches to family violence by a broad range of 'helping' professions in almost all industrialized nations (see Hanmer, Radford, and Stanko, 1989). Medical practice and social work have subsequently developed approaches aimed at improved detection of cases of wife battery and their referral to appropriate support services, including treatment programs for battering men (see Ahluwalia, 1987). In the area of criminal justice, two major legislative changes were in place in Canada by 1983: changes in the wording of sexual-assault legislation permitted a wife to charge her husband; and amendments to the *Canada Evidence Act* expanded the situations in which both husbands and wives could be compelled to give evidence against a spouse in the cases of wife assault and child abuse. At the level of the courts, a number of 'designated' crown attorneys specifically trained to deal with wife battering have been appointed. These attorneys meet with battered women before court proceedings, counsel women who want to drop charges, and in some cases communicate the wishes of the wife to the judge before sentencing. In provinces or territories where designated crown attorneys have not been appointed, attorneys have been educated about the issues of wife battery and instructed to handle these cases 'more sensitively' (MacLeod, 1987: 84). At the same time, a number of provinces are assessing the alternatives to court on an experimental basis and taking steps to reduce the inordinate delays experienced in both waiting for trial after charge and completing trial. During the same period, the RCMP has developed an aggressive charging policy under the directives of the solicitor-general. Since 1982, all provincial/territorial governments have instructed the police (and in most cases the crown attorneys) to rigorously investigate and prosecute wife battering. Reflecting these changes, the London (Ontario) city police force instituted a policy of presumptive arrest. Appearing in a memo, the directive instructed officers at all ranks that: "Commencing immediately, charges are to be laid by our Force in all cases where there are reasonable and probable grounds revealed in the investigation. The practice of directing the victim to lay private informations is to cease" (in Burris and Jaffe, 1983: 312). In an assessment of police responses to these directives, Burris and Jaffe (1983) report that officers perceived this policy as reflecting a changed public attitude about the seriousness of wife assault and as a consequence welcomed the opportunity to act more decisively. In reviewing police statistics, Burris and Jaffe (1983: 316) note that the directives were followed by a sharp increase in assault charges.[11] The authors point out that because officers have always had the authority to arrest and charge in domestic assault cases, this trend cannot necessarily be interpreted as reflecting an increase in the real incidence and severity of wife assault, but rather should be seen as evidence of attitudinal changes among police officers. Burris and Jaffe conclude that: "This change in police policy obviously affects attitudes as well and may serve to protect and support women who call the police. In the long run, decisive police action may help to interrupt the cyclical pattern of violence and possibly prevent more serious injury and death" (1983: 317).[12]

While these conclusions are clearly speculative, Sherman and Berk (1984a,b) present empirical evidence to support the notion that arrest makes a positive difference in the behaviour of battering men. This support comes from an influential and controversial experiment conducted in a Minneapolis police jurisdiction. Between March 1981 and August 1982, officers responded to domestic-violence calls with the assigned options of arrest, separation, or advice. In each given instance, the appropriate choice of category was determined by reference to a set of report forms that were colour-coded for action and placed in random order. The effect of each intervention was determined through follow-up personal and telephone interviews that measured the degree of victimization by the suspect after police intervention and from criminal-justice reports during a six-month follow-up period (1984b: 263). The initial experiment was conducted in two precincts with the highest density of domestic-violence crime reports and arrests, with 33 of the 34 officers participating for one year.

Within the academic literature, the results of this experiment have been presented as a test of deterrence theory, specifically as to whether punishment — operationalized as arrest — deters battering men. These findings were translated directly into policy implications, appearing in a *Police Foundation Report*. In both discussions, Sherman and Berk (1984b) concluded that arrest significantly reduced repeated occurrences of domestic assault. They reported a recidivism rate of 19 per cent for arrested abusers, compared to 35 per cent in cases dealt with by mediation only. Sherman and Berk (1984a) suggest "that arrest and initial incarceration alone may produce a deterrent effect," and use these findings to advance a policy of mandatory arrest. This position was subsequently supported by data from a U.S. National Crime Survey indicating that the appearance of police in a domestic-violence situation may, in and of itself, be punishing to the suspect. The basis for this claim was the finding that of married women who did not call the police after a physical attack by a husband, 41 per cent were attacked again within six months, compared to 15 per cent of wives who did contact police (Goolkasian, 1986). Despite the fact that the evidence on deterrence is not unambiguously in favour of arrest (see Pasternoster et al., 1983), U.S. data supporting aggressive policing was quickly incorporated into public debates in the United States as well as abroad (see Stanko, 1989). In March 1986, *Newsweek* added to publicity surrounding the Minneapolis experiment, featuring an article with the subtitle, "cops take a hard line to combat domestic violence." While referring specifically to the success of the Minneapolis police, it cited dramatic examples of the impact of the experiment on the cities of Denver and Phoenix. Following the Minneapolis model, within 12 months the Denver police had arrested almost 4,000 men involved in domestic disputes, while researchers said that battered women in Phoenix were pleased with a new policy of mandatory arrest because it resulted in real differences in their husbands' responses. To the public it would appear that the demands of battered women had been satisfactorily met. Furthermore, it might also appear that wife battery had been successfully transformed from a 'private trouble' into a 'public issue.'

IS CRIMINALIZATION A VICTORY FOR WOMEN ?

While the type of evidence provided by criminologists appears to lend support to both the commonsense and academic wisdom that arrest deters the use of physical force against women, the intervening years have witnessed a serious reconsideration of both the effectiveness and desirability of the criminalization of wife battery. From a purely academic standpoint, Binder and Meeker (1988) have challenged both the internal and external validity of the Minneapolis experiment, which had become the basis for nationwide policies of mandatory arrest. To begin with, they point out problems that arose during implementation of the project — problems that resulted in many officers failing to follow the experimental procedures. The response rate was under 50 per cent with 28 per cent of the case reports coming from only 3 of the 33 officers. However, the most damaging criticisms relate to reanalyses of the data. After completing a number of statistical tests appropriate to the experimental design but ignored by the original researchers, Binder and Meeker (1988: 352-3) were unable to demonstrate a significant difference in recidivism rates between the options of arrest and advise: They found that variations in police responses explained only 1.8 per cent of the variation in the likelihood of future violence. In terms of policy considerations, they note that while arrest is thus no better than advice, arrest is far costlier to the system in terms of overcrowded jails, intrusion by the state into domestic affairs, and increased drain on police resources. They argue that a broad range of cost-benefit considerations should be evaluated before arrest is widely accepted, including the effects of arrest upon children in the household, future employment prospects, the likelihood that a spouse will call police in the future, and the operation of the CJS. While they concede that the Minneapolis study suggests interesting trends that are worthy motivators of further research, Binder and Meeker conclude: "If one uses or sees the study in terms of a critical, or even a significant, determiner of national police policy, one might be accused of foolishness bordering on irresponsibility" (1988: 354). In closing they remind readers, "Even if arrest is the best *police* response, it may not be the best *societal* response" (emphasis ours). More recently Sherman et al. (1991) report that both a reanalysis of the Minneapolis experimental data and results from numerous other similar studies seems to strongly suggest that short-term arrests lead to short-term deterrence, which is eclipsed by long-term recidivism. They conclude: "Policymakers and criminologists should therefore consider the possibility that a little jail time can be worse than none" (1991: 846). To this we might add that the next logical step is the observation that a longer period in jail can be better than a little jail time — an observation that smacks with the punitive logic of law and order solutions. Clearly, in Canada and the U.S. where prison terms are amongst the longest in the world, recidivism rates are equally high by comparison.

While no similar quantitative approach has been applied to the Canadian context, the CACSW commissioned a review and assessment of the sweeping changes that followed *The Vicious Cycle*. This second study, published in 1987 and again authored by MacLeod, acknowledges that the action focus of the previous report, which emphasized provision of shelters, use of police and courts, and referral to agencies, cannot be claimed as an unqualified success (MacLeod, 1987: 6). MacLeod warns that the threefold increase in the number of transition houses in Canada during the intervening years cannot be seen as an unequivocal success for the women's movement. This is because government support has been "both a facilitator and a product of changes in philosophy among many shelter workers" (1987: 54). MacLeod highlights the growing tendency to hire staff with formal educational credentials and professional qualifications. While many workers welcome this because it promotes credibility in the community and helps to link transition houses with other professional services, it has transformed the relationship between battered women and transition-house workers (see Morgan, 1981), as well as creating a division between grassroots workers and professionals. While boards of directors previously consisted of staff and community members who shared the philosophical orientation and goals of the staff, newer boards are fashioned on a 'business model' with members chosen primarily for the influence they wield in the community (MacLeod, 1987: 57). As a consequence directors are more likely to be lawyers, accountants, teachers, or social workers. Reflecting this changing structure, those involved in the delivery of services are struggling over the questions of who 'owns' the issue of wife battering and how this ownership creates or changes the definition of the problem, as well as over the type and quality of services provided. While no one can 'own' a social problem, as MacLeod points out, "Social reactions to that problem and service development are largely decided by who controls the money" (1987: 59).

More importantly, however, problems are revealed when MacLeod explores the perspective of battered women themselves. Here she notes that although many women welcomed police protection and the opportunity to use the courts, others argued that mandatory arrest policies make the police a less desirable option.[13] Similarly, in a follow-up study of women using shelters in Saskatchewan, Smith (1984) reports that only 6 per cent of respondents considered police involvement as the best way to stop men from being violent, so that only 12 per cent of women saw the increased effectiveness of police or the legal system as a first priority. Instead, battered women themselves saw the provision of shelters and public education as the most desirable option. This dissatisfaction is not simply the result of police inefficiency: Women in the CACSW study said that mandatory arrest is unsuitable:

> I've thought so many times about calling the police. If truth be known, I've thought about it for years — to teach him a lesson, to make him see what he's doing. But I always figured it would do more harm than good.... I call

the police, and bang, he's out of a job, and jobs aren't so easy to come by here. Then where are we at? Things'll just get worse. We'll have no money. He'll start drinking more. He'll be even more angry at me and he'll hit me more. So where's the sense calling the police? (1987: 79)

I needed someone to stop him, just so he could see some sense. But when they got here, they started talking about arresting him, about me going to court. Well I didn't want that.... I don't want to hurt him more. I want to help him. (1987: 80)

Interpreting similar findings in the Netherlands, Zoomer (1989) points out that while women may call the police because they do indeed need immediate physical protection, many believe the presence of police will facilitate a redefinition of the situation. In other words, the police symbolize to those involved that the use of physical force against women is wrong, no matter what the pretext, and often that the husband needs help. Calling the police thus cannot necessarily be equated with a punitive motive or with the commonsense view that arrest is accepted by battered women as a way to deter future violence. From the perspective of battered women, the need for police intervention can reflect powerlessness in both their immediate, as well as their general social, situations. At the same time, Ahluwalia (1991) reminds us that women's orientations to the police differ significantly. In particular, people who are visibly non-European in ancestry, or are recent immigrants, may be subject to racist policing practices (see chapter 13). This means that women from visible minorities may not look to the police for 'justice.'

MacLeod concludes that earlier campaigns by Canadian feminists failed "the test of reality," of *women's* realities. Specifically, battered women do not always "support the simplistic 'bad man/good woman' assumption at the basis of most crisis responses" (MacLeod, 1987: 6). Women do not always want to support a service- and crisis-response network that gives support to *her* as an individual but does not offer support to the batterer or to their children. Regarding the earlier report, MacLeod concedes:

And so to take action we have simplified the problem — focussed on the physically violent act, provided support and protection to individuals. It became unpopular to even talk about relationships when dealing with wife battering. Wife battering was reduced to a series of acts — violent acts of a man against a woman for which a man must take responsibility. For the purposes of action, wife battering was individualized.... Criminal justice intervention which is based in individual responsibility was stressed. Individual counselling programs, particularly for the battered, multiplied. Psychological theories of battering proliferated. A concern with incidence, with numbers of charges, with numbers of women needing shelter grew. Pressure was put on services to prove their importance through the number of battered women or batterers with whom they dealt. (1987: 6-7)

What does this tell us about liberal responses to radical demands for social justice ?

RETHINKING RESPONSES TO WIFE BATTERING

The momentum to transform wife battery from a private trouble into a public issue has its origins in a grassroot movement to provide refuge for women from male violence. While there is considerable diversity in feminist analyses about the origins of this violence, in general it is recognized as an issue of differential power and linked to the structural rather than personal nature of the bourgeois, patriarchal family. On this basis, shelter workers explicitly rejected the therapeutic approach favoured by the 'helping professions,' stressing instead how the experience of 'women helping women' can become the basis for a broader political movement (see Mies, 1983; Barnsley, 1980; Chalmers and Smith, 1988). As a broader political movement, wife battery is a problem linked to women's disadvantaged position in the Canadian economy, their subsequent dependency upon men, and their isolation within a privatized family setting. The notion of transforming wife battery into a 'public issue' rather than 'private trouble,' therefore, was seen as a challenge to the status quo, and within it the legal system (see Comack, 1987b). The limitation of current programs of intervention is that wife battery has been incorporated into existing institutions: In the move to broaden the mandate of both the police and the courts, wife abuse has been accommodated within the CJS while the fundamental challenges that gender equality demands have not been addressed in any way. Because the only line of action open to the CJS is more arrests and convictions, a focus on wife abuse as a criminological issue does not allow the development of other avenues of intervention and change.[14] As a consequence, politicization has strengthened institutional rather than community-based and more radical responses. Central to institutional responses are the commonsense notions, legitimated as social-scientific claims, that increased law enforcement is symbolic of public sentiments that condemn personal violence; and that the law therefore, in both fact and in operation, will deter wife battery. Following from this, the general cry is for more resources to accelerate responses by the CJS and to make these more efficient through their integration with medical and social-work programs. This is what Barnsley (1985) and others refer to as "the institutionalization of women's issues." While there is no doubt that many women welcome police protection and the opportunity to use the courts, wife battery as a social issue has been transformed into a policing issue. Within this discourse the issues concern legal rights, police protection, and criminal justice: technical issues that can be safely met within the current system without any meaningful redistribution of power. For this reason, the effect of intervention could well be the strengthening of the very same processes and institutions that gave rise to the demand for justice in the first place. At the same time, CJS intervention simultaneously gives the impression that the state has dealt with the problem. In the public's mind, feminist demands have been satisfactorily addressed, making it more difficult and less acceptable to criticize the state or to demand more action (see Barnsley, 1985: 84). In this way, while the need for protection from male violence is a real, experienced need, satisfying this need has been conflated with solving the problem of inequality between men and women. As the state increasingly can argue that it has met the needs of victims, feminist demands are being defined as redundant or excessive, and because of this they are being called upon to justify their very existence (see Price, 1988).

For these reasons, a number of writers are beginning to question both the usefulness and the desirability of increased policing as the solution to violence against women. Snider (1991), for example, argues:

> The criminal justice system is not an ally the feminist movement can reliably use to achieve humanistic and liberating goals. Structurally, states in capitalist societies benefit by the existing patterns of class and gender dominance; tactically, feminists cannot control the writing of laws, nor the uses to which they are put after they are passed. The historical record of the initiatives of the recent and distant past, and their near-universal failure to achieve the goals envisaged, is striking. The major consequence has been to increase state control over lower and working class women as well as men, to the benefit of neither. (259-60)

What does this mean for 'critical' criminologists engaged in the struggles for justice ?

Criminological as well as other 'academic' research has provided legitimation for the "institutionalization" of women's issues and the shift from 'welfare' justice to one focused upon individual accountability and punitive responses to deviance (see chapter 4). In assessing the impact of 'experiments' such as that conducted in Minneapolis, Binder and Meeker (1988) note that an array of political rather than strictly scientific factors has been behind the rapid and dramatic reaction to wife abuse in the United States. These factors include a generalized concern for law and order; the prevalence of punitive rather than rehabilitative counselling approaches to criminal deviance; arguments by individuals and groups taking feminist positions that the police have not responded with enough vigour in wife-abuse contexts because they generally support a husband's right to control his wife; the rise of victim rights organizations and the inclusion of victims in the advocacy process; and police departments' general fear of liability in response to the expansion of legal theories of negligence, problems of insurance, and the vehemence of the various advocacy groups in the realm of wife abuse. In terms of the translation of rather insubstantial evidence into national policy, they point to the propaganda generated by the agencies that participated in the Minneapolis research — the National Institute of Justice and the Police Foundation (1988: 348).

From this perspective, it is interesting to pay attention to the stated purposes of the CACSW's second investigation into wife battery. In *Battered But Not Beaten*, these are explicitly given as:

- to applaud the progress which has been made over the past few years in responses to wife battering, and to *encourage continued, appropriate government efforts* in this area;
- to *speculate on the limits of* a sensitive and appropriate government

response, by exploring the ramifications for battered women, their children, their batterers, and for society of a *continued increase in government intervention* and of institutional rather than less formal family and community responses to wife battering;

* to help give battered women and front-line workers a voice in policy making *so that the initiatives supported and developed by governments* will reflect the varied and changing experiences of women who are battered; (MacLeod, 1987: 7; emphasis ours)

Not surprisingly, the Canadian state endorsed the recommendations of the Advisory Counsel report, which largely included extensions of earlier recommendations:[15] continuing training of all police officers (rather than only new recruits) to encourage consistency in the application of policies relating to wife battering; education for judges and crown attorneys that would make them more sensitive and supportive of women and would thereby "prevent the problem of women refusing to testify, and so deflect the unnecessary and harsh use of contempt charges against women who are feeling frightened, vulnerable, and confused"; and better record-keeping systems by police agencies. By accepting these recommendations — if only at the rhetorical level — the Progressive Conservative Party linked itself to the progressive image provided by the CACSW through its platform of reform on 'women's issues.'[16] In reviewing the CACSW report, the minister responsible for the status of women declared, "The issue of wife assault is one of the issues Prime Minister Brian Mulroney cares about the most." In response to its recommendations, the minister announced:

Research being undertaken by the Departments of Health and Welfare, Solicitor General, Justice, and the Secretary of State and the RCMP and my own Department ... will lead to program proposals for pilot projects dealing with family violence, as well as developing programs related to policing, corrections, prosecutions and the courts.... Under this particular initiative ... the Solicitor General is supporting an assessment of the needs for an integrated *intervention* strategy linking *police, social,* and *health* agencies. (Minister's Response to *Battered But Not Beaten*, 1987:3; emphasis in original)

Within the Canadian context, Havemann (this book) links the current transformation of juvenile justice to the dismantling of the liberal welfare state, management of the fiscal and ideological crises via corporatism, and the gradual evolution of 'an exceptional state.' In terms of reforms within this context — including those advocated by the Advisory Council on the Status of Women — it is important to remember that liberalism as a philosophy and as a practice is supportive of, and consistent with, capitalism. While liberalism expresses a desire to modify the most glaring inequities resulting from the protection of the private realm and capitalist exploitation, liberal critiques entail neither an assessment of the system itself that generates social problems nor a critical examination of how liberal definitions of these problems and programs of intervention maintain rather than challenge the status quo.[17] Pitch (1985) points out that equating the use of criminal justice with 'justice' for women implies an acceptance of the liberal guarantees and formal safeguards inherent in the bourgeois CJS; the demise of the notion of rehabilitation/re-education and a tangential interest in retribution are seen as more compatible with formal safeguards; abandonment of the notion of prevention becomes a way of eliminating at least some of the contradictions that supposedly generate both crime and victimization; and the analytical collapsing together of the notions of 'needs,' interests, demands, and institutional responses means that demands for more repression are usually seen as signals of real needs. On this last point, the tendency has been not so much to take seriously and analyse the nature and effects of social demands, but to postulate the 'real' needs behind them. Criminologists mistakenly interpret the request by women for more policing as indication of a *real* — even an *objective* — problem of crime, which current programs literally address as the goal of intervention. What gets neglected is the real goal, which is to develop solutions to more fundamental problems that cannot be addressed by policing *per se*.[18]

As a question of 'radical' practice, this chapter suggests a number of immediate agendas for critical criminology. One question concerns the need for more careful investigation of the long-term effects of police intervention at the empirical level. It is clear that the needs and desires of women vary. For this reason, both in research and in framing strategies of intervention, a criminal-justice perspective needs to be replaced — at least momentarily — by a woman-centred approach (see Eichler, 1987; Faith, 1989). One problem with the criminal-justice model is that although it is based upon a case-by-case approach, it does not allow for real diversity in intervention. Not only does it equate fairness with the notion that each individual/incident is equivalent regardless of the context (although we have seen that this is not the actual practice), in a number of unusual cases mandatory arrest has led to the prosecution of battered women. In an assessment of presumptive arrest policies in Arizona, for example, Ferraro (1989) documents the arrest of women who had been assaulted by husbands, while in Canada women have been charged with contempt of court for refusing to testify against husbands charged with assault.

Clearly, the nature of the problem of wife battery is rooted in social structures, such as the structure of the current family and the nature of family life, as well as in women's generally disadvantaged social position. Some writers are increasingly drawing attention to these processes as the real failure of individualistic programs of intervention. The question remains as to why liberal models based on individual needs and rights prevail rather than those based upon more radical and feminist approaches that stress the collective nature of the problem. From this perspective, the issue of 'accountability' reaches far beyond the police and criminal-justice agents: for critical criminologists it includes academic accountability and involves explication of how radical critiques — such as those behind early initiatives to politicize wife battery — become transformed into liberal responses that unproblematically equate state-controlled 'human services' with 'the public good.' Herein lies the real challenge for critical criminology: to take seriously the feminist struggle to politicize personal relations of dependency and victimization.

We would like to thank Pelly Shaw (Department of Anthropology and Sociology, University of British Columbia) in particular for assistance in the preparation of this chapter.

NOTES

1. See Errington, 1977.
2. Here the term 'radical' refers to the call for structural rather than 'cosmetic' changes and thus does not imply a specific theoretical orientation.
3. While all feminists support the notion of freedom from personal violence, this is not the same as the more radical demand for the end of societal violence.
4. For this reason, perhaps somewhat paradoxically, liberal feminists have framed the right of access to abortion as an issue that upholds the principle of privacy of choice, rather than advancing the more radical position based on abortion as a social necessity.
5. The term "First Wave" refers to the women's movement that emerged in the later part of the nineteenth century, while the contemporary movement is described as the "Second Wave" (see Adamson, Briskin and McPhail, 1988).
6. Many of the arguments developed here about the CJS apply to the case of rape, which is not specifically discussed here. For a discussion of changes in the *Criminal Code* provisions concerning rape see Gunn and Minch (1988); for a critical assessment of problems with these changes, see Smart (1989) and Los (1990).
7. An injunction is a court order prohibiting a husband from entering the matrimonial home and/or restraining him from molesting or interfering with his wife.
8. At that time the legal definition of rape was "the act of forcible, fraudulent or otherwise coercive sexual intercourse committed by a male person upon a female person who is not his wife" (Section 143, *Criminal Code of Canada*). At the same time, civil law was also designed to protect family unity. In most provinces a woman could not sue her husband (or vice versa) after divorce for an assault committed during marriage or for injuries received from beatings. This stipulation did not apply to common-law marriages, although this legal right was weak. Both of these areas were to become the focal point for political activity by feminists.
9. In fact, 14.6 per cent of the 41 Canadian policemen killed between 1961 and 1973 were killed while responding to domestic complaints (Levens and Dutton, 1980: 9).
10. For an overview of sexist attitudes in other cultural contexts, see Hanmer, Radford and Stanko (1989).
11. A similar finding is reported following the adoption of this type of directive by the Winnipeg Police Department during 1983 (see Ursel and Farough, 1985).

12. For a more critical assessment of this policy in the U.S. context, see Ferraro, 1989.

13. This echoes the claim by Caputo and Kozak (1986) that only a small majority (55 per cent) of battered women in their U.S. study wanted husbands arrested. See also Radford (1987).

14. This trend towards single issues has been a characteristic of the Canadian women's movement more generally (see Adamson, Briskin and McPhail, 1988).

15. While it is true that MacLeod (1987) acknowledges the need for further community-based programs as desirable responses in Canada, her recommendations overwhelmingly translate these possibilities into initiatives on the part of the Minister of Health and Welfare Canada, the Secretary of State, the Solicitor-General of Canada, and the Department of Justice.

16. Similarly, in British Columbia the Social Credit minister responsible for women used her 'credentials' as a battered wife to endorse a campaign of police intervention, within a context where funding of shelters had been dramatically threatened.

17. Thus the values that writers like Geller (1989) identify as the source of the failure of the current administration of justice — such as the adversarial nature of criminal justice and the individualism of social services — are integral and not incidental to liberal practice.

18. Given the limitations of the current format, this chapter does not deal with the related but complex issue of whether women can play a meaningful role in the policing of male violence against women through their integration into current policing forces. For an interesting and critical discussion on this issue see Radford (1989).

Chapter Thirteen

Reconstituting Social Order and Social Control: Police Accountability in Canada

Dawn H. Currie/Walter S. DeKeseredy/Brian D. MacLean

Despite the important role of police in the reproduction of social order, there is a lacuna in critical criminological literature about policing in democratic societies. As a consequence, the mistaken impression is fostered that policing in Canada is not problematic. This chapter challenges that view, documenting the extent of police malpractice in Canada and raising the question of the need for police accountability. The authors review a number of incidences of police malpractice and summarize the observations made by the Royal Commission Inquiry into Metropolitan Police Practices chaired by Justice Morand.

The authors discuss three forms that police accountability has taken historically: judicial inquiries such as the Ontario Race Relations and Policing Task Force and the Manitoba Native Justice Inquiry; community police monitoring groups, such as CIRPA in Toronto; and consultative liaison panels, such as those developed in England and Wales. They note that all three models depend upon the police for information about the nature of crime and policing, making them susceptible to dominant discourses about policing. A potential fourth form is the left-realist model, a form of police accountability that emerged in Britain during the 1980s and is characterized by the production of an alternative discourse on crime and police practices based on locally conducted and controlled victimization surveys. The extent to which this practice of police accountability might be relevant to the Canadian context remains to be explored. The authors note in closing, however, that this is an empirical and not a theoretical question, meaning that Canadian criminologists must become more practical and less academic in their discourses of social control.

Dawn H. Currie is Assistant Professor in Sociology at the University of British Columbia, Walter S. DeKeseredy is Associate Professor in Sociology at Carleton University, Brian D. MacLean is a Criminologist resident in Vancouver

"A riot is at bottom the language of the unheard."
(Rev. Martin Luther King Jr., 1967)

INTRODUCTION

The different aspects of organized state practices, which are generally referred to as agencies of social control, are central to the conception of social order in contemporary society. The enforcement branch of the state, particularly the police, represents the single most important agency responsible for the reproduction of social order. When one considers the breadth of literature pertaining to criminal justice specifically, and the administration of justice generally, however, it is clear that the policing role is a political one and the social order that this institution serves to reproduce is generally defined within a discourse that is not public in nature. In short, there is little room within policing discourse for public conceptions of social order, of how social order is constituted, or how it should be reproduced. In Canada, the reproduction of social order is often left to the 'experts,' whose role is not simply to reproduce order but also to produce public acceptance of this expert status and the organized set of practices associated with it.

In this chapter we briefly review the scarce critical literature on police in Canadian society. The inattention given to policing by Canadian critical criminology fosters the mistaken impression that policing is not problematic despite the fact that the Canadian policing institution is plagued with malpractice and scandal, which can only be resolved by effective police accountability. From this perspective, we begin by assessing the need for police accountability. Following this, we review three models of police accountability and consider their appropriateness for Canada. We argue that none of the three traditional forms are promising, and for this reason we identify a fourth model *that appears to have greater potential* — the left realist-model as advanced in Britain.

REVIEW OF THE LITERATURE

Most literature on police in society, whether North American or British, tends to classify the function of policing into two broad categories, each of them contributing to the reproduction of order in society. *Crime control* is that aspect of police work dealing with instances of criminal infractions, which can involve both reactive policing — in which the police respond to crime as it comes to their attention — and pro-active policing — in which specific practices contribute to crime prevention before it occurs. *Public order* refers to a variety of civil and political processes that can threaten the established order. Police might be found at political rallies that are voicing dissent, or they may be found surveilling a variety of political and quasi-political organizations, such as the labour movement, the peace movement, and the environmental movement, under the assertion that these organizations present a threat to the public order (in that they wish to change society somehow). Thus progressive organizations tend to be watched more closely by police simply because they desire a change in the status quo. Alternatively, as Fleming (1981, 1983) illustrates, the targeting of specific marginal groups in Canadian society for focused policing is often the product of police intolerance masquerading as concern for public order.

While policing as crime control has a number of potentials for abuse of power and unfair policing of the community, public-order policing presents the greatest threat to the suspension of democratic civil liberties, and it can easily be seen how the police might be used by their political superiors to stem the tide of legitimate political opposition. A good example of the police breaching the law for such purposes occurred in Quebec in the aftermath of the October Crisis, during which both federal and municipal police broke into offices and stole computer tapes containing the membership lists of the Parti Québécois (Dion, 1982).

One difficulty associated with the conception of police as agents of public order is that the guidelines are blurred between what constitutes legitimate political dissent as opposed to a threat to the rule of law in a democracy. Brown (Chapter nine) outlines numerous scandals that have surrounded the deployment of RCMP agents for purposes of surveilling certain populations, and the continuous infractions of civil liberties in which the policing institution has been engaged in Canada. Indeed, the McDonald Inquiry and the Keable Commission were appointed and charged with the task of investigating the extent of RCMP illegalities and eventually led to the creation of the Canadian Security Intelligence Service (CSIS) (Goff and Reasons, 1986), itself riddled with scandal since its inception. Gorman and McMullan (Chapter 10) discuss how the RCMP was used to control the unemployed labour force during the 1930s. They argue that this population posed a political threat to the party in power, which used the RCMP to fulfil partisan political objectives.

The question raised by such investigation is "Who is responsible for policing the police in a democracy?" In other words, if the police are in part responsible for the reproduction of social order, the question of *whose order* or *in whose interest* must be addressed. Should the police be responsible only to partisan political leadership, or should they be performing a non-political role? If the latter, does this mean that the political party in power has no control over the police and, if not, who does? If political supervision of the police invites partisan manipulation, does this mean that the judiciary is the only agency capable of assuring that policing is done fairly and not carried out in the interests of a particular political or social group? If the courts are the only agency capable of monitoring policing, surely they cannot do this adequately, because it is only during or at the conclusion of a policing crisis that the courts become involved. There is no real structure within the administration of justice that ensures fair and non-partisan policing in our society. All of these questions have been repeatedly debated at length in the House of Commons and the provincial legislatures. If there is a fine line between public safety and the suspension of the civil liberties boasted by democratic social formations, there is no single issue of greater importance than the democratic accountability of the police to the public they serve, as insurance against that line being breached. For purposes of this discussion, then, police accountability can be defined as a process by which fair and non-partisan policing is ensured by a structure allowing democratic control over policing practices. In this structure the police would be open to full public scrutiny by the communities they serve. Sometimes, accountability might be direct, at other times it might be indirect in that the police would be accountable to representatives of the community. Sometimes accountability might mean investigations *after* alleged police malpractice; at other times it might mean prevention of such instances before they occur. Accountability, therefore, is what distinguishes democratic social formations from police states.

Despite the importance of police accountability, there is a curious lacuna of criminological discourse that critically examines the contemporary policing institution in Canada. There has been some critical research; however, this has been largely restricted to studies of the RCMP, and usually conducted by authors who would not identify themselves as criminologists. Labour historians Brown and Brown (1978) have produced the most complete historical examination of the formation and deployment of the RCMP in Canada. Dion (1982) and Pelletier (1971), both journalists, have produced detailed critical assessments of the 'October Crisis' and the 'Mountygate' scandal that followed. Another journalist, Richard Fidler (1978), has analysed the role of the RCMP as the guardian of public order and places RCMP officers into the camp of *agents provocateurs* in what he calls "Ottawa's Secret War on Democratic Rights." Except for a small number of academic papers in scholarly journals, such as those by Taylor (1986) and Brogden (1990), the RCMP have gone largely unnoticed by Canadian critical criminologists, who have elected instead to direct their attention more towards the correctional enterprise in Canada and the formation and interpretation of the law. To the extent that there has been a critical discourse surrounding the police, it remains a discourse largely about law-enforcement biases, which have their basis in the wide degree of discretion that the police enjoy in enforcing the law. For example, in his anthology, Shearing (1981) attempts to illustrate that police deviance is structural in nature and must be understood within the sociopolitical reality of police work.

If the RCMP has received comparatively little attention from critical criminologists, local and municipal police forces have received even less. Exceptions to this are Ericson (1981, 1982) and Ericson and Baranek (1982), whose studies of the Metropolitan Toronto Police Force and its objects of policing practices are unparalleled in Canadian critical criminology. Also, Stenning (1981) examines the history and structure of municipal police boards and discusses the relationship between these and democratic accountability of the police, while Lowman (1990) investigates local policing practices in relation to Vancouver prostitutes and their customers. The significance of this vacuum in critical Canadian discourse is even more striking given the jurisdictionally structured relationship between the police and the public. This means that how the relations between the

Metropolitan Toronto police and the residents of the Jane-Finch corridor evolve can be quite different than how community-police relations are constructed in Vancouver's West Point Grey, for example. In short, the nature of community-police relations is geographically, politically, and historically specific, so that to grasp the sociological processes involved in the construction of these relations criminologists are required to carry out in-depth local studies of the police and the communities they operate in. Nevertheless, local police forces in anglophone Canada have been overlooked in the process of critical criminological scrutiny.

THE NEED FOR POLICE ACCOUNTABILITY IN CANADA

Perhaps even more striking than the absence of critical studies of policing at the local level is the degree of scandal associated with virtually every major metropolitan police force in Canada. In 1988 alone, there were scandals amongst the metropolitan police forces in Vancouver, Edmonton, Calgary, Saskatoon, Winnipeg, Toronto, Montreal, and a host of smaller cities across Canada. Incidents involved everything from murder to the dismissal of a deputy police commissioner for conduct unbecoming a police officer when he was caught *flagrante delicto* with a prostitute in the back of a police van. Police officers have been involved in the distribution of narcotics, bank robberies, and the murder of their wives, in addition to the rash of slayings that has resulted from the use of excessive force upon arrest. One example involved the November 11, 1987, shooting of Anthony Griffin, a 19-year-old member of Montreal's black community by Constable Allan Gosset. After being arrested for being unable to pay a taxi fare and for being in possession of a bag of cigarettes, Griffin was shot to death as he stood "immobilized seven metres away in Station 15 in Notre Dame de Grâce" (*The Gazette* (Montréal), Dec.,23, 1987). Although Roland Bourget, Director of the Montréal Urban Community Police Department (MUCPD), at first claimed that there were no racial overtones in the shooting (*The Gazette*, Nov. 12, 1987), two days later it was discovered that Gosset had severely beaten another black suspect in 1981 and had been subsequently sued by the Quebec Human Rights Commission. The action resulted in an out-of-court settlement in the amount of $2,450 (*The Gazette*, Nov. 13, 1987). Combined with Bourget's reluctance to accept the possibility of widespread police malpractices in the MUCPD and the minimal charge of manslaughter in the case, this new knowledge led to a protest march by over 2,000 citizens (*The Gazette*, Nov. 23, 1987).[1] Bourget pleaded with the community not to "blame the entire police force" for the Griffin slaying and argued that despite a few 'rotten apples' "we're doing a good job" (*The Gazette*, Nov. 21, 12, 1987).

The difficulty with the 'bad apple theory' is that it deflects public attention away from institutional practices and individualizes police malpractices (MacLean, 1986a). One officer is arrested for an incident that results in widespread public outcry, and the difficulty seems to be resolved when the officer is sanctioned. Despite his reference to a few 'rotten apples,' Director Bourget admitted that at the time of the Griffin shooting there were 189 damage suits being faced by the MUCPD for wrongful arrest, brutality, or racism (*The Gazette*, Nov. 12, 1987). About the time that Bourget made his statement, the Superior Court awarded $14,000 to a deaf and mute 110-pound, 17-year-old boy who had been struck in the head by a police flashlight, had a gun pointed at him, had been nearly suffocated, had been handcuffed, and had his head banged against the police-car door frame — a case of mistaken identity. In all such instances, the MUCPD itself handles the complaints against its own officers. Very few complainants are compensated, and only after lengthy court proceedings. In 1987 alone the MUCPD had 12 court judgments filed against it for a total of $275,000 in damages, and 49 new suits were launched, demanding a total of $5,389,500 (*The Gazette*, Dec. 30, 1987). It seems that the only structure of police accountability in Montreal is the already overburdened court.

In Toronto, community-police relations appear to be worse than in Montreal. The Metropolitan Toronto Police Force has a lengthy history of allegations of police wrongdoing, which has resulted in a series of public inquiries (McMahon and Ericson, 1984). In 1974 Justice Donald R. Morand of the Ontario Supreme Court was appointed as commissioner for the Royal Commission Inquiry into Metropolitan Police Practices (Morand, 1976). A brief analysis of the Morand Commission's findings illustrates the limitations of the full judicial inquiry into policing practices.

Although the Morand Commission received a total of 155 allegations of police brutality, it heard evidence in only 17 cases that the commissioner felt were representative of all the cases that came to his attention. The conservative pro-police bias of the commission is, perhaps, best illustrated by the report's introductory discussion. The report states that in 1975 the Metropolitan Toronto police made over 94,352 arrests and in addition had approximately 1.2 million other occasions of police-public contacts (Morand, 1976). According to Commissioner Morand:

> The Metropolitan Police Department polices an area of 243 square miles containing approximately 2,700,000 people. There are 3100 miles of roadways. There are approximately 5500 police personnel and 800 civilian employees in the Metropolitan Police Department.
>
> When we compare the number of complaints made to the Royal Commission complaining about excessive use of force with the total number of arrests, it quickly becomes apparent that on a percentage basis the number of complaints are an extremely small percentage. Even that percentage may be reduced when one considers that a substantial number of complaints were without merit. There were undoubtedly however other incidents about which no complaint was made to the Royal Commission. No estimate can be made as to the number of such incidents.
>
> Of course, one occurrence is one too many, but so long as policing is done by human beings dealing with other human beings, perfection will never be achieved. (Morand, 1976: xviii-xix)

The introduction serves to sensitize the reader to the 'fact' that a certain level of police brutality is inevitable; however, given the magnitude of the task that policing Toronto represents, the few instances of reported brutality remain very low. This royal commission clearly attempts to minimize the frequency of police malpractice. Despite its conservative bias, however, the commission found convincing evidence for, among other things, the systematic use of a mechanical device to extract confessions from alleged offenders. In one case, the complainant, Thomas Gordon Henderson, 18, had his apartment door kicked in by police and was subsequently arrested for possession of small quantities of hashish and LSD. He complained not only of excessive force upon arrest, but also of having a mechanics' claw used on his nose and genitals by police officers (Morand, 1976). In reviewing the evidence, Commissioner Morand concludes:

> Although it is difficult to believe that conduct such as that alleged by Henderson could occur in this city, I have come to the conclusion that Henderson's allegations concerning the violence and threats made upon him at the police station did, in fact, occur.... I am satisfied that the mark on Henderson's penis was consistent with the application of the type of device that he described in evidence.... It is with a great deal of regret that I have come to the conclusion that Henderson's allegations concerning his treatment in the police station were true. I am satisfied that Officers Rusk and Jilek placed the vise grips and the claw upon Henderson when he stripped in the police station.... The probable purpose of this was to intimidate rather than to injure Henderson. This, of course, far from being a justification. (1976: 6-7)

Clearly, while the commissioner was satisfied that such flagrant malpractice did occur, his conclusion is framed within an apologetic discourse that serves to minimize the severity of such behaviour.

In another case, a university student, Gary Bain, who had a previous record of stealing a book, was arrested for possession of three ounces of marijuana. During the course of his interrogation Bain made police aware of the location of several other ounces. He complained that in addition to a variety of threats and violence, the police stapled his penis. Commissioner Morand concludes:

> Evidence had been previously given ... concerning an allegation ... that ... he had been threatened with a similar device, which was described as a vise-like chest expander.... I am satisfied that there was such a device as described by Bain on the premises and that [the officer] deliberately misled me about it and that the other officers ... must have known of its existence.... I am satisfied that threats were made to him and that these threats could have and did have no other effect but to terrorize Bain. I am further satisfied that while in the police station, a stapler was applied to Bain's penis.... I must reluctantly hold that ... Bain was subjected to excessive force and threats of force which were unjustifiable. (1976: 14-5)

In addition to the evidence for substantiated claims of police brutality, Morand (1976) also finds evidence of false arrests, police cover-ups, false charges laid to mask police malpractice, and collusion between officers to protect each other from critical scrutiny by the courts. It is also important to note here that while the commission concludes that the extent of police malpractice is not widespread, the commissioner does imply that he would react most strongly to those incidents that might be viewed as the police usurping the authority of the court's most important function, weighing evidence for the purpose of determining guilt:

> I have heard it said that the police feel that they are the last thin line protecting the citizen from the barbarian hordes who wish to destroy society, that they are frustrated in that they make arrests and the courts either render inadequate sentences or let the accused go free.... To the extent that this belief is held, police therefore feel it is necessary and justifiable to take the law into their own hands, to decide the question of guilt, and then to administer the punishment.... From the statistics quoted elsewhere in this Report, it is obvious that this inference is not true. I am sure that at some time during their careers, police officers feel frustrated when a person they believe to be guilty is acquitted or punished lightly. *It is trite, but deserves to be reiterated, that a policeman's duty is to gather evidence and to submit that evidence to a court of law. It is not for them to determine guilt or innocence, beyond the point of deciding that there is sufficient evidence to lay a charge. It is solely the function of a judge or jury to decide guilt or innocence.* (Morand, 1976: 122, emphasis ours)

Morand (1976) concludes his report with a series of recommendations for policing reform, including a more effective police-complaints procedure and involving the community in some form of structure that would provide a participatory role in policing.

Ironically, the Morand inquiry does not investigate complaints raised by women against the police, except in one instance that helps to illustrate the masculine bias of both the police and the commission appointed to investigate them. In the Patricia Murphy case (Morand, 1976), four female complainants alleged that while out drinking at a tavern one evening, they were verbally molested by a drunken male patron who called them 'dykes' for not succumbing to his unwanted sexual advances. After complaining unsuccessfully to the manager, the four women proceeded to make use of the equipment on a stage provided for "patron entertainment." After singing a "'lesbian-feminist' song set to the tune of 'I enjoy being a girl,'" they were asked to leave the premises, a request they refused. As a consequence the four were physically removed by police, who arrested them and transported them to the police station. After being released they returned to the tavern where they were once more arrested and taken to the station. It was at this point that they were allegedly assaulted. Morand concludes:

> I am satisfied that on no occasion throughout the evening did the police officers use excessive force. I am further satisfied that the attitude of the four women, particularly Patricia Murphy, was very antagonistic to the police who were only carrying out their duties. It became clear from the evidence that the women considered that they were making a declaration to the public on behalf of homosexuals.... It may be that they felt that the management and the police were discriminating against homosexuals ... and the police were justified not only in requesting the women to leave but also in forcibly removing them when they refused to leave.... The only fault

that I find with the conduct of the police is that some of the officers, the identity of whom it is impossible to determine, did use abusive language in addressing the women. This was in response to the abusive language used by the women to the police ... this does not excuse the police who should have been professional enough in their approach to maintain a dignified silence and not descend to the level of the people whom they were arresting. (1976: 70-1)

This citation clearly indicates both an anti-female and anti-lesbian bias on the part of the Commissioner. Despite any evidence of 'homosexuality,' he assumes this to be the sexual predisposition of the women. Even if this were a fact, it is irrelevant to the case. Nevertheless, while not formally condoning the police officers' behaviour, the commissioner finds it understandable, given the 'level of people' with whom the police must regrettably deal.

The treatment of women as 'offenders' is not the only aspect of 'undignified' policing practice. Recent research points to unsatisfactory practices when the police deal with requests for assistance from victims of crime. The Canadian Urban Victimization Survey (CUVS), for example, notes that 'fear of the police' is a major factor for women who decide not to report an assault (Canada, Ministry of the Solicitor General, *Bulletin 4*, 1984: 10). Clark and Lewis (1977: 58) found that police officers share general prejudices about appropriate behaviour for women, which adversely affects their classification of rape reports, while Gunn and Minch (1988:57) report that police evaluate the validity of women's complaints according to stereotypical notions of how a victim should act. In terms of domestic violence, the Canadian Advisory Council on the Status of Women complains that the police may respond too slowly, fail to act altogether, or respond in a sexist manner. In a well-publicized case, the officer involved was quoted as saying, "If it had been my house, I would have beaten my wife for the condition it was in" (in MacLeod, 1980: 38). In this way, like the testimony of alleged offenders, the experiences of victims of crime document the need for police accountability in Canada.

THREE MODELS OF POLICE ACCOUNTABILITY

There is sufficient evidence, then, both in the recorded incidents of police malpractice and the recommendations of judicial inquiries, to conclude that there is a need for some form of police accountability in Canada. Historically, police accountability has been attempted in three ways. The first form is the *judicial inquiry*, such as the royal commission. The role of such inquiry has been to isolate on a case-by-case approach instances in which specific police officers have abused their authority and which ultimately result in a set of recommendations that the judiciary view as being safeguards against future infractions. While these inquiries have been successful in identifying individual cases, they have not been successful in making the police accountable, nor have they been successful in eliminating either unfair policing, police abuse of powers, or police racism and sexism. It is this recognition that leads the Morand Inquiry to recommend the second form, a *community monitoring group* that will help to ensure that complaints about policing will be dealt with independently and not covered up through a procedure controlled by those being complained against. The third form involves some method of *consultative liaison panel* in which members of the public, democratically elected to a panel, engage in regular meetings with police personnel to ensure that the police know about community concerns around crime and policing. This model can be contrasted with the community monitoring group in that the monitoring group is an adversarial structure while the consultative liaison panel is supposed to operate more as a vehicle of constructive public feedback.[2]

1. Judicial Inquiries

The police shootings of two black men in the Metropolitan Toronto area and a Native leader in Winnipeg generated the creation of two judicial inquiries, with mandates to examine how the police and courts treat visible minorities: The *Race Relations and Policing Task Force* (Lewis et al., 1989a) and the *Manitoba Native Justice Inquiry* (*Calgary Herald*, Aug. 22, 1989).

A. The Race Relations and Policing Task Force

In December 1988, two black men, Lester Donaldson and Michael Wade Lawson, were killed in separate incidents by police officers from different departments in the Metropolitan Toronto area. These slayings caused a major breakdown in relations between visible minorities and the police. In fact, they led to what one person viewed as "an atmosphere of mutual mistrust and pessimism" (Lewis et al., 1989a: 3). In response to this crisis, Joan Smith, Ontario's solicitor-general, announced the creation of the Race Relations and Policing Task Force on December 13, 1988.

On December 15, 1988, Smith told the legislature that the task force was required to study and report on six specific issues:

1. The training members of police forces currently receive as it relates to visible minorities.
2. Ways to improve this training and education, for both recruits and serving officers.
3. Police hiring practices and promotional processes, including the establishment of employment equity programs.
4. Ways to improve the interaction of the police with the visible minority communities through the establishment of liaison officers, committees, community education programs, and race relations training.
5. Ways in which a monitoring system may be established to provide a regular review of the interaction between visible minorities and the police.
6. The policies and practices of the police relating to the use of force (Lewis et al., 1989b: 4).

The data reported in this study came from several sources. Firstly, 118 oral presentations were submitted by individual citizens, members of community groups, and representatives from police forces and commissions to public hearings in Toronto, Ottawa, Windsor, and Thunder Bay. In addition, 127 written briefs were submitted (Lewis et al., 1989b: 4). Secondly, information was gleaned from 121 police forces. In total, 99 questionnaires and "private information gathering sessions" with members of the Ontario Police College, the C.O. Bick Police College, the Firearms Branch of both the Centre of Forensic Sciences and the Metropolitan Toronto Police, and private consultants were completed. Thirdly, a computer-assisted review of relevant literature was conducted. Finally, a review of previous reports and recommendations made to the government was also carried out (Lewis et al., 1989a: 4-5).

In the summary of its report, the task force stated that it was convinced that "Visible minority communities do not believe that they are policed in the same manner as the mainstream, white community. They do not believe that they are policed fairly, and they made a strong case for their view which cannot be ignored" (Lewis et al., 1989a: 5-6). Black youths reported being both physically and verbally abused by police officers, while another example of racist policing practices was the differential policing response to victims of domestic assault. In responding to battered women, some officers gave lesser assistance to women of colour than to their white counterparts (1989a: 153-4).

To alleviate these and other related problems, 57 recommendations were presented to the solicitor-general. Among the most important are:

1. The development, by statute, of the Ontario Race Relations and Policing Review Board, consisting of three to five civilians.
2. Mandatory employment equity programs for all Ontario police forces.
3. Race relations training for police.
4. Legal restrictions on the use of deadly force and civilian members of police shooting investigation teams.
5. The inclusion of definitions of and sanctions for racism in the *Police Act*.
6. The formation of community policing and community consultation committees representative of various ethnic groups.
7. A study of Native justice systems in Ontario (Lewis et al., 1989b: 10-27).

These recommendations are the result of an intensive investigation that yielded such compelling evidence of rampant institutional racism that a new police act for the province of Ontario was drafted. Nevertheless, the new act was delayed in the legislature, and it is doubtful that the recommendations of the Lewis report will be acted upon in the near future. Perhaps the more recent incident of yet another black youth shot by a Metropolitan police constable is sufficient evidence to support our pessimistic view that this form of accountability is of limited practical utility.

Another reason for our scepticism is that recent examples of police racism are not limited to Ontario, where there is a lengthy history of strained community-police relations. Minority residents in Western Canadian provinces, such as Manitoba, are victims of brutality, verbal abuse, and the deadly use of force. Native people are at greater risk for being victimized by such malpractice, as a recent inquiry held in Winnipeg substantiates.

B. The Manitoba Native Justice Inquiry

Consistent with the catalyst for the creation of the Race Relations and Policing Task Force in Ontario, the March 9, 1988, police shooting of a Native leader, J.J. Harper, in Winnipeg contributed to the commissioning of the Manitoba Native Justice Inquiry to examine the treatment of Natives by the justice system. Even though Constable Robert Cross mistook Harper for a car thief, Cross was cleared of any misconduct by an internal police investigation and an inquest into Harper's slaying (Canadian Press, Nov. 6, 1989). Consequently, Manitoba's Native community reacted with anger, allegations of racism, and demands for a public inquiry.

The inquiry is also, in part, a reaction to Native outrage with the response of the Manitoba criminal-justice system to the sexual assault and murder of Helen Betty Osborne, which occurred in The Pas, Manitoba, in 1971. Four men killed her; however, only one, Dwayne Archie Johnston, was convicted of second-degree murder, and only then in 1987 — some 16 years later (Canadian Press, Nov. 6, 1989).

The Harper inquiry began in the fall of 1988 and ended on Wednesday, November 22, 1989. It heard 700 hours of testimony from 1,050 witnesses and produced 21,000 pages of transcripts. Over two years later the final report had still not been released, and although it was expected in the near future, its contents had not been divulged. However, during the inquiry a four-page suicide note written by Inspector Ken Dowson, the officer in charge of the internal police investigation into the murder of Harper, reveals that the police conducted a sloppy investigation. Judges heading the inquiry intimated that they would call for a separate justice system for Manitoba's Native community (*Canadian Press*, Nov. 23, 1989).

These two inquiries illustrate the limitations of this model of accountability. Firstly, inquiries are generally commissioned only after a policing crisis has emerged. In this sense they are at best reactive and more concerned with political damage control than progressive social change. Secondly, to the extent that these inquiries have attempted to provide proactive and progressive changes in the form of recommendations, if taken seriously such recommendations often take years to implement. In the meantime, as the case of Toronto illustrates, more crises emerge and various segments of the community become disgruntled and further alienated. These inquiries are not good value for limited community resources. They are conducted at a considerable expense; however, even when serious attempts to interview a broad cross-section of the community are made, they result in far too few briefs and testimonies to generalize to the population at large. Nevertheless, the reports of judicial inquiries do make such generalizations, contributing to the dubiousness of their scientific merit. Finally, as demonstrated by the Morand Inquiry, there is a serious danger that the inquiry will 'descend to the level' of policing discourse. Since it has been demonstrated that discursive policing practices are often sexist, racist, and homophobic, adoption of this discourse by a judicial inquiry means that institutionalized biases remain unaddressed.

2. Police Monitoring Groups

Perhaps the best recent example of a police monitoring group stems from the Morand Inquiry and was formed in Toronto in 1981 (McMahon and Ericson, 1984). Ericson (1987) argues that a number of critical incidents in which allegations of police racism were unsuccessfully dealt with by the Police Complaints Board led to the formation of the Citizen's Independent Review of Police Activities (CIRPA), a police watchdog committee consisting of a number of lawyers and concerned citizens in Metropolitan Toronto. In reviewing the history of CIRPA, Ericson suggests that while at first the relationship between CIRPA and the police was quite confrontational, as time passed CIRPA became sensitized to policing discourse and eventually became more or less co-opted. What started out as a challenge to certain police activities became an agency that facilitated police rationalization of police activities. In this way, rather than engaging in debate with police — a process that might be seen as the clash of two discourses — CIRPA found itself adopting the policing discourse and thereby accepting the police definition of the situation. The process of co-optation to which Ericson refers is a subtle process through which CIRPA came to debate the issues on terms established by the police. Ericson (1987) concludes that such a process is inevitable for agencies such as CIRPA. Thus police monitoring committees, or watchdog groups such as CIRPA, have historically proved to be ineffective at bringing the police under democratic accountability.

Another contemporary example of this form of police accountability is located in London, England, where during the mid-1980s the Greater London Council (GLC) funded a number of monitoring groups. The mandate of these organizations was: (1) to take up on a case-by-case, individualistic approach complaints against the police; (2) to take an adversarial stance vis à vis the police in a fashion not dissimilar to what Ericson (1987) and McMahon and Ericson (1984) document in the early stages of CIRPA; and (3) to engage in an education/propaganda campaign that attempts to sensitize the public to the negative aspects of the metropolitan police. Figure 13-1 serves as an example of the kind of materials distributed. It depicts a card produced and widely distributed by Police Accountability for Community Enlightenment (PACE), a monitoring group funded by the GLC. Needless to say, the result of such publications was a concerted countercampaign undertaken by the central government, the media and the metropolitan police, which together characterized these groups as anti-police while depicting the members of the GLC as the 'looney left' (MacLean, 1989). While the battle for control over the image of the police was waged in the public arena, the Thatcher government quietly passed legislation eliminating the County Councils in Britain, including the GLC-funded police monitoring groups (Seccombe, 1987). Thus, from the British experience, it would seem that Ericson's pessimism is well founded. Either the monitoring group adopts the policing discourse and is co-opted, as in the case of CIRPA, or it maintains an oppositional discourse that can be legislated away politically, as in the case of the GLC-funded monitoring groups.

Perhaps one of the contributing factors to the failure of both judicial inquiries and community monitoring groups has been their insistence on reviewing police activities in an individualistic case-by-case fashion. In this reactive manner every incident that comes to the attention of these structures of accountability can be explained in a variety of ways, so that in the unlikely case that an officer is found to be culpable, his dismissal acts as evidence for the fact that these forms of accountability are working. In this way, the structure and process of policing tend to be ignored — and an examination of this structure and process is necessary for the achievement of progressive changes to the policing institution.

3. Consultative Liaison Panels

A third way in which policing can be brought under democratic accountability is through the creation of some form of consultative liaison panel. In this form of accountability, a representative group of community members meets with the police to discuss incidents of police indiscretion and wider policy issues. Examples of the policy issues might include: police training, the deployment of police resources to specific areas of the community, the split between crime control and public order, police procedures of arrest, and race and gender relations. The difficulty with this approach, however, is similar to the problems that Ericson (1987) identifies for police monitoring groups. Because the police have a monopoly of knowledge over crime and policing processes, liaison panels ultimately come under police domination. Panels cannot easily challenge police rationalizations for specific policies and practices because they lack the empirical basis for proper debate. Both the police and the panel are dependent upon police statistics for their description of crime and policing patterns, and as a consequence the policing discourse, which is directly related to this description, prevails in meetings. Unless such liaison panels can produce an alternative set of empirical information that describes crime and policing processes, they will also be co-opted into policing discourse.

Unlike judicial inquiries and police monitoring groups, consultative liaison groups are yet to be firmly established in Canada. Thus the extent to which liaison panels equipped with an alternative set of information can be successful is an empirical question and can only be answered as such. However, recent developments in Britain provide some data. After the Brixton riots in 1981, Lord Scarman recommended in his report to Parliament that community liaison panels be established:

> 8.39. Community involvement in the policy and operations of policing is perfectly feasible without undermining the independence of the police or destroying the secrecy of those operations against crime which have to be kept secret. There is a need to devise means of enabling such involvement. ... I *recommend* that a statutory duty should be imposed on Police authorities and on Chief Officers of Police to co-operate in the establishment of such consultative arrangements. I also *recommend* that meanwhile Police

Authorities and Chief Officers of Police should act at once under their existing powers to set up such arrangements...

8.40. In London, I do not recommend any change in the law substituting some other body for the Secretary of State as Police Authority. I do, however, *recommend* that a statutory framework be developed to require local consultation between the Metropolitan Police and the community at Borough or Police District level. The possibility of an Advisory Board or other consultative arrangements between the Home Office, the Commissioner, and the London Boroughs at force level should also be studied. (Scarman, 1981: 130)

Figure 13-1: Card Distributed by Police Accountability For Community Enlightenment (PACE)

ARRESTED?

GENERAL
DO NOT answer any police questions- you have the right to remain silent.

DO give your name and address.

NOTE the identity of all police officers you deal with.

ALWAYS try to be polite and calm.

STOP AND SEARCH
Ask why you have been stopped.

If you are asked to go to the Police Station, ask if you are being arrested.

The police have the right to search you on reasonable suspicion for drugs, firearms, terrorist articles and stolen goods. If you are searched ask why and try to have an independent witness present. You may be taken to the Police Station to be searched if it cannot be done in the street. This is not an arrest. You may leave the Station afterwards.

TROUBLE WITH THE POLICE?   **263·1075 24 HOURS**

TROUBLE WITH THE POLICE?   **263·1075 24 HOURS**

AT THE POLICE STATION
Apart from giving your name and address, say nothing until a solicitor is present. Ask to make a phone call and keep asking. Do not get drawn into casual conversations. Do not sign any statements or make any admissions before contacting a solicitor.

HOUSE SEARCH
The Police do not need your permission or a warrant to enter your house to arrest a person suspected of a serious offence. They should name the person. In general the police need a warrant before they can search your house for property. If your house is searched ask to see the warrant. You are entitled to demand the reason for the search, but barring their entry could be an offence. Always try to have an independent person to witness the search.

If the Police Bill becomes law, some of these points will not apply. Contact PACE for a new card.

P.A.C.E.   Islington Police Monitoring Group

301 Hornsey Road London N 19

Except in the London Borough of Lambeth, the location of the Brixton riots, the consultative liaison panels recommended by Scarman were optional for the London boroughs. This recommendation was rejected by Labour-controlled inner-city London boroughs because they believed that consultative liaison was a sham constructed by the Home Office to appease public demand (Christian, 1983) and that they were a front for racism. For example, in a press release produced by the Stoke Newington and Hackney Defence Campaign, the Hackney Council is urged not to adopt consultative liaison, and the public is encouraged to lobby the council for this purpose:

> The Stoke Newington & Hackney Defence Campaign says that the disgusting racist torturer Newman [Commissioner of The Metropolitan Police] should resign and that one and all should join with us on the 13th [September, 1982] and actively demand of Hackney Council's police committee that they resist Newman's style of 'contact between police and public' and say NO CLOAK FOR THE POLICE TO HIDE THEIR VILE DEEDS!! NO POLICE CONSULTATIVE COMMITTEE IN HACKNEY!! CRIME IS NOT THE ISSUE — RACIST POLICING IS
> (unpublished leaflet)

While the police committees of the Labour-controlled London boroughs uniformly decided not to participate in Home Office efforts to construct liaison committees, a different view was taken by The London Borough of Islington Council (LBI), which proceeded to negotiate the composition of such a committee with the Home Office. Under Home Office guidelines adopted directly from Scarman, each borough would separately negotiate the actual structure and representation of the community liaison panels. Due to the mass rejection by other boroughs, Islington succeeded in negotiating a committee that consisted of: 10 elected councillors, no more than 5 senior members of 'N' District of the Metropolitan Police, the 2 Labour MPs from Islington, the 3 local GLC councillors, and no less than 13 members of the community approved by the others.[3] Islington took the initiative to lobby tenants associations and other community organizations to produce a total of 33 members for the committee, the majority of them sympathetic to the views on policing held by the Islington Council Police Committee (MacLean, 1989). The initial position taken by the LBI Police Sub-Committee was similar to the other Labour-controlled boroughs, as illustrated in the minutes of the early meetings of the committee:

> The Policy and Programme Planning Officer informed the Sub-Committee the G.L.C. had provided funding for two staff in the financial year 1982/83 and in this connection a sum of £23,000 was proposed to be included as a committed growth item in the 1983/84 Programme Plan.
>
> Members were of the view that some provision should be made for clerical/admin[istrative] support staff for the Police Unit, campaign expenses and for grants to outside bodies such as the Independent Monitoring Group, although it was hoped such groups would also benefit from G.L.C. funding or Partnership Grants.[4]

Thus LBI was not opposed to monitoring groups but felt that the GLC should fund these as well as the committee support staff positions. And on the issue of consultative liaison, the committee was adamant about having itself recognized by the Home Office as a Consultative Liaison Committee:

> The Sub-Committee noted that the Queen's Speech had included proposals for a statutory consultation framework and therefore any local structure may be short-lived and information available gave little indication as to the level of discretion available to the Commander. Since publication of the Speech, negotiations with the Home Office as to the role of the Islington Police Sub-Committee has ceased.
>
> Members stressed the need to maintain the Sub-Committee so as to be able to develop democratic forms of control over the Police. The Council should not agree to take part in any consultative machinery, other than to discuss normal policing issues.[5]

Thus the Islington Council was not initially unlike other Labour-controlled boroughs in that it rejected the idea of consultation as formulated by the Home Office, and in that it wanted to support the idea of monitoring groups. It did differ from other boroughs, however, by the fact that it did not fund its own committee and wanted to depend on GLC funding for both staffing and support of police monitoring groups. Unlike the other boroughs, however, this strategy changed considerably. The new strategy can be attributed to the influence from a left-realist position on the utility of liaison, as argued by Lea and Young (1984):[6]

> In the absence of proper accountability the newly constituted liaison committees will be in a position of searching ground for significant groupings or representatives of the local community to consult. So, for example, the Home Office guidelines for the constitution of such bodies stipulate that membership should include the local Community Relations Council representatives.... Despite the ambiguities of, and police opposition to, Scarman's recommendations for statutory police-community liaison, the police themselves have put a considerable effort into such schemes, particularly in areas like Brixton. This can be seen partly as an attempt to short-circuit the growing campaign of a future Labour government and partly as realization that the drift to military style policing is indeed counter-productive.... Under such circumstances, police-community 'liaison' by means of a few representatives drawn from CRCs and local government which at the end of the day leaves policy-making exactly where it was to begin with, firmly in the hands of the police themselves, does nothing to end the political marginalization of the young unemployed. It is hardly surprising, therefore, that the bulk of the local community should see little point in participation in such enterprises and that the police should feel hamstrung by consultation procedures tying them to talks and discussions with local individuals whose representative credentials they regard as highly suspect.... This brings us to the second issue. *In our opinion it would be a mistake to try and ignore the police liaison schemes.* (249-61, our emphasis)

Thus, while liaison was hardly seen as the solution, it was certainly seen as a step towards a solution, and the strategy adopted by LBI was to use the structure as a means not only to strike a committee — the majority of which agreed with council initiatives — but also to provide a public forum for the open discussion of issues. Furthermore, this forum would be the ideal location for a challenge to the crime and policing knowledge held by the police provided by the results of a local crime survey. In short, the Islington Police Sub-Committee successfully outmanoeuvred the Home Office in the formation of its Consultative Liaison Committee, to the extent that the Home Office, in recognition of this, later amended its guidelines so that no more than five councillors from the local governments could be on these committees.[7] With the passing of the *1984 Police and Criminal Evidence Act*, it is now compulsory for all London boroughs to have these panels, with or without the support of the Local Council (MacLean, 1989). The battle for greater council representation, which was won by Islington in taking an active role in the political developments on the police, has now been lost by other Labour-controlled London boroughs in that these committees will be struck with or without the support of the councils; however, should the councils choose to participate it is with comparatively minimal representation.

This brief review of models of police accountability shows that none provide an optimistic potential for achieving meaningful and effective structures of police accountability. In the case of judicial inquiries and police monitoring groups, the tendency is to adopt policing discourse, which results in an *acceptance of* rather than *challenge to* current policing practices. While the consultative liaison group has potential, its dependency upon police information makes it susceptible to police domination. It is with this insight that in England, where this model has been advanced, local governments failed to endorse such committees. The exception of the London Borough of Islington stands as a marked contrast. Under the influence of a group of realist criminologists, the council not only endorsed consultative liaison, but did so in combination with a commitment to conducting a program of local crime survey research. These two developments combine to form the left-realist model of police accountability.

THE LEFT-REALIST MODEL OF POLICE ACCOUNTABILITY

In addition to its position on consultative liaison, Islington Council can be distinguished from other Labour-controlled London boroughs by its continued commitment to the Islington Crime Survey (Jones, MacLean, and Young, 1986).

Shortly after the Police Sub-Committee was established in 1982, it went on record as supporting the idea of a large multiborough criminal victimization survey: "The Police Support Unit advised members that the Middlesex Polytechnic had begun consultations with local interest groups including tenants associations and women's organizations in conjunction with the Race Relations Unit, on the victimization survey being carried out in the Borough."[8] Researchers from the Middlesex Polytechnic had engaged five inner-city boroughs in talks aimed at carrying out such a survey in the London boroughs of Greenwich, Newham, Camden, Hackney, and Islington. While the initial response of the police committees was favourable, community organizations, again funded by GLC resources, lobbied their councils to vote against the proposed research while demonstrating against the project at council meetings in the various boroughs. Perhaps the strongest criticism was aimed at John Lea and Jock Young, who were portrayed as racists due to their analysis of race and crime in *Policing The Riots* (Cowell, Jones, and Young, 1982). The result of such popular resistance by community organizations was the defeat of the proposed project in all of the boroughs (Gutzmore, 1983), except Islington which continually reiterated its support by vote at meetings of its Police Sub-Committee. The position taken by Lea and Young on surveys was later published in *What Is to Be Done About Law and Order?* (1984):

> On the first issue, some boroughs are going ahead with the idea of a victimization survey conducted by the police committee. This is of considerable importance: it generates an alternative set of statistics about the incidence of crime to the police arrest statistics or statistics for victim-reported crime (much crime is unreported where it is felt that the police could not be bothered anyway). These can be used as part of a public debate about policing needs. Such surveys can also include questions not normally considered relevant by the police, such as the incidence of domestic violence, illegal acts by police officers, and the specific problems of ethnic minorities. The Community can then get a clearer picture of what it is facing than it can from the police statistics. (1984: 261)

Thus Islington was influenced by and committed to a two-pronged strategy of producing alternative statistics via the survey and the use of a liaison committee as the vehicle for making these statistics known, a position directly attributable to the left-realist discourse. Since the formation of the liaison committee was already being negotiated, its utility would be severely diminished unless an alternative informational base was constructed, such as that promised by a local crime survey.

It is within the specific political and social milieu of policing and police accountability in England and Wales that the left-realist model of police accountability was constructed (MacLean, 1989). More specifically, the left realists at Middlesex Polytechnic were influential in the development of this model; however, the political specificity of LBI, and the discourse in which it was framed, were also influential in the construction of left-realist discourse (MacLean, 1989).[9] The product of this relationship was a *discursive practice* that included both a specific structure within which the political struggle with the police was waged, and the literature based upon it. In political conflict with other discursive practices such as that being produced by the GLC, the left-realist discourse won the struggle (Pease, 1990). The result has been a host of local crime survey research funded by local councils (Bottomley, 1988) and used in tandem with consultative liaison panels endorsed by those councils (MacLean and DeKeseredy, 1990). Finally, despite the specificity of the left-realist model of police accountability, the fact that it is a practical discourse means that it has relevance for a variety of local jurisdictions.

CONCLUSIONS

Britain provides an example, then, of a structure of accountability consisting of community liaison panels and information gleaned from large-scale in-depth local crime surveys. Based upon the newly emerging left-realist discourse, these panels make use of information from the surveys to challenge the police in the public forum rather than accepting police definitions of crime and policing processes. Left-realist discourse is the practical application of discourse theory, Marxist political economy, and feminism in the struggle for a more fair administration of justice and construction of social order. The struggle for democratic accountability of the police by left realists in England provides us with the opportunity to evaluate both the potential effectiveness of police accountability and the potential importance of the left-realist model of police accountability to the Canadian administration of justice. There are two central aspects to this model. Firstly, the formation of community liaison panels is essential to public accountability. Such panels would consist of a representative cross-section of the community, so that changes in the social, racial, and demographic character of the community are reflected in the membership of the committee. Secondly, the left-realist strategy provides an alternative set of information derived from probability surveys of the community in which respondents reply to a variety of questions as indicators for crime and policing processes.

In England and Wales, left realism recognized that the Thatcher government had been successful in its political agenda on law and order for two important reasons. Firstly, as the current government, it possessed a monopoly on the legislative process. But secondly, and perhaps more importantly, it had a monopoly on knowledge of crime and policing. This monopoly is the result of the police having the formal responsibility for creating crime and policing statistics, allowing them to become the experts on the frequency and distribution of crime, and consequently, on the methods of dealing with these trends. Significantly, these statistics become the empirical evidence for the political arguments given by the right in the public forum. For this reason the Islington Council was convinced that because the debate was framed in a neoconservative discourse it was necessary to generate its own information base, which would serve to challenge the monopoly of knowledge and push the debate forward. By allowing themselves to be influenced by a left-realist position on crime and policing, the strategy followed by the LBI Police Sub-Committee can be distinguished from other Labour-controlled boroughs while the left-realist position itself can be seen as being influenced by the concerns of LBI Council. The GLC, largely influenced by what Young (1979) has called the left idealists, promoted a very different strategy, which eventually led to its demise. Thus what began as a struggle for dominance between left-wing academics in discourse became a practical struggle between government institutions at different levels. The substance of the struggle was academic but the arena for the contest was located in the local government structures, with the ICS a direct and successful product of this struggle.

As a local crime survey, ICS paid considerable attention to measuring all moments in the crimes process, eliminating the sexist and conservative biases of other crime survey research and reducing the costs of data collection through proxy interviewing while attempting to cope with the sampling error engendered by such a data collection strategy (MacLean, 1989). In so doing, the ICS became a valuable source of information for the Islington Council in its struggle for police accountability; however, the questions still remain: *To what extent might a similar strategy be useful within a Canadian context? While it seems to be a promising alternative, where and how is this technology likely to develop?* The answers depend upon a number of key political and academic questions. For example, how likely is it that local authorities will undertake such research initiatives independently? The recent *Report of the Race Relations and Policing Task Force in Ontario* (1989) was an attempt to identify the scope of police racism and find ways to improve community-police relations, particularly in the minority communities of Metropolitan Toronto. Although this was a lengthy and expensive exercise, it is doubtful that the findings from this form of judicial review will have much impact upon policing. Perhaps such a body might greatly benefit from information derived from local crime surveys; however, such a step can only be decided politically, and for this reason critical criminologists must become more practically involved in these debates — which is the basic premise of left-realist discourse.

Can a defensible, relatively accurate, alternative source of information be generated by such technology to help local councils and local police in Canada resolve their crime and policing differences? To what extent can the descriptive statistics provided by these surveys be of use in explaining crime and policing trends? Finally, can these surveys provide a less politically biased account of crime and policing trends than other measures of crime? Whether political or academic, such questions are practical and can only be answered practically. Critical criminology must be distinguished from other criminological discourses by its practice. Critical discourse divorced from critical practice degenerates into mere literary criticism, the value of which is *a purely scholastic question.* If the advance represented by left-realist discourse and practice is to take root within the Canadian context and assist in the formation of structures for democratic police accountability, it rests with the critical criminologists to advance such a model within practical political fora at the local level.

Reprinted with the kind permission of The Journal of Human Justice, *Vol. 2, No. 1:29-53 (Autumn, 1990)*

NOTES

1. The potential for open rebellious protest in the streets is reminiscent of the gloomy prediction voiced in the King quotation at the beginning of this chapter.

2. In the following discussion we necessarily examine each of the three models separately. Clearly, however, at different times and in different

places these overlap or operate in combination. Our purpose here is to articulate the logic of each model to identify the inherent practical limitations of each of them.

3. Islington Police Sub-Committee minutes, Jan. 8, 1985 (agenda item 12).

4. LBI Police Sub-Committee minutes, Nov. 11, 1982 (minute 26).

5. LBI Police Sub-Committee minutes, Nov. 11, 1982 (minute 28).

6. For a full discussion of the relationship between the Middlesex Group and the LBI see MacLean, 1989.

7. Home Office Guidelines adopted from the 1984 *Police and Criminal Evidence Act*.

8. LBI Police Sub-Committee minutes, Nov. 8, 1984 (Agenda Item 12).

9. For a thorough review of the history of police in England and Wales see Critchley, 1978; for a discussion of the politics of policing in England and Wales see Reiner, 1985.

Bibliography

Abel, R. 1982. "Torts." Pp185-200 in D. Kairys (ed.), *The Politics of Law: A Progressive Critique*. New York: Pantheon Books.

Ad Hoc Committee of Women on the Constitution. 1988. "We Can Afford a Better Accord: The Meech Lake Accord." *Resources for Feminist Research*. Vol. 17, No. 3: 143-146.

Adachi, Ken. 1974. *The Enemy That Never Was: A History of the Japanese Canadians*. Toronto: McClelland and Stewart.

Adamson, Nancy, Linda Briskin and Margaret McPhail. 1988. *Feminist Organizing for Change: The Contemporary Women's Movement in Canada*. Toronto: Oxford University Press.

Adelberg, Ellen and Claudia Currie (eds.). 1987. *Too Few to Count: Canadian Women in Conflict with the Law*. Vancouver: Press Gang.

Ahluwalia, Seema K. 1987. "A History of Domestic Violence: Implications for Medical Intervention in Saskatchewan." Unpublished M. A. thesis, Department of Sociology, University of Saskatchewan.

Ahluwalia, Seema K. 1991. "Currents in British Feminist Thought." *The Critical Criminologist: A Newsletter*. Vol. 3, No. 1(Spring).

Alberta Gaming Commission. 1988. *1987 Annual Review*. Edmonton.

Allen, J. M. and M. A. Straus. 1980. "Resources, Power and Husband-Wife Violence." Pp188-208 in M. A. Straus and G. T. Holtaling (eds.), *The Social Causes of Husband-Wife Violence*. Minneapolis: University of Minnesota Press.

Althusser, L. 1971. *Lenin and Philosophy*. New York: Monthly Review Press.

Aries, Phillippe. 1962. *Centuries of Childhood*. New York: Alfred A. Knopf.

Asch, Michael, Douglas Hudson, Mark Lathrop, Ken Luckhardt and Pat McCormack. 1976. "The People Speak." *This Magazine*. Vol. 10, No. 3 (June-July):18-21.

Asch, Michael and Patrick Macklem. 1991. "Aboriginal Rights and Canadian Sovereignty: An Essay on *R. v Sparrow*." *Alberta Law Review*. Vol. 24, No. 2:498-517.

Asch, Michael. 1984. *Home and Native Land: Aboriginal Rights and the Canadian Constitution*. Toronto: Methuen.

Atcheson, M. Elizabeth, Mary Eberts and Beth Symes. 1984. *Women and Legal Action: Precedents, Resources and Strategies for the Future*. Ottawa: Canadian Advisory Council on the Status of Women.

Atkins, Susan and Brenda Hoggett. 1984. *Women and the Law*. New York: Basil Blackwell.

Badgely, R.F., D. F. Caron and M. G. Powell. 1977. *Report of the Committee on the Operation of the Abortion Law*. Ottawa: Minister of Supply and Services.

Baines, Beverley. 1987. "Gender and the Meech Lake Committee." *Queen's Quarterly*. Vol. 94, No. 4:807-816.

Baines, Beverley. 1988. "Women and the Law." Pp157-183 in Sandra Burt, Lorraine Code and Lindsay Dorney (eds.), *Changing Patterns: Women in Canada*. Toronto: McClelland and Stewart.

Bakan, Joel. 1991. "Constitutional Interpretation and Social Change: You Can't Always Get What You Want (Nor What You Need)." *Canadian Bar Review*. Vol. 70 (June):307-328.

Bakan, Joel. 1990. "Strange Expectations: A Review of Two Theories of Judicial Review." *McGill Law Journal.* Vol 35, No. 2: 439-458.

Bakhtin, M. 1986. *Speech Genres and Other Late Essays.* C. Emerson and M. Holquist (eds.). Austin, Texas: University of Texas Press.

Bakhtin, M. 1981. *The Dialogical Imagination.* Austin, Texas: University of Texas Press.

Balkin, D. 1987. "Deconstructive Practice and Legal Theory." *Yale Law Journal.* Vol 96:743-786

Balbus, I. 1973. *The Dialectics of Legal Repression.* New York: Russel Sage.

Bannister, S. and D. Milovanovic. 1990. "The Necessity Defense, Substantive Justice and Oppositional Linguistic Praxis." *International Journal of Sociology of Law.* Vol. 18, No. 1:179-198.

Baran, P. and Sweezy, P. 1966. *Monopoly Capital: An Essay on the American Economic and Social Order.* New York: Modern Reader Paperbacks.

Barley, S. 1983. "Semiotics and the Study of Occupational and Organizational Cultures." *Administrative Science Quarterly.* Vol 28:393-413.

Barnsley, Jan. 1985. *Feminist Action, Institutional Reaction: Responses to Wife Assault.* Vancouver: Women's Research Centre.

Barnsley, Jan. 1980. "'Battered and Blamed' — A Report on Wife Assault From the Perspective of Battered Women." Vancouver: Vancouver Transition House and the Women's Research Centre.

Barthes, R. 1974. *S/Z.* New York: Hill and Wang.

Barrett, M. and M. McIntosh. 1982. *The Anti-Social Family.* London: Verso.

Baudrillard, J. 1981. *For a Critique of the Political Economy of the Sign.* St. Louis: Telos Press.

Bayda, E. D. 1980-81. "The Adequacy of the Public Inquiry Process for Assessing Major Nuclear Facilities." *Saskatchewan Law Review.* Vol. 45, No. 1:3-12.

Bayda, E. D. 1978a. *Final Report: Cluff Lake Board of Inquiry.* Regina: Department of Environment.

Bayda, E. D. 1978b. *Transcripts, Cluff Lake Board of Inquiry.* Regina: Department of Environment.

Becker, Howard S. 1963. *Outsiders: Studies in the Sociology of Deviance.* New York: Free Press.

Bell, Daniel J. 1984. "The Police Response to Domestic Violence: A Replication Study." *Police Studies.* Vol. 7, No. 3:136-144.

Bell, Daniel J. 1986. "Domestic Violence in Small Cities and Towns: A Pilot Study." *Journal of Crime and Justice.* Vol. 9:163-181.

Bell, Daniel J. 1987. "The Victim-Offender Relationship: A Determinant Factor in Police Domestic Dispute Dispositions." *Marriage and Family Review.* Vol. 12, Nos. 1-2: 87-102.

Bender, Barbara. 1975. *Farming in Prehistory: From Hunter-Gatherer to Food-Producer.* London: John Baker.

Bennet, W. and M. Feldman. 1981. *Reconstructing Reality in the Courtroom.* New Brunswick, New Jersey: Rutgers University Press.

Benveniste, E. 1971. *Problems in General Linguistics.* Coral Gables, Florida: University of Miami Press.

Berk, Fenstermaker S. and D. R. Loseke. 1980-81. "'Handling' Family Violence: Situational Determinants of Police Arrest in Domestic Disturbances." *Law and Society Review.* Vol. 15, No. 2:317-346.

Berlin, I. 1981. *Russian Thinkers.* London: Hogarth Press.

Bertell, R. 1985. *No Immediate Danger: Prognosis for a Radioactive Earth..* Toronto: Women's Press.

Biderman, A. 1967. "Surveys of Population Samples for Estimating Crime Incidents." *Annals of the American Academy of Political and Social Science.* No. 374 (November):16-33.

Binder, Arnold and James W. Meeker. 1988. "Experiments as Reforms." *Journal of Criminal Justice*. Vol. 16:347-358.

Black, D. 1976. *The Behavior of Law*. New York: Academic Press.

Blau, Peter M. 1964. *Exchange and Power in Social Life*. New York: John Wiley and Sons.

Boateng, P. 1982. *Foreword Policing London: The Policing Aspects of Lord Scarman's Report on The Brixton Disorders*. London: Greater London Council (March 9).

Bogue, R. 1989. *Deleuze and Guattari*. New York: Routledge.

Borch-Jacobsen, M. 1991. *Lacan: The Absolute Master*. Stanford, California: Stanford University Press.

Borch-Jacobsen, M. 1988. "What is Called Subject? A Note on Lacan's 'Linguistery.'" Paper presented to the Annual Congress of the Society for Phenomenology and Existential Philosophy, Northwestern University, Chicago, October.

Bottomley, K. 1988. "Review Article: Victims of Crime." *International Journal of Sociology and Social Policy*. Vol. 8, No. 5:51-54.

Bottoms, Anthony E. 1983. "Neglected Features of Contemporary Penal Systems." Pp166-202 in Garland and Young (eds.), *The Power to Punish: Contemporary Penality and Social Analysis*. London: Heinemann Educational Books.

Bourdieu, P. 1987. "The Force of Law: Toward a Sociology of the Juridical Field." *The Hastings Law Journal* . Vol 38: 814-853.

Bowles, S. and H. Gintis. 1976. *Democracy and Capitalism*. New York: Basic Books.

Bowles, S. and H. Gintis. 1976. *Schooling in Capitalist Society*. New York: Basic Books.

Bowman, Myrna. 1981. "From Bad to Worse in One Easy Step: Proposed Transfer of Divorce Jurisdiction: An Assessment." Pp77-93 in Audrey Doerr and Micheline Carrier (eds.), *Women and the Constitution*. Ottawa: Canadian Advisory Council on the Status of Women.

Box, S. 1987. *Recession, Crime and Punishment*. London: Macmillan.

Boyd, Susan and Elizabeth Sheehy. 1989. "Feminism and the Law in Canada." Pp255-292 in Caputo, Kennedy, Reasons and Brannigan (eds.), *Law and Society: A Critical Perspective*. Toronto: Harcourt Brace Jovanovich.

Boyle, Christine. 1984. "Home Rule for Women: A Contribution to the Feminist Analysis of Representation." *Socialist Studies*. Vol. 2:131-148.

Braverman, Harry. 1974. *Labor and Monopoly Capital*. New York: Monthly Review Press.

Briggs, J. and F. D. Peat. 1989. *Turbulent Mirror*. New York: Harper and Row.

British Columbia Gaming Commission. 1988. *Report on the Status of Gaming in British Columbia*. Victoria. January 1.

British Columbia Legislative Assembly. 1929-34. *Finance Department, Budget Address*. Victoria: King's Printer.

Broadfoot, B. 1973. *Ten Lost Years: Memories of Canadians Who Survived the Depression*. Toronto: Doubleday Books.

Brogden, M. 1990. "Law and Criminal Labels: The Case of the French Metis." *The Journal of Human Justice*. Vol. 1, No. 2:13-32.

Brophy, J. and C. Smart (eds.). 1985. *Women in Law: Explorations in Law, Family, and Sexuality*. London: Routledge and Kegan Paul.

Brown, Caroline and Lorne Brown. 1978. *An Unauthorized History of the RCMP*. Toronto: James Lorimer.

Brown, D. and R. Hogg. 1992. "Law and Order Politics, Left Realism and Radical Criminology: A View from Down Under." In R. Matthews and J. Young (eds.) *Issues in Realist Criminology*. London: Sage.

Brown, Lorne. 1987. *When Freedom Was Lost*. Montreal: Black Rose Books.

Brown, Lorne. 1978. "Unemployment Relief Camps in Saskatchewan 1933-36." Pp190-218 in W.K. Greenaway and S.L. Brickey (eds.), *Law and Social Control in Canada*. Scarborough, Ontario: Prentice Hall.

Brown, R. 1977. *A Poetic For Sociology.* Cambridge: Cambridge University Press.

Brown, S. E. 1984. "Police Responses to Wife Beating: Neglect of a Crime of Violence." *Journal of Criminal Justice* . Vol. 12, No. 3:277-288.

Brownmiller, Susan. 1975. *Against Our Will: Men, Women, and Rape.* New York: Simon and Schuster.

Bruce, M. 1966. *The Coming of the Welfare State.* New York: Schocken Books.

Buck, P. 1977. "Seventeenth Century Political Arithmetic: Civil Strife and Vital Statistics." *Isis.* Vol 68:67-84.

Buhay, Beckie. 1932. "Political Arrests Since January, 1931." *Canadian Labour Defender.* August.

Bundred, S. 1982. "Accountability and the Metropolitan Police: A Suitable Case for Treatment." Pp58-81 in D. Cowell, T. Jones and J. Young (eds.), *Policing The Riots.* London: Junction Books.

Burris, C. A. and P. Jaffe. 1983. "Wife Abuse as a Crime: The Impact of Police Laying Charges." *Canadian Journal of Criminology.* Vol. 25, No. 3:309-328.

Burstyn, Varda. 1985. "Masculine Dominance and the State." Pp45-89 in Varda Burstyn, Dorothy Smith and Roxanna Ng (eds.), *Women, Class, Family and the State..* Toronto: Garamond Press.

Burstyn, Varda (ed.). 1985. *Women Against Censorship.* Vancouver: Douglas and McIntyre.

Burt, Sandra. 1988. "Legislators, Women and Public Policy." Pp129-155 in Sandra Burt, Lorraine Code and Lindsay Dorney (eds.), *Changing Patterns: Women in Canada.* Toronto: McClelland and Stewart.

Burton, F. and P. Carlen. 1979. *Official Discourse.* London: Routledge and Kegan Paul.

Buzawa, E. S. 1982. "Police Officer Response to Domestic Violence Legislation in Michigan." *Journal of Police Science and Administration.* Vol. 10, No. 4:415-424.

Cain, Maureen. 1983. "Gramsci, the State, and the Place of Law." In D. Sugarman (ed.), *Legality, Ideology, and the State.* London: Academic Press.

Cairns, Alan. 1988. "Citizens (Outsiders) and Governments (Insiders) Constitution-Making: The Case of Meech Lake." *Canadian Public Policy.* Vol. 14, Supp: S121-S145.

Calgary Police Service. 1985. "Report on Casino Gambling." Unpublished report. March.

Callwood, June. 1984. *Emma.* Toronto: Stoddart Publishing.

Campbell, C. S. 1981. "Parasites and Paradoxes: Legalized Casino Gaming in Alberta, Canada." In William R. Eadington (ed.), *The Gambling Papers.* Proceedings of the Fifth International Conference on Gambling and Risk Taking, University of Nevada, Reno.

Campbell, C. S. and J. Rick Ponting. 1984. "The Evolution of Casino Policy in Alberta." *Canadian Public Policy.* Vol. 10, No. 2:142-155.

Campbell, T. 1977/78. "Abortion Law in Canada: A Need for Reform." *Saskatchewan Law Review.* Vol 42:221-250.

Canada, Department of Labour. 1936. *Unemployment and Relief in Canada.* Ottawa: King's Printer.

Canada, Department of National Defence. 1932-37. *Annual Report.* Ottawa: King's Printer.

Canada, House of Commons. 1930-38. *Official Report of Debates.* Ottawa: King's Printer.

Canada, Ministry of the Solicitor General. 1975. *Young Persons In Conflict With The Law.* Ottawa.

Canada, Ministry of the Solicitor General. 1984. *Legalized Gambling: An Overview.* Research Report 1984-13, Ottawa.

Canada, Ministry of the Solicitor General, Research and Statistics Group, Programs Branch. 1984. *The Canadian Urban Victimization Survey, Bulletin 2: Reported and Unreported Crimes.* Ottawa: Minister of Supply and Services.

Canada, Ministry of the Solicitor General (Programs Branch). 1985. *Canadian Urban Victimization Survey, Bulletin 5: Cost of Crime to Victims.* Ottawa: Minister of Supply and Services.

Canada, Ministry of the Solicitor General, Programs Branch. 1985. *Canadian Urban Victimization Survey, Bulletin 4: Female Victims of Crime.* Ottawa: Minister of Supply and Services.

Canadian Bar Association Committee Report. 1985. *The Appointment of Judges In Canada.* Ottawa: Canadian Bar Foundation.

Capra, F. 1982. *The Turning Point.* New York: Simon and Schuster.

Caputo, Richard K. and Conrad M. Kozak. 1986. "Police Response to Domestic Violence: Two Urban Police Districts. Part II."

Caputo T.C. 1987. "The Young Offenders Act: Childrens' Rights, Childrens' Wrongs." *Canadian Public Policy - Analyse de Politiques.* Vol. 13:125-143.

Carlo, A. 1975. "Review of C.P. Kindelberger's The World in Depression." *Telos.* Vol. 24 (Summer):173-176.

Carriere, K. and R.V. Ericson. 1989. *Crime Stoppers.* Toronto: Centre For Criminology, University of Toronto.

Cassidy, H.M. 1939. "Relief and Other Social Services for Transients." Pp172-221 in L. Richter (ed.), *Canada's Unemployment Problem.* Studies of Institute of Public Affairs at Dalhousie University, Halifax: Macmillan.

Catlin, G. and S. Murray. 1979. *Report of Canadian Victimization Survey Methodological Pretests.* Ottawa: Statistics Canada.

Chadwick, E. 1825. "First Report from the Select Committee of the House of Commons on the Laws Respecting Friendly Societies." *Westminister Review.* July:384-421.

Chalmers, Lee and Pamela Smith. 1988. "Wife Battering: Psychological, Social and Physical Isolation and Counteracting Strategies." Pp221-244 in A. Tigar McLaren (ed.), *Gender and Society: Creating a Canadian Women's Sociology.* Toronto: Copp Clark Pitman.

Chesney-Lind, M. 1985/86. "Sexist Juvenile Justice: A Continuing International Problem." *Resources for Feminist Research.* Vol. 13:7-9.

Chesney-Lind, M. 1974. "Juvenile Delinquency: The Sexualization of Female Crime." *Psychology Today.* July:43-46.

Christian, L. 1983. *Policing By Coercion.* London: GLC Police Committee Support Unit.

Christiansen, E.M. 1985. "Illegal Gambling." In V. Abt, J.F. Smith and E.M. Christiansen (eds.), *The Business of Risk.* Lawrence: University of Kansas Press.

Cixous, H. 1981. "Castration or Decapitation?" *Signs.* Vol. 7, No. 1:41-55.

Clark, Lorenne and Debra Lewis. 1977. *Rape: The Price of Coercive Sexuality.* Toronto: Women's Press.

Clarke, Dean H. 1978. "Marxism, Justice and the Justice Model." *Contemporary Crises.* Vol. 2, No. 1:27-62.

Clarke, John. 1985. "Whose Justice? The Politics of Juvenile Control." *International Journal of the Sociology of Law.* Vol. 13:407-421.

Clement, C. 1983. *The Lives and Legends of Jacques Lacan.* New York: Columbia University Press.

Cohen, Stan. 1972 (reprinted 1987). *Folk Devils and Moral Panics: The Creation of Mods and Rockers.* London: MacGibbon and Kee.

Cohen, Stan. 1983. "Social Control Talk: Telling Stories about Correctional Change." Pp101-129 in Garland and Young (eds.), *The Power to Punish: Contemporary Penality and Social Analysis.* London: Heinemann Educational Press.

Cohen, Stan. 1983/1985. *Visions of Social Control..* Cambridge: Polity Press.

Cohen, Stan. 1987. "Taking Decentralization Seriously." Pp358-379 in Lowman, R.J. Menzies and T.S. Palys (eds.), *Transcarceration: Essays in the Sociology of Social Control.* Aldershot: Gower.

Cohen, Stan. 1989. "The Critical Discourse on 'Social Control': Notes on the Concept as Hammer." *International Journal of Sociology of Law*. Vol. 17, No. 3:347-357.

Collins, Anne. 1985. *The Big Evasion: Abortion, The Issue That Won't Go Away*. Toronto: Lester and Orpen Dennys.

Collins, L. D. 1982. "The Politics of Abortion: Trends in Canadian Fertility Policy." *Atlantis*. Vol. 7, No. 2 (Spring):2-20.

Collins, R. 1971. "Functional and Conflict Theories of Educational Stratification." *American Sociological Review*. Vol. 36:1002-1019.

Comack, Elizabeth. 1990. "Law-and-Order Issues in the Canadian Context: The Case of Capital Punishment." *Social Justice*. Vol. 17, No. 1:70-97.

Comack, Elizabeth. 1987a. "Theorizing the Canadian State and Social Formation." Pp225-240 in Ratner, R.S. and J. McMullan (eds.), *State Control: Criminal Justice Policies in Canada*. Vancouver: U.B.C. Press.

Comack, Elizabeth. 1987b. "Women Defendants and the 'Battered Wife Syndrome': A Plea for the Sociological Imagination." *Crown Counsel's Review*. Vol. 5, No. 11 (December):6-10.

Conway, J. F. 1983. *The West: The History of a Region in Confederation*. Toronto: James Lorimer and Company.

Coombe, Rosemary. 1989a. "Room for Manoeuver: Towards a Theory of Practice in Critical Legal Studies." *Law and Social Inquiry*. Vol. 14 (1): 69-121.

Coombe, Rosemary. 1989b. "Same As It Ever Was: Rethinking the Politics of Interpretation." *McGill Law Journal*. Vol 34 (3):604-652.

Coordinated Law Enforcement Unit (CLEU). 1979. *Third Findings Report on Organized Crime in British Columbia*. Victoria: Ministry of Attorney General.

Coordinated Law Enforcement Unit (CLEU). 1974. *Initial Findings Report on Organized Crime in British Columbia*. Victoria: Ministry of Attorney General.

Cornell Law Project. 1977. *Development of the Law of Gambling: 1776-1976*. Washington, D.C.: National Institute of Law Enforcement and Criminal Justice.

Corrado, Raymond R. 1983. "Introduction." Pp1-27 in Corrado, Trepanier and LeBlanc (eds.), *Current Issues in Juvenile Justice*. Toronto: Butterworths.

Cousin, G., B. Fine and R. Millar. 1985. "The Politics of Policing." Pp 227-236 in B. Fine and R. Millar (eds.), *Policing The Miners' Strike*. London: Lawrence and Wishart.

Cowell, D., T. Jones and J. Young. 1982. *Policing The Riots*. London: Junction.

Critchley, T.A. 1978. *A History of Police in England and Wales*. London: Constable.

Cross, Arthur Lyon. 1928. *Eighteenth Century Documents Relating to the Royal Forests, the Sheriffs and Smuggling*. New York: The Macmillan Company.

Cullen, F.T. and Gilbert, K. E. 1982. *Re-affirming Rehabilitation*. Cincinatti, Ohio: Anderson.

Currie, Dawn H. 1992. "Representation and Resistance: Feminist Struggles Against Pornography." Pp191-208 in D. H. Currie and V. Raoul (eds.), *The Anatomy of Gender: Women's Struggle for the Body*. Ottawa: Carleton University Press.

Currie, Dawn H. 1990. "Battered Women and the State: From a Failure of Theory to a Theory of Failure." *The Journal of Human Justice*. Vol. 1, No. 2:77-96.

Currie, Dawn H. 1989. "State Intervention and the 'Liberation' of Women: A Feminist Exploration of Family Law." Pp271-292 in T. C. Caputo, M. Kennedy, C. E. Reasons and A. Brannigan (eds.), *Law and Society: Critical Perspectives*. Toronto: Harcourt Brace Jovanovich.

Currie, Dawn H. 1988. "Reproductive Decision-making and Choice About Motherhood: A Case Study of Deferred Motherhood." Unpublished Ph.D. dissertation, London School of Economics.

Currie, Dawn H. 1986. "Female Criminality: A Crisis in Feminist Theory." Pp232-246 in B.D. MacLean (ed.), *The Political Economy of Crime: Readings for a Critical Criminology*. Toronto: Prentice-Hall.

Currie, Dawn H., Walter DeKeseredy and Brian D. MacLean. 1990. "Reconstituting Social Order and Social Control: Police Accountability in Canada." *The Journal of Human Justice.* Vol. 2, No. 1(Autumn):29-54.

Currie, Dawn H. and Marlee Kline. 1991. "Challenging Privilege: Women, Knowledge and Feminist Struggles." *The Journal of Human Justice.* Vol. 2, No. 2:1-36.

Currie, E., 1985. *Confronting Crime.* New York: Pantheon Books.

Currie, E., 1990. "Crime and Market Society." Paper presented to the conference on Crime and Policing, Islington, London.

Dalton, Clare. 1985. "An Essay in the Deconstruction of Contract Doctrine." *Yale Law Journal.* Vol 94, No. 5:997-1116.

Daly, K. and M. Chesney-Lind. 1988. "Feminism and Criminology." *Justice Quarterly.* Vol. 5:101-143.

DeKeseredy, Walter. 1989. "Woman Abuse in Dating Relationships: An Exploratory Study." *Atlantis.* Vol. 14:55-62.

DeKeseredy, Walter and Ronald Hinch. 1991. *Woman Abuse: Sociological Perspectives.* Toronto: Thompson Educational Publishing, Inc.

DeKeseredy, Walter and Brian D. MacLean. 1991. "Exploring the Gender, Race and Class Dimensions of Victimization: A Left Realist Critique of the Canadian Urban Victimization Survey." *International Journal of Offender Therapy and Comparative Criminology.* Vol. 35, No. 2:143-161.

DeKeseredy, Walter and Brian D. MacLean. 1990. "Researching Woman Abuse in Canada: A Realist Critique of the Conflict Tactics Scale." *Canadian Review of Social Policy.* Issue No. 25:19-27.

DeKeseredy, W.S. and M. D. Schwartz, 1992. "British and U.S. Left Realism: A Critical Comparison." *International Journal of Offender Therapy and Comparative Criminology,* 35 (3): 248-262.

Deleuze, G. and F. Guattari. 1987. *A Thousand Plateaus.* Minneapolis: University of Minnesota Press.

Deleuze, G. and F. Guattari. 1986. *Kafka: Toward a Minor Literature.* Minneapolis: University of Minnesota Press.

De Michel, P. 1983. "The Subjected Body: An Analysis of the Occupational Health and Safety Apparatus in New South Wales." *Australian Journal of Law and Society.* Vol. 41(2):5-44.

Devereux, G. 1976. *A Study of Abortion in Primitive Societies.* New York: International Universities Press.

Dickens, B. M. 1981. "Legal Aspects of Abortion." Pp16-29 in Sachdev (ed.), *Abortion: Readings and Research.* Toronto: Butterworths.

Dickens, B. M. 1976. "The Morgentaler Case: Criminal Process and Abortion Law." *Osgoode Hall Law Journal.* Vol. 14, No. 2 (October):229-274.

Dickson, P. 1967. *The Financial Revolution in England.* London: Macmillan.

Dion, Robert. 1982. *Crimes of the Secret Police.* Montreal: Black Rose Books.

Dobash, R. E. and R. Dobash. 1979. *Violence Against Wives.* New York: The Free Press.

Dodge, R. 1977. "Analysis of Screen Questions on The National Crime Survey." Washington, D.C.: Crime Statistics Analysis Staff, U.S. Census Bureau Memorandum. December 22.

Doerr, Audrey. 1981. "Overlapping Jurisdictions and Women's Issues." Pp123-148 in Audrey Doerr and Micheline Carrier (eds.), *Women and the Constitution.* Ottawa: Canadian Advisory Council on the Status of Women.

Dolon, R., J. Hendricks and M. S. Meagher. 1986. "Police Practices and Attitudes Toward Domestic Violence." *Journal of Police Science and Administration.* Vol. 14, No. 3:187-192.

Domagalski, Marilyn. 1986. "The Role of Canadian Women in Federal and Provincial Politics." Pp39-43 in Robert Fleming (ed.), *Canadian Legislatures: The 1986 Comparative Study.* Queen's Park, Toronto: Office of the Assembly.

Dombrink, J. D. 1981. "Outlaw Businessmen: Organized Crime and the Regulation of Casino Gambling." Unpublished Ph.D. dissertation, University of California, Berkeley.

Dominion-Provincial Conference. 1935. *Memoranda on Unemployment and Relief*. Ottawa: King's Printer.

Donovan, Josephine. 1986. *Feminist Theory: The Intellectual Traditions of American Feminism*. New York: Ungar.

Donzelot, Jacques. 1979. *The Policing of Families*. New York: Pantheon Books.

Dreyfus, H. and Rainbow, P. 1983. *Michel Foucault: Beyond Structuralism and Hermeneutics*. 2nd Edition. Chicago: University of Chicago Press.

Dunhill, Christina (ed.). 1989. "The Boys in Blue." Pp102-122 in C. Dunhill (ed.), *The Boys in Blue: Women's Challenge to the Police*. London: Virago.

Dutton, D. and L. Kennedy. 1987. "The Incidence of Wife Abuse in Alberta." In *Edmonton Area Series Report No.53*. University of Alberta, Edmonton: Population Research Laboratory.

Dworkin, Ronald. 1984. "Liberalism." In Michael Sandell (ed.), *Liberalism and Its Critics*. Oxford: Basil Blackwell.

Eayrs, J. 1964. *In Defence of Canada: From the Great War to the Great Depression*. Toronto: University of Toronto Press.

Edie, J. 1972. "Husserl's Conception of 'The Grammatical' and Contemporary Linguistics." In Lester Embrie (ed.), *Life-World and Consciousness*. Evanston, Illinois: Northwestern University Press.

Eichler, Margrit. 1987. "The Relationship Between Sexist, Nonsexist, Woman-Centred and Feminist Research." Pp 31-61 in A. Tigar McLaren (ed.), *Gender and Society: Creating a Canadian Women's Sociology*. Toronto: Copp Clark Pitman Ltd.

Eisenstein, S. 1975. *The Film Sense*. New York: Harcourt Brace Jovanovic.

Eisenstein, Zillah R. 1988. *The Female Body and the Law*. Berkeley: University of California Press.

Eisenstein, Z. 1984. *Feminism and Sexual Equality: The Crisis in Liberal America*. New York: Monthly Review Press.

Empey, Lamar T. 1982. *American Delinquency: Its Meaning and Construction*. Homewood, Illinois: The Dorsey Press.

Endicott, Stephen. 1980. *James G. Endicott: Rebel Out of China*. Toronto: University of Toronto Press.

Ennis, P. 1967. *Criminal Victimization in the United States: A Report of a National Survey, President's Commission on Law Enforcement and the Administration of Justice*. Field Studies II. Washington, D.C.: USGPO.

Erickson, E. A. 1972. "The Great Crash of October 1929." Pp3-12 in H. van der Wee (ed.), *The Great Depression Revisited: Essays on the Economics of the Thirties*. The Hague: Martinus Nijhoff.

Ericson, R.V. 1981. *Making Crime: A Study of Detective Work*. Toronto: Butterworths.

Ericson, R.V. 1982/84. *Reproducing Order: A Study of Police Patrol Work*. Toronto: University of Toronto Press.

Ericson, R.V. 1987. "Reforming the Police and Policing Reform." Pp38-68 in R.S. Ratner and J. McMullan (eds.), *State Control: Criminal Justice Politics in Canada*. Vancouver: U.B.C. Press.

Ericson, R.V. and P. M. Baranek. 1982. *The Ordering of Justice: A Study of Accused Persons as Dependents in the Criminal Process*. Toronto: University of Toronto Press.

Ericson, R.V., P. M. Baranek and J. Chan. 1987. *Visualizing Deviance*. Toronto: University of Toronto Press.

Errington, Gene B. 1977. *Family Violence — Is It a Woman's Problem?* Address to the Symposium on Family Violence, Vancouver, British Columbia (March 1977). Vancouver: Women's Research Centre.

Evans, J. and G. Leger. 1979. "Canadian Victimization Surveys." *Canadian Journal of Criminology*. Vol. 21, No. 2 :166-183.

Faith, Karlene. 1989. "Justice, Where Art Thou? And Do we Care?" *The Journal of Human Justice*. Vol. 1, No. 1:77-98.

Farmer, Lindsay. 1987. "The Politics of Legal Signification: Press Coverage of Urban Disorder in 1985." *Liverpool Law Review*. Vol 9, No. 1:3-22.

Fearon, P. 1979. *The Origins and Nature of the Great Slump of 1939-1932: The Economic History of Society*. London: Macmillan Press.

Ferrajoli, L., 1989. *Diritto e Ragione*. Bari, Italy: Laterza.

Ferraro, Kathleen J. 1989. "Legal Responses to Woman Battering in the United States." Pp155-184 in Hanmer, Radford and Stanko (eds.), *Women, Policing, and Male Violence: International Perspectives*. London: Routledge.

Fidler, R. 1973. *RCMP: The Real Subversives*. Toronto: Vanguard.

Fine, B. 1986. "Young Marx's Critique of Law and the State: The Limits of Liberalism." Pp42-55 in B. D. MacLean (ed.), *The Political Economy of Crime: Readings for a Critical Criminology*. Scarborough, Ontario: Prentice-Hall.

Fine, B. 1984. *Democracy and the Rule of Law*. London: Pluto Press.

Finley, Lucinda M. 1989. "Breaking Women's Silence in Law: The Dilemma of the Gendered Nature of Legal Reasoning." *Notre Dame Law Review*. Vol 64, No. 5:886-910.

Fitzpatrick, F. J. E. 1921. *Sergeant 331*. New York, published by the author.

Fleming, T. 1983. "Criminalizing a Marginal Community: The Bawdy House Raids." Pp37-60 in T. Fleming and L. Visano (eds.), *Deviant Designations: Crime, Law and Deviance in Canada*. Toronto: Butterworths.

Fleming, T. 1981. "The Bawdy House Boys: Some Notes on Media, Sporadic Moral Crusades and Selective Law Enforcement." *Canadian Criminology Forum*. Vol. 3, No. 2.

Foucault, M. 1984. "The Juridical Apparatus." Pp201-221 in W. Connolly (ed.), *Legitimacy and the State*. New York: New York University Press.

Foucault, M. 1980. *History of Sexuality (Volume 1)*. New York: Vintage.

Foucault, M. 1977. *Discipline and Punish. The Birth of the Prison*. Harmondsworth, Middlesex: Peregrine Books.

Foucault, M. 1972. *The Archeology of Knowledge*. New York: Pantheon.

Foucault, M. 1970. *The Order of Things*. London: Tavistock.

Fox, Bonnie J. 1988. "Conceptualizing 'Patriarchy.'" *Canadian Review of Sociology and Anthropology*. Vol. 25, No. 2:163-182.

Francome. C. 1984. *Abortion Freedom: A Worldwide Movement*. London: George Allen and Unwin.

Frankel, B. 1982. "On the State of the State: Marxist Theories of the State after Leninism." Pp257-273 in A. Giddens and D. Held (eds.), *Classes, Power and Conflict: Classical and Contemporary Debates*. Berkeley: University of California Press.

Freeman, Alan. 1982. "Antidiscrimination Law: A Critical Review." Pp96-116 in David Kairys (ed.), *The Politics of Law: A Progressive Critique*. New York: Pantheon Books.

Freire, P. 1985. *The Politics of Education*. South Hadley, Massachusetts: Bergin and Garvey.

Freud, S. 1914. *The Psychopathology of Everyday Life*. New York: Macmillan.

Freud, S. 1965. *The Interpretation of Dreams*. New York: Avon Books.

Friedrichs, D. 1989. "Narrative Jurisprudence and Other Heresies: Legal Education at the Margin." *Legal Studies Forum*.

Friedrichs, D. 1980. "The Legitimacy Crises in the United States: A Conceptual Analysis." *Social Problems*. Vol. 27:540-554.

Friel, C. M. and J. B. Vaughn. 1987. "A Consumer's Guide to the Electronic Monitoring of Probationers." *Federal Probation*. Vol. 50, No. 3:3-14.

Gabel, P. and J. Feinman. 1982. "Contract Law as Ideology." Pp172-184 in D. Kairys (ed.), *The Politics of Law: A Progressive Critique.* New York: Pantheon Books.

Gallop, J. 1982. *The Daughter's Seduction: Feminism and Psychoanalysis.* Ithaca, New York: Cornell University Press.

Garland, David and Peter Young. 1983. *The Power to Punish.* London: Heinemann Educational Books.

Gavigan, Shelley. 1988. "Law, Gender, and Ideology." Pp283-295 in A. F. Bayefsky (ed.), *Legal Theory Meets Legal Practice.* Edmonton: Academic Printing and Publishing.

Gavigan, S. 1986. "Women and Abortion in Canada: What's Law Got to do With It ?" Pp263-284 in H.J. Maroney and M. Luxton (eds.), *Feminism and Political Economy: Women's Work, Women's Struggles.* Toronto: Methuen.

Geller, G. 1987. "Feminism and Criminal 'Justice': An Uneasy Partnership." *Resources for Feminist Research.* 17 (3):100-102.

Geller, G. 1987. "Young Women in Conflict With the Law." Pp113-126 in E. Adelberg and C. Currie (eds.), *Too Few to Count: Canadian Women in Conflict with the Law.* Vancouver: Press Gang.

Gelsthorpe, L. and A. Morris. 1988. "Feminism and Criminology in Britain." Pp93-110 in P. Rock (ed.), *A History of British Criminology.* Oxford: Clarendon Press.

Gilder, G. 1981. *Wealth and Poverty.* New York: Bantam Books.

Gilman, R. 1988. "The War of All Against All: The Political Role of Parent Metaphors in Philosophical Reading and Writing." Unpublished manuscript.

Giroux, H. 1988. *Schooling and the Struggle for Public Life.* Minneapolis: University of Minnesota Press.

Glasbeek, Harry and Michael Mandel. 1984. "The Legalization of Politics in Advanced Capitalism: The Canadian Charter of Rights and Freedoms." *Socialist Studies/ Etudes Socialistes.* Vol 2.

Goff, C. and C. E. Reasons. 1986. "Organizational Crimes Against Employees, Consumers, and the Public." Pp204-231 in B. D. MacLean (ed.), *The Political Economy of Crime: Readings for a Critical Criminology.* Toronto: Prentice-Hall.

Goff, C. and C. E. Reasons. 1978. *Corporate Crime in Canada: A Critical Analysis of Anti-Combines Legislation.* Toronto: Prentice-Hall.

Goffman, E. 1967. *Interaction Ritual.* New York: Anchor Books.

Gold, D.A., C. Y. H. Lo and E. O. Wright. 1975. "Recent Developments in Marxist Theories of the Capitalist State." Part Two, *Monthly Review.* November: 36-51.

Goode, William. 1971. "Force and Violence in the Family." *Journal of Marriage and the Family.* Vol. 33, No. 4:624-636.

Goodrich, Peter. 1987. *Legal Discourse.* Houndmills, Hampshire: The Macmillan Press.

Goodrich, Peter. 1986. *Reading the Law: A Critical Introduction to Legal Method and Techniques.* Oxford: Blackwell.

Goodrich, Peter. 1984. "Rhetoric as Jurisprudence: An Introduction to the Politics of Legal Language." *Oxford Journal of Legal Studies.* Vol 4:88-122.

Goolkasian, G. A. 1986. *Confronting Domestic Violence: A Guide for Criminal Justice Agencies.* Washington, D.C.: U. S. Government Printing Office.

Gorman, L. and J. McMullan. 1987. "In Defence of the Law of the Land: Social Control and the Unemployed Movement in the Dirty Thirties in British Columbia." *Canadian Criminology Forum.* Vol 8:84-102.

Gosden, P. 1973. *Self-Help.* London: B.T. Batsford.

Gough, I. 1979. *The Political Economy of the Welfare State.* London: The Macmillan Press.

Gramsci, A. 1971. *Selections from the Prison Notebooks of Antonio Gramsci.* Translated and edited by Q. Hoare and G. Nowell Smith. New York: International Publishers.

Green, Eileen, Sandra Hebron and Diana Woodward. 1987. "Women, Leisure and Social Control." Pp75-92 in Jalna Hanmer and Mary Maynard (eds.), *Women, Violence and Social Control.* London: Macmillan Press.

Green, Jim. 1986. *Against the Tide: The Story of the Canadian Seamen's Union.* Toronto: Progress Publishers.

Greenberg, David F. 1983. "Reflections on the Justice Model Debate." *Contemporary Crises.* Vol. 7:313-327.

Greenwood, M. 1948. *Some British Pioneers of Social Medicine.* New York: Books For Libraries Press.

Greenwood, V. and J. Young. 1976. *Abortion in Demand.* London: Pluto Press.

Gregory, J. 1986. "Sex, Class, and Crime: Towards a Non-Sexist Criminology." Pp317-335 in B. D. MacLean (ed.), *The Political Economy of Crime: Readings for a Critical Criminology.* Toronto: Prentice-Hall.

Greschner, Donna. 1991a. "A Checklist of Current Constitutional Processes." *New Breed.* March:21-34.

Greschner, Donna. 1991b. "Coming to Consensus: Behind the Scenes with Elijah Harper." *NeWest Review.* December/January:17-20.

Greschner, Donna. 1986. "Can Constitutions Be For Women Too?" Pp21-34 in D. H. Currie and B. D. MacLean (eds.), *The Administration of Justice.* Saskatoon: Social Research Unit.

Gross, B. 1980. *Friendly Fascism: The New Face of Power in America.* New York: M. Evans and Co. Inc.

Grosz, E. 1990. *Jacques Lacan: A Feminist Introduction.* New York: Routledge.

Gumbert, Marc. 1984. *Neither Justice Nor Reason.* St Lucia: University of Queensland Press.

Gunn, Rita and Candice Minch. 1988. *Sexual Assault: The Dilemma of Disclosure, The Question of Conviction.* Winnipeg: University of Manitoba Press.

Gusfield, J. 1963. *Symbolic Crusades.* Urbana: University of Illinois Press.

Gutzmore, C. 1983. "Capital, 'Black Youth' and Crime." *Race and Class.* Vol. 25, No. 2:13-30.

Habermas, J. 1987. *The Theory of Communicative Action. Vol. Two. Lifeworld and System: A Critique of Functionalist Reason.* Trans. T. McCarthy. Boston: Beacon Press.

Habermas, J. 1984. *The Theory of Communicative Action. Vol. One. Reason and the Rationalization of Society.* Trans. T. McCarthy Boston: Beacon Press.

Habermas, J. 1975. *Legitimation Crises.* Boston: Beacon Press.

Hacking, I. 1975. *The Emergence of Probability.* Cambridge: Cambridge University Press.

Haig, G. T. 1979. *Manitoba Lotteries Review Committee Final Report.* Province of Manitoba. January.

Hall, R. 1985. *Ask Any Woman: A London Inquiry into Rape and Sexual Assault.* London: Fallingwall Press.

Hall, Stuart (ed.). 1982. *Managing Conflict, Producing Consent.* Unit 21. Milton Keynes: Open University Press.

Hall, Stuart. 1979. "The Great Moving Right Show." In S. Hall and M. Jacques (eds.). *The Politics of Thatcherism.* London: Lawrence and Wishart.

Hall, S., C. Critcher, T. Jefferson, J. Clarke and B. Roberts. 1978. *Policing the Crisis: Mugging, the State, and Law and Order.* London: Macmillan.

Halley, E. 1963. "Degrees of Mortality of Mankind." *Philosophical Transactions of the Royal Society of London.* Vol. XVII, No. 198: 654-656.

Hanmer, Jalna, Jill Radford and Elizabeth A. Stanko (eds.). 1989. *Women, Policing, and Male Violence: International Perspectives.* London: Routledge.

Hanmer, Jalna (1989). "Women and Policing in Britain." Pp90-124 in Hanmer, Radford and Stanko (eds.). *Women, Policing, and Male Violence: International Perspectives.* London: Routledge.

Harding, J. 1988. *Aboriginal Rights and Government Wrongs: Uranium Mining and Neo-Colonialism in Northern Saskatchewan*. The Public Interest Series, Prairie Justice Research, University of Regina, Working Paper No 1.

Harding, J. 1986. "A Content Analysis of Attitudes Towards Uranium Mining Expressed in the Local Hearings of the CLBI." *Impact Assessment Bulletin*. Vol. 4, Nos. 1-2: 189-209.

Harding, J. et al. 1987. *Ten Years After: Findings From Follow-up Study of Participants in the Uranium Inquiries*. Report to SSHRC (Human Context of Science and Technology), Prairie Justice Research, University of Regina.

Harris, R. and David Webb. 1987. *Welfare Power and Juvenile Justice*. London. Tavistock Publications.

Hatch, Alison and Karlene Faith. 1989/90. "The Female Offender in Canada: A Statistical Profile." *Canadian Journal of Women and the Law*. Vol. 3, No. 2:432-456.

Hatty, Suzanne E. 1989. "Policing and Male Violence in Australia." Pp70-89 in Hanmer, Radford and Stanko (eds.), *Women, Policing, and Male Violence: International Perspectives*. London: Routledge.

Havemann, Paul. 1986a. "From Child Saving to Child Blaming: The Political Economy of the Young Offenders Act, 1908-1984." Pp225-242 in S. Brickey and E. Comack (eds.), *The Social Basis of Law*. Toronto: Garamond Press.

Havemann, Paul. 1986b. "Marketing the New Establishment Ideology in Canada." *Crime and Social Justice*. Vol. 26:11-37.

Havemann, Paul, Keith Couse, Lori Foster and Rae Matonovich. 1985. *Law and Order for Canada's Indigenous People*. Regina: Prairie Justice Research, University of Regina. March.

Hayles, K. 1990. *Chaos Bound*. New York: Cornell University Press.

Heath, S. 1981. *Questions of Cinema*. Bloomington, Indiana: Indiana University Press.

Heaven, Olga and Maria Mars. 1989. "Policing Irish Women in Britain." Pp219-231 in C. Dunhill (ed.), *The Boys in Blue: Women's Challenge to the Police*. London: Virago.

Heilbroner, R.L. 1980. *The Making of Economic Society*. Sixth Edition. Englewood Cliffs, New Jersey: Prentice-Hall.

Henry, F. 1986. "Crime — A Profitable Approach." Pp182-203 in B. D. MacLean (ed.), *The Political Economy of Crime: Readings for a Critical Criminology*. Toronto: Prentice-Hall.

Henry, S. and D. Milovanovic. 1991. "Constitutive Criminology." *Criminology*. Vol. 29, No. 2:293-315.

Herman, Didi. 1990. "Are We Family?: Lesbian Rights and Women's Liberation." *Osgoode Hall Law Journal*. Vol 28:789-815.

Hill, E.D. 1951. "The Regional Administration of Public Welfare in British Columbia: A Survey of the Present Administration in Light of its Historical Development." Unpublished M.S.W. thesis, School of Social Work, University of British Columbia.

Himes, N. 1936. *Medical History of Contraception*. London: George Allen and Unwin.

Hindell, K. and M. Simms. 1971. *Abortion Law Reformed*. London: Peter Owen.

Hirst, Paul. 1979. *On Law and Ideology*. London: Macmillan Ltd.

Hoar, V. 1973. *Recollections of the On-To-Ottawa Trek*. Toronto: McClelland and Stewart.

Home Office Research and Planning Unit. 1984. *Research Programme 1984/85*. London: HMSO.

Horkheimer, M. and T. Adorno. 1975. *Dialectic of Enlightenment*. New York: Continuum.

Horrall, S.W. 1972. "Sir John A. Macdonald and the Mounted Police Force for the Northwest Territories." *Canadian Historical Review*. Vol. LIII, No. 2 (June).

Horton, J. and L. Kennedy. 1985. "Coping with the Fear of Crime." Unpublished paper presented at Canadian Research Institute for the Advancement of Women annual conference, Saskatoon.

Hosek, Chaviva. 1983. "Women and Constitutional Process." Pp280-300 in Banting and Simeon (eds.), *And No One Cheered: Federalism, Democracy and the Constitution Act*. Toronto: Methuen.

Hough, M. and P. Mayhew. 1983. *The British Crime Survey*. London: HMSO.

Howard, V. 1974. "The Vancouver Relief Camp Strike of 1935: A Narrative of the Great Depression." *Canada: An Historical Magazine*. Vol. 1, No. 3. Toronto: Holt, Rinehart and Winston of Canada.

Howard, V. 1976. "The On to Ottawa Trek, Parts One and Two." *Canada: An Historical Magazine*. Vol. 3, Nos. 3 and 4. Toronto: Holt, Rinehart and Winston of Canada.

Hoy, David Couzens. 1985. "Interpreting The Law: Hermeneutical and Poststructuralist Perspectives." *Southern California Law Review*. No. 58.

Hudson, Barbara. 1987. *Justice through Punishment: A Critique of the 'Justice' Model of Corrections*. London: Macmillan Education.

Humphreys, J. C. and W. O. Humphreys. 1985. "Mandatory Arrest: A Means of Primary and Secondary Prevention of Abuse of Female Partners." *Victimology*. Vol. 10:267-280.

Hunt, Alan. 1990. "The Big Fear: Law Confronts Postmodernism." *McGill Law Journal*. Vol 35, No. 3:507-540.

Hunt, Alan. 1985. "The Ideology of Law: Advances and Problems in Recent Applications of the Concept of Ideology to the Analysis of Law." *Law and Society Review*. Vol 19 (1):11-37.

Hutchinson, Allan. 1989. "That's Just the Way It Is: Langille on Law." *McGill Law Journal*. Vol 34 (1): 145-159.

Hutchinson, Allan 1988. *Dwelling on The Threshold: Critical Essays on Modern Legal Thought*. Agincourt: Carswell.

Huzel, J.P. 1986. "The Incidence of Crime in Vancouver During the Great Depression." *B.C. Studies*. Nos. 69/70 (Spring/Summer):211-248.

Information Canada. 1970. *Royal Commission on the Status of Women*. Ottawa: Minister of Supply and Services.

International Association of Chiefs of Police (IACP). 1929. *Uniform Crime Reporting*. New York: I.A.C.P.

Irigaray, L. 1985. *Speculum of the Other Woman*. Ithaca: Cornell University Press.

Jackson, B. 1988. *Law, Fact and Narrative Coherence*. Merseyside, U. K.: Deborah Charles.

Jackson, B. 1985. *Semiotics and Legal Theory*. New York: Routledge and Kegan Paul.

Jaggar, A. 1983. *Feminist Politics and Human Nature*. Sussex: Harvester Press.

Jakobson, R. 1971. "Two Aspects of Language and Two Types of Aphasic Disorders." Pp55-82 in R. Jakobson and M. Halle (eds.), *Fundamentals of Language*. Paris: Mouton.

Jamieson, Stuart. 1968. *Times of Trouble: Labour Unrest and Industrial Conflict in Canada, 1900-66*. Task Force on Labour Relations Study No. 22. Ottawa: Information Canada.

Jankovic, I. 1980. "Labour Market and Imprisonment." Pp93-104 in A. Platt and P. Takagi (eds.), *Punishment and Penal Discipline: Essays on the Prison and the Prisoners' Movement*. San Francisco: Crime and Social Justice Associates.

Jessop, B. 1977. "Recent Theories of the Capitalist State." *Cambridge Journal of Economics*. Vol. 1:353-373.

Jewers, G.O. 1983. *The Private Operators in Lotteries Inquiry Final Report*. Province of Manitoba. June.

Johnson, J. 1980. "An Ex-Mountie in the Eye of Gambling Storm." *The Edmonton Sun*. January 7:15.

Jones, T., Brian D. MacLean and Jock Young. 1986. *The Islington Crime Survey: Crime, Victimization and Policing in Inner-City London*. London: Gower.

Kairys, David (ed.). 1982. *The Politics of Law: A Progressive Critique*. New York: Pantheon Books.

Kalish, C. n.d. *Crimes and Victims: A Report on The Dayton-San Jose Pilot Survey of Victimization*. Washington, D.C.: National Criminal Justice Information and Statistics Service, Printing Office.

Kaplan, William. 1987. *Everything That Floats: Pat Sullivan, Hal Banks and the Seamen's Union of Canada.* Toronto: University of Toronto Press.

Keane, J. 1978. "The Legacy of Political Economy: Thinking With and Against Clause Offe." *Canadian Journal of Political and Social Theory.* Vol. 2, No. 3 (Fall):49-92.

Kendal, G. H. 1980. *Facts.* Toronto: Butterworths.

Kelly, Liz. 1987. "The Continuum of Sexual Violence." Pp46-60 in Jalna Hanmer and Mary Maynard (eds.), *Women, Violence and Social Control.* London: Macmillan Press.

Kennedy, Duncan. 1987. "Toward a Critical Phenomenology of Judging." In A. Hutchinson and P. Monahan (eds.), *The Rule of Law: Ideal or Ideology?* Toronto: Carswell Co.

Kennedy, Duncan. 1982. "Legal Education as Training for Hierarchy." Pp40-61 in D. Kairys (ed.), *The Politics of Law: A Progressive Critique.* New York: Pantheon Books.

Kennedy, W. 1913 (reprinted 1964). *English Taxation 1640-1799.* New York: Augustus M. Kelley.

Kessler-Harris, Alice. 1987. "Equal Employment Opportunity Commission v Sears, Roebuck and Company: A Personal Account." *Feminist Review.* Vol 25:46-49.

Kettle, M. and L. Hodges. 1982. *Uprising: The Police, the People and the Riots in Britain's Cities.* London: Pan Books.

King, D. 1939. "Employment and Direct Relief." Pp59-110 in L. Richter (ed.), *Canada's Unemployment Problems.* Toronto: Macmillan.

Kinsey, R. and J. Young. 1982. "Police Autonomy and The Politics of Discretion." Pp118-134 in D. Cowell, T. Jones and J. Young (eds.), *Policing The Riots.* London: Junction Books.

Kinsey, R., J. Lea and J. Young. 1986. *Losing The Fight Against Crime.* Oxford: Basil Blackwell.

Kish, L. 1965. *Survey Sampling.* New York: Wiley.

Kitsuse, J. and A. Cicourel. 1963. "A Note on the Use of Official Statistics." *Social Problems.* No. 11:131-139.

Klare, K. 1982. "Critical Theory and Labour Relations Law." Pp65-88 in D. Kairys (ed.), *The Politics of Law: A Progressive Critique.* New York: Pantheon Books.

Knight, Rolf and Maya Koizumi. 1976. *A Man of Our Times.* Vancouver: New Star.

Kojeve, A. 1969/80. *Introduction to the Reading of Hegel.* Ithaca: Cornell University Press.

Kolb, Trudy M. and Murray A. Straus. 1974. "Marital Power and Marital Happiness in Relation to Problem-Solving Ability." *Journal of Marriage and the Family.* Vol. 36 (November):756-766.

Kome, Penny. 1983. *The Taking of Twenty-Eight.* Toronto: Women's Educational Press.

Kristeva, J. 1984. *Revolution in Poetic Language.* New York: Columbia University Press.

Kristeva, J. 1980. *Desire in Language.* New York: Columbia University Press.

Kuhn, T. 1962. *The Structure of Scientific Revolutions.* Chicago: University of Chicago Press.

LaBerge, Danielle. 1991. "Women's Criminality, Criminal Women, Criminalized Women? Questions In and For a Feminist Perspective." *The Journal of Human Justice.* Vol. 2, No. 2:37-56.

Lacan, J. 1988. *The Seminar of Jacques Lacan, Book II. The Ego in Freud's Theory and in the Technique of Psychoanalysis 1954- 1955.* Cambridge: Cambridge University Press.

Lacan, J. 1981. *The Four Fundamental Concepts of Psycho-Analysis.* New York: W.W. Norton and Co.

Lacan, J. 1977. *Ecrits: A Selection.* Trans. A. Sheridan. New York: Norton.

Laclau, E. 1977. *Politics and Ideology in Marxist Theory: Capitalism, Fascism, Populism.* London: New Left Books.

Lahey, Kathleen A. 1984. "Implications of Feminist Theory for the Direction of Reform of the Criminal Code." Paper prepared for the Law Reform Commission of Canada.

Lane, M. 1966. "Unemployment During the Depression: The Problem of the Single Unemployed Transient in British Columbia." Unpublished Hons. B.A. essay, History Department, University of British Columbia.

Laplanche, J. and J. Pontalis. 1973. The Language of Psycho-Analysis. New York: Norton and Co.

Lasch, C. 1977. Haven in a Heartless World: The Family Besieged. New York: Basic Books.

Lauretis, T. de. 1984. Alice Doesn't. Bloomington: Indiana University Press.

Lautard, E. E. J. 1965. "An Evaluation of a Municipal Work-for-Relief Project." Unpublished M. S. W. thesis, School of Social Work, University of British Columbia.

Laycraft, J. H. 1978. Royal American Shows Inc. and Its Activities in Alberta: Report of a Public Inquiry. Edmonton: Queen's Printer,.

Lea, J. and J. Young. 1984. What is to be Done About Law and Order. Harmondsworth: Penguin.

Lea, J. and J. Young. 1982. "The Riots in Britain 1981: Urban Violence and Political Marginalisation." Pp5-20 in D. Cowell, T. Jones and J. Young (eds.), Policing The Riots. London: Junction Books.

Lea, J. and J. Young. 1986. "A Realistic Approach to Law and Order." Pp358-364 in B.D. MacLean (ed.), The Political Economy of Crime: Readings for a Critical Criminology. Toronto: Prentice-Hall.

Lecercle, J. 1990. The Violence of Language . New York: Routledge.

Lecercle, J. 1985. Philosophy Through the Looking Glass: Language, Nonsense, Desire. London: Hutchinson.

Lee, Patricia M. 1989. "Feuding Factions and Federalism in the British Columbia Abortion Debate." Unpublished paper, Department of Anthropology and Sociology, University of British Columbia.

LeFresne, G. M. 1961. "The Royal Twenty Centres: The Department of National Defence and Federal Unemployment Relief 1932-1936." Unpublished B. A. thesis, Royal Military College, Kingston.

Lemaire, A. 1977. Jacques Lacan. Trans. D. Macey. New York: Routledge and Kegan Paul.

Leon, Jeffrey S. 1977. "The Development of Juvenile Justice: A Background for Reform." Osgoode Hall Law Journal . Vol. 15, No. 1:71-106.

Leonard, E. 1982. Women, Crime and Society: A Critique of Criminological Theory. New York: Longmans.

Levens, Bruce R. with Donald G. Dutton. 1980. The Social Service Role of Police — Domestic Crisis Intervention . Ottawa: Minister of Supply and Services.

Lewis, C. (Chair). 1989. Executive Summary of the Report of the Race Relations and Policing Task Force. Toronto: Government of Ontario.

Lewis, C., R. Agrad, K.J. Gopic, J. Harding, T.S. Singh and R.Williams. 1989. The Report of the Race Relations and Policing Task Force. Toronto: Solicitor General of Ontario.

Leyton, Elliot. 1979. The Myth of Delinquency. Toronto: McClelland and Stewart.

Lipton, Charles. 1968. The Trade Union Movement of Canada, 1827-1959. Toronto: Canadian Social Publications.

Littleton, James. 1986. Target Nation: Canada and the Western Intelligence Network. Toronto: Lester and Orpen Dennys.

Liversedge, R. 1973. Recollections of the On-to-Ottawa Trek. Toronto: McClelland and Stewart.

Loney, Martin. 1986. The Politics of Greed: The New Right and the Welfare State. London: Pluto Press.

Los, Maria. 1990. "Feminism and Rape Law Reform." Pp160-172 in L. Gelsthorpe and A. Morris (eds.), Feminist Perspectives in Criminology. Milton Keynes: Open University Press.

Love, N. 1986. Marx, Nietzsche, and Modernity. New York: Columbia University Press.

Loving, N. and M. Quirk. 1982. "Spouse Abuse: The Need for New Law Enforcement Responses." *Law Enforcement Bulletin*. Vol. 51, No. 12:10-16.

Lowman, J., 1992. "Street Prostitution Control: Canadian Reflections on the Finsbury Park Experience." *British Journal of Criminology*, 32 (1): 1-17.

Lowman, J. 1990. "Notions of Formal Equality Before The Law: The Experience of Street Prostitutes and Their Customers." *The Journal of Human Justice*. 1 (2) (Spring): 55-76.

Lowman, J., R. J. Menzies and T. S. Palys (eds.). 1987. *Transcarceration: Essays in the Sociology of Social Control*. Aldershot: Gower.

Lowman, J. and T. S. Palys. 1991. "Interpreting Criminal Justice System Records of Crime." Pp349-369 in M. A. Jackson and C. T. Griffiths (eds.), *Canadian Criminology: Perspectives on Crime and Criminality*. Toronto: HBJ, Canada.

Luker, K. 1984. *Abortion and the Politics of Motherhood*. Berkeley: University of California Press.

MacCabe, C. 1985. *Tracking the Signifier*. Minneapolis: University of Minnesota Press.

MacCabe, C. 1979. *James Joyce and the Revolution of the Word*. London: Macmillan Press.

MacDonald, Edythe. 1988. "Notes For Address to be Given by the Honourable Edythe I. MacDonald, Judge, District Court of Ontario, to the National Association of Women Lawyers," Royal York Hotel, Toronto, August 6.

MacDonald, W. A., C. T. McHattie and E. Branden. 1935. *Report of the Royal Commission to Enquire into Conditions in the Relief Camps in British Columbia*. Ottawa: King's Printer.

Mackenzie, Maxwell. 1969. *Royal Commission on Security Report*. Ottawa: Government Printer.

MacKinnon, Catharine. 1983. "Feminism, Method, Marxism and the State: Toward Feminist Jurisprudence." *Signs*. Vol. 8, No. 4:635-658.

MacKinnon, Catharine. 1985. "Privacy v. Equality: Beyond Roe v. Wade (1983)." Paper presented at a conference, *Who Governs Reproduction?* New Haven, Connecticut. November 2.

MacLean, Brian D. 1991. "In Partial Defense of Socialist Realism." *Crime, Law and Social Change*. Vol. 15:213-254.

MacLean, B. D. 1989. "The Islington Crime Survey 1985: A Cross-Sectional Study of Crime and Policing in The London Borough of Islington." Unpublished Ph.D. dissertation, London School of Economics and Political Science.

MacLean, B. D. 1988. "The New Victimology: Political Praxis or Left Unrealism." Unpublished paper presented to the Learned Societies Annual Meetings, Windsor, Ontario. June 5.

MacLean, B.D. 1986a. "Critical Criminology and Some Limitations of Traditional Inquiry." Pp1-20 in B.D. MacLean (ed.), *The Political Economy of Crime: Readings for a Critical Criminology*. Toronto: Prentice-Hall.

MacLean, B. D. (ed.) 1986b. *The Political Economy of Crime: Readings for a Critical Criminology*. Toronto: Prentice-Hall.

MacLean, B. D. 1985. "Review of Ruth Hall: Ask Any Woman." *British Journal of Criminology*. Vol 25, No.4:390-391.

MacLean, B.D. and W.S. DeKeseredy. 1990. "Taking Working Class Victimization Seriously: The Contribution of Left Realist Surveys." *International Review of Modern Sociology*. Vol. 20 (Autumn):211-228.

MacLean, Brian D., Trevor Jones and Jock Young. 1986. *The Preliminary Results of the Islington Crime Survey, Report to The London Borough of Islington Police Sub-Committee*. London: London Borough of Islington.

MacLean, B. D. and D. Milovanovic, (eds.), 1991. *New Directions in Critical Criminology*. Vancouver: The Collective Press.

MacLean, Brian D. and R. S. Ratner. 1987. "An Historical Analysis of Bills C-67 and C-68: Implications for the Native Offender." *The Native Studies Review*. 3 (1) :31-58.

MacLeod, Linda. 1980. *Wife Battering in Canada: The Vicious Circle*. Ottawa: Minister of Supply and Services.

MacLeod, Linda. 1987. *Battered But Not Beaten: Preventing Wife Battering in Canada*. Ottawa: Canadian Advisory Council on the Status of Women.

MacNeil, Michael. 1989. "Courts and Liberal Ideology: An Analysis of the Application of the Charter to Some Labour Law Issues." *McGill Law Journal*. Vol 34 (1):86-118.

Magnusson, W., William K. Carroll, Charles Doyle, Monika Langer and R.B.J. Walker. 1984. *The New Reality: The Politics of Restraint in Canada*. Vancouver: New Star Books.

Mahoney, Kathleen. 1988. "Women's Rights." Pp159-170 in Roger Gibbins (ed.), *Meech Lake and Canada: Perspectives From the West*. Edmonton: Academic Printing and Publishing.

Major-Poetzl, P. 1983. *Michel Foucault's Archaeology of Western Culture*. Chapel Hill: The University of North Carolina Press.

Majury, Diana. 1987. "Strategizing In Equality." *Wisconsin Women's Law Review*. Vol. 3:169-187.

Maltz, Michael D. 1977. "Crime Statistics: A Historical Perspective." *Crime and Delinquency*. Vol. 23:32-40.

Mandel, Michael. 1989. *The Charter of Rights and the Legalization of Politics in Canada*. Toronto: Wall and Thompson.

Manitoba Association of Women and the Law. 1988. *Gender and Equality in the Courts*. Winnipeg Regional Office of Canadian Advisory Council on the Status of Women.

Mann, E. and T. A. Lee with Norman Penner. 1979. *The RCMP vs. the People*. Don Mills, Ontario: General Publishing.

Manning, P. 1988. *Symbolic Communication: Signifying Calls and the Police Response*. Cambridge, Mass.: MIT Press

Manning, P. 1979. "Metaphors of the Field: Varieties of Organizational Discourse." *Administrative Science Quarterly*. Vol. 24: 660-671.

Matthews, Roger. 1989. "Reflections on Recent Developments in 'Social Control.'" Paper given at the British Criminology Conference, Bristol.

Maxfield, M. 1984. *Fear of Crime in England and Wales*. London: HMSO.

Mayhew, H. 1972. "London Labour and the London Poor." Pp47-62 in S. Sylvester (ed.), *The Heritage Of Modern Criminology*. Cambridge, Mass.: Schenkman Publishing Company.

Mcauley, Chris. 1989. "Nationalist Women and the RUC." Pp138-148 in C. Dunhill (ed.), *The Boys in Blue: Women's Challenge to the Police*. London: Virago.

McBarnet, D. 1983. *Conviction: Law, the State and the Construction of Justice*. London: Macmillan.

McCall, W. W. 1988. "Presentation to the National Symposium on Lotteries and Gambling." Le Meridien Hotel, Vancouver. May 26-28.

McCandless, Robert. 1985. *Yukon Wildlife: A Social History*. Edmonton: University of Alberta Press.

McDonald, Mr. Justice D.C. 1981a. *Commission of Inquiry Concerning Certain Activities of the Royal Canadian Mounted Police. Freedom and Security Under the Law*. Second Report, Vols. I, II.

McDonald, Mr. Justice D.C. 1981b. *Certain RCMP Activities and the Question of Government Knowledge*. Third Report.

McDonnell, K. 1984. *Not an Easy Choice: A Feminist Re-examines Abortion*. Toronto: The Women's Press.

McLaren, A. 1978. "Birth Control and Abortion in Canada, 1870-1920." *Canadian Historical Review*. Vol 59, No. 3:319-340.

McLaren, J. and J. Lowman. 1988. "Prostitution Law Enforcement in Canada, 1892-1920: Unravelling Myth and Reality." Unpublished manuscript.

McMahon, M.W. and R.V. Ericson. 1984. *Policing Reform: A Study of the Reform Process and Police Institution in Toronto.* Toronto: Centre for Criminology, University of Toronto.

NcNeill, Sandra. 1987. "Flashing: Its Effect on Women." Pp93-109 in Jalna Hanmer and Mary Maynard (eds.), *Women, Violence and Social Control.* London: Macmillan Press.

Medvedev, P. Bakhtin. 1978. *The Formal Method in Literary Scholarship.* Baltimore: The John Hopkins University Press.

Messerschmidt, J. 1986. *Capitalism, Patriarchy, and Crime: Toward A Socialist Feminist Criminology.* Totowa, N.J.: Rowman and Littlefield.

Metz, C. 1982. *The Imaginary Signifier.* Bloomington: Indiana University Press.

Michalowski, R., 1991. "Niggers, Welfare Scum, and Homeless Assholes: The Problems of Idealism, Consciousness, and Context in Left Realism."   B. D. MacLean and D. Milovanovic (eds.). *New Directions in Critical Criminology.* Vancouver: The Collective Press: 31-38.

Mies, Maria. 1983. "Towards a Methodology for Feminist Research." Pp117-139 in G. Bowles and R. Duelli Klein (eds.), *Theories of Women's Studies.* London: Routledge and Kegan Paul.

Mika, H. and J. Thomas. 1988. "The Dialectics of Prisoner Litigation: Reformist Idealism or Social Praxis?" *Social Justice.* Vol. 15:48-71.

Millett, Kate. 1970. *Sexual Politics.* New York: Avon.

Mills, C. Wright. 1959. *The Sociological Imagination.* New York: Oxford University Press.

Milovanovic, D. fc. "Law, Semiotics and Reality Construction" (in progress).

Milovanovic, D. 1991a. "Humanistic Sociology and the Chaos Paradigm: A Review Essay of N. Katherine Hayles, *Chaos Bound: Orderly Disorder in Contemporary Literature and Science.*" *Humanity and Society.* Vol. 15, No. 1 February: 135-146.

Milovanovic, D. 1991b. "Images of Unity and Disunity in the Juridic Subject and the Movement Toward the Peacemaking Community." Pp209-227 in R. Quinney and H. Pepinsky (eds.), *Criminology as Peacemaking.* Bloomington: Indiana University Press.

Milovanovic, D. 1990a. "Law and the Challenge of Semiotic Analysis: A Review Essay of Bernard Jackson's 'Law, Fact and Narrative Coherence.'" *Legal Studies Forum.* Vol. 14, No. 1:71-84.

Milovanovic, D. 1989. *Weberian and Marxian Analysis of Law: Structure and Function of Law in a Capitalist Mode of Production.* Aldershot, England: Gower Publishers.

Milovanovic, D. 1988a. *A Primer in the Sociology of Law.* Albany, New York: Harrow and Heston.

Milovanovic, D. 1988b. "Jailhouse Lawyers and Jailhouse Lawyering." *International Journal of the Sociology of Law.* Vol. 16, No. 4: 455-475.

Milovanovic, D. 1988c. "Review Essay: Critical Legal Studies and the Assault on the Bastion." *Social Justice.* Vol. 15:161-172.

Milovanovic, D. 1987. "The Political Economy of 'Liberty' and 'Property' Interests." *Legal Studies Forum.* Vol. 11:267-293.

Milovanovic, D. 1986. "Juridico-Linguistic Communicative Markets: Towards a Semiotic Analysis." *Contemporary Crises.* Vol. 10:281-304.

Milovanovic, D. 1985. "Anarchism, Liberation Theology and the Decommodification of the Juridic and Linguistic Form." *Humanity and Society.* Vol. 9 (May):182-196.

Milovanovic, D. and Jim Thomas. 1989. "Overcoming the Absurd: Legal Struggle as Primitive Rebellion." Unpublished manuscript, available on request.

Ministry of Solicitor General, Programs Branch. 1983/4. *Ministry of The Solicitor General Annual Report.* Ottawa: Minister of Supply and Services.

Moi, Toril. 1985. *Sexual/Textual Politics.* London: Methuen.

Montero, G. 1979. *We Stood Together: First Hand Accounts of Dramatic Events in Canada's Labour Past.* Toronto: James Lorimer.

Morand, Justice D.R. (Chair). 1976. *The Royal Commission Into Metropolitan Police Practices.* Toronto: Government of Ontario.

Morgan, E.C. 1970. "The North-West Mounted Police, 1873-1883." Unpublished M. A. thesis, University of Regina.

Morgan, G. 1983. "More on Metaphor: Why We Cannot Control Tropes in Administrative Science." *Administrative Science Quarterly.* Vol. 28:601-607.

Morgan, G. 1980. "Paradigms, Metaphors, and Puzzle Solving in Organizational Settings." *Administrative Science Quarterly.* Vol. 25: 605-622.

Morgan, Nicole. 1988. *The Equality Game: Women in the Federal Public Service (1908-1987).* Ottawa: Canadian Advisory Council on the Status of Women.

Morgan, P. 1981. "From Battered Wife to Program Client: The State's Shaping of Social Problems." *Kapitalistate.* Vol. 9:17-41.

Morris, A. 1987. *Women, Crime and Criminal Justice.* Oxford: Basil Blackwell.

Morris, P. and H. Giller. 1980. *Providing Criminal Justice for Children.* London: Macmillan.

Mount, Ferdinand. 1984. *The Subversive Family.* London: Unwin Paperbacks.

Munche, P. B. 1981. *Gentlemen and Poachers: The English Game Laws 1671-1831.* Cambridge: Cambridge University Press.

Myers, Gustavus. 1972. *A History of Canadian Wealth.* Toronto: James Lewis and Samuel.

National Action Committee on the Status of Women. 1987. *Brief on the 1987 Constitutional Accord.* Ottawa.

Naylor, R. T. 1975. *The History of Canadian Business, 1867-1914 , Vol. I.* Toronto: Lorimer.

Newman, O. 1975. "The Ideology of Social Problems: Gambling, A Case Study." *Canadian Review of Sociology and Anthropology.* Vol. 12 (November):541-550.

Newman, Sir Kenneth. 1985. *Report of the Commissioner of Police of the Metropolis for the Year 1984.* London: HMSO.

Nicholoson, R., (ed.), 1990. *Feminism/Postmodernism.* New York: RKP.

Nietzsche, F. 1969. *The Will to Power.* New York: Random House.

Nietzsche, F. 1968. *Twilight of the Idols and the After-Christ.* New York: Penguin.

Nietzsche, F. 1967. *Beyond Good and Evil.* New York: Vintage Books.

O'Barr, W. M. 1982. *Linguistic Evidence: Language, Power, and Strategy in the Courtroom.* New York: Academic Press.

O'Connor, James. 1984. *The Accumulation Crisis.* Oxford: Basil Blackwell.

O'Connor, James. 1973. *The Fiscal Crisis of the State.* New York: St. Martin's Press.

Offe, C. 1975. "The Theory of the Capitalist State and the Problem of Policy Formation." In L.N. Lindbert et al. (eds.), *Stress and Contradiction in Modern Capitalism.* Toronto: Lexington Books, D.C. Heath and Co.

Offe, C. 1985. "Legitimation Through Majority Rule?" Pp259-299 in J. Keane (ed.), *Disorganized Capitalism.* Cambridge: Polity Press.

Offe, C. 1984. *Contradictions of the Welfare State.* Cambridge, Mass.: The MIT Press.

Offe, C. 1980. "The Separation of Form and Content in Liberal Politics." *Studies in Political Economy.* No. 3 (Spring):5-15.

Offe, C. 1972a. "Political Authority and Class Structures — An Analysis of Late Capitalist Societies." *International Journal of Sociology.* Vol. 2, No. 1:73-107.

Offe, C. 1972b. "Advanced Capitalism and the Welfare State." *Politics and Societies.* Summer: 479-448.

Offe, C. and H. Wiesenthal. 1980. "Two Logics of Collective Action: Theoretical Notes on Social Class and Organizational Form." *Political Power and Social Theory.* Vol. 1:67-115.

Offe, C. and V. Ronge. 1982. "Theses on the Theory of the State." Pp249-256 in A. Giddens and D. Held (eds.), *Classes, Power and Conflict: Contemporary Debates.* Berkeley: University of California Press.

Ontario Coalition for Abortion Clinics. 1988. "State Power and the Struggle for Reproductive Freedom: The Campaign for Free-standing Abortion Clinics in Ontario." *Resources for Feminist Research.* Vol. 17, No. 3:109-114

Ormsby, M. 1958. *British Columbia: A History*. Toronto: Macmillan of Canada.

Osborne, J. A. and C. S. Campbell. 1988. "Recent Amendments to Canadian Lottery and Gaming Laws: The Transfer of Power Between Federal and Provincial Governments." *Osgoode Hall Law Journal.*. Vol. 26, No. 1:19-43.

Pagels, H. 1983. *The Cosmic Code*. New York: Bantam Books.

Palmer, Bryan D. 1987. *Solidarity: The Rise and Fall of an Opposition in British Columbia*. Vancouver: New Star.

Panitch, Leo and D. Swartz. 1988. *The Assault on Trade Union Freedoms*. Toronto: Garamond.

Parnas, Raymond I. 1972. "The Police Response to the Domestic Disturbance." In L. Radzinowitz and M. E. Wolfgang (eds.), *The Criminal in the Arms of the Law*. New York: Basic Books.

Pashukanis, E. 1980. "The General Theory of Law and Marxism." Pp37-131 in P. Beirne and R. Sharlet (eds.), *Pashukanis: Selected Writings on Marxism and Law*. New York: Academic Press.

Paternoster, Raymond, L. E. Saltzman, G. P. Waldo, and T. G. Chiricos. 1983. "Perceived Risk and Social Control: Do Sanctions Really Deter?" *Law and Society Review*. Vol. 17, No. 3:457-479.

Paternoster, R. and T. Bynam. 1982. "The Justice Model as Ideology: A Critical Look at the Impetus for Sentencing Reform." *Contemporary Crises*. Vol. 6:7-24.

Pearson, Geoffrey. 1983. *Hooligan: A History of Respectable Fears*. London: Macmillan.

Pease, K. 1990. "The Local Crime Survey: Pitfalls and Possibilities." Paper presented at *Realist Criminology: Crime Control and Policing in the 1990s*. Vancouver, Harbour Centre. May 25.

Pecheux, M. 1982. *Language, Semantics and Ideology*. New York: St. Martin's Press.

Peirce, C. S. 1931. *The Collected Papers of Charles Sanders Peirce*. C. Hartshorne and P. Weiss, (eds.). Cambridge: Harvard University Press.

Peitchinis, S. 1985. "Microelectronics, The Concept of Work and Employment." Pp193-212 in A. Brannigan and S. Goldenberg (eds.), *Social Responses to Technological Change*. Westport, Connecticut: Greenwood Press.

Parnas, Raymond I. 1972. "The Police Response to the Domestic Disturbance." In L. Radnowitz and M. E. Wolfgang (eds.), *The Criminal in the Arms of the Law*. New York: Basic Books.

Pelletier, G. 1971. *The October Crisis*. Toronto: McClelland and Stewart.

Pelrine, E. Wright. 1971. *Abortion in Canada*. Don Mills, Ontario: PaperJacks.

Pelrine, E. Wright. 1975. *Morgentaler: The Doctor Who Couldn't Turn Away*. New York: Signal Books.

Petchesky, R. 1984. *Abortion and Woman's Choice: The State, Sexuality, and Reproductive Freedom*. New York: Longman.

Pfohl, Stephen J. 1985. *Images of Deviance and Social Control*. New York: McGraw-Hill.

Phillips, Paul. 1982. *Regional Disparities*. Toronto: James Lorimer and Company Publishers.

Pitch, Tamar. 1985. "Critical Criminology, the Construction of Social Problems, and the Question of Rape." *International Journal of Sociology of Law*. Vol. 13:35-46.

Pitkin, H. 1971. *Wittgenstein and Justice*. Berkeley: University of California Press.

Pizzey, Erin. 1974. *Scream Quietly or the Neighbours Will Hear*. London: Penguin Books.

Platt, A. and P. Takagi. 1980. "Perspective and Overview." Pp1-5 in A. Platt and P. Takagi (eds.), *Punishment and Penal Discipline: Essays on the Prison and the Prisoner's Movement*. San Francisco: Crime and Social Justice Associates.

Platt, Anthony. 1969. *The Child Savers*. Chicago: Chicago University Press.

Pratt, John 1989. "Corporatism — The Third Model of Juvenile Justice." *British Journal of Criminology*. Vol. 29, No. 3:236-254.

Price, Lisa A. 1988. *Women's Interests: Feminist Activism and Institutional Change.* Vancouver: Women's Research Centre.

Pupo, N. 1988. "Preserving Patriarchy: Women, the Family and the State." Pp207-237 in N. Mandell and A. Duffy (eds.), *Reconstructing the Canadian Family: Feminist Perspectives.* Toronto: Butterworths.

Quinney, Richard. 1974. *Criminal Justice in America: A Critical Understanding.* Boston: Little, Brown.

Radford, Jill. 1989. "Women and Policing:Contradictions Old and New." Pp70-89 in Hanmer, Radford and Stanko (eds.), *Women, Policing, and Male Violence: International Perspectives.* London: Routledge.

Radford, Lorraine. 1987. "Legalizing Women Abuse." Pp135-151 in J. Hanmer and M. Maynard (eds.), *Women, Violence and Social Control.* London: Macmillan.

Ragland-Sullivan, E. 1986. *Jacques Lacan and the Philosophy of Psychoanalysis.* Chicago: University of Illinois Press.

Ratner, R. S. (ed.). 1986. "Introduction to a Conjunctural Analysis of Social Control in Canada." *Crime and Social Justice.* No. 26:1-10.

Ratner, R.S. 1984. "Inside The Liberal Boot: The Criminological Enterprise in Canada." *Studies in Political Economy: A Socialist Review.* Vol. 13 (Spring):145-164.

Ratner, R. S. and J. McMullan (eds.). 1987. *State Control: Criminal Justice Politics in Canada.* Vancouver: U.B.C. Press.

Ratner, R. S. and J. McMullan. 1983. "Social Control and the Rise of the 'Exceptionalist State' in Britain, the United States and Canada." *Crime and Social Justice.* (Summer):31-43.

Reich, Charles A. 1970. *The Greening of America.* New York: Random House.

Reiner, R. 1985. *The Politics of the Police.* Brighton: Wheatsheaf Books.

Repka, William and Kathleen Repka. 1982. *Dangerous Patriots.* Vancouver: New Star Books.

Reuben, William A. 1955. *The Atom Spy Hoax.* New York: Action Books.

Reuter, P. and J. Rubinstein. 1982. *Illegal Gambling in New York.* Washington, D. C.: National Institute of Justice.

Roberts, Barbara. 1988. *Whence They Came: Deportation from Canada, 1900-1935.* Ottawa: University of Ottawa Press.

Rooke, Patricia and R. L. Schnell. 1982. *Studies in Childhood History: A Canadian Perspective.* Calgary: Detselig Enterprises.

Rosecrance, J. 1988. *Gambling Without Guilt.* Pacific Grove, California: Brooks/Cole.

Rossi, Alice S. 1973. *The Feminist Papers: From Adams to de Beauvoir.* New York: Bantam.

Rothman, D. 1980. *Conscience and Convenience: The Asylum and its Alternatives in Progressive America.* Boston, Mass.: Little Brown.

Royal Canadian Mounted Police. 1984. "Gambling, Corruption, and Racketeering In Canada." Unpublished research report.

Rusche, Georg and Otto Kirchheimer. 1939. *Punishment and Social Structure.* New York: Columbia University Press.

Russell, D. 1982. "The Prevalence and Incidence of Forcible Rape and Attempted Rape of Females." *Victimology: An International Journal .* Vol. 17:81-93.

Ryan, H.R.S. 1981. "Abortion and Criminal Law." *Queen's Law Journal .* Vol. 6:362-371.

Sagoff, Mark. 1983. "Liberalism and Law." Pp12-24 in D. Maclean and C. Mills (eds.), *Liberalism Reconsidered.* Totawa: Rowman and Allanhead.

Sallot, Jeff. 1979. *Nobody Said No.* Toronto: Lorimer.

Sandel, Michael. 1982. *Liberalism and the Limits of Justice.* Cambridge: Cambridge University Press.

Sandel, Michael (ed.). 1984. *Liberalism and Its Critics.* Oxford: Basil Blackwell.

Sarup, Madan. 1989. *An Introductory Guide to Post Structuralism and Postmodernism.* Athens: The University of Georgia Press.

Saunders, S. A. 1939. "Nature and Extent of Unemployment in Canada." Pp1-58 in L. Richter (ed.), *Canada's Unemployment Problems.* Toronto: Macmillan.

Saussure, F. de. 1966. *Course in General Linguistics.* New York: McGraw-Hill.

Savage, Robert. 1985. *Personal Interview.* Vancouver, May 31.

Sawatsky, John. 1984. *Gouzenko: The Untold Story.* Toronto: Macmillan of Canada.

Sawatsky, John. 1980. *Men in the Shadows.* Toronto: Doubleday.

Scarman, Rt. Hon. Lord. 1981. *The Brixton Disorders 10-12 April 1981.* Report to Parliament, London: HMSO, 1981.

Schechter, Susan 1982. *Women and Male Violence: The Visions and Struggles of the Battered Women's Movement.* Boston: South End Press.

Scheerer, S., 1986. "Towards Abolitionism." *Contemporary Crises,* 10 (1): 5-20.

Schmidt, A.K. 1987. "Electronic monitors." *Federal Probation.* Vol. 50, No. 2:42-49.

Schwartz, Bryan. 1987. *Fathoming Meech Lake.* Winnipeg: University of Manitoba.

Schweinitz, K. de. 1961. *England's Road to Social Security.* New York: A.S. Barnes and Co.

Schwendinger, J. and H. Schwendinger. 1985. *Adolescent Subcultures and Delinquency.* New York: Praeger Publishers.

Schwendinger, J. and H. Schwendinger. 1983. *Rape and Inequality.* Beverly Hills: Sage Publications.

Scott, Robert and A. Scull. 1987. "Penal Reform and the Surplus Army of Labour." Pp147-158 in W. K. Greenaway and S. L. Brickey (eds.), *Law and Social Control in Canada.* Scarborough, Ontario: Prentice-Hall.

Seccombe, W. 1987. "Sheila Rowbotham on Labour and The Greater London Council." *Canadian Dimension.* Vol. 21, No. 2:32-37.

Selva, L. and R. Bohm. 1987. "Law and Liberation: Toward an Oppositional Legal Discourse." *Legal Studies Forum.* Vol. 11:243-266.

Sentes, R. 1988. "Developing Occupational Exposure Standards for Asbestos: The Federal Experience 1972-1982." Paper presented at the Socialist Studies Sessions of the Learned Societies Conference, Windsor, Ontario. June 4.

Serres, M. 1982. *Hermes: Literature, Science and Philosophy.* Baltimore: John Hopkins.

Shearing, C. D. (ed.) 1981. *Organizational Police Deviance.* Toronto: Butterworths.

Sheils, Jean and B. Swanky. 1977. *Work and Wages: Semi-documentary Account of the Life and Times of Arthur H. (Slim) Evans.* Vancouver: Trade Union Research Bureau.

Sherman L. W. and R. A. Berk. 1984a. *The Minneapolis Domestic Violence Experiment.* Police Foundation Reports, No. 1. Washington, D.C.: Police Foundation.

Sherman L. W. and R. A. Berk. 1984b. "The Specific Deterrent Effects of Arrest for Domestic Assault." *American Sociological Review.* Vol. 49: 261-272.

Sherman, Lawrence, Janell D. Schmidt, Dennis P. Rogan, Patrick R. Gartin, Ellen G. Cohen, Dean J. Collins and Anthony R. Bacich. 1991. "From Initial Deterrence to Longterm Escalation: Short Custody Arrest for Poverty Ghetto Domestic Violence." *Criminology.* Vol. 29, No. 4:821-850.

Sieghart, P. 1979. *The Big Public Inquiry: A Proposal for the Impartial Investigation of Projects with Major National Implications.* London: The Outer Unit Policy Unit, June.

Silverman, K. 1983. *The Subject of Semiotics.* New York: Oxford University Press.

Skogan, W. 1981. *Issues in the Measurement of Victimization.* Washington, D.C.: U.S. Goverment Printing Office.

Skolnick, J. H. 1979. "The Social Risks of Casino Gambling." *Psychology Today.* July:52-64.

Skolnick, J. H. 1978. *House of Cards.* Boston: Little, Brown.

Skolnick, J. H. 1988. "The Social Transformation of Vice." *Law and Contemporary Problems.* Vol. 51, No. 1:9-29

Slobodin, R. 1962. *1962 Band Organization of the Peel River Kutchin*. Ottawa: National Museum of Man Bulletin, No. 179.

Smart, Carol. 1990a. "Feminist Approaches to Criminology or Postmodern Woman Meets Atavistic Man." Pp70–84 in L. Gelsthorpe and A. Morris (eds.), *Feminist Perspectives in Criminology*. Milton Keynes: Open University Press.

Smart, Carol. 1990b. "Law's Power, the Sexed Body, and Feminist Discourse." *Journal of Law and Society*. Vol 17 (2):194-210.

Smart, Carol. 1989. *Feminism and the Power of Law*. London: Routledge and Kegan Paul.

Smart, Carol. 1976. *Women, Crime and Criminology: A Feminist Critique*. London: Routledge and Kegan Paul.

Smith, D. 1983. *Police and People in London: Vol.1, A Survey of Londoners*. London: Policy Studies Institute.

Smith, Lynn. 1988. "The Distinct Society Clause in the Meech Lake Accord: Could It Affect Equality Rights for Women?" Pp35-54 in Katherine Swinton and Carol Rogerson (eds.), *Competing Constitutional Visions: The Meech Lake Accord*. Carswell: Toronto.

Smith, Lynn. 1986. "A New Paradigm for Equality Rights." *Canadian Human Rights Reporter Inc*. Volume 7.

Smith, M. 1987a. "The Incidence and Prevalence of Woman Abuse in Toronto." *Violence and Victims*. Vol. 2, No. 3:173-187.

Smith, M. 1987b. "Women's Fear of Violent Crime: An Exploratory Test of a Feminist Hypothesis." Paper presented at the American Society of Criminology Annual Meetings, Montreal, November.

Smith, M. 1985. *Woman Abuse: The Case for Surveys by Telephone*. Lamarsh Research Program on Violence and Conflict Resolution Report No. 12. York University, Toronto.

Smith, Pamela. 1984. *Breaking Silence: Descriptive Report of a Followup Study of Abused Women Using a Shelter*. Ottawa: National Clearinghouse on Family Violence.

Smith, P. 1988. *Discerning the Subject*. Minneapolis: University of Minnesota Press.

Snider, Laureen. 1991. "The Potential of the Criminal Justice System to Promote Feminist Concerns." Pp238-260 in E. Comack and S. Brickey (eds.), *The Social Basis of Law* (2nd ed.). Halifax, Nova Scotia: Garamond.

Sparks, R. 1981. "Surveys of Victimization — An Optimistic Assessment." Pp1-60 in M. Tonry and N. Morris (eds.), *Crime and Justice: An Annual Review*. Chicago: University of Chicago Press.

Sparks, R. 1982. *Research on Victims of Crime: Accomplishments, Issues and New Directions*. Rockville, Maryland: U.S. Department of Health and Social Services.

Sparks, R., H. Genn and D. Dodd. 1977. *Surveying Victims: A Study of the Measurement Of Criminal Victimization, Perceptions of Crime and Attitudes Towards Criminal Justice*. Chichester: Wiley.

Spector M. and J. Kitsuse. 1977. *Constructing Social Problems*. Menlo Park, California: Cummings.

Spencer, S. 1985. "The Eclipse of the Police Authority." Pp34-53 in B. Fine and R. Millar (eds.), *Policing The Miners' Strike*. London: Lawrence and Wishart.

Spitzer, S. 1975. "Toward a Marxian Theory of Crime." *Social Problems*. Vol. 22:229-258.

Stanko, Elizabeth A. 1989. "Missing the Mark? Policing Battering." Pp46-69 in Hanmer, Radford and Stanko (eds.), *Women, Policing, and Male Violence: International Perspectives*. London: Routledge.

Statistics Canada. 1990. *Women in Canada: A Statistical Report*. Ottawa: Minister of Supply and Services. March.

Statistics Canada. 1985. *Women in Canada: A Statistical Report*. Ottawa: Minister of Supply and Services. March.

Statistics Canada. 1981. *Juvenile Delinquents*. Ottawa: Minister of Supply and Services.

Steele, Sam. 1914. *Forty Years in Canada*. Winnipeg: Russell Long and Co.

Stenning, P.C. 1981. "The Role of Police Boards and Commissions as Institutions of Municipal Police Governance." Pp161-208 in C. D. Shearing (ed.), *Organizational Police Deviance*. Toronto: Butterworths.

Stephan, E. 1976. *Die Stuttgarter Opferbefragung*. Wiesbaden Germany: Bundeskriminalamt.

Steward, J. 1955. *Theory of Cultural Change*. Champaign: University of Illinois Press.

Straus, Murray A. 1976. "Sexual Inequality, Cultural Norms, and Wife Beating." *Victimology: An International Journal*. Vol. 1, No. 1:54-70.

Straus, Murray A. 1980. "Sexual Inequality and Wife Beating." Pp86-93 in M. A. Straus and G. T. Holtaling (eds.), *The Social Causes of Husband-Wife Violence*. Minneapolis: University of Minnesota Press.

Strong-Boag, Veronica. 1986. "Wages for Housework: Mother's Allowances and the Beginnings of Social Security in Canada." Pp91-106 in Brickey and Comack (eds.), *The Social Basis of Law*. Toronto: Garamond.

Struthers, J. 1983. *No Fault of Their Own: Unemployment and the Canadian Welfare State 1914-1941*. Toronto: University of Toronto Press.

Sugarman, David (ed.). 1983. *Legality, Ideology and the State*. London: Academic Press.

Sumner, Colin. 1979. *Reading Ideologies*. London: Academic Press.

Sutherland, N. 1976. *Children in English-Canadian Society: Framing the Twentieth Century Consensus*. Toronto: University of Toronto Press.

Swanson, R. 1985. "Recognizing Battered Wife Syndrome." *Canadian Family Physician*. Vol. 31, No. 1:823-825.

Sweezy, P. 1980. "The Crisis of American Capitalism." *Monthly Review*. Vol. 32, No. 5 (October):3-5.

Swettenham, John. 1968. *McNaughton*. Toronto: Ryerson Press.

Tanner, Julian, G.S. Lowe and Harvey Krahn. 1985. "Youth Unemployment and Moral Panics." Pp285-289 in T. Fleming (ed.), *The New Criminologies in Canada*. Toronto: Oxford University Press.

Taub, N. and E. Schneider. 1982. "Perspectives on Women's Subordination and the Role of Law." Pp117-139 in D. Kairys (ed.), *The Politics of Law: A Progressive Critique*. New York: Pantheon Books.

Taylor, I., P. Walton and J. Young. 1973. *The New Criminology*. London: Routledge and Kegan Paul.

Taylor, Ian. 1987. "Theorizing the Crisis in Canada." Pp198-224 in R. S. Ratner and J. McMullan (eds.), *State Control: Criminal Justice Politics in Canada*. Vancouver: U.B.C. Press.

Taylor, Ian. 1986. "Martyrdom and Surveillance: Ideological and Social Practices of Police in Canada in the 1980's." *Crime and Social Justice*. No. 26:60-78.

Taylor, Ian. 1983a. *Crime, Capitalism and Community: Three Essays in Socialist Criminology*. Toronto: Butterworths and Co.

Taylor, Ian. 1983b. "Some Reflections on Homicide in Canada." Pp83-113 in I. Taylor, *Crime, Capitalism and Community: Three Essays in Socialist Criminology*. Toronto: Butterworths and Co.

Thomas, J. 1988. *Prisoner Litigation: The Paradox of the Jailhouse Lawyer*. Totowa, N.J.: Rowman and Littlefield.

Thomas, J. 1984. "Law and Social Praxis: Prisoner Civil Rights and Structural Mediations." Pp141-170 in S. Spitzer and A. Scull (eds.), *Research in Law, Deviance and Social Control* (V1). Greenwich, Conn.: J. A. I. Press.

Thompson, E. P. 1981. "The Rule of Law." Pp130-137 in P. Beirne and R. Quinney (eds.), *Marxism and Law*. New York: John Wiley and Sons.

Todorov, T. 1984. *Mikhail Bakhtin: The Dialogical Principle*. Minneapolis: University of Minnesota Press.

Tolmie, S. F. 1981. *Papers of S.F. Tolmie*. Special Collections Division, Vancouver: University of British Columbia Library.

Tong, Rosemarie. 1989. *Feminist Thought: A Comprehensive Introduction*. Boulder and San Francisco: Westview Press.

Trojanowitz, R. 1978. *Juvenile Delinquency: Concepts and Control*. Englewood Cliffs, New Jersey: Prentice-Hall.

Tuchfarber, A. and W. Klecka. 1976. *Random Digit Dialing: Lowering The Cost of Victimization Surveys*. Washington, D. C. Police Foundation.

Tucker, E. 1984. "The Determination of Occupational Health and Safety Standards in Ontario, 1860-1982: From the Market to Politics to ...?" *McGill Law Journal*. Vol. 29, No. 2.:261-311.

Turner, A. 1977. *An Experiment to Compare Three Interview Procedures in The National Crime Survey*. Washington D.C.: Statistical Research Division, U.S. Bureau of Census Memorandum. March.

Turner, F. J. 1921. *The Frontier in American History*. New York: Henry Holt.

Turner, John Peter. 1950. *The North West Mounted Police, 1873-1893., Vol. II*. Ottawa: King's Printer.

Ursel, E. Jane and Dawn Farough. 1985. *The Legal and Public Response to the New Wife Abuse Directive in Manitoba* . Winnipeg Area Study Report, Number 4, Department of Sociology, University of Manitoba.

Usher, Peter. 1984. "Property Rights, the Basis of Wildlife Management." Pp389-415 in *Proceedings of National and Regional Interests in the North*. Canadian Arctic Resources Committee.

Valk, A. de. 1974. *Morality and Law in Canadian Politics: The Abortion Controversy*. Montreal: Palm Publishers.

Volosinov, V. 1986. *Marxism and the Philosophy of Language*. Cambridge, Massachusetts: Harvard University Press.

Volosinov, V. 1976. *Freudianism: A Marxist Critique*. New York: Academic Press.

Voumvakis, S. E. and R. V. Ericson. 1984. *News Accounts of Attacks on Women*. Centre of Criminology, University of Toronto.

Vygotsky, L. 1972. "Thought and Word." Pp180-213 in P. Adams (ed.), *Language in Thinking*. Middlesex, England: Penguin Books.

Walker, Leonore. 1979. "The Cycle of Theory of Violence." Pp55-77 in L. Walker (ed.), *The Battered Woman*. New York: Harper and Row.

Ward, W. P. 1966. *Administration of Justice in the North-West Territories, 1870-87*. Unpublished M. A. thesis, University of Alberta.

Wardell, W. 1985. "The Young Offenders Act." *Saskatchewan Law Review*. Vol. 47, No. 2:381-388

Warnock, J. 1988. *Free Trade and the New Right*. Toronto: Lorimer.

Watkins, M. 1978. *Dene Nation: The Colony Within*. Toronto: University of Toronto Press.

Weber, M. 1978. *Economy and Society*. Two Volumes. G. Roth and C. Wittich (eds.). Berkeley: University of California Press.

Weisbord, Merrily. 1983. *The Strangest Dream*. Toronto: Lester and Orpen Dennys.

West, Gordon. 1984. *Young Offenders and the State: A Canadian Perspective on Delinquency*. Toronto: Butterworths.

West, Robin. 1988. "Jurisprudence and Gender." *University of Chicago Law Review*. Vol 1.

Westergaard, H. 1932 (reprinted 1969). *Contributions to the History of Statistics*. New York: Augustus M. Kelley.

Whitaker, Reg. 1987. *Double Standard: The Secret History of Canadian Immigration*. Toronto: Lester and Orpen Dennys.

Whitehurst, R. 1974. "Violence in the Husband-Wife Interaction." Pp143-174 in S. Steinmetz and M. Straus (eds.), *Violence in the Family*. New York: Harper and Row.

Whorf, B. 1956. *Language, Thought, and Reality*. New York: John Wiley and Sons.

Whyte, John. 1988. "The 1987 Constitutional Accord and Ethnic Accommodation." Pp263-270 in Katherine Swinton and Carol Rogerson (eds.), *Competing Constitutional Visions: The Meech Lake Accord*. Toronto: Carswell.

Williams, Daniel. 1988. "Law, Deconstruction and Resistance: The Critical Stances of Derrida and Foucault." *Cardozo Arts and Entertainment Law Journal*. Vol 6, No. 2:359-410.

Williams, R. 1977. *Marxism and Literature*. Oxford: Oxford University Press.

Williamson, J. 1987. *Decoding Advertisement*. New York: Marion Boyars.

Willox, P. 1980. *The Capital Crisis and Labour: Perspectives on the Dynamics of Working Class Consciousness in Canada*. Ph.D. thesis, Upsala University, Stockholm, Sweden: Almqvist and Wiksell International.

Wittgenstein, L. 1958. *The Blue and Brown Books*. New York: Harper and Row.

Woltman, H. and J. Bushery. 1978. "Results of the NCS Maximum Personal Visit - Maximum Telephone Interview Experiment." Washington, D.C.: U.S. Bureau of Census mimeo.

Women's Research Centre. 1982. *A Study of Protection for Battered Women*. Vancouver: Press Gang.

Wood, D. 1983. *Survey of Londoners: Technical Report*. London: SCPR.

Wood, D. 1984. *British Crime Survey: Technical Report*. London: SCPR.

Wood, S. T. 1941. "Tools for Treachery." *RCMP Quarterly*. April.

Woods, Raymond. 1985. Personal Interview. Westbank, British Columbia, May 23.

Worden, R. E. and A. A. Pollitz. 1984. "Police Arrests in Domestic Disturbances: A Further Look." *Law and Society Review*. Vol. 18, No. 1:105-119.

Young, J., 1992. "Ten Points of Realism." R. Matthews and J. Young, (eds.), *Rethinking Criminology*. London: Sage.

Young, J. 1986. "The Failure of Criminology: The Need For a Radical Realism." Pp4-30 in R. Matthews and J. Young (eds.), *Confronting Crime*. London: Sage Publications.

Young, J. 1979. "Left Idealism, Reformism and Beyond: From New Criminology to Marxism." Pp11-28 in B. Fine et al. (eds.), *Capitalism and the Rule of Law*. London: Hutchinson.

Young, T. R. 1990. "Marx and the Postmodern." Unpublished manuscript.

Young, T. R. 1991. "Chaos Theory and Symbolic Interactional Theory." *Symbolic Interaction*. Vol 14, No. 3.

Zaretsky, E. 1982. "The Place of the Family in the Welfare State." Pp188-224 in B. Thorne and M. Yalow (eds.), *Rethinking the Family: Some Feminist Questions*. New York: Longmans.

Zizek, S. 1989. *The Sublime Object of Ideology*. New York: Verso.

Zoomer, Olga J. 1989. "Policing Woman Beating in the Netherlands." Pp125-154 in Jalna Hanmer, Jill Radford and Elizabeth A. Stanko (eds.), *Women, Policing and Male Violence: International Perspectives*. London: Routledge.

Miscellaneous Archival Materials and Documents

British Columbia Provincial Archives, Correspondence Files, 1931. Victoria: Government of British Columbia.

British Statutes. 1971. *Wild Creatures and Forest Law Act of 1971*. Statutes of Westminister.

Budget Address of British Columbia Legislative Assembly, 1929-1934. Victoria: Government of British Columbia.

Canada, *Proceedings of Standing Senate Committee On Legal and Constitutional Affairs*, 1st Session, 33rd Parliament, 1984-85, Issues 32 and 33, Dec. 11,12,13, 1985.

Canadian Annual Review of Public Affairs, Toronto: C.A.R. Publishing, 1920.

Committee to End the Marion Lockdown. *Can't Jail the Spirit: Political Prisoners in the U.S. A Collection of Biographies, 1988* (monograph available: Committee to End the Marion Lockdown, 343 S. Dearborn, Suit 1607, Chicago, Ill. 60604).

Constitution Act. 1982, being Schedule B of the *Canada Act, 1982,* c. 11 (U.K.).

Constitutional Accord (The Meech Lake Accord). 1987.

Department of Indian Affairs and Northern Development (DIAND). 1984. *The Western Arctic Claim: The Inuvialuit Agreement.* Ottawa: DIAND.

First Ministers Conference on the Constitution: Verbatim Transcript. 1987. Canadian Intergovernmental Conference Secretariat: Ottawa, June 3.

Hansard 1819. *Parliamentary Debates* (Volume 39).

House of Commons Debates. 1963. April 4, 1922; May 31, 1963; June 3.

Matthews, J. S. 1935. "Unemployment and Relief" Additional Manuscripts 54, Volume 8, Number 2. Vancouver, British Columbia:Vancouver City Archives.

Matthews, J.S. 1935a. "Unemployment and Relief" Additional Manuscripts 54, Volume 13. Vancouver: Vancouver City Archives, 1935.

Matthews, J.S. 1935b. "Unemployment and Relief" Additional Manuscripts 54, Volume 8, Number 3. Vancouver, British Columbia, Vancouver City Archives.

Matthews, J.S. 1936-37. "Unemployment and Relief" Additional Manuscripts 54, Volume 8, Number 4. Vancouver, British Columbia: Vancouver City Archives.

Matthews, J.S. 1931-32. "Unemployment and Relief" Additional Manuscripts 54, Volume 8, Number 1. Vancouver City Archives, Vancouver, British Columbia.

McGeer, G.G. *Original Papers.* Victoria: Provincial Archives of British Columbia, 1913-47.

Oxford Dictionary of the English Language. 1976.

The James Bay Agreement. Quebec: Editeur Officiel du Québec, 1976.

Vancouver City Archives (VCA). "Administrative History Files." Volumes 5, 28, 30, 31, 32, 33. Vancouver: City of Vancouver.

Vancouver City Archives (VCA). "City Clerk's Files." Volumes 141, 155, 166, 195. Vancouver: City of Vancouver.

Vancouver City Archives (VCA). "City Clerk's Series One Operational Files." Correspondence Inward 1888-1946. Vancouver: City of Vancouver.

Vancouver City Archives (VCA). "City Records." Location Numbers 33, 75. Vancouver: City of Vancouver.

Vancouver City Archives (VCA). "Public Record Files, Mayor." Volumes 5, 8, 9, 10. Vancouver: City of Vancouver.